D1581167

# LEARNING EUROPEAN LAW

A Primer and Vade-mecum

AUSTRALIA
LBC Information Services
Sydney

CANADA and USA
Carswell
Toronto Ontario

NEW ZEALAND
Brooker's
Auckland

SINGAPORE and MALAYSIA
Thomson Information (S.E. Asia)
Singapore

# LEARNING EUROPEAN LAW

## A Primer and Vade-mecum

## By Tom Kennedy

Published in 1998 by
Sweet & Maxwell Limited
100 Avenue Road
Swiss Cottage
London NW3 3PF
(http://www.smlawpub.co.uk)

Typeset by York House Typographic Ltd
Printed in Great Britain by Butler and Tanner Ltd.

*A CIP catalogue record for this book is available from the British Library*

ISBN 0–421–63620–3

All rights reserved.
No part of this publication may be
reproduced or transmitted, in any form
or by any means, electronic, mechanical, photocopying,
recording or otherwise, or stored in any retrieval
system of any nature, without the written permission
of the copyright holder and the publisher, application
for which shall be made to the publisher.

©
TOM KENNEDY
1998

# PREFACE

"Some experience of popular lecturing had convinced
me that the necessity of making things plain to unin-
structed people was one of the very best means of
clearing up the obscure corners in ones own mind."

T.H. Huxley, *Man's place in nature* (1894).

"La dernière chose qu'on trouve en faisant un ouvrage,
est de savoir celle qu'il faut mettre la première".

Pascal, *Pensées* (1670).

The germ of the idea for this book came many years ago when I
first thought that it would be helpful to provide journalists and
newspaper editors with a one or two page stylesheet essentially
distinguishing the (then) two European Courts from each other
and giving a small amount of guidance on some of the legal
terminology surrounding them. That stylesheet is now the "style-
guide" in the Vade-mecum and the work has vastly outgrown my
initial conception.

In the course of frequent lecturing to groups of law students,
judges and practising lawyers as well as lay people visiting the
European Court of Justice I realised that there were many other

areas of confusion and misconceptions as to the operation of, in particular, the European Community legal system. As time passed the system has become increasingly complex with the development of the European Communities into the European Union, the creation of the European Economic Area and the establishment of two new European Courts, the EFTA Court and the Court of First Instance of the European Communities.

As a result, since I first proposed to Sweet & Maxwell to write a general introductory book to the area (which, I see from my correspondence, was as long ago as 1992), the need for such a work has seemed to me to grow ever stronger. Nonetheless the increasing activity at the European Court of Justice and Court of First Instance meant that the demands of my daytime job made it impossible to begin work seriously on the project. I am therefore immensely grateful to the Alexander Maxwell Law Scholarship Trust whose generosity enabled me to take leave of absence from that job for a few months during 1997 thus enabling me to get the project off the ground. Information about the Trust is on p. ix.

Even during the writing of the book the speed of change in the area of European law, taken in its widest sense, has not slackened. Firstly, the Eleventh Protocol to the European Convention on Human Rights, which radically changes the enforcement machinery of that Convention was adopted. Ratification was completed in 1997 and that Protocol comes into force tomorrow. The Member States of the European Union opened an Inter-Governmental Conference in 1996 which resulted in the adoption of the Treaty of Amsterdam on October 2, 1997. That Treaty, which was intended to carry out some fine-tuning of the novel European Union structure, in fact included a number of major developments which I have included in the text of this book. In the United Kingdom the Labour government elected in 1997 has made good its promise to incorporate the Human Rights Convention into its national law, and the Human Rights Act 1998 will have received the Royal Assent by the time this book goes on sale.

It is not yet clear how the new machinery provided for by the Eleventh Protocol will operate in practice, and at the time of drafting this preface it looks as if another six months will elapse before final ratification and entry into force of the Treaty of Amsterdam. I have therefore given certain hostages to fortune by treating both texts as if they were already in operation.

No undertaking of this sort can ever be a wholly solo operation and I am greatly indebted to all those who "directly or indirectly, actually or potentially", and I might add, knowingly or unknowingly, helped in the realisation of it. Special thanks are due to Sally Harris who more than amply compensated for my lack of skill with the wrd prcessr, and to Gillian Byrne for her invaluable assistance in compiling the Vade-mecum. Those who provided suggestions, inspiration, practical help in the form of re-reading certain chapters or sections of the book in which their expertise was greater than mine, or just beer and encouragement are listed under the acknowledgements on the next page. I would also like to thank Joshua Rozenberg of the BBC for his kind words in the Foreword and Ingram Pinn of the *Financial Times* for allowing me to use his drawing on the cover.

Any errors or omissions remaining must be blamed on the dog. If any readers are kind enough to contact me through the publishers' web-site at http://www.smlawpub.co.uk, I will bring them to his attention. Suggestions for changes, should a second edition be called for, are also welcome.

Last but not least I would like to thank my wife, Liv-Ellen, for her forbearance (mostly) of my neglect of household and horticultural duties for the past two years.

Tom Kennedy,
Schoenfels,
October 31, 1998

# FOREWORD

When I began to study law as an undergraduate exactly thirty years ago, European Law was not on the syllabus. The course was far from insular: Roman Law was compulsory and even International Law was available as an option. Neither of these was likely to have much practical value unless one turned out to be a slave or a state. On graduating, I took the solicitors' qualifying examinations. These were supposed to be fiercely practical: all that double-entry book-keeping was meant to keep solicitors on the straight and narrow. But again, no mention of European Law.

I suppose there was not so much of it around in those days. We in Britain had only recently allowed individuals to take the Government to the European Court of Human Rights; nobody quite understood what this meant. We were not yet in the Common Market, as we then called it. Lord Denning had yet to tell us, in *Bulmer v. Bollinger*, that the "incoming tide" of Community law could not be held back — a statement of the obvious that had apparently passed people by when parliament voted for the European Communities Act in 1972.

Since my studies ended I have been trying to learn as much European Law as I can. This is not because I want to improve my mind: my motives are entirely selfish. Together with Public Law, which regulates the powers of ministers, European Law in its broadest sense is one of the most fruitful sources of news stories. One definition of news is something that is new, true and interesting. Cases from the European Courts are all those — and important too.

This book will be a valuable guide for those of us who are still trying to pick up enough European Law to get by. The author has fun at the expense of those journalists who don't know their Human Rights Court from their Court of Justice — while conceding that if ever a system was named to confuse, this was it. Who, after all, decided there should be *two* major European Courts, each located in a city ending in *bourg*? Who decided that we should have a Council of Europe as well as a European Council, or a European Parliament sharing a debating chamber with a Council of Europe Parliamentary Assembly? Why were there two different Commissions? And what, in heaven's name, is an Advocate General? He is certainly not a General, nor even an advocate. Mr Kennedy helpfully tells us we may think of him as a duck-billed platypus.

This book can be read on several levels. At its simplest, it is a handy reference guide to all those strange European bodies with similar names. For students, it should provide an easily digestible introduction to an important area of study. And for those who are trying to understand a system of law that has a profound effect on our daily lives, it will prove to be a valuable source of insight.

*Joshua Rozenberg*
BBC Legal Affairs Correspondent

# ACKNOWLEDGMENTS

The following names are in no particular order:

Kieran Bradley; Patricia Shaughnessy; Peter Galezowski; the two Nevilles, Brown and March Hunnings; Jules Lonbay; Rod Liddell; Martin Johansson; Adela Klirova; Christian Kohler; Geoff Meade; Veerle Deckmyn; Ian Frame; Paul Farmer; Charlie Nordling; Nic Lockhart; Dorothy Donald-Little; Timothy Millett.

### The Alexander Maxwell Law Scholarship Trust

Maurice W. Maxwell, whose family founded Sweet & Maxwell the law publishers, by his Will established a charitable trust to be known as The Alexander Maxwell Law Scholarship Trust in memory of his great great grandfather. The Trust is committed to promoting legal research and writing at various levels by providing financial assistance to authors whether they be experienced legal practitioners, those in the early years of practice or at post-graduate level.

The author of this book received financial assistance from the Trust to enable him to complete the work.

The Trust calls for applications from time to time. Anyone interested in its work should write to The Clerk to the Trustees, The Alexander Maxwell Scholarship Trust, c/o Sweet & Maxwell, 21 Alva Street, Edinburgh, EH2 4PS.

# CONTENTS

# PART ONE:
# THE CONTEXT

# 1. WHY STUDY EUROPEAN LAW?

*"We prefer world law, in an age of self-determination,
to world war in an age of mass extermination".*

*John F. Kennedy.[a]*

I was once asked to speak at an afternoon meeting of a provincial
lawyers' association. Over lunch my hosts (who had paid my fare)
generously thanked me for having travelled all the way from
Luxembourg to meet them, and said that although they were
extremely interested in what I had to say, European affairs did not
really impinge much upon life in general or the practice of law in
that particular region. From the remarks heard over coffee I
concluded that the reason that my talk on European law and the
role of the Court of Justice was so well attended was that the
professional authorities, in their wisdom, would award those
attending a significant proportion of the credits which they needed to satisfy for their profession's continuing vocational
education requirements for that year.

When I got up to speak, departing from the prepared text of
which I had sufficient printed copies in my briefcase to supply
several such meetings, I first asked whether any of those present

---

a    Address to General Assembly of the United Nations,
     September 25, 1961.

had dealt with a case with the European law element, and if so, would he or she show his or her hand[1] – no hands were shown.

I then asked whether any of those present had ever represented a client who was a national of one of the other (then twelve) Member States (two hands were raised); whether any of them had clients who traded goods or services with other Member States (eight hands were raised); whether any of them had clients who were farmers (just over half their hands were raised); and finally, whether any of them had clients who were businesses or traders registered for VAT purposes, or indeed whether they were registered for VAT themselves. By that stage all of the hands had been raised.

With a few examples drawn from the recent case law of the European Court of Justice,[2] the point was quickly made and accepted by those present that no legal practitioner in that (or any other) Member State could afford to be unaware of a potential European law dimension to his work. The remainder of my talk was listened to with a degree of attention uncommon for post-prandial lectures and a lively discussion followed.

I do not, however, want to give the impression that European law is only of interest to legal practitioners (and by extension to those students who aspire to practise the law, of whom more anon), only that it is indispensable for them. Some understanding of the institutions and mechanisms of European organizations and of the legal rules which underpin them, the relationship between those rules and the rules of the various national legal systems through which they are applied, and the remedies which may be available in case of a breach of those rules as well as an ability to deploy the vocabulary of European law accurately and effectively are, I suggest, essential pieces of kit for a variety of professionals. The list may include politicians (whether at local, regional, national or European level), people in business, journalists, local and national government officials, teachers (particularly of history, geography, political science, economics or languages) and campaigners for the protection of the environment, as well as myriad other special interest groups.

Opening almost any newspaper will illustrate the extent to

---

1   Notwithstanding tenets of political correctness I propose hereafter to follow Section 6 of the Interpretation Act 1978 which provides that " ... unless the contrary intention appears (a) words imparting the masculine gender include the feminine; (b) words imparting the feminine gender include the masculine".

2   Dozens of other examples might have been used covering areas such as consumer protection, local government procurement, environmental protection, labour law, intellectual property or social security.

which European law permeates our economic and political life.
On the day this part of the chapter was drafted[3] the *Financial Times*
carried reports on:

- a judgment of the Court of Justice of the European Communities in which it essentially upheld Sweden's State monopoly on the sale of wines and spirits;

- a report of a vote in the European Parliament amending the draft of a directive prepared by the European Commission on the composition of chocolate;

- a request from music recording companies throughout the world for the Commission to take action through the World Trade Organisation against Bulgaria in connection with music piracy;

- an article on the British Government's reaction to a ruling by the World Trade Organisation's disputes resolution body over the claim by Latin-American banana producers that the Community's preferential regime for Caribbean producers was discriminatory and contrary to the GATT; and

- a report on the way in which the United Kingdom proposes to incorporate the European Convention on Human Rights into British domestic law.

The same edition of the newspaper carried further reports on
political issues relating to the future enlargement of the European
Union, the United Kingdom's position on whether or not to join
the single currency under the plans for Economic and Monetary
Union (EMU) and letters from readers relating to the effects of
competition policy within the European Union, EMU and the
problem of banana imports already mentioned. While I admit that
this game is easier to play with the *Financial Times* than with
almost any other newspaper, I have also played it successfully
with *The International Herald Tribune*, *La Repúbblica*, *Les Echos de la
Bourse* and even *The Daily Mail*.

No national politician of any claim to credibility can any longer
ignore the impact of Europe on domestic politics. Immensely
important and complex questions of constitutional law, international relations and economic management, including the pros
and cons of monetary union, are under constant discussion in the
political milieux of the Member States. It is no exaggeration to say
that those issues have dominated the British political stage during
the 1990s. Nonetheless, few politicians, even those from a legal
background, have more than the haziest grasp of the legal principles underlying their debates, or of the jurisdiction and working

3  Friday, October 24, 1997.

of the various European courts. Thus a judgment of any of those courts which is perceived to be adverse to national or sectoral interests is more likely to be greeted with apoplectic bluster than with informed and measured criticism, where that is justified. All too often ignorance is demonstrated by attributing judgments of the European Court of Human Rights to the European Community (or vice versa), or by suggesting that since the judgment was clearly adopted by ignorant foreign judges it can safely be ignored.

The same politicians however must scrutinize legislation whose purpose is to give effect in the national legal system to rules adopted at European level, they may wish to apply for aid for a declining industry in their constituency and therefore need to know the limitations placed on the granting of such aid or, conversely, what to do if a competing manufacturer in another Member State apparently receives such aid, thus putting it in a stronger competitive position than a company in his own constituency. Members of the European Parliament frequently forward letters which they have received from constituents asking about the possibilities of legal redress at European level in cases ranging from apparent discrimination in the payment of Armed Forces' pensions, to delay in the recovery of import duties wrongly claimed by the customs authorities of another Member State. For the advice which may be given in such cases see the final section of Chapter 6 entitled "How do I bring a case before the European Court?".

While the specialists in the European Parliament's Legal Service can be relied upon to defend vigorously the Parliament's prerogatives in proceedings before the Court of Justice, the MEPs' effectiveness whether at constituency level, in any of the various parliamentary committees, or in the plenary session, can only be enhanced by a better understanding of the legislative processes and of the consequences of Community legislation within the Member States.

One of the main tasks of journalists is to call politicians to account by exposing inconsistencies in the positions which they take or by demonstrating that those positions are based upon false premises. While it is no doubt easier, and possibly more entertaining, simply to reproduce the soundbites fed to them by politicians or their spin doctors, a journalist can only accurately assess the veracity or credibility of a politician if she knows at least as much about the subject as the politician concerned.

While I do not suggest that all journalists should have a postgraduate level knowledge of European law, in this context a basic understanding of the differences between the various European courts and the main elements of the procedure (although not necessarily the niceties of it) are essential. As can be seen from the headlines on page 8, even the most reputable newspapers are not immune from committing howlers (editors must take responsibility too for solecisms committed by the journalists and sub-editors who work for them). In order to avoid such gaffes, journalists should at least know in which cities the courts are located, the difference between a preliminary ruling, interim measures and an Advocate General's Opinion[4] and, while explaining complex legal situations in ordinary language, not, in doing so, slip into sloppy or inaccurate terminology (beware of adjectives).

The broadcast media arguably have an even greater responsibility because of their wide audience and, in particular, the immediate impact of television images. In this context there can be no excuse for introducing the story about a case before the European Court of Human Rights in Strasbourg with a picture of either the building or the members of the Court of Justice in Luxembourg, as happens all too often, nor of suggesting that, as one BBC Radio journalist recently did, that a complex property dispute which had been the subject of litigation in Italy for over 150 years might ultimately have to be resolved by the European Court at The Hague.

In the business world too, European law must be regarded as a fact of life. Even companies not involved in trading with other Member States (for whom of course the rules on free movement of goods and freedom to provide services provide the central underpinning of their business) must take account of European competition law, that is to say the rules derived from Articles 85 and 86 of the EC Treaty whose aim is to ensure the famous "level playing field". Moreover, businesses must ensure that they comply with the rules on equal pay for men and women employees, with the principle of equal treatment implying equal opportunities for professional training, promotion and other aspects of working conditions (including the length of the working week), the provision of written conditions of employment and the protection of workers' rights in the case of acquiring a new business or of making workers redundant, all of which derive from rights protected under European Community law.

On the wider scene there is progressive harmonization of the rules governing the conduct of business, including the adoption of common accounting standards and reporting practices, the disclosure of company statutes, rules on mergers and on corporate structure. Indeed, a report published by the Department of Trade and Industry in 1993[5] said that almost 70 per cent of future

---

4   See the style guide in Vade-mecum I for the answer.
5   Review of the implementation and enforcement of EC law in the UK.

## Some Newspaper Howlers

Not even the most reputable newspapers are immune from these mistakes.

1. *Times Law Report*, October 2, 1998;  2. *ABC*, November 5, 1997;
3. *The Times*, July 10, 1992;  4. *Financial Times*,                    1992;
5. *Liberation*, June 11, 1997;  6. *Financial Times*, April 23, 1998.

business law was likely to be derived from the European Community. While it is true that most company directors and managers will have access to legal advice, they should at least be able to understand the system upon which that advice is based and to identify situations in which advice should be sought.

On a day-to-day basis European law, especially European Community law, is applied by both national and local civil servants. Thus the customs officers in every sea and airport of the Community apply the common customs tariff which is the essential badge of a common market[6]; central, regional and local offices of the Ministries of Agriculture administer the common agricultural policy, including the complexities of commodity price support, set aside payments and sheepmeat clawback. Other rules affect the very working methods of administrative authorities. Thus planning procedures will involve the inclusion of environmental impact studies, and something as banal as buying new office furniture or special paint for road markings must be carried out in compliance with the rules on public procurement which are derived from a series of important and complex European Community directives.

Environmental and other special interest campaigners can increase their effectiveness by an understanding and use of the remedies available under European law. For example, complaints by environmental groups to the European Commission in Brussels have led to legal proceedings against Germany and France, and the Royal Society for the Protection of Birds in Britain sought judicial review in the British courts of a decision by the Minister for the Environment to allow the construction of new port facilities at Lappel Bank in northern Kent.[7] The latter case was referred to the Court of Justice which ruled that a minister was not entitled to decide that economic benefits of the proposed development outweighed its negative environmental impact without an explicit examination of that question. Gay rights campaigners have supported proceedings in both the European Court of Human Rights and in the European Court of Justice in accordance with the respective scope of the jurisdiction of those two bodies,[8] and prisoners' rights organizations have supported proceedings in the

---

6  See Chapter 2 below, at p. 21.
7  Case C-44/95, *R v. Secretary of State for the Environment, ex p. RSPB*, [1996] ECR I–3805.
8  On July 30, 1998 I received several 'phone calls from journalists and one from a reputable and long-established equal rights organisation asking me for information about a case concerning transsexuals which had been decided that day at the European Court of Human Rights (based in Strasbourg), *Sheffield and Horsham v. United Kingdom* (unreported).

Human Rights Court over the extent of the right of prison authorities to intercept prisoners' mail.

Of course businessmen, campaigners and civil servants may
sooner or later have to turn to lawyers for professional advice and
for representation of their interests before regulatory authorities,
national courts and tribunals or, ultimately, the European courts.
The examples already given, which are by no means exhaustive,
clearly illustrate the broad scope of European law. Indeed, in the
introduction to the report mentioned above the Department of
Trade and Industry stated that "over a third of existing UK
legislation arises from an obligation to implement EC law and this
proportion is likely to increase". For those reasons the two governing bodies of the legal professions in Scotland, in collaboration
with the Scottish university law faculties, decided that with effect
from Autumn 1991 a pass in a paper in European Community
law, either during the university studies or subsequently during
the professional legal exams, would be compulsory for all new
entrants to the legal profession. After some hesitation based on
fears that an additional compulsory element might overload an
already heavily-charged professional training schedule, the English legal professions have followed suit with effect from 1995. It is
perhaps surprising that only a minority of the Member States have
such a requirement.

The Single European Act, a treaty adopted in February 1982 by
the then twelve Member States of the European Communities,
included a requirement for the Economic Community (EEC as it
was then called) to "adopt measures with the aim of progressively
establishing the internal market over a period expiring on 31
December 1992". The catalogue of some three hundred legislative
measures required to be adopted by the Community in order to
achieve that aim and the political impetus which it gave to the
development of the Communities, focused attention on their legal
aspects. It was emphasized that the success of that massive legislative programme depended upon the effective and uniform
application of the rules within the Member States. As indicated
above, this effort in turn required diligence on the part of the
national administrative authorities responsible for applying the
new rules. It was also necessary for the legal professions and the
judiciaries of the Member States to understand the rules themselves, their own role in ensuring the correct application of those
rules and more widely the relationship between national law and
European Community law. Increasingly it was ʀecognized that
the protection of the interests of individuals (whether workers,
consumers, farmers or others) or businesses depended upon the
ability of lawyers to deploy European law effectively in the
national courts. Moreover, a lack of knowledge of European
Community law in particular by the national judges and by the

legal professions was identified as a potential obstacle to the realization of the single market programme.

While it is the law of the European Communities which has permeated the domestic law of the Member States the most deeply, and which has the most diverse and wide-ranging impact on national law, the law of the European Convention on Human Rights has also grown in importance, sufficiently for its implementation into United Kingdom domestic law to have been a manifesto commitment of the Labour Government elected in May 1997, which they have honoured with the Human Rights Bill currently before Parliament. In that regard a prominent criminal lawyer recently said that the Convention "should be the constant companion of the criminal law practitioner" and yet it is rarely mentioned in the main practitioners' manuals or student textbooks on criminal law.

Obviously matters relating to individual liberty such as powers of detention, the right to a fair and speedy trial and freedom from retroactive criminal offences or punishment are matters which may potentially arise in almost any criminal case. The right to privacy has been much discussed in connection with examples of intrusive journalistic practices and the Lord Chief Justice of England has said that, when the Human Rights Convention has been incorporated into the law of the United Kingdom, the judges will be able to develop principles of the protection of privacy on the basis of Article 8 of the Convention. Article 9, guaranteeing freedom of religion and Article 12, the right to marry and to found a family, are rights which may also develop within the scope of family law, an area not usually associated with ideas of fundamental rights.

Similarly, the world of commerce and business is not normally associated with the Convention. Nonetheless, there is no reason to suppose that its underlying ethos of the protection of individual interests against arbitrary power should not be applied here as well. Thus, for example, the right to freedom from expropriation of property without compensation might be of relevance, as would the right to a fair hearing before a regulatory authority, by analogy with an individual's right to a fair trial. This should include full information as to the "charges faced" and access to all of the documents relied upon. The recent Ernest Saunders case[9] shows that this right too may have application in a commercial context.

By now it should be clear that, even without the compulsory requirements for admission to one of the professions, no practitioner can afford to be without some idea of the workings of the European legal system. Nonetheless, European law should not be

---

9 *Ernest Saunders v. United Kingdom* (1996) Reports VI, 2044.

regarded as simply another specialised subject area (albeit with many variants) in which a certain number of rules must be learned for their practical application by lawyers in court or advising clients.

As will be seen in the following chapters, European law has arisen as a result of political pressure on States to integrate their economies and to subscribe to common standards of protection of individual liberties. This is a historic process which took on particular momentum after the Second World War but which has its roots decades or even centuries earlier. This historical background must always be borne in mind as it conditions much of the thinking behind the process of integration through law. Moreover, European law can hardly be understood without reference to economic principles, whether of microeconomics governing the behaviour of individual enterprises, or broader considerations such as the workings of international trade upon which the GATT and the World Trade Organization are based. The pace of change both via legislation and jurisprudential developments limits the usefulness of spending an excessive amount of time learning detailed rules in certain specific areas, save in so far as they illustrate the legislative process or the approach of the judiciary.

For all those reasons European law is also an area of study which should be strongly commended to those students whose intentions do not include entering into one of the legal professions. Indeed with a growing gap between the increasing numbers of law graduates and those holding a professional legal qualification and a relatively static number of opportunities to enter legal practice, the awareness of the broader horizons of European law and the ability to adapt to a different conceptual and methodological framework are benefits which will help students to adapt to careers in other areas.

These elements and the political excitement surrounding the realization of the single market programme in the years up to 1992 may explain the great increase in numbers of students opting for Community law courses. That those numbers have been maintained in the United Kingdom is probably due to the fact that European law has become a compulsory subject in many universities and, as mentioned above, for those who wish to enter legal practice. Nonetheless, in Britain at least, a political climate which was hostile to further integration during the mid 1990s, and the increasing complexity of the European Union which led the subject to be regarded as a difficult one, appear to have led to a diminution in the number of students going beyond the compulsory elements of European law courses (which generally cover institutional matters, remedies and one or two of the fundamental freedoms) to examine certain specific areas of European law in greater depth. Moreover some teachers report that the results obtained by students, even those who have performed well on other courses, are increasingly disappointing.

## SCOPE OF THE BOOK

Despite the title of this book it is not intended to be a guide to acquiring or refining studying techniques and skills.[10] Neither is it intended as a quick overview of the subject such as the many revision aids which are available. Of course, if the book proves helpful in either of those respects I will be only too pleased. Furthermore, the book is not only addressed to those who are following or planning to follow a formal course in European law, or those for whom the question at the head of this chapter is superfluous because the course on European law is a compulsory part of their study programme (although they will, I hope, form a substantial part of the readership). In most cases members of this group will already have spent a year or more studying the law and will have covered certain theoretical and conceptual aspects of the subject as well as some of the substantive law subjects of the legal system in which they are working, in particular its constitutional law and legal history as well as some of the law of property, the law of contractual obligations or criminal law. Necessary though those elements are in the course of legal training, they cannot prepare the student for the culture shock of embarking on the study of European law.

There are many thousands of legal practitioners and judges who, like me, completed their legal training having had little, if any, contact with European law. I hope that they will find this work helpful in providing a starting point from which to approach the subject and an outline of the context in which European law operates. Moreover, as we shall see, the impact of European law is now so great within the economic, political and social fabric of European States and beyond, that it is necessary even for non-lawyers to have some grasp of the basic mechanisms and how they work. Here I am thinking particularly of journalists, politicians and teachers of or researchers in other disciplines.

In short, the aim of the book is to provide a primer of European law on the one hand for those embarking on its study in the hope

---

10   For an excellent general manual on study skills see Andrew North-edge, *The Good Study Guide* (Open University, 1990). For the more particular requirements of studying law and using legal materials, in addition to Glanville Williams' immortal, *Learning the Law* (11th ed., 1994) see Bradney & Others, *How to Study Law* (Sweet and Maxwell, 1986) and Holland and Webb, *Learning Legal Rules* (2nd ed., Blackstone Press, 1994).

of easing them over the hurdle of arcane terminology and a plethora of overlapping organisations and institutions, and on the other hand to demystify the legal aspects of those organisations and institutions, for those who encounter European law in its various forms in their day-to-day work.

To that end the next chapter will trace the post-war history of intergovernmental co-operation and the creation of various European organisations, drawing a distinction between inter-governmental co-operation and economic integration. Definitions of the five different degrees of economic integration are also given. The remainder of the chapter includes brief outlines of the organisation and competences of the major European intergov-ernmental organisations divided into those responsible for economic and political co-operation, for security and defence co-operation and for co-operation in specific technical fields, in particular co-operation in the area of nuclear energy. Chapter 3 charts the progress of European integration from the establish-ment of the European Coal and Steel Community to the European Union as it is now shaped under the Treaty of Amsterdam. Here the institutions of the European Communities and the Union are treated in some depth and attention is also given to certain other organisations because of their close connection with the European Union, in particular the Benelux Union, the European Economic Area and the countries covered by the Schengen Convention.

Part Two of the book goes to the heart of the matter. First I will attempt an overall definition of European law in all its diversity. Here it is necessary to look at some of the components of Euro-pean law, namely public international law, the nature and characteristics of treaties, the definition of a State and the crucial and controversial characteristic which States have, that of sover-eignty. For convenience private international law is also mentioned at this point. The remainder of the chapter deals with the sources of European law taking in turn the founding treaties, the different forms of Community legislation, then moving on to the general principles of law, decisions of the courts, legal writing and "soft" law.

Chapter 5 deals with the complex, delicate and fascinating question of the impact of European law, in all its manifestations, within the national legal systems of States involved. Here we look first at the ways in which different States make constitutional arrangements in order to comply with their obligations under international law, and then in turn examine the impact of the European Convention on Human Rights within the Member States of the Council of Europe, before moving on to European Community law and the vital doctrines of direct effect and pri-macy which characterise the European Community legal order.

The relationship between the law of the European Union and

that of the European Economic Area and their respective Member States is summarised, and finally the chapter contains a section on the interaction between the protection of fundamental rights under the European Convention and under European Community law.

There is permanent confusion between the titles, functions and even location of the various European courts and Chapter 6 is aimed to dispel this. In a series of sections laid out in identical manner the title, location, composition, jurisdiction and procedure of all of the European courts are outlined. For the sake of completeness the International Court of Justice at The Hague is treated in the same fashion and brief mention is made of certain other specialised international law tribunals which happen to be based in Europe. The chapter ends with a brief guide to bringing cases before the European courts.

Part Three of the book consists of two chapters which together constitute a sort of user's manual for materials on European law including how to locate legislation or case-law which might be needed in order to answer an essay assignment or to give advice to a client. Chapter 7 also deals with forms of citation which, with the increasing use of electronic retrieval systems and databases are actually becoming more rather than less important than in the past. In addition to law students and legal practitioners this section should also be helpful to librarians and documentalists in universities, government departments and law firms who are often asked to hunt for authorities with only the scantiest clues to follow.

Given the different purpose and origin of the rules and principles of European law it is hardly surprising that the methods for working with them and, above all, the principles for interpreting them differ somewhat from those familiar within national legal systems. Such differences in approach, far from being an abstract, priestly mystery, may have very important and direct consequences for the effect of the rules under consideration which may be at variance with the result of applying purely national approaches. Chapter 8 therefore outlines the methods and approach to interpretation, in particular of the European Court of Justice and of the European Court of Human Rights.

Part Four of the book deals with some of the special features of studying European law, placing emphasis on the importance of learning languages as well as simply the rules of the various legal systems. Specific features such as traineeships in European Community institutions and the contribution of European Community law to student mobility through the recognition of diplomas are also covered. For professionals not having received any training in European law during their formal training, Chapter 9 includes a section on continuing education. Chapter 10 on the practical application of European law as a part of one's professional equipment deals with joining and working within both the European and national civil service, joining the legal professions and using European law both in domestic practice and for the purposes of appearing before the European courts. That section also includes a brief outline of the legislation and case law on establishing oneself as a lawyer in a Member State other than the one in which you obtained your legal qualification. The chapter, and the text part of this book concludes with an illustration of the wide range of applications of European law for professional purposes outside the narrow scope of the legal professions, thus rejoining the theme of the first part of this chapter.

The final part of the book is a Vade-mecum intended as a practical manual for students, practitioners and other users of European law. Thus there is a brief style guide containing warnings of the main solecisms committed by journalists and others in writing about European law. A list of some of the many abbreviations and acronyms which are encountered in dealing with the subject are included, as well as a list of cases often referred to by their nicknames and which without this sort of cross-referencing are nearly impossible to trace.

To sum up, I hope that, by placing the development of European law in the wider context of European organizations and by explaining some of the specific concepts and legal methods which are peculiar to European law, students will be able to embark on its study in greater confidence. For those who are not in pursuit of a legal qualification but who do encounter European law in their professional work I hope that this book will better enable you to appreciate the impact of European law in your field and to handle its vocabulary with confidence.

# 2. EUROPEAN ORGANISATIONS: INTERGOVERNMENTALISM

*"Eutia non sunt multiplicanda praeter necessitatem."* William of
Occam, *early fourteenth century.*[10a]

The urgent need for economic reconstruction in Western Europe
after the Second World War, the longer term concern to create
conditions in which any future such conflagration would be
unthinkable, and the perceived threat of the Communist regimes
to the east of the Iron Curtain, could only be dealt with successfully through concerted action by the countries concerned with
the active help of former allies such as the United States and
Canada. These different objectives and varying political conditions and priorities in the countries concerned resulted in the
establishment in the late 1940s and early 1950s of a series of
organisations and groupings of states, each dealing with a more or
less widely defined aspect of the three basic problems. These
groupings included various fora[11] within which those issues could

10a This principle, known as "Occam's Razor", may be translated in
various ways: a literal version might be "Things (or bodies) should
not be multiplied except from necessity"; a pithier paraphrase might
be "keep it simple".
11 To call them "mere fora" would be to do an injustice both to the
importance of the matters discussed and to Winston Churchill's
aphorism that "to jaw jaw is better than to war war" (in a speech at
the White House, June 26, 1954).

be discussed between governments, with a view to establishing a common approach and consensus while leaving intact the sovereign freedom of those governments. Others, as we shall see, had a clearly defined mandate and included the creation of institutions with powers to regulate and manage certain areas of activity.

Unfortunately for the average citizen and all but a few lawyers or specialists in international relations, the names, and worse still the acronyms, given to these institutions are based on an extremely limited vocabulary, in which, quite apart from the ubiquitous adjective "European", the words "association", "organisation", "council" and "economic" recur, often meaning different things according to their context. Moreover, perhaps inevitably, the internal structure of these organisations includes elements (variously called "institutions", "bodies" and "organs") in which the words "council" (again), "commission" and "agency" recur.

Given that the central purpose of this book is to provide an introduction to European law, I propose to concentrate on the organisations and institutions which have contributed most to the development of that law, in particular the European Communities, covered in the next chapter, and the Council of Europe. However, it is necessary to introduce the other organisations which have contributed to European integration, partly to resolve confusion and to avoid terminological inexactitude, and partly because many of their functions and tasks are complementary to each other, though rarely overlapping more than partially.

The terminological difficulties referred to above are compounded by the difficulties in classifying the various institutions concerned. Broadly speaking, two categories may be identified. On the one hand there are those which represent the traditional approach to international co-operation in which efforts are directed to reaching a consensual position between sovereign independent states. This form of organisation is sometimes called intergovernmental and was famously supported by Mrs Thatcher, then Prime Minister of the United Kingdom, in a speech made in Bruges on September 20, 1988. The other category of organisation is that whose purpose is closer integration of states, including the creation of supranational institutions whose power can override that of the states themselves and which are sometimes, rightly or wrongly, described as federalist in tendency.

Such a neat distinction between categories might be easy to grasp and apply were it not for the fact that the two categories are not mutually exclusive. That is to say sovereign States may, and do, belong quite happily to bodies which co-operate for certain purposes or which involve different combinations of states, while at the same time belonging to other associations or groupings whose aim is deeper integration. Moreover, the waters are further muddied by a hybridization between the two categories so that, for example, the Council of Europe, which in many ways is a traditional vehicle for intergovernmental co-operation, has adopted the European Convention on Human Rights and Fundamental Freedoms and established an effective supranational mechanism to ensure its proper observance in all signatory States. By contrast the European Community, which refers in the preamble to its principal treaty to a desire to create "an ever closer union among the peoples of Europe" and which established a most sophisticated system of supranational institutions and procedures, has evolved into the European Union in which two significant elements (Common Foreign and Security Policy and Justice and Internal Affairs[12]) are explicitly stated to be based on intergovernmental co-operation. These two elements, while operating through the institutions which were originally created to further integration, in large measure exclude the intervention of those which could result in co-operation going further than consensual discussion.

## THE DISTINCTION BETWEEN INTERGOVERNMENTAL CO-OPERATION AND INTEGRATION

So far as States are concerned, intergovernmental co-operation is characterised by the search, through more or less structured meetings and discussions, for a freely arrived at consensus. Organisations whose principal aim is co-operation usually have a straightforward institutional structure consisting of a body formed by representatives of the States which is supported by a small secretariat to prepare and organise meetings. They may also have other institutions which, however, are either subordinate to the intergovernmental body or are merely consultative. Even where States are required by the agreements or treaties establishing such organisations to discuss particular issues in that forum, their conclusions do not affect the sovereignty of those States. This is either because they bind only those States which have agreed to be so bound, or because they are required to adopt positions on the basis of unanimity.

Legally such accords are no more than international agreements or even draft international agreements. Even if the acts or decisions adopted by such bodies did not require any approval through national constitutional procedures, in such organisations the legal problems only arise from the internal operation of the organisation. Important organisational tasks do not depend on a

---

12 The Justice and Internal Affairs "pillar" of the European Union is now entitled "Provisions on Police and Judicial Co-operation in Criminal Matters", and has (to a large extent) been incorporated into the Community structure. See below, Chapter 3 at pp. 83–84.

complex legal order and the organisation can therefore manage without a court to resolve disputes. It will have little or no legal impact because all of its powers are those relating to the external relations which the Member States guard so closely. The clearest examples of such organisations are those which are established for an important though limited technical purpose such as the European Organisation for Nuclear Research (known as CERN from the initials of its French title *Conseil Européen pour la Recherche Nucléaire*) or the European Conference of Postal and Telecommunications Administrations (or CEPT from the French, *Conférence Européenne de l'Administration Postale et des Télécommunications*). The organisations which fall most squarely within this category are those whose principal concern is defence (such as NATO and the Western European Union, see below) or those whose objective is broad, cultural or economic co-operation such as the Council of Europe or the OECD.

So far as integrationist organisations are concerned the main characteristics are that their institutions are endowed with their own powers similar to those exercised by States in their respective internal constitutional orders. Moreover, in the institutions in which the Member States are represented, at least some of the decisions may be adopted by majority vote while bodies or institutions composed of persons who do not directly represent the states have a part in the decision-making process. Finally, and most importantly, the powers of the organisation are exercised directly without going through the intermediary of national governments. Such organisations inevitably have powers closely circumscribed by specific and detailed rules which in many cases may evolve into a fully-fledged legal order and which in any case require the supervision and constraining authority of a court.

As I have already mentioned, the distinction between intergovernmental or co-operative organisations and those whose purpose is closer integration is not a sharp one and should be used with caution. In the first place, the distinction has no legal significance since, for example, co-operative institutions may have very extensive powers within their fields of activity. Conversely, integrationist organisations may depend upon unanimous agreement among their members in order to take certain measures, even where those fall clearly within the competence of the organisation concerned. However, one of the distinctive characteristics of integrationist organisations is that they do more than simply establish a framework within which States may work together in a particular field: they also create institutions which, by independently pursuing the aims for which they were established, may further contribute to the integration process.

Finally, given that the process of European integration (in the broader sense of that term) is conducted in the real world by human beings and political parties within the different Member States which both guide and follow public opinion, the process does not lend itself to any neat, scientific categorization. For present purposes, however, the distinction is helpful in describing the various organisations but it should always be borne in mind that, in practical terms, the difference between them may be less wide than at first sight appears.

## Forms of Integration

Although economic integration is itself a major objective of many of the international organisations described in this and the next chapter and such integration is itself a stepping-stone towards political integration, it may take many different forms according to the degree of integration desired by the parties. Five different forms of integration may be identified and are present in the various European organisations described below and in the next chapter.

In ascending order of the degree of integration there are first a *free trade area* in which customs tariffs and quantitative restrictions on trade between the participating countries are abolished. However each Member State retains its own tariffs in respect of goods imported from non-member countries. This necessitates complex rules for the establishment of the origin of goods to prevent deflection of trade from third countries entering the free trade area through a country whose third party tariff is low to be sold on, under the free trade area's rules, to a country in which a direct import would have been charged a higher tariff. EFTA (see pp. 28 *et seq*) is the classic example of such an organisation.[12a] That problem is avoided in the second stage, the establishment of a *customs union* which, in addition to abolishing discrimination affecting trade in commodities within the union, results in the equalization of tariffs for trade with non-member countries and the establishment thereby of a common external customs tariff. This system is neatly summarized in Article 23 (ex Article 9) EC which provides that "the Community shall be based upon a customs union which shall cover all trade in goods and which shall involve the prohibition between Member States of customs duties on imports and exports and of all charges having equivalent effect, and the adoption of a common customs tariff in their relations with third countries."

A *common market* takes integration one stage further enabling not only goods but labour, capital and services to be freely traded

12a A Central European Free Trade Area (CEFTA) was established in 1992 by the Czech Republic, Poland, Hungary, Slovakia and Slovenia. Romania joined in 1997 and Bulgaria will become a member in January 1999.

between the Member States free of tariff protection, restrictive technical regulation or other impediment. Article 8(1) of the EEC Treaty originally provided that "the Common Market shall be progressively established during a transitional period of twelve years", that is to say by 1970 in so far as the original six Member States were concerned. In order to avoid having to make the damaging admission that the Emperor had no clothes, the Single European Act[13] set a new target, that of achieving an internal market by December 31, 1992. Article 14 (ex Article 7(a)) EC defines the internal market as "an area without internal frontiers in which the free movement of goods, persons, services and capital is ensured".

The fourth stage, that of an *economic union*, combines the elimination of restrictions on the movement of goods and the factors of production with a certain degree of harmonization of national economic and social policies in order to remove distortions arising from the disparities in those policies between the Member States. This stage may include monetary union with the use of a single currency and progressive alignment of fiscal policy. Finally, *total economic and political integration*, such as that which exists in the United Kingdom between Scotland, England, Wales and Northern Ireland, requires the unification of monetary, fiscal, social and other policies under the supervision of supranational bodies whose decisions are binding on and enforceable against the Member States.

## INTERGOVERNMENTAL ORGANIZATIONS

In common with most of the textbooks on European law, I take as my starting point the flowering of European organisations that took place just after the Second World War, a conflict which is generally given the credit for giving political impetus to the integration process. While that approach makes a convenient starting point, it should not be forgotten that the idea of Europe as an entity did not begin with Sir Winston Churchill's famous Zurich speech in which he proposed to "recreate the European family . . . and provide it with a structure under which it can dwell in peace, in safety and in freedom. We must build a kind of United States of Europe".[14]

It may not be necessary to go back so far as the peopling of the world by the sons of Noah in which, we are told, that Japheth and his seven sons and their wives were given the responsibility for providing Europe with its population. Readers should however be aware of the earlier history of Europe during the 19th and 20th centuries. Thus the impact of the great Depression of the 1930s

---

13   Which, despite its title, was adopted on February 17, 1986 in Luxembourg and again eleven days later in The Hague.
14   September 19, 1946.

was still relatively fresh in the minds of political leaders in the 1940s and 50s, as was the equally horrific, albeit geographically more limited carnage of the First World War. To a lesser extent the Franco-Prussian War, the unification of Germany under Bismarck and of Italy under Garibaldi and Cavour, all played a part in creating a climate of opinion favourable to greater solidarity between European nations.

While bearing in mind that the following classification is adopted mainly for convenience in description, and is not a rigid or infallible one, one can divide intergovernmental organisations into three categories: those whose purpose is economic or political co-operation, those concerned with matters of security and defence and those responsible for co-operation in specific technical fields.

## Economic and Political Co-operation

### *Organisation for Economic Co-operation and Development ("OECD")*

Once the immediate chaos and disruption caused in Europe by the Second World War had subsided, the Government of the United States of America realized that the United Kingdom, Germany and the formerly occupied countries were too debilitated and their infrastructures too disrupted to enable them to play a full part in maintaining the peace, and in international relations generally. Moreover they lacked the financial resources to be able to import food for their populations and the equipment and materials necessary for the reconstruction effort.

So, on June 5, 1947 in a speech at Harvard University, the then Secretary of State, George Marshall, announced the establishment of a European recovery programme under which the United States would give massive financial assistance to provide a platform for the resumption of normal economic and political life. A conference was convened in Paris in July 1947 whose aim was to establish the needs and priorities for the re-establishment of economic life in Europe. Recognizing, however, that it might be resented, even if it were possible, for the United States actually to implement this aid programme, the Americans proposed that a European organisation be set up to supervise the application of the aid.

That organisation, established on April 16, 1948, was the Organisation for European Economic Co-operation ("OEEC"). The fifteen original Member States were joined by the Federal Republic of Germany after its foundation in 1949 and by Spain in 1959. The United States and Canada had become associate members in 1950.

By 1956 the success of the European Coal and Steel Community (see below) had encouraged the six Member States of that organisation to open discussions within the OEEC with a view to closer integration. Those talks, following a conference held in Messina in 1955, ultimately led to the creation of the European Economic Community (EEC) and the Atomic Energy Community ("Euratom"). The United Kingdom and six other European States for whom the European Communities then represented too high a degree of integration established a free trade area (EFTA) in May 1960.

Those developments and the effective completion of the Marshall aid programme[15] led to the winding-up of the OEEC. and its re-establishment in December 1961 as the OECD, which now includes in its membership the United States, Canada, Australia, New Zealand, Japan, Korea and Mexico, as well as all of the European Union Member States. Its task, as its name suggests, is to encourage economic co-operation between industrialized States, to co-ordinate development assistance to the Third World and to provide a forum for the discussion and resolution of problems affecting world trade and economic growth. Under the aegis of the OECD the Group of seven ("G7"),[16] a group of leading industrialized countries, was set up and has now been extended to eight nations to include the Russian Federation. The OECD provided the framework which resulted in the establishment of the European Bank for Reconstruction and Development ("EBRD") in May 1990 with a view to encouraging economic restructuring and the development of open markets in former Communist countries, an exercise with obvious parallels to the original Marshall plan.

The principal authority of the OECD is its council composed of a representative, usually at ambassador level, from each member country and from the European Commission. Once per year the council meets at ministerial level with Ministers of Foreign Affairs, Finance and Trade to establish the political and economic priorities for the work of the Organisation for the coming year. The council may take decisions which are binding on the Member States (though such decisions can only be adopted on the basis of unanimity) and may make recommendations to Member States. The Secretariat co-ordinates the activities of the organisation and monitors the economic performance of the Member States, resulting in reports which are highly authoritative and keenly followed by other states and by the international financial and commodity markets. Typically for an intergovernmental organisation, the OECD has no machinery for enforcement of its decisions, no obligatory system for resolving disputes, nor is it accountable either to a parliamentary assembly or to national parliaments for its activities.

15   Which by now had disbursed some US$ 13 billion.
16   See Vade-mecum XII. G Spot.

*The GATT and the World Trade Organisation*

As its very name suggests the work of the World Trade Organisation ("WTO") and the application of the principal legal instrument upon which it is based, the General Agreement on Tariffs and Trade ("GATT"), have an impact far beyond the boundaries of Europe. However, an awareness of the basic purpose and organisation of the WTO and the GATT is essential to a proper understanding of one of the most important aspects of the activity of the European Community, namely its trade with non-Member States. In that context the European Community must observe the rules of international trade which have been codified in the GATT. Moreover, although each of the Member States of the European Communities is also a member of the WTO, the European Community as a legal entity is also a member in its own right. In the field of international trade the Commission conducts negotiations on behalf of the Community as a whole and on the basis of a mandate given to it by the Council of the European Union in accordance with Article 133 (ex Article 113) of the EC Treaty.

The original GATT, signed by the governments of 23 countries, was opened for signature on October 30, 1947 and entered into force on a provisional basis on January 1, 1948. The fact that it remained in force on that basis for nearly 50 years makes it a striking example of the durability of such "provisional" arrangements. Now nearly all of the world's trading nations are signatories to the GATT. The agreement lays down the principal rules governing international trade, the main object being to increase the volume of trading by reducing tariff barriers and other obstacles to trade and hence to increase world prosperity generally. This aim is of particular importance to developing countries for whose trade specially favourable conditions are available.

The agreement requires signatory states to reduce tariffs on the trade of goods between each other and not to take any steps likely to damage such trade, while at the same time allowing for states who consider themselves to have been the victims of such measures to take retaliatory action. It is based on a principle of non-discrimination (so-called "most favoured nation" status) under which trading privileges granted to one trading partner must be open to all others within the agreement. An exception to this principle is made for members of customs unions. The agreement has been renegotiated several times in so-called "rounds"[17] of

---

17  The seven previous rounds have been known successively as the First Geneva Round (1947), the Annecy Round (1949), the Torquay Round (1950), the Second Geneva Round (1956), the Dillon Round (1960–61), the Kennedy Round (1964–67) and the Tokyo Round

negotiation, most recently under the Uruguay Round between 1986 and 1993.

The Final Act embodying the results of the Uruguay Round of multilateral trade negotiations, signed by 117 nations at Marrakesh on April 15, 1994, is an astonishingly complex document[18] which incorporates the Marrakesh agreement establishing the World Trade Organisation and some 28 other agreements running to several hundred pages of legal texts. A further 26,000 pages of schedules are appended to the Final Act. I would suggest that reading the WTO agreement is an exercise which should only be embarked upon by those with a real need to know about the intricacies of international trade, preferably equipped beforehand with a sound basic knowledge of the subject and a textbook to serve as a guide. For present purposes a brief outline of the agreement will suffice.

The agreement itself sets up the World Trade Organisation and lays down the rules governing its functions, its structure and its voting procedures. It provides that all of the existing contracting parties to GATT in 1947 become the original Members of the WTO and lays down a uniform accession procedure for new members. By contrast with the Secretariat General of the GATT, its predecessor, the WTO is a formal and permanent organisation with its own legal personality.

The WTO agreement has six annexes, the first of which itself has a complex content. Moreover, the structure and terminology adopted lend themselves to terminological confusion. Thus Annex 1(a) includes the GATT 1994. The GATT 1994 itself consists of several elements including the GATT 1947, as amended and consolidated over the years, and separate instruments adopted pursuant to the GATT 1947. It also includes a series of understandings on the interpretation of various of the rules included in the GATT 1994 and the Marrakesh protocol to the GATT 1994 which deals with several issues concerning tariffs. The GATT 1994 has not replaced the GATT 1947 which continues to exist for certain purposes and between certain contracting states.

(1973–79). The principal achievement of those seven rounds was the reduction of average tariff levels on goods imported between the contracting parties from just over 40 per cent to approximately 5 per cent by the time the Tokyo Round tariff cuts were completed.

18    The text of the Final Act and its various annexes and accessory agreements is published itself as an annex to the Decision of the Council of the European Communities No. 94/800/EC of December 22, 1994 (1994 OJ L 336), approving the Marrakesh agreements. A helpfully annotated copy of the text edited by Philip Raworth and Linda C. Reif, *The Law of the WTO, final text of the GATT Uruguay Round Agreements* (Oceana, 1995) is available in "The Practitioner's Deskbook Series".

## The Structure of the WTO Agreement:

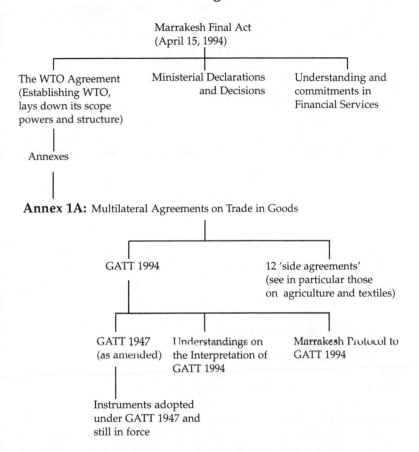

Marrakesh Final Act
(April 15, 1994)

The WTO Agreement
(Establishing WTO,
lays down its scope
powers and structure)

Ministerial Declarations
and Decisions

Understanding and
commitments in
Financial Services

Annexes

**Annex 1A:** Multilateral Agreements on Trade in Goods

GATT 1994

12 'side agreements'
(see in particular those
on agriculture and textiles)

GATT 1947
(as amended)

Understandings on
the Interpretation of
GATT 1994

Marrakesh Protocol to
GATT 1994

Instruments adopted
under GATT 1947 and
still in force

**Annex 1B:** General Agreement on Trade in Services (GATS)
**Annex 1C:** Agreement on Trade Related Aspects of Intellectual
Property Rights (TRIPS)
**Annex 2:** Understanding on Rules and Procedures Governing the
Settlement of Disputes (DSU)
**Annex 3:** Trade Policy Review Mechanism
**Annex 4:** Plurilateral Trade Agreements:      Civil Aircraft
Government Procurement
Dairy Products

Annexes 1(b) and 1(c) include a new "General Agreement on Trade in Services" ("GATS") and an agreement on "Trade-Related aspects of Intellectual Property Rights" (known as "TRIPS"). So far as the European Community was concerned the problem arose of whether or not the European Community as such, or its Member States, or both jointly were competent to conclude those agreements. That question was put to the Court of Justice which concluded[19] that the Community acting through the Commission had exclusive competence with respect to trade in goods, including action where necessary against counterfeit goods, although it shared its competence with the Member States so far as trade in services and intellectual property rights were concerned.

The other important annex is Annex 2, "Understanding on Rules and Procedures governing the settlement of Disputes" (known for short as the "Disputes Settlement Understanding" or "DSU"). The DSU established a "Dispute Settlement Body" ("DSB") to provide a formalised structure for the resolution of trade disputes. Under that scheme, where mediation or conciliation fail to resolve any dispute, a panel may be constituted from whose decisions an appeal on points of law may lie to a standing Appellate Body which is a court in all but name.[20]

*The European Free Trade Association (EFTA)*

As mentioned above, EFTA was established at the initiative of the United Kingdom in large measure in response to the setting up of the EEC by six of the Member States of the OEEC. While wishing to avoid the degree of economic integration proposed by the six founding EEC States, the United Kingdom and six other OEEC. members (Switzerland, Denmark, Norway, Austria, Portugal and Sweden) thought that liberalization of trade between them would bring significant economic benefits. Moreover, as a trading group, they would carry more weight in the international arena than any of them could muster individually.

The association came into being by the Stockholm Convention of January 3, 1960 with the aim of establishing the free movement of goods between the Member States while reducing tariffs and quotas in parallel to the reductions taking place between the members of the EEC, a procedure which left open the possibility of a collective negotiation for the accession of EFTA to the EEC. Contrary to the EEC however, the EFTA Convention did not cover agricultural or fisheries products, nor did it include any common economic policy. So far as external trade was concerned, the

19   Opinion 1/94 (World Trade Organisation) [1994] ECR. I–5267.
20   See Chapter 6 at p. 204 below.

association was limited to making slight clarifications or adjustments to the principles set out in the GATT, and indeed among its aims was to make a contribution to "the harmonious development and expansion of world trade", a phrase used in the GATT. The membership of EFTA has ebbed and flowed with the successive accession of Member States to the European Communities and other developments. Thus Finland, because of its special relationship with the Soviet Union, became an associate member in 1961 and a full member in 1986. Iceland joined in 1970, while Denmark and the United Kingdom withdrew in January 1973 as did Portugal in 1986. Liechtenstein, which as a result of its customs union with Switzerland, had a special status within EFTA and became a member in 1991. Since the accession of Austria, Finland and Sweden to the European Union in January 1995 it is one of the four remaining EFTA States, namely Iceland, Liechtenstein, Norway and Switzerland.

As originally conceived in the Stockholm Convention EFTA had only one institution, the EFTA Council, which contained representatives of member governments meeting at either ministerial or civil level. As a typical intergovernmental organisation, decisions normally require unanimity, each Member State therefore effectively having a veto. A committee of parliamentarians from the EFTA States was established in 1977 in order to discuss matters of common interest and which could be consulted by the Council on certain questions. There is also a Consultation Committee comprising representatives of both sides of industry as well as numerous working parties of officials from the member governments.

This clear picture of EFTA as an intergovernmental organisation was seriously muddied by the establishment of the European Economic Area (EEA) by the Oporto Agreement, signed between the then twelve Member States of the European Communities and seven Member States of EFTA. Switzerland, whose people and cantons both rejected the Agreement in a referendum held on December 6, 1992, did not ratify the Agreement. Liechtenstein however, in a referendum held a few days later, did approve the Agreement, and became a member of the EEA in 1996 after special negotiations necessitated by its monetary and customs unions with Switzerland.

The EEA institutions will be described in the next chapter. However, it should be mentioned that, as originally drafted, the EEA Agreement envisaged the creation of an EEA Court of Justice which would have been composed jointly of judges from the EFTA countries and from the European Court of Justice. However, the latter court, asked for its opinion on the compatibility of the proposed agreement with the EC Treaty under Article 228 of that Treaty, ruled that such an arrangement was incompatible with the prerogatives of the Court of Justice as laid down in the EEC Treaty and with the autonomy of the legal order of the Community.[21] The Agreement was hurriedly revised to provide for the establishing of an EFTA Court whose jurisdiction is discussed in Chapter 6.

*The Council of Europe*

This is perhaps the least widely understood of all the European organisations and, when it does enter into consideration, it is all too often and understandably confused with the European Council or the Council of the European Union, these latter two being parts of the European Union. Such lack of recognition is a pity given the important work carried out by the organisation in many fields, most notably the protection of human rights, and the role it has assumed more recently in helping to develop and consolidate the emerging democracies in the Central and Eastern European countries. Most of the latter countries have now joined the Council of Europe which, as a result, now has 40 Member States with five further candidates awaiting membership and holding "special guest" status. Three non-European countries, Canada, the United States and Japan, also have observer status.

The Council of Europe was established by a treaty signed on May 5, 1949 in the light of ideas debated at the Congress of Europe held at The Hague a year earlier. In the event, the ambitious plans discussed at that Congress by some 800 delegates from nearly all of the States of Europe were not realized and the Council of Europe began as an organisation of 10 States with a straightforward institutional arrangement reflecting its intergovernmental nature. The three institutions are: the Committee of Ministers, which is the central decision-making body; the Parliamentary Assembly, which may deliberate on matters of current interest and address resolutions to the Committee of Ministers; and thirdly the Congress of Local and Regional Authorities of Europe, a consultative body in which, as its name suggests, local and regional authorities are represented and which may also submit resolutions to the Committee of Ministers. It should be noted that none of the members of those three institutions is directly elected. Thus for example the Member States are represented in the Committee of Ministers by the Minister for Foreign Affairs or for certain purposes his or her deputy or permanent representative. The Parliamentary Assembly (initially called the Consultative Assembly) is composed of 245 delegates appointed by national parliaments from among their own membership. Similarly, the

21   See Opinion 1/91, [1991] ECR. I–6079.

Congress of Local and Regional Authorities consists of 286 members designated from among elected local or regional authorities. The three institutions are supported by a single, permanent Secretariat. The work of the Council of Europe may touch on virtually any political, social or cultural issue which faces Europe as a whole, with the exception of defence and security matters. Thus recent conventions have dealt with matters such as the prevention of torture, spectator violence at sporting events, data protection, the protection of regional or minority languages and wildlife and natural habitats.

Such conventions, once adopted, do not have direct legal effect in the Member States unless and until each Member State[21a] has individually signed and ratified the convention concerned. According to the respective constitutional requirements of the Member States it may then be necessary to adopt further implementing legislation in order to incorporate the principles and rules of the relevant convention into domestic law so that it can be applied in specific circumstances by the national courts of the Member States. Those conventions therefore constitute an important source of European law. Moreover, the process of deliberating upon a particular issue and then drafting and agreeing the text of a convention to deal with it represents a process of crystallization of a political consensus which will inform and influence the treatment of the question within domestic politics and legislative activity even in the absence of formal ratification and implementation of a convention. Other less formal instruments which may be adopted by the Committee of Ministers include charters, codes of practice and recommendations.

By far the best known of the Council of Europe conventions, and probably its most outstanding achievement, is the Convention for the Protection of Human Rights and Fundamental Freedoms signed in Rome on September 4, 1950.[22] That Convention has been complemented by a series of protocols (adopted in the same manner as the Convention itself), intended to protect certain rights and freedoms other than those already included in the Convention itself. The sixth protocol concerns the abolition of the death penalty. Although the Universal Declaration of Human Rights had already been adopted by the United Nations on

21a Certain conventions designated "Council of Europe Conventions" may be open to signature and ratification by non-Member States. Conventions open only to Member States are known as "European Conventions".

22 87 UNTS, 103; ETS 5. Often abbreviated to the European Convention on Human Rights or the Human Rights Convention. For a list of the rights protected under the Convention and its protocols, see Vademecum VI.

December 10, 1948, the important and original feature of the European Convention was that it not only enumerated the rights whose protection was to be ensured but also set up enforcement procedures and institutions. The States signatory to the Convention were therefore obliged not only to agree to observe its principles and standards, but also to confer rights on individuals under international law.

The enforcement machinery is explained in more detail in Chapter 6 below. However, it may be mentioned here that, as originally conceived, the machinery was based upon a two-tier structure. First, the European Commission of Human Rights[23] whose task is to establish the admissibility of complaints and having done so to establish the facts of a particular case and to seek to promote an amicable settlement between the parties. In the absence of such a settlement the Commission draws up a report, including an expression of an opinion as to the existence or otherwise of an infringement of the Convention. The report is adopted by a simple majority and may have dissenting opinions annexed to it. The second tier is the European Court of Human Rights whose role is to make a definitive adjudication on the existence or otherwise of an infringement.

In May 1994, an eleventh protocol to the Convention was adopted whose purpose was to restructure the control machinery established by the Convention. That protocol entered into force in November 1998 whereupon the Commission (after a transitional year to complete outstanding cases) ceased to exist so that the entire review procedure now takes place under the auspices of the Court itself.

*The Nordic Council*

The Nordic Council provides a vehicle for political co-operation in limited spheres between the parliaments and governments of the five member countries. Originally established by an agreement between Denmark, Iceland, Norway and Sweden in 1952, the Union was formalized by the Treaty of Helsinki, signed on March 23, 1962, Finland having joined the four founder members in 1955. Under that Treaty the Nordic Council itself consists of 87 members made up of delegations designated by the national parliaments of each of the five States. The Finnish delegation consists of seven members, including one representative of the Åland Islands. Each of the other delegations consists of twenty

23  Since this has absolutely nothing to do with the Commission of the European Communities, it is best to avoid the expression "European Commission" and, where necessary, to abridge the name to "Human Rights Commission" or if the context allows of no possible confusion, simply "the Commission" as in the text of the Convention itself.

members, the Danish delegation including representatives of the autonomous territories of Greenland and the Faroe Islands.

Following amendments to the Helsinki Treaty in 1971, a new body, the Nordic Council of Ministers, was established in which a Minister from each of the five governments with specific responsibility for Nordic co-operation meet. The Council of Ministers is assisted by a secretariat based in Copenhagen, whereas the Nordic Council itself has a permanent secretariat in Stockholm.

The full Council, which in principle meets once a year, discusses matters of common interest in the fields of communications and transport, cultural matters, economic policy, legal and social affairs and the protection of the environment, those areas being enumerated in the Helsinki Treaty. The Council operates by proposing and monitoring co-operation in specific areas and by submitting recommendations or opinions to the Nordic Council of Ministers and to the member governments. While such recommendations and opinions have no legal force, the fact that they originate from parliamentarians of the member countries (which are accustomed to consensual politics) means that such proposals very often result in action by the governments concerned. The Council of Ministers and the individual governments may themselves put forward matters to be discussed within the Nordic Council.

The most tangible result of the Nordic Council, and one of its earliest successes, was the establishment of a passport union which was completed in 1958 and which enables both nationals of the five States and travellers from third countries to move freely between the five countries once they have entered the territory of the Union. The desire on the part of Denmark, Finland and Sweden to maintain the Nordic Passport Union made it difficult for them to accede to the Schengen Convention (see p. 91 below). However, a Co-operation Convention between Norway and Iceland on the one hand and the Schengen countries on the other resolved the problem.

### Security and defence co-operation

This is an area which is rarely, if ever, dealt with in textbooks on European law. This is understandable given that, on the one hand, the issues which arise are matters of high politics concerning the direct exercise of state sovereignty and are thus pre-eminently matters which are dealt with through intergovernmental means where co-operation is sought at all. Equally, where the law does intervene it is rather traditional international law[24] than any set of

---

24   See Chapter 4 below at p. 100.

rules internal to the organisations involved or adopted collectively by the States concerned and which might conveniently be labelled European law. Nonetheless, for three particular reasons, I believe that an awareness of defence and security issues and of the existence and structure of the principal organisations involved is essential for a proper understanding of the development of European law and the context in which it operates.

First, of course, the desire of all participants, whether citizens or governments, European States or those further afield, to avoid renewed and disastrous conflict led more naturally to the establishment of defence coalitions than it did towards economic and political integration. Secondly, the establishment of a Common Foreign and Security Policy ("CFSP") as one of the pillars of the European Union, incorporating a direct relationship with the longstanding Western European Union ("WEU") brings the issues much closer to other policies of the European Union. In addition, since the Treaty of Amsterdam, the European Parliament and the European Commission as well as the Council play a role in formulating policy in this context. Thirdly, as the Gulf War of 1991 and the disastrous civil war in the former Yugoslavia have shown, expectations of the world at large and Europe's citizens in particular are that an entity with the economic and political weight of the European Union should equally be able to exercise influence in security matters.

The first stage in the process was a treaty between the United Kingdom and France signed, symbolically, at Dunkirk on March 4, 1947. That treaty provided for consultation and for mutual assistance in case of external aggression. The continued consolidation of Communist regimes in countries occupied by Russia and, in particular, developments in Czechoslovakia, led the three Benelux countries to join France and the United Kingdom in adopting the Treaty of Brussels of March 17, 1948 which provided for mutual military assistance and economic, social and cultural co-operation. Although the latter provisions were never followed up or developed, that treaty laid the ground plan for both the WEU and the North Atlantic Treaty Organisation ("NATO").

Following the establishment of the European Coal and Steel Community among the Benelux countries, France, Germany and Italy, the French Government submitted a plan named after its Minister of Defence, René Pléven, for a European Defence Community ("EDC"), with the same institutional structure as that of the Coal and Steel Community. A treaty establishing the European Defence Community was signed in Paris on May 27, 1952 but, ironically, it was the French failure to ratify that treaty which led to its demise. Nonetheless, that particular failure led the six ECSC Member States to consider other forms of integration and to

## European Security and Defence Co-operation

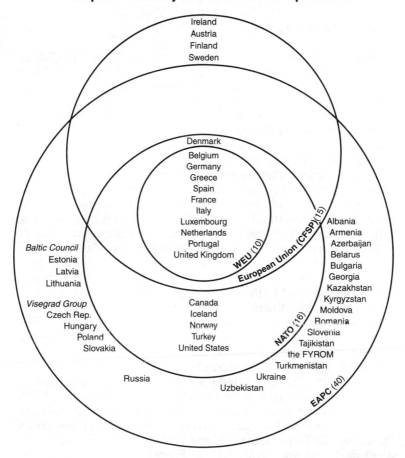

lay the groundwork for the establishment of the European Economic Community and EURATOM at a conference in Messina in June 1955.

## Western European Union

Following the setback of the EDC the United Kingdom Government convened a meeting of the signatories of the Brussels Treaty (that is the UK itself, France and the three Benelux countries), the two other ECSC Member States, Germany and Italy, and the former allies Canada and the United States. The key result of that conference was that the then newly emerged Federal Republic of Germany was allowed to re-arm (although not to construct, hold, or use atomic, biological or chemical weapons) and the Western European Union was established between the original seven Member States by a treaty signed on May 6, 1955. Nonetheless, the fact that NATO had already been established to cover defence matters and the assumption by the Council of Europe of responsibility for social and cultural affairs meant that, for many years, the WEU was practically moribund. It was kept in existence principally as a vehicle for the United Kingdom to maintain direct contact with the six original Member States of the European Communities prior to the United Kingdom's accession.

However, since the mid 1980s the fortunes of the organisation have improved. First in 1984 it was decided to reactivate the WEU as a vehicle to enable the addition of a security dimension to political co-operation between the European Community Member States. The WEU was expanded by the accession of Portugal and Spain in 1990 and Greece in 1995. However, the defining event in the resurrection of the WEU was its inclusion in the Common Foreign and Security Policy established by the European Union in the Maastricht Treaty. In Article J4 of that treaty, the European Union requested the WEU to elaborate and implement decisions and actions of the European Union which have defence implications. In that article the WEU was referred to as "an integral part of the development of the [European] Union".

A certain number of practical measures were also taken such as moving the headquarters of the WEU from London to Brussels, and the representatives of the Member States to the Alliance and to the European Union were empowered to "draw on a double hatting formula"[25] for the purposes of their representation on the WEU Council. Subsequent developments have included observer

---

25  This bizarre expression appears only to mean that the Permanent Representatives of the Member States to the E.U. may also sit in the WEU Council.

status for Austria, Denmark, Finland, Ireland and Sweden, associate membership for the remaining European NATO States, namely Iceland, Norway and Turkey, and "associate partner" status for 10 Central and Eastern European countries. Operationally the WEU has taken part in joint actions in the Gulf. As part of the complex jigsaw of peace initiatives in the former Yugoslavia the WEU operates a naval patrol force in the Adriatic Sea jointly with NATO forces, it provides an independent police force in the divided city of Mostar (Bosnia) and a mission on the River Danube to enforce the embargo on trade with Yugoslavia. A Eurocorps was formed in November 1993 consisting of French, German, Belgian, Luxembourg and Spanish troops.

These aspects of the WEU's activities and its incorporation into the structure of the wider European Union have been further consolidated by the Treaty of Amsterdam which provides for complete replacement of the former Articles J to J.11 of the TEU. Now Article 17 (ex Article J.7) TEU, while reiterating that the WEU is an integral part of the development of the E.U., requires the latter to "foster closer institutional relations with the WEU with a view to the possibility of the integration of the WEU into the [European] Union". The article also states that the tasks which may be conferred on the WEU in this context include "humanitarian and rescue tasks, peacekeeping tasks and tasks of combat forces in crisis management, including peacemaking".

## NATO

The North Atlantic Treaty Organisation (NATO) has already been mentioned in the context of the evolution of the WEU. Nonetheless, because of its close affinity with the WEU already mentioned and its central role in the development of European politics, a further brief mention is appropriate.

The organisation was established by the Treaty of Washington signed on April 4, 1949[26] between Belgium, Canada, Denmark, France, Iceland, Italy, Luxembourg, the Netherlands, Norway, Portugal, United Kingdom and the United States. In 1952 Greece and Turkey joined the organisation. In 1955 Germany was admitted and Spain joined in 1982. As a purely intergovernmental organisation, each of its decision-making bodies comprises representatives of the Member States. Thus the North Atlantic Council comprises the foreign ministers of each Member State with the assistance of permanent representatives, while the defence ministers of the Member States sit both in the Defence Planning Committee and the Nuclear Planning Group. Finally, the Military

26   34 UNTS 243.

Committee comprises senior generals and admirals of each Member State as well as two supreme allied commanders, one covering Europe, the other the Atlantic. The infrastructure for the various meetings and the vehicle for ensuring that all delegations are fully informed of developments is provided by a permanent secretariat which has no independent powers, although the Secretary General is an influential figure who has authority to speak on behalf of the Organisation. The North Atlantic Assembly, while not strictly a part of the NATO structure, has existed since 1955 and now comprises 188 members of the parliaments of the 16 NATO countries. At its twice yearly meetings it may adopt recommendations and resolutions, although its principal function is to provide a broader parliamentary forum for the discussion of defence and security issues and, more recently, to develop parliamentary links with the countries of Central and Eastern Europe.

Since the ending of the Cold War in 1989 NATO and its Member States have had to re-appraise the role of the organisation and re-orient its policies. While maintaining the security of the Member States remains the central function of the organisation, great importance has been placed on the establishment of security links with the States of Central and Eastern Europe and those of the former Soviet Union, including Russia itself. This has been effected by the conclusion of "partnerships for peace" with those States. These relations are developed through the North Atlantic Co-operation Council established by the NATO States in 1991 in order to create a forum for discussion of security issues with those States, while not imposing upon them the benefits and obligations of full membership of the organisation. It is likely that three of the former Warsaw Pact countries, Poland, Hungary and the Czech Republic, will become full members of NATO in 1999.

These relationships were consolidated and developed through the North Atlantic Co-operation Council ("NACC") established by the Nato States in 1991, in order to create a discussion forum for the debate of security issues with the former Warsaw Pact countries and the CIS, while not imposing on the latter the full obligations of membership of NATO.

The NACC was superseded in 1997 by the Euro-Atlantic Partnership Council ("EAPC") which provides a framework for closer political and security related consultations and co-operation. EAPC now has 40 members – while as participants in the wider but looser grouping "Partnership for Peace", Austria, Finland, Sweden and Switzerland have observer status in EAPC.

*Organisation for Security and Co-operation in Europe ("OSCE")*

The Organisation for Security and Co-operation in Europe ("OSCE") with some 55 members (plus seven other "partner" states) is the largest of the European organisations. All of the Member States of the European Union and the Council of Europe are also members of the OSCE and, since the organisation takes a broad view of security as including the development of democratic institutions and economic stability, once again its existence must be borne in mind as part of the context for the development of European law. Originally formed as the Conference on Security and Co-operation in Europe ("CSCE"), like many other bodies it was created as a forum for dialogue rather than as an organisation with power of independent action. The result of the first conference was the signing of the Final Act in Helsinki on August 1, 1975 between 33 European countries, including all of the Warsaw Pact countries, and the United States and Canada. The Final Act covered four areas, curiously known as "baskets", the first dealing with security and disarmament, the second with economic, scientific and technical co-operation, including the protection of the environment. The third was entitled "co-operation in humanitarian and other fields", and the fourth dealt with mechanisms for monitoring and following up the commitments entered into in the first three baskets.

The day-to-day operation of the organisation is ensured by the Permanent Council which meets weekly at its headquarters in Vienna. Its work is supervised and directed by the Senior Council comprising the political directors of participating States who meet three times a year in Prague. At a higher level again the foreign ministers of participating States hold an annual ministerial council meeting and every two years a summit of all of the Heads of State or Government is convened. Among the activities of the organisation are electoral monitoring and the development of national electoral institutions, the provision of technical assistance for the development of national legal institutions, the training of human rights monitors and journalists, the promotion of arms control and conflict prevention.

*Common Foreign and Security Policy*

As its name suggests, the Common Foreign and Security Policy ("CFSP") is not a separate organisation. However, it is convenient to deal with it here partly because of the subject-matter concerned and partly because of its affinity with the WEU as already mentioned. The CFSP constitutes the second of the three pillars which together make up the European Union established by the Maastricht Treaty. The purpose of CFSP is to ensure that, so far as possible, in all matters of foreign relations (with the exception of international trade which falls within the competence of the European Community) the Member States of the Union speak with one voice and do not pursue divergent objectives.

The principal difficulty in achieving such an aim, however desirable it may be in theory, is that the capacity to manage foreign relations is one of the essential ingredients of national sovereignty and indeed is a touchstone of the very existence of an independent state. Moreover, each of the Member States, over the course of their respective histories, has forged particular links with other countries and may thus have specific responsibilities or antagonisms which may not be shared by all or any of the other members.

Arising out of discussions between Member States on foreign policy issues outside the scope of the Community treaties, a series of informal intergovernmental arrangements evolved, providing for regular exchanges of information and meetings between foreign ministers outside the Council meetings. In this area the Commission had no power of initiative, the Parliament might be consulted or informed at the discretion of the ministers and the Court of Justice had no jurisdiction. Following a report in 1981 these informal arrangements were refined in order to provide the capacity for responding to crises more rapidly and, on the institutional level, the Commission was associated with the work of European political co-operation (now formalized and given its own acronym, EPC). A small secretariat was established in Brussels. Those arrangements were consolidated and given a formal existence in Title III of the Single European Act which was headed "Treaty provisions on European co-operation in the sphere of foreign policy". It was specified that "the Commission shall be fully associated with the proceedings of political co-operation" and that the "High Contracting Parties"[27] shall ensure that the European Parliament is closely associated with European political co-operation". To that end the European Parliament was to be regularly informed of the foreign policy issues being examined within EPC, and the presidency was to ensure that the views of the European Parliament were duly taken into consideration.

The Maastricht Treaty replaced EPC with CFSP. The provisions of Title V of the TEU, while still maintaining CFSP at an intergovernmental level, took further steps towards incorporating those issues into the Community structure. Thus, the Council (not just the individual Member States or High Contracting Parties) became the central institution within which Member States were to inform and consult each other on matters of foreign security

---

27    The use of that term makes it clear that, although the High Contracting Parties were in fact the Member States of the European Communities, they were not engaging in political co-operation in that capacity, despite the involvement of the Commission and Parliament.

policy of general interest, while it is for the European Council to "define the principles of and general guidelines for the Common Foreign and Security Policy". The Council is required to act unanimously, except on procedural questions. However, in the context of joint action already agreed in order to achieve one of the aims of CFSP, it may decide that certain matters for which follow-up decisions were to be taken could be dealt with by a qualified majority. Finally, the administrative expenditure arising out of CFSP is charged to the budget of the European Communities, although the Council may also decide that operational expenditure arising from the CFSP be charged either to the budget of the European Communities or to the Member States in accordance with a scale to be decided.

The difficulties of trying to achieve unity in the areas of foreign and security policy were starkly illustrated by the lack of success of the European Union in its interventions in the complexities of the Yugoslav and Rwandan civil wars. Therefore, the need to ensure effective action in these areas led the Member States, by the Treaty of Amsterdam, to completely recast and restructure the CFSP provisions while still maintaining their intergovernmental character. Nonetheless the involvement of the Community institutions is taken one step further in that the Secretary General of the Council is given the tasks of High Representative for the CFSP, the European Parliament is to be kept regularly informed by the presidency and the Commission of the development of the foreign and security policy and it is explicitly given the power to ask questions of the Council or to make recommendations to it. For its part, in addition to being "fully associated with the work carried out in the Common Foreign and Security Policy field", as was the case under the Maastricht Treaty, the Council may request the Commission to submit to it any appropriate proposals relating to the CFSP to ensure the implementation of joint action.

Finally, although it is once again specified that "decisions under this title shall be taken by the Council acting unanimously", it is also provided that abstentions by members shall not prevent the taking of decisions and that abstaining members, while not being obliged to apply any such decision will refrain from any action likely to conflict with it. Moreover, in a number of circumstances by derogation from the principle of unanimity, the Council may act by a qualified majority when adopting joint actions, common positions or taking any other decision on the basis of a common strategy. (As already mentioned in the context of the description of the Western European Union above, the WEU is effectively integrated into the European Union in order to elaborate and implement decisions and actions of the Union regarding defence implications).

## Technical and Scientific Co-operation

### Nuclear Energy

Nuclear energy is a field which, not so much lends itself to co-operation between states but positively demands it. The reasons for this are the massive economic potential of nuclear power as an energy source and the equally huge appetite which it has for investment in research and development as well as the construction of the power stations themselves. Furthermore, the environmental risks inherent in the production of nuclear power require a strong and enforceable regulatory framework including a safety inspectorate covering not only the work of research centres and power stations but also aspects of transport and trade in fissile materials. Finally, of course, the potential for those same fissile materials to be used in the manufacture of nuclear weapons adds a security and defence dimension to the field. Those considerations have led to the establishment of both integrationist and co-operative organisations.

The first such organisation was established under the auspices of the United Nations whose General Assembly adopted the statute of the International Atomic Energy Agency ("IAEA") in 1956.[28] The agency is based in Vienna where its day-to-day management is ensured by a Board of Governors which is ultimately responsible to the General Conference, in which representatives of all of the Member States meet once a year. Various committees are responsible for carrying out specific tasks and the management is under the responsibility of a Secretariat headed by a Director General. Its functions, which are based on voluntary co-operation, without giving rise to significant rights and obligations between the members, include the sharing and dissemination of scientific and technical information, promotion of research and development for peaceful use of atomic energy and technical assistance between the Member States.

The European Atomic Energy Community ("EAEC"), normally called EURATOM, was established by "the other" Treaty of Rome, signed by France, Italy, Germany and the Benelux countries on March 25, 1957.[29] According to Article 2 of the Euratom Treaty, the Community's aim of fostering the conditions necessary for the speedy establishment and growth of nuclear

28   276 UNTS 3.
29   The same day as the treaty establishing the European Economic Community, which is the one more generally referred to as *the* Treaty of Rome. The existence of two treaties equally entitled to that designation should give rise to caution in using it and perhaps its restriction to circumstances where no ambiguity is possible.

industries is to be achieved by the promotion of research and dissemination of technical information, the establishment of uniform safety standards for the health of workers in the industry and the general public as well as the application of those standards, to facilitate investment, to ensure that all users receive a regular and equitable supply of ores and nuclear fuels, and to make certain, by appropriate supervision, that nuclear materials are not diverted to purposes other than those for which they are intended. For those purposes the Community was equipped with the same four institutions as those of the ECSC and the EEC[30] of which the Parliamentary Assembly and the Court of Justice were, from the beginning, common to all three communities. The EAEC Council and Commission were merged with those of the other two communities by the Merger Treaty in 1965.

The emphasis on the promotion of research was confirmed in Article 8 of the Euratom Treaty which provided for the establishment of a joint research centre. This now consists of nine distinct research institutes, of which six are based at Ispra near Turin in Italy, and the remaining three at Geel in Belgium, Karlsruhe in Germany, and Petten in the Netherlands. Under the Maastricht Treaty on European Union ("TEU") a new European science and technology observatory has been set up in Seville whose task is to monitor all research both within and outwith the European Union which has a bearing on the policies and objectives of the Union. Outside the structure of the joint research centres, the Joint European Torus ("JET") based at Culham, England, is essentially a European Union based research project, although Switzerland also participates. Its aim is to develop nuclear fusion as a safer and, in the long run, more sustainable and efficient source of nuclear power than the traditional nuclear fission.

Following the creation of EURATOM by six of the Member States of the then OEEC, in 1958 the remaining countries established a European Nuclear Energy Agency. However, in 1972 the adjective "European" was dropped and membership of the agency was extended to non-European countries. The 27 Member States now include Australia, Canada, Japan, Korea, Mexico and the United States. The overlapping and hybridization of international organisations already mentioned is again illustrated by the fact that the Commission of the European Communities, acting under the Euratom Treaty, takes part in the work of the NEA and that a co-operation agreement is in force between the NEA and the IAEA. Furthermore, with a view to ensuring that the use of materials, equipment or services made available by the agency are not diverted to or made available for any military

---

30 To those the Court of Auditors was added by Article I(1) of the Treaty on European Union.

purpose, a control and inspection service similar to that of the IAEA has been established. However, going further than the IAEA and approaching the integrationist approach of Euratom, the NEA has created an independent tribunal to which governments may appeal against decisions of the inspection and control authorities. The tribunal may also decide claims by national undertakings for compensation in the event that inspection procedures give rise to exceptional damage.

At the purely scientific level the European Organisation for Nuclear Research (known as CERN from the French acronym for *Conseil Européen pour la Recherche Nucléaire*) was established by a convention of July 1, 1953 in order to construct and operate a laboratory and various other types of experimental equipment which were too expensive for individual states. These include a massive particle accelerator built inside a purpose-made circular tunnel 12km in circumference. Apart from an annual budget which dwarfs that of many of the world's nations and scientific successes which often consist of events lasting only for nano-seconds, perhaps the most visible success of CERN was the development by one of its scientists, Tim Berners-Lee, of the Worldwide Web as a vehicle for transmitting and sharing research and data in advanced physics with other research institutes around the world. The rest, as they say, is history.

**Other areas of Co-operation**

The selection of organisations whose purpose and structures are summarized below are engaged in activities generally confined to a limited technical area. Nonetheless the myriad agencies with specific tasks also have a role to play in creating a situation where a *de facto* solidarity may lead to increasing vertical integration. Indeed this was the approach which inspired Robert Schumann's famous declaration of May 9, 1950 in which he proposed the merger of French and German coal and steel production. It is worth mentioning just a few of those organisations.

The European Organisation for the Safety of Air Navigation, known as Eurocontrol, was established in 1963 with a view to bringing the regulation of air traffic under one agency. Despite the increasing overcrowding of the skies over Europe this has not yet happened, owing to Member States' reluctance to relinquish control over their air space and the sheer cost of harmonizing the many different technical systems of air traffic control in existence.

The European Space Agency ("ESA") was established in 1975 on the basis of two pre-existing space research bodies, the European Space Research Organisation ("ESRO") and the European Organisation for the Development and Construction of Space

Vehicle Launches ("ELDO"). With headquarters in Paris and a launching facility in French Guyana, the ESA has developed the Ariane series of rockets which have successfully launched many space satellites.

Monetary and financial corporations have obviously been of prime importance even before the plan for economic and monetary union ("EMU") crystallized in the Maastricht Treaty. Thus the Bank for International Settlements ("BIS"), based in Basle, was established in 1930 to facilitate co-operation and financial transactions between central banks around the world. More recently, the European Bank for Reconstruction and Development ("EBRD") was created in 1989 at the initiative of the President of France, François Mitterand, in order to provide specialized assistance and support to encourage the economic restructuring and the development of market economies in the former Communist countries of Central and Eastern Europe and the former Soviet Union. The European Investment Bank ("EIB") established under the EEC Treaty[31] was set up to contribute to the balanced and steady development of the Common Market by making loans and giving guarantees for infrastructure projects which are of such a size or nature that they cannot be financed by the means available in the individual Member States or for developing Europe's less developed regions.

Transport and communications have an obvious role in facilitating closer co-operation and integration. In the nineteenth century it was already recognized that even non-riparian states had an interest in the principle of freedom of navigation over major international rivers and this was included in the final protocol of the Vienna Congress in June 1815. That protocol applied to the Rhine, the Neckar, the Main and was extended to the Danube by the Paris Treaty of 1856. The latter treaty is of particular interest in the present context since it provided for the establishment of independent commissions which were created to supervise the observance of the Treaty, and which included several non-riparian states. These commissions were arguably the first truly supranational institutions. Later, the Treaty of Versailles in 1919, which embodied the final settlement of the First World War, added non-riparian Member States to the Central Commission for Navigation on the Rhine which had been established by the Convention of Mannheim in 1868. That regime, which was revised and updated after the Second World War, is still in force.

Railway companies from over sixty countries co-operate internationally through the International Union of Railways, which was founded in 1922, although, for obvious practical reasons such

---

31  See now Articles 266 (ex 198d) and 267 (ex 198e) of the EC Treaty.

as the compatibility of gauges and rolling stock, international co-operation between both states and commercial undertakings has been a feature of the railway industry since the period of its greatest expansion in the mid-nineteenth century. Such co-operation involves matters such as ticketing, synchronization of timetables and, in the days before the Schengen Agreement, procedures for customs clearance and passport control on long-distance sleeper trains which might cross several borders in the course of a night journey. At European Community level, the co-operation is co-ordinated by the Community of European Railways which, in addition to the fifteen Member States of the Union, includes Switzerland.

Like the railways, the development of postal communications across state boundaries in the early part of the nineteenth century fostered a need for an international framework for co-operation between postal administrations. At the international level the Universal Postal Union ("UPU") was established at a conference in Berne, Switzerland, in 1874 and since 1947 the UPU has been recognized as one of the specialized agencies of the United Nations. So far as telecommunications are concerned, the International Telegraph Union was established in 1865 and as the International Telecommunication Union it too became a UN specialized agency in 1948. At the European level the European Conference of Postal and Telecommunications Administrations (known generally by its French acronym "CEPT") was set up within the UPU in 1959.

# 3. EUROPEAN INTEGRATION: FROM COAL AND STEEL TO EUROPEAN UNION

As has already been indicated in the previous chapter, the evolution of organisations of states towards integration represents a qualitative departure from the traditional models of intergovernmental co-operation with important consequences for the States involved. Undoubtedly the greatest progress towards economic and political integration has been made by the European Union which in turn is based on the three European Communities. An account of that evolution is the central part of this chapter. Given their close relationship with the European Communities and the Union it is also appropriate to deal in this chapter with the Benelux Economic Union, the European Economic Area and the Schengen Agreement since, although all three groups were conceived and established on intergovernmental lines, they each have special connections with the European Union and have certain features of an integrationist nature making them (each in their different ways) a hybrid which sets them apart from traditional intergovernmental organisations. For its part, the Schengen system will, on final ratification of the Treaty of Amsterdam, become fully integrated into the Community structure.

## BENELUX

The most venerable of those organizations is the Benelux Economic Union which had a precursor in the Belgo-Luxembourg
Economic Union ("BLEU"). The BLEU Convention was signed in
1921 and came into force on May 1, 1922. Most of the activities of
the BLEU were subsequently taken over by the Benelux Economic
Union and later by the EEC. The BLEU also established a monetary union supervised by the Belgo-Luxembourg Monetary
Institute which still manages the gold and foreign exchange
reserves of the two countries.

The BLEU was dissolved when the two countries were occupied in 1940 but, by 1944 their exiled governments as well as that
of the Netherlands were holding discussions which resulted in the
signature of a convention establishing the Benelux Customs
Union on September 5, 1944. The BLEU was resurrected immediately after the war and still forms the basis of the economic
partnership between the two countries.

The Benelux Customs Union came into force on January 1, 1948
resulting in the immediate abolition of internal customs duties
and a common external customs tariff. Over the following decade
various other steps were taken such as liberalizing capital move-
ments between the three states providing for the free movement
of labour between them and certain measures relating to trade
policy were adopted in common. Moreover, the three countries
became even more closely associated with each other through
their joint membership of the European Coal and Steel Community ("ECSC"), which had been established in 1951, and the
European Economic Community (EEC) established in 1957.

Nonetheless to consolidate their own moves towards economic
union they signed the treaty establishing the Benelux Economic
Union on February 3, 1958. It is worth noting that the EEC Treaty
(now the EC Treaty) made special provision for the BLEU and the
Benelux Economic Union in Article 233 (now Article 306), which
provides that "the provisions of this Treaty shall not preclude the
existence or completion of regional unions between Belgium and
Luxembourg or between Belgium, Luxembourg and the Netherlands to the extent that the objectives of these regional unions are
not attained by application of this Treaty". This recognition of the
progress already made by the Benelux countries towards attaining the goals of the European Economic Community (EEC)
justifies Benelux regarding itself as a model and a laboratory for
closer European economic integration.

Notwithstanding its integrationist ideals, the central authority
and decision-making body of the Benelux Union is its Committee
of Ministers composed of the three Ministers for Foreign Affairs
or, where necessary, the ministers responsible for specific areas

such as transport, agriculture and so forth. Within the scope of the Treaty of Union, the Committee of Ministers may adopt a decision which will bind all three governments which must take the necessary steps to implement the decision through their own national legislation. In areas not specifically covered by the Treaty but falling within its general scope, the Committee may make recommendations to the three governments and in areas which fall wholly outwith the scope of the Union Treaty, the ministers may draw up conventions which must then be signed by the governments of each of the three countries and ratified like other international treaties. The General Secretariat of the Union has its headquarters in Brussels where a staff of about 90 provides the necessary administrative and technical support for the Committee of Ministers and liaison between the Union and the three Member States.

In November 1955 an "Interparliamentary Consultative Benelux Council", known for short as the Benelux Parliament was established. It may be consulted upon proposed decisions or conventions or adopt opinions on the progress and functioning of the economic union between the three States, co-operation in the field of foreign policy and other matters of common interest. The Benelux Parliament is composed of 49 members designated by the parliaments of the three Member States, 21 each from Belgium and the Netherlands and seven from Luxembourg.

Given the number of Benelux rules which have been adopted and subsequently implemented in the three Member States, and with the successful example of the Court of Justice of the European Communities before it, a Court of Justice of Benelux[32] was established by a treaty signed on May 11, 1974 to ensure uniformity in the interpretation of specified common rules. It should be noted that the Benelux Court of Justice does not have jurisdiction to interpret all of the rules common to the three countries, nor can it enforce compliance by the three Benelux States with their treaty obligations.

## THE EUROPEAN UNION

The European Union (E.U.) established by the Treaty on European Union ("TEU") by the Treaty of Maastricht[33] now has fifteen Member States and a complex structure including both integrationist and intergovernmental elements, known as "pillars". According to the TEU the Union is founded on the European Communities (Article 1 (ex Article A)) and is served by a single institutional framework (Article 3 (ex Article C)). Nonetheless,

---

32  See further Chapter 6 below at p. 203.
33  OJ C 191, July 29, 1992.

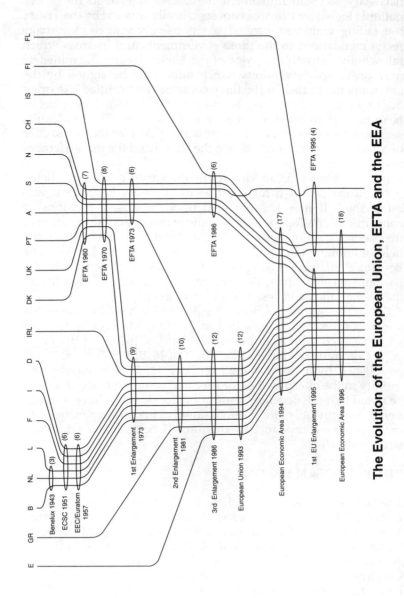

The Evolution of the European Union, EFTA and the EEA

there are important legal differences between the European Communities on the one hand and the European Union (of which the Communities form a part, called the first pillar) on the other. In order to understand those differences and the structure of the Union it is necessary to be acquainted with the evolution of the European Communities since the establishment of the Coal and Steel Community (ECSC) in 1951. That evolution falls into four parts:

(i)   the establishment of the three European Communities;

(ii)  the step-by-step enlargement from six to fifteen Member States;

(iii) political pressures and developments both between the Member States and on the wider geopolitical scene;

(iv)  major structural changes brought about by the Single European Act ("SEA"), the TEU and the Treaty of Amsterdam.

## The European Communities

By 1950 the work of the OEEC was proceeding smoothly and Jean Monnet, then responsible for the management of the plan for French economic recovery, suggested to Robert Schuman, the French Foreign Minister, that fusion of the French and German coal and steel industries under a supranational authority would be an important first step towards a lasting peace between the two countries. Schuman agreed and in a declaration made on May 9, 1950[34] he stated:

"Europe will not be made all at once, or according to a single general plan. It will be built through concrete achievements, which first create a *de facto* solidarity. ... The French Government proposes to place all Franco-German production of coal and steel under a common High Authority in an organisation open to other European countries".

The Benelux countries, which as we have already seen had already taken steps towards a certain integration of their economies by establishing a customs union, and Italy joined France and

---

34  That date is now taken as the date of foundation of the European Communities and May 9 is celebrated as Europe Day, a date upon which the officials of the European Community institutions are given a holiday, for which they revere Robert Schuman.

Germany and together they signed the Treaty of Paris[35] on April 18, 1951.

The Treaty, once ratified by the six States, created completely independent supranational institutions endowed with their own powers to take decisions and other measures binding on the Member States without those states having played a part in their formulation and without any national consent, ratification or implementation being required. That approach represented a dramatic shift from the pre-existing intergovernmental approach to international relations and it remains the single most important characteristic of all three European Communities. As Konrad Adenauer pointed out in a speech to the German Bundestag "for the first time in history, countries want to renounce part of their sovereignty, voluntarily and without compulsion, in order to transfer it to a supranational structure", words echoed a decade later by the Court of Justice in the *Van Gend en Loos* case.[36] That structure consisted of a High Authority (the precursor of the Commission), a Common Assembly (the forerunner of the European Parliament), a special Council of Ministers and a Court of Justice (in that order, Article 7 of the ECSC).

One feature of the ECSC Treaty (apart from its rather superfluous use of the adjectives "high", "common" and "special" in establishing the institutions) is that that treaty was expressly concluded for a duration of only 50 years. When that period expires in 2002, and in the absence of any specific arrangements the coal and steel industries and the products which they produce will presumably fall under the aegis of the general rules laid down in the EC Treaty.

Notwithstanding its temporary nature the ECSC operated effectively from the outset resulting in a substantial increase in trade in the products covered by the treaty while the institutions created established their working methods and a reputation for effectiveness and independence. Those successes led the six Member States to contemplate closer integration at a broader political level and to develop plans for a European defence community and a European political community. The time, however, was not propitious for such developments and the plans were eventually abandoned. Nonetheless, the six were still keen to build upon the

---

35 Treaty establishing the European Coal and Steel Community (ECSC Treaty) 261 UNTS 140, published with amendments effected by the Merger Treaty, the Convention on common institutions, various accession treaties and the TEU (see references at Vade-mecum IV) in Book 1, Volume II, selected instruments taken from the treaties, Office for official publications 1995.

36 Case 26/62 *Van Gend en Loos v. Nederlandse Administratie der Belastingen* [1963] ECR I; see Chapter 5 at p.000 below.

experience of the ECSC and to extend the application of a Community structure to other areas of economic activity. At a conference held in Messina in June 1955, an intergovernmental committee was established under the chairmanship of Paul-Henri Spaak, whose report led to the drafting of two new treaties between the Six, one establishing a European Economic Community (EEC) and the other a European Atomic Energy Community (Euratom).

Each of those two communities followed the same institutional model as the ECSC, although the four institutions were designated slightly differently and were, perhaps significantly, listed in a different order in the two new treaties, thus the institutions were an Assembly, a Council of Ministers, a Commission and a Court of Justice. At the same time as the signature of the two Treaties of Rome, a Convention on Certain Institutions common to the European Communities was signed which provided for a single Parliamentary Assembly and a single Court of Justice to exercise the functions required of them for each of the three communities. Nearly a decade later the 1965 Merger Treaty came into force creating a single Council of Ministers and a single Commission for all three communities, the latter absorbing and taking over the powers of the former High Authority of the ECSC.

## The Community Institutions

That four-part institutional structure has since remained essentially unchanged although the TEU added the Court of Auditors, which had existed since 1975, to the list of institutions. The Court of Justice is described in more detail in Chapter 6[36a] and the task of the Court of Auditors, although of course it is governed by the treaties and other Community legal texts, falls outside the scope of this book. The role in the legislative process of the three political institutions is dealt with in the next chapter. However, it is appropriate to summarise their organisation and principal functions here.

### The European Parliament

None of the institutions has developed or changed more in its organisation or character than the European Parliament during the history of the Communities. Whether in terms simply of the number of its members, the scope of its powers and privileges or its influence on Community affairs, it has steadily grown in both scale and political stature.

36a At pp. 169 *et seq.*

The old "Common Assembly" of the ECSC had been composed of 78 members, divided among the Member States approximately in proportion to their respective populations, an approach which has prevailed to the present day albeit with some weighting in favour of the smaller Member States (particularly Luxembourg) and to the detriment of the larger states. The number of members of the institution was nearly doubled by the EEC and Euratom treaties and has been steadily increased on the successive accessions of new Member States so that it now stands at 626 members divided between the 15 current states. It is generally accepted that this steady growth cannot continue as an already unwieldy institution would risk becoming completely unmanageable. Therefore, in accordance with the wishes of the Parliament itself, the Treaty of Amsterdam provides for a permanent ceiling of 700 to be set on the number of members of the Parliament. Once that ceiling has been reached any further enlargements of the Communities will have to be accommodated by reducing the numbers of the existing delegations of each State.

Although the ECSC Treaty envisaged from the outset that the members of the Assembly would be directly elected, it was nearly 30 years before that became a reality. In 1976 the Member States adopted a Direct Elections Act[37] which fixed the total number of members of the Parliament at 410, and allowed elections to take place on different days over a four-day period in the different Member States in order to accommodate their various electoral traditions. Although the Act re-iterated the Parliament's power (set out in the three founding treaties) to draw up a uniform voting system and a number of attempts have been made to define such a system both by members of the Parliament and various academic groups, this chimera appears to be as elusive as ever.

The seat of the European Parliament has been a vexed question since the earliest days of its existence as the Common Assembly of the ECSC. Thus, although it had been agreed by the governments of the six original Member States that all of the institutions would be provisionally based in Luxembourg, and the then tiny Secretariat of the Common Assembly was established there, there were at that time no facilities in Luxembourg for the organisation of plenary sessions to be conducted in four languages. The first plenary session was therefore held in Strasbourg, an *ad hoc* solution which the French Government has since jealously defended. Again, for practical reasons, the committees of the Assembly started meeting in Brussels and the resulting peripatetic existence of the European Parliament has continued to this day.

37   Act concerning the election of the representatives of the Assembly by direct universal suffrage (OJ L 278, October 8, 1976, p. 10).

Although the European Parliament has adapted its working methods to these circumstances, the fact that it must work in three different centres is undoubtedly expensive, time-consuming and disruptive. It weakens the efficiency of the institution both at an internal level and in terms of the degree of control and influence it can exercise over the Council and the Commission as well as diminishing its authority and credibility in the eyes of the citizens of the Member States.

The powers of the Parliament fall essentially into five categories:

(i) Its participation in the *legislative process*, which is dealt with in the next chapter.

(ii) In relation to the *budget* of the European Union, the Parliament's powers to determine the allocation of expenditure have increased significantly since the financial treaties of 1970 and 1975[38] so that the Parliament now constitutes, jointly with the Council, the budgetary authority of the European Union.

(iii) In the area of the *conclusion of international agreements* between the European Communities and non-member countries or international organisations, the powers of the European Parliament have been steadily increased. Now the Parliament must be kept informed of the progress of those negotiations by the Commission and the Council and be informed of the outcome of negotiations before signature of the treaty concerned. These arrangements extend to "all significant international agreements concluded by the Communities".[39] Under Article 49 (ex Article O) TEU, the European Parliament must give its assent to the application of any European State to become a member of the European Union.

(iv) The Parliament has general *supervisory powers* over the other institutions of which the most draconian is its power to pass a motion of censure on the activities of the Commission (Article 201, (ex Article 144) EC). Such a motion, if carried by a two-thirds majority of the votes cast, representing at the same time an absolute majority of the members of the Parliament, requires the Commission to

38 Treaty amending Certain Budgetary Provisions (1972) and Treaty amending Certain Financial Provisions (1975) of the Merger Treaty, for full titles and references see Vade-mecum IV.
39 A solemn declaration on European Union made following the European Council meeting in Stuttgart on June 19, 1983, known for short as the Stuttgart Declaration.

resign as a body. In addition, under Article 193 (ex Article 138(c)) EC, the European Parliament may set up temporary committees of enquiry to investigate alleged contraventions of or maladministration in the implementation of Community law. It may also receive petitions from individuals or corporations in the Member States on any matters within the Community's fields of activity, and the members of Parliament may submit written or oral questions to the Commission or to the Council, the questions and their respective answers being published in the Official Journal. Finally, under a power conferred upon it by the TEU the European Parliament has appointed an Ombudsman who may receive and investigate complaints concerning instances of maladministration in the activities of the Community institutions or other bodies (except for the Court of Justice or the Court of First Instance acting in their judicial roles).

The Parliament has also steadily increased its authority and its capacity to supervise the other institutions through *litigation*, and in so doing has contributed to the development of the constitution of the Communities. Initially, as a purely consultative body, there was no need for the treaties to provide for any procedure for judicial review of the Parliament's activities, nor for the Parliament to seek judicial review of acts of the other institutions. Nonetheless, Article 38 of the ECSC Treaty provided that a Member State might apply to the Court of Justice to have an act of the European Parliament declared void and, in the first of a series of cases relating to the seat of the European Parliament,[40] Luxembourg's challenge to a resolution of the Parliament which purported to decide that its future sessions should be held in Strasbourg was found to be admissible under Article 38.

Subsequently however, the development of the Parliament's role in the budgetary process led the Court of Justice to find that, since measures adopted by the Parliament might encroach on the powers of the Member States or of the other institutions or otherwise exceed the limits on the Parliament's powers laid down in the treaties, it was necessary for the possibility of judicial review of acts having legal effects with regard to third parties to be susceptible of judicial review by the Court.[41] Four years

40  Case 230/81, *Luxembourg v. European Parliament* [1983] ECR 255.
41  Case 294/83, *Partie écologiste Les Verts v. European Parliament* [1986] ECR 1339.

later in the *Chernobyl* case,[42] the Court similarly concluded (reversing an earlier judgment[42a] on this point) that the institutional balance of the Communities and the system of judicial review created by the treaties enabled the Parliament to challenge acts of the Council or the Commission where such a challenge was necessary to protect its prerogatives.

(v) The Parliament is responsible for the *organisation of its own work*, thus it draws up its own rules of procedure, sets its own agenda for the work both of the plenary session and its committees. However, as we have seen above, this power of internal organisation does not extend to deciding where it should have its seat or places of work or even the number of sessions which it must hold in Strasbourg each year.[43]

## The Council

Trying to describe the Council is somewhat like wrestling with jelly, because it has a number of distinct but overlapping functions which, in national constitutional systems, are exercised by separate powers. Thus the Council has been described as resembling "a head of State in status, a legislature in function and an assembly of constituent States in structure". This conceptual difficulty is compounded by a degree of terminological duplication which is all too likely to lead to the confusion of students and journalists, not to mention the general public. To deal with the latter point first I must emphasise that this section deals with one of the principal political institutions of the European Communities. It has nothing whatsoever to do with the Council of Europe (described above at pp. 30 *et seq*) and although it is closely related to, it is distinct from the European Council (see below).

As we have seen, the Council was first established by the ECSC Treaty as the "Special Council of Ministers". Although the adjective "special" is no longer used, the expression "the Council of Ministers" is still used even when referring to matters under the EC or Euratom treaties. While not strictly accurate this usage has some merit in that it gives an idea of the composition of the institution. Like the EC and Euratom treaties, the TEU refers only

42  Case 70/88, *European Parliament v. Council* [1990] ECR I–2041. The case is so nicknamed because the Parliament was seeking the annulment of a Council regulation adopted to deal with the consequences of nuclear accidents following the accident at Chernobyl in April 1985.

42a  See n. 57 at p. 66.

43  See Case C–345/95, *France v. European Parliament* [1997] ECR I–5215.

to "the Council" simpliciter.[44] However, after the entry into force of the TEU, and given the role of the Council in matters relating to the two non-Community pillars of the European Union, the Council decided to redesignate itself "the Council of the European Union".

According to Article 203 (ex Article 146) EC the Council consists of a representative of each Member State at ministerial level who is authorised to commit the government of that Member State.[45] While that wording makes it clear that the Council must always have a representative of each Member State, it enables the Council to be constituted differently according to the specific subject-matter which it needs to deal with. Thus the General Affairs Council is that composed of the foreign ministers of the Member States through whom, in accordance with traditional rules of public international law, relations between states are conducted. Alternatively, the Council may from time to time be composed of, for example the agriculture, environment or justice ministers of each Member State. Occasionally, two or more groups of ministers may be combined to deal with matters of common interest in a so-called "jumbo Council", for example combining transport and environment ministers or agriculture and trade ministers. The composition of the institution is therefore constantly changing in accordance with the subject at hand (and with changes of government in the Member States), and it is not possible to take a snapshot at any given time and say *"This* is the membership of the Council".

The holder of the presidency of the Council has a vital role in setting the agenda for discussion at each meeting, in ensuring that all points of view are sufficiently aired without allowing futile discussions to become interminable, and in trying to reconcile opposing positions between the Member States by drafting and proposing compromise solutions. Given the importance of this role it is perhaps surprising that the treaty provides that the office of President shall be held in turn by each Member State in the Council for a term of six months in an order decided by the Council acting unanimously.[46] Moreover, the representatives of

44   See for example Article 3 (ex Article C) TEU and Article 5 (ex Article E) TEU.
45   Prior to the TEU this provision simply read that "the Council shall consist of the representatives of the Member States".
46   Article 203 (ex Article 146) EC The present order for this rotation is laid down in a Council decision of January 1, 1995 determining the order in which the office of President of the Council shall be held ([1995] OJ L 1 220). That order incorporates the three new Member States in such a way that each successive *troika* of which they form a part will always include at least one of the five larger Member States.

the Member State holding the presidency of the Council also preside over the meetings of COREPER and the *ad hoc* working groups in which they participate. The risk of dissipation or duplication of effort which such a fragmented structure might entail is diminished, if not altogether eliminated, in two ways. First, although each successive presidency establishes its own agenda and priorities, the Member State holding the presidency works in close collaboration with both its immediate predecessor and the next country which will take on the presidency. These three form the so-called *troika*, ensuring that actions agreed under one presidency will be continued under the succeeding presidencies.

Second, although the Council itself may be a somewhat ephemeral body changing both according to its subject-matter and with political developments in each Member State, it is supported by two more permanent bodies, namely its own secretariat and COREPER.[47] The Secretariat includes a legal service and other specialist divisions which act as the long term memory of the Council.

The preparatory work for the ministerial councils is carried out by COREPER and by specialised working groups of national civil servants. COREPER, or the Committee of Permanent Representatives is "responsible for preparing the work of the Council and for carrying out the tasks assigned to it by the Council".[48] The permanent representatives of each Member State have the status of ambassadors of their respective countries and are permanently based in Brussels, meeting every week. They vet all decisions that are ready to be submitted to the full Council (whatever the formation of the latter) and agreement on a point of principle or a detailed text at COREPER level is very often tantamount to definitive adoption of the measure concerned.

In more difficult cases the COREPER will identify the points of strong disagreement between different delegations. The representative of the Member State holding the presidency of the Council will then draw up the agenda for the particular Council in two parts, so-called A points, upon which agreement has been established and only the rubber stamp of the authority of the Council is required. The representative will then draw up B points which require political resolution of a disagreement or other difficulty. The work of COREPER itself is in turn divided into A and B points on the basis of the work already carried out by working groups of which there may be as many as 200 at any given time.

47 The acronym derives from the French, *Comité des représentants permanents*.
48 Article 207 (ex Article 151 EC).

As already indicated, the Council has a number of different functions including policy co-ordination, legislative and other decision-making powers, and executive powers. Each of these is to a large extent shared, with the European Council in the policy area, with the European Parliament in the legislative area and shared with or delegated to the Commission in executive matters. Again, the legislative role will be dealt with in the next chapter. Here a certain number of general remarks will be made. The main task of the Council is to enable the interests of the Member States to be represented in the activities of the European Union.[49] While the advent of a greater range of subjects which may be decided by majority voting has given the Council more of the character of an integrationist institution, it has not developed into a truly collegiate body or a kind of upper chamber of the legislature as the authors of the treaties may once have intended. Instead (subject to those areas in which majority voting applies) it operates more in the manner of a traditional intergovernmental organisation seeking to adopt decisions by consensus wherever possible. This inevitably involves some watering down of proposals and compromises or agreements to differ which are often castigated as "fudges".

The tendency towards intergovernmentalism was accelerated in 1965 when France, under President De Gaulle, was unable to accept Commission proposals for the Community to have its own financial resources with which to finance the Common Agricultural Policy or for the European Parliament to play a more important role in the budgetary process. French ministers therefore refused to attend Council meetings and the French Permanent Representative was withdrawn from COREPER. This period is known as the "empty chair" crisis.

The resulting paralysis of both legislative and other activities in the Communities was only resolved six months later at a meeting held in Luxembourg which thereby had the unwanted distinction of giving its name to the notorious "Luxembourg compromise". Although the compromise enabled the Community's work to restart, the substance of it was little more than an agreement to disagree and it effectively eliminated the Community's ability to act on the basis of majority voting, even in matters where the treaties required it to do so. The substance of the compromise was that, in areas where majority voting was provided for and where "very important interests of one or more partners are at stake" the members of the Council would endeavour to reach solutions which could be adopted unanimously.

This effectively gave any Member State the veto over any action by the Community in an area in which it could declare, uni-

49   Including of course those of the European Communities.

laterally, and without any requirement to substantiate its claim, that its important interests were at stake. This inevitably put a serious brake on progress towards achieving the aims of the treaties with new legislation slowed to a mere trickle, a situation which became known as "Eurosclerosis". The emergence of the European Council (see below) as a higher political decision-making authority consolidated that tendency since even the General Affairs Council (composed of Ministers of Foreign Affairs) preferred to defer the most important decisions to the higher body. Moreover, the expansion of the Communities from six to nine and then 10 Member States, meant that there was a wider range of "very important interests" which might give rise to such blockages in the decision-making process.

The situation was only resolved on the eve of the accession of Spain and Portugal by the adoption of the Single European Act which amended the EEC Treaty so as to require a wider range of decisions to be taken by majority voting. This was reinforced by the clear political will of the Member States to realise the economic benefits of the Common Market (now re-baptised the Single Market), including a willingness to acquiesce (albeit sometimes with a bad grace) when outvoted by other Member States on a particular issue. There are three different methods of voting in the Council in order to reach a decision. The fallback or "default" position is laid down in Article 205 (ex Article 148)(1) according to which, unless otherwise provided by the Treaty, the Council shall act by a majority of its members. In almost all cases however it is "otherwise provided".

Thus certain important decisions such an agreement to open negotiations for accession with candidate States or decisions on the harmonisation of fiscal legislation must be adopted by unanimous vote within the Council. However, for this purpose, abstentions by certain States cannot prevent the adoption by the Council of acts which require unanimity. Alternatively, and in an increasing number of areas, the Council may have recourse to "qualified majority voting", often abridged to QMV. Under this system the vote of each Member State is given a weighting with a view to reflecting (very approximately) the size of their population and economy.[50] The purpose of the system is on the one hand to prevent the larger Member States from permanently dominating the Council and from steamrollering decisions through,

---

50  It is interesting to note in this context that Article 28 of the ECSC Treaty which lays down the voting procedure for the Council of that Community also includes provision for the votes to be weighted in accordance with the proportion of the Community output of coal and steel of each Member State.

possibly against the wishes of the smaller countries (as would be the case if the voting system were completely proportionate to the populations of the respective countries for example), while at the same time preventing the more numerous smaller Member States from being able to gang up on the larger ones. Thus, for a measure to be adopted, the five largest Member States require the support of at least three of the smaller countries, while only three of the large Member States may together form a blocking minority.

Under the QMV weighting system, Germany, France, Italy and the United Kingdom may each cast 10 votes, Spain eight votes, Belgium, Greece, Netherlands and Portugal five votes, Austria and Sweden four votes, Denmark, Ireland and Finland three votes and Luxembourg two votes. For a decision to be adopted, 62 votes must be cast and in addition, where the Council is acting other than on a proposal from the Commission, these must include the votes of at least 10 Member States. To look at it another way, a measure may be blocked by a group of Member States which can muster at least 26 votes between them. This is the so-called "blocking minority".

It follows from this system that the votes of the larger Member States would be, to a small extent, "diluted" by the accession of new Member States. This caused the United Kingdom, during the negotiations for the adoption of the Treaty of Accession for Austria, Norway, Finland and Sweden to resist a simple proportionate extension of the QMV scheme. The United Kingdom's obduracy resulted in another agreement now known as the "Ioannina compromise".[51] As a result, although the voting rules set out in the treaties themselves (as now amended by the Act of Accession) did simply change the votes in direct proportion to the enlargement of the Communities, if a proposed measure is opposed by Member States representing between 23[52] and 25 votes (*i.e.* one short of a blocking minority), the Council agrees that it will "do all in its power" to find a solution which can be adopted by States representing at least 65 votes. The United Kingdom's obdurate and discreditable struggle to obtain this marginal refinement to the voting system seems to have been dictated mainly by considerations of internal British politics rather than by any wish to improve the efficiency of the Community system. The issue of QMV as a whole however proved too

---

51  Council decision of March 29, 1994, OJ C 105, April 13, 1994, p. 1 as amended by the decision of January 1, 1995, OJ C 1, January 1, 1995, p. 1, taking into account Norway's failure to ratify the accession treaty.

52  The blocking minority prior to the accession of the new Member States.

sensitive to be reopened during the 1996 Intergovernmental Conference but will inevitably have to be re-examined as progress is made towards the accession of new Member States.

## The European Council

The European Council brings together the heads of state or of government of the Member States of the European Community as well as the President of the Commission. The meetings, which are often called "summits" (because they take place at the highest level[53]) take place at least twice per year under the chairmanship and in one of the major cities of the Member State holding the presidency. The practice has developed that a summit takes place towards the end of each presidency, providing, in addition to other matters for discussion, an opportunity to take stock of the achievements of the presidency and to look forward to the agenda for the next six-month period. Where necessary other meetings of the European Council may be convened on an *ad hoc* basis in order to deal with particular issues. In 1986 the existence of the European Council was formally recognised in the Single European Act, Article 2 of which is in terms similar to the opening sentence of this paragraph.

Article 4 (ex Article D) TEU now provides that "the European Council shall provide the Union with the necessary impetus for its development and shall define the general political guidelines thereof". That article also provides that the European Council is to submit to the European Parliament a report after each of its meetings and an annual written report on the progress achieved by the Union. Otherwise, decisions arrived at by the European Council are announced in the form of conclusions of the presidency announced at the end of each summit. In addition to providing political guidance the European Council is responsible for co-ordinating, planning, and managing the common foreign and security policy (CFSP) provided for by the TEU, for supervising and taking the main decisions involved in preparation for economic and monetary union, and for making important appointments such as the President of the European Commission and now the President of the European Central Bank.

As an intergovernmental body (and not a European Community institution), decisions are arrived at by consensus, in other words by unanimity which, while providing a degree of authority for the outcome, may again result in unsatisfactory compromises where one Member State "takes hostage" a given issue in order to

53 Continuing the mountaineering metaphor the senior civil servants and political delegates who prepare summit meetings are referred to as "Sherpas".

get satisfaction on another. Such horse trading has, however, been surprisingly successful on many occasions in breaking political impasses, and thereby enabling the other institutions to carry out their work of legislation and implementation within a clear policy framework.

*The Commission*

The Commission is possibly the most visible, and certainly the most maligned, of all of the European Community institutions. Often referred to disparagingly as a "vast army of Eurocrats" who are seen as bent upon interfering in matters which are properly the preserve of the Member States and their national administrations it is in fact nothing of the sort. Legally speaking, the institution consists only of the 20 Commissioners themselves who collectively exercise the powers conferred upon it by the treaties or delegated to it by the Council. In common parlance however, reference to the Commission usually includes or implies a reference to the departments or services which provide the necessary infrastructure for the work of the Commission itself. Even the staff of the services are not particularly numerous, including, for the 1998 budgetary year, only 20,600 officials.[54] This number compares with the staff of a medium-sized government department in any of the larger Member States or the number of employees of a medium-sized city. To check this assertion find out for yourself the number of employees of, for example, the Transport or Environment Ministry of your country or of the administration of any city of around 250,000 inhabitants.

According to Article 213 (ex Article 157) of the EC Treaty, the Commission, which since the accession of Austria, Finland and Sweden consists of 20 members, must include at least one national of each of the Member States but may not include more than two members having the nationality of the same State.[55] To achieve this there are two Commissioners from each of the five larger Member States and one from each of the 10 smaller countries.

The Commissioners are chosen on the grounds of their general competence and independence and are generally appointed from among senior political figures, usually with ministerial experience in their respective countries. Since the entry into force of the TEU, the governments of the Member States first nominate by common

---

54   Including the staff of Joint Research Centres (see Chapter 2, p. 43 above), the Office for Official Publications and two other decentralised bodies. There are, in addition, just under 900 temporary staff.

55   Article 213 (ex Article 157) EC.

accord (*i.e.* unanimously), after consulting the European Parliament, the person whom they intend to appoint as President of the Commission.[56] Thereafter, in consultation with the nominee for President of the Commission the Member States nominate the other persons whom they intend to appoint as members of the Commission. The President and the other members of the Commission thereby nominated are submitted collectively to a vote of approval by the European Parliament. Subject to that approval the President and the other members of the Commission are appointed by common accord of the governments of the Member States.

The independence of the Commissioners referred to in Article 213 (ex Article 157) is not merely a pious hope. Various provisions of the treaties combine to secure the independence, in particular from the governments, but also from the other institutions both of individual commissioners and of the college as a whole. Thus commissioners must neither seek nor take instructions from any government or from any other body. Reciprocally the Member States undertake to respect that principle and not to seek to influence the members of the Commission in the performance of their tasks. On taking up their duties new Commissioners make a solemn declaration before a plenary session of the Court of Justice which amounts to a public affirmation of those commitments.

Secondly, the Commissioners are protected from individual pressure by the collegiate nature of the body. Thus although individual Commissioners may make statements or declarations relating to their individual spheres of responsibility, or may even exercise individually, by delegation, certain of the powers conferred upon the Commission as a whole, all Commission decisions are those of the College and dissenting opinions by the Commissioners are not publicly expressed (although, as in national politics, leaks to the media are not unheard of). Decisions taken by the full Commission are adopted by a simple majority (Article 219 (ex Article 163)).

Each Commissioner appoints his or her personal staff, including a so-called *Chef de Cabinet* (Chief of Staff) whose role is to co-ordinate the work of the Commissioner with that of the other Commissioners as well as with the various Directorates General of the Commission's administration. The staff will also include specialists in the subject areas dealt with by the Commissioner, political advisers and a press spokesman as well as appropriate clerical staff.

The remainder of the Commission's staff is headed by the Secretary General and divided up into 26 Directorates General, each with a specific area of responsibility, such as competition

56   Article 214 (ex Article 158) EC.

("DGIV"), agriculture ("DGVI") or the internal market ("DGXV"). Also attached to the Secretariat General are services responsible for protocol in order to deal with the huge number of visiting heads of State, government ministers and leaders of international organisations who regularly visit the Commission, the translation service and the joint interpreting service (who between them account for some 2,000 of the Commission's staff). The Office for Official Publications of the European Communities ("EUR-op"), one of the world's largest publishers, is also a part of the Commission. Its most important responsibility is producing the daily editions of the Official Journal containing legislation and notices of decisions which, in the absence of such publication in eleven languages, may be invalid (see Chapter 7 below).

The Commission works in close collaboration with and under the supervision of a series of highly specialised and influential committees of which there may be several hundred in existence at any given time. The existence of these committees and their hierarchy is referred to collectively as "comitology". Pursuant to the Single European Act the Council adopted a decision[57] which essentially codified the existing, rather anarchic committee system by identifying three different types of committees. These are the advisory committees, management committees and regulatory committees. The proposal for any given legislation or other important decision specifies which level of committee is to be involved so as to avoid later procedural wrangling.

The Commission's powers and duties are essentially laid down in Article 211 (ex Article 155) EC and fall into four main categories. First the Commission must ensure that the provisions of the treaties and measures adopted for their implementation are properly applied and, as a result, it is occasionally referred to as the "guardian of the treaties". This task involves it in monitoring the legislation and administrative activities of the Member States for which purpose it may collect any information and carry out any checks required for the performance of its duties[58] and receive complaints from individuals or companies who believe that a

57   Council Decision 87/373 of July 13, 1987 laying down the procedures for the exercise of implementing powers conferred on the Commission (OJ L 197 July 18, 1987, p.33). The European Parliament sought the annulment of that decision in Case 302/87 *European Parliament v. Council* [1988] ECR 5615, known as the "*Comitology*" case in which the Court found that the European Parliament had no *locus standi* under Article 173 of the EC Treaty as it then stood. In an enigmatic declaration to the Treaty of Amsterdam (No.31) the Member States here called upon the Commission to submit a proposal to the Council for the modification of that Decision.

58   Article 284 (ex Article 213) EC.

Member State may be infringing their rights under Community law. If as a result of these monitoring activities or complaints the Commission finds that a Member State appears to be failing to fulfil its obligations under the treaties it may open so-called infringement proceedings, first by drawing the apparent infringement to the Member State's attention then, in the absence of a satisfactory response, by issuing a reasoned opinion requiring the Member State to end the infringement within a set time. Ultimately, if necessary, it can bring proceedings before the European Court of Justice for a declaration that the Member State has failed to fulfil its obligations.

Secondly, the Commission may make recommendations or deliver opinions on matters covered by the treaty.

Thirdly, the Commission has its own power of decision and participates in the preparation and adoption of measures taken by the Council and by the European Parliament. This refers principally to the Commission's role in the legislative process, including its all important privilege of initiating the legislative process. In addition the Commission exercises its "own power of decision" in a number of important areas, such as competition policy where it may investigate potential infringements of the competition rules (Articles 81 (ex Article 85) and 82 (ex Article 86) EC), and in agriculture where it may, under supervision of various management committees, adopt regulations fixing Community price levels and other procedures for regulating the market in various agricultural products.

Finally, it exercises powers delegated to it by the Council.

Other provisions confer specific responsibilities on the Commission. Thus, for example, Article 274 (ex Article 205) EC requires the Commission to implement the Community's budget, having already participated closely in drawing up that budget, in particular by preparing the preliminary draft budget to be placed before the Council. Where the Union intends to enter into a bilateral or multilateral international agreement it is the Commission, acting under a mandate laid down by the Council, which conducts the relevant negotiations (Article 133(3) (ex Article 113(3)) EC and Article 300(1) (ex Article 228(1)) EC).

In order to both promote and defend its work under its various heads of competence, the Commission, with the advice and support of its legal service, frequently engages in litigation before the Court of First Instance and the European Court of Justice. At this level in the infringement proceedings mentioned above it acts in a role analogous to that of a public prosecutor by bringing defaulting Member States before the Court. The Commission's own actions may be subject to challenge by means of an action for annulment brought by a Member State, the Council or under certain particular circumstances by the European Parliament or

even private individuals or corporations. Thus the United Kingdom recently secured the annulment of a Commission decision to
undertake certain expenditure intended to combat social exclusion on the ground that the Commission had exceeded its power
to undertake feasibility studies or to initiate pilot projects.[59] In the
area of competition law, the exercise of the Commission's powers
frequently gives rise to challenges by the undertakings concerned
who may have been fined extremely substantial amounts and
who may seek the annulment of the Commission's decision by the
Court of First Instance. Thirdly, the Commission invariably submits written and oral observations to the Court of Justice in
proceedings submitted to it under Article 234 (ex Article 177)
EC.

Through its involvement in all of these procedures and, in
particular, its participation in the preliminary ruling procedure
where the Commission acts more as an *amicus curia* than as a party
with a particular position to defend, the Commission is able to
make a further important contribution to the development of
European Community law. Thus it can inform the Court of the
policy considerations behind, and the legislative history of, the
particular instrument which the Court is called upon to interpret
and it may look beyond the narrow interests of the parties to
wider questions of the development of the law.

## Enlargement

From the outset it was envisaged that membership of the Communities would be open to other States. Thus Article 98 ECSC
provided "any European State may apply to accede to this
treaty", leaving open the question of what is a "European State"
for this purpose. A somewhat speculative application for membership of the Communities by the Kingdom of Morocco in 1987
was turned down by the Council on the grounds that Morocco
was not a European State. Although her request to open accession
negotiations has been turned down on other grounds it appears to
be accepted that Turkey is a European State for this purpose
(indeed it would be difficult not to do so given that Turkey is a
European member of NATO).

The first applications for membership during the 1960s were led
by the United Kingdom which was supported by Denmark,
Ireland and Norway, as well as, on the second occasion, Sweden.
Despite the progress made in negotiations, these applications
were blocked by the intransigence of the President of France,
General de Gaulle. Finally, under a new French President, Denmark, Ireland and the United Kingdom became Member States of

---

59   Case C–106/96 *UK v. Commission*, [1998] ECR I–2729.

the European Communities with effect from January 1, 1973, while Norway, which had signed the Accession Treaty, failed to ratify it as a result of a negative result in a referendum. By the second enlargement, which took place in 1981, Greece joined the Communities to be followed in 1986 by Spain and Portugal.[60] The Community accepted, with open eyes, the problems arising from the relative poverty of those three countries and the difficulties which they would inevitably have in assuming the obligations of membership as the price to be paid for helping to consolidate their newly re-established democracies following periods of dictatorial or military rule.

The fourth enlargement took place without the requirement of a treaty amendment since it arose from the dissolution of the German Democratic Republic and the reunification of its six *Länder* with those of the Federal Republic on October 3, 1990. While the economic burden of that development fell largely on Germany's shoulders the repercussions for the Communities were considerable.

Before any further accessions could take place the (now 12) Member States of the European Communities concluded the Treaty on European Union which came into force on November 1, 1993. Among other things the TEU reformed the procedure for the accession of new States (by Article O, now Article 49) and it is important to remember that, henceforth, all accessions are now to the European Union as a whole including, but not limited to, accession to the European Communities.

Under Article 49 (ex Article O) not only must candidate States be "European" but they must also respect the principles set out in Article 6 (ex Article F(1)), namely the principles of liberty, democracy, respect for human rights and fundamental freedoms, and the rule of law.

In June 1993 the European Council meeting in Copenhagen, in addition to those requirements, laid down certain political criteria for membership. These included the effective functioning of a pluralist democracy and the rule of law ensuring in particular, the protection of fundamental human rights and the rights of minorities, the stabilisation of the economies and the development of the capacity to cope with competitive pressures and market forces within the European Union, the ability to assume the obligations of membership within the various spheres of activity of the Union and the administrative and judicial capacity to apply the *acquis communautaire*.

---

60　The precise dates of the accession treaties and the dates of accession of each Member State are contained in the list of key dates in part III of the Vade-mecum. References to the treaties are contained in part IV.

On receipt of an application the Council must consult the Commission and the European Parliament. The Commission's opinion drawn up in the light of detailed information obtained from the candidate country will review the economic and political consequences of accession of the country concerned, and point to any specific areas in which the candidate country may require a permanent or temporary derogation from normal Community rules or a transitional period in order to be able to adapt to those rules. In the light of this opinion the European Parliament may give its assent to the application which must be by an absolute majority of the members. Subject to a unanimous decision of the Council, detailed accession negotiations and the drafting of the accession treaty will then proceed and, once concluded, the accession treaty must be ratified not only by the candidate State but also by each of the existing Member States of the Union.

The first accessions to the European Union following its establishment were those of Austria, Finland and Sweden in January 1995, Norway once again having negotiated and signed an accession treaty but failing to ratify it as a result of a negative referendum result.

In the light of the Copenhagen criteria the Commission prepared opinions on the applications of 10 Central and Eastern European countries[61] and the European Council held in Luxembourg on December 12 and 13, 1997 decided to launch the accession process comprising those 10 states and Cyprus. Initially bilateral intergovernmental conferences have been convened to begin negotiations with Cyprus, Hungary, Poland, Estonia, the Czech Republic and Slovenia on the conditions for their entry into the Union.

Enlargement of the European Union is more than a simple matter of increasing the territorial scope of Community law and the population to which it applies. It gives rise to substantial problems at institutional, political and practical levels. As already mentioned above, the number of members of the European Parliament will in future be limited to a maximum of 700 while any substantial increase in the number of Member States, say to 20 or more, will inevitably call in question the possibility for each Member State to nominate one member of the Commission. Prior to the signature of the Amsterdam Treaty it was suggested that the Commission might adopt a two-tier structure with a smaller central Commission of perhaps 12 or 15 Commissioners with a

---

61   Hungary, Poland, Romania, Slovakia, Latvia, Estonia, Lithuania, Bulgaria, the Czech Republic and Slovenia. The 10 reports were published as supplements to the monthly bulletin of the European Communities.

larger body of "Junior Commissioners" below them having responsibility for the day-to-day management of individual policy areas. Even the Court of Justice, in its evidence to the Intergovernmental Conference which led to the drawing up of the Amsterdam Treaty,[62] expressed concern that in the context of further enlargement of the European Union:

> "Any significant increase in the number of judges might mean that the plenary session of the Court would cross the invisible boundary between a collegiate court and a deliberative assembly."

At the political level the problems which will arise for the decision-making process in the Council may already be guessed at in the light of the problems which arose for QMV on the accession of Austria, Finland and Sweden and the Ioannina compromise mentioned above. The current group of candidate countries includes one large state (Poland), three smaller ones (Hungary, the Czech Republic and Slovenia) and two very small states (Estonia and Cyprus). Moreover, although the increasing diversity of the states is a source of enrichment to the Union, their differences of background, outlook and simple geographical situation may make reaching a consensus in those areas where unanimity is required increasingly difficult to attain, especially in questions arising under the common foreign and security policy.

Finally, on a purely practical level, the politically sensitive question of languages will become progressively harder to avoid. Continued extension of the current rule that for discussions within the Council or in the European Parliament documents must be available in all of the official languages and members must be able to express themselves in any of those languages, will become harder to maintain as the number of languages increases, risking effective paralysis of the decision-making process or wildly increasing costs.[63]

---

62  Report of the Court of Justice on certain aspects of the application of the Treaty on European Union, published in *The Annual Report of the Court of Justice*, 1995, p. 19, at p. 28.

63  For the purposes of translation and interpretation it must be borne in mind that the number of languages (L) causes a geometric increase in the number of combinations (C) which must be catered for. The formula is $C = L \times (L-1)$, thus the current 11 languages give rise to 110 different language combinations, while four additional languages will take the number of combinations to 210.

## Political Developments

Some of the political developments which have shaped the European Communities have already been alluded to. Thus the empty chair crisis and the Luxembourg compromise, and the emergence of the European Council and its consolidation as a recognised authority in the Community process, were dealt with in describing the Council, while the reunification of Germany in 1990 was mentioned in the context of enlargement of the Communities. A number of other developments may also usefully be mentioned.

First, the Council decided in April 1970[64] that the European Communities should acquire their *own financial resources*. The existence of this system of own resources is another important distinction between the European Union and other international organisations, reinforcing as it does the Union's independence from its constituent Member States and enabling it to take action without depending on authorisation or financing from those States. The own resources now include the customs duties levied in accordance with the common external customs tariff, levies on agricultural products arising from trade with non-member countries and duties on sugar and isoglucose produced within the Member States, a maximum of 1.4 per cent of the VAT revenue of each Member State, and finally a contribution from each Member State in proportion to its gross national product at a rate determined each year in the light of the overall budget situation. These own resources are subject to a ceiling of 1.2 per cent of the total GNP of the European Union. This development in turn led to a strengthening of the budgetary powers of the European Parliament by two treaties in 1970 and 1975,[65] which represented the first step in giving the European Parliament real political power as opposed to a mere consultative role.

Also in the early 1970s *foreign policy* questions were first discussed among the Member States at the meetings which eventually became the European Council. These discussions formed the embryo of political co-operation by the Member States, albeit at intergovernmental level separate from the work of the European Communities. This co-operation was given a more structured form by Article 30 of the Single European Act and eventually became the second pillar (Common Foreign and Security Policy) of the European Union under the Maastricht Treaty (see Chapter 2 at p. 000 above).

*Economic and Monetary Union* ("EMU") is a natural complement

---

64  Council Decision 70/243, April 21, 1970 on the replacement of financial contributions from the Member States by the Community's own resources, OJ En.Sp.Ed. 1970 (I), p. 224.
65  See Vade-mecum IV for full references.

to (although not the inevitable consequence of) the establishment of a single market. Its undoubted economic importance arising from the elimination of the costs and risk of exchange transactions between traders in different Member States, the extra weight which the European Community will have in its trade on world markets, and the reduction in vulnerability to volatile forces on the money markets, are all tempered by sensitive political issues. Thus participating Member States lose the right to issue their own currency, one of the badges of statehood, and perhaps more importantly, they lose the capacity to conduct domestic monetary policy through control of the money supply. Some critics of monetary union claim that its existence makes it inevitable that fiscal powers will sooner or later also become centralised.

Although many of the developments leading to EMU are in the political and economic sphere and, as matters at present stand, only 11 out of the 15 E.U. Member States are taking part in it, many of the institutions and structures required to implement it have been given legal form, in particular in the TEU. Under EMU, all of the Community institutions have a part to play in its operation. It is therefore appropriate briefly to summarise the matter here.

The ambition to establish monetary union goes back at least to 1970 when Pierre Werner, then the Prime Minister of Luxembourg, submitted a report to the heads of government of the then six Member States with a proposal for a three-stage programme similar in its broad pattern to that which is presently under way. Economic and political difficulties in the early 1970s meant that the plan never came to fruition. When he became President of the Commission in 1977, Roy Jenkins put forward a less ambitious proposal for the creation of a European Monetary System (EMS) which was endorsed by meetings of the European Council at Bremen and in Brussels in 1978.

The establishment of the EMS in 1979 included the adoption of a European Currency Unit ("ECU"), a notional currency based on a so-called "basket" of national currencies of the Member States. It does not have notes or coins but the budget and accounts of the European Communities and the institutions are kept in ECUs. The EMS also included an Exchange Rate Mechanism ("ERM") designed to reduce fluctuations between the values of the currencies of the Member States. Each of the currencies included in the EMS is allocated a fixed exchange rate with the ECU, and a range within which it may fluctuate against the other currencies. If it approaches the upper or lower limits to that range the central banks may intervene on the money markets in order to make the necessary adjustments. However, massive currency speculation in September 1992 went beyond the capacity of the central banks to counteract it, even by concerted action. This led to the withdrawal of Sterling and the Italian lire from the ERM. Those traumatic events (known as Black Wednesday) have conditioned much of the subsequent debate on EMU, particularly in the United Kingdom.

The establishment of the EMS required no more authority than the political will of the Member States expressed at the European Councils as already mentioned. Nonetheless the Single European Act, referring to those two Councils in its preamble, added a new chapter to the EEC Treaty headed "Co-operation in Economic and Monetary Policy (Economic and Monetary Union)". The single article in that chapter only required Member States to co-operate with a view to encouraging economic stability and made no institutional changes. Following the entry into force of the SEA, the Member States once again considered the possibility of progressing towards EMU, and at the European Council of Hanover in 1988 asked for a report to be drawn up by the governors of the national central banks under the chairmanship of Jacques Delors, the Commission President. Like the earlier Werner Report, the Delors Report identified three phases in progressing towards EMU. The first stage required the members to co-ordinate more closely within the EMS in order to ensure that the underlying economic conditions for EMU existed while at the same time preparing the necessary legal and institutional changes. To that end an intergovernmental conference was to be established, one of two which led ultimately to the adoption of the TEU at Maastricht.

The Maastricht Treaty, when it came into force on November 1, 1993, marked the opening of the second stage of EMU including fixing the composition of the ECU basket of currencies, establishing a European Monetary Institute ("EMI") to co-ordinate the necessary preparatory work for the third phase and to act as an embryonic European Central Bank ("ECB") which would take responsibility for managing the new single currency. Other amendments to the EC Treaty enable the future ECB to bring legal proceedings before the Court of Justice for the purpose of protecting its prerogatives (Article 230 (ex Article 173) EC) while the Court of Justice itself was given jurisdiction to give preliminary rulings concerning the validity and interpretation of acts of the ECB (Article 234 (ex Article 177) EC).

Finally, the TEU provides for the third stage of EMU to begin at the latest on January 1, 1999 at which date the Council will irrevocably fix the conversion rates of the participating currencies against the Euro and against each other, the ECB will take up its duties and over the following three years the ECB and the ESCB will gradually implement the replacement of national coins and bank notes by Euro coins and notes.

The *completion of the Single Market* by the identification and elimination of the remaining barriers to trade between the Member States was one of the key priorities of the Commission newly constituted in 1985 under the Presidency of Jacques Delors. To that end the Commissioner responsible for the internal market, Lord Cockfield, drew up a report known as a white paper[66] submitted to the European Council, which, at its meeting in Milan in June 1985 decided to establish an intergovernmental conference with a view to effecting the necessary changes to the Community treaties. The Cockfield white paper identified the need to adopt nearly 300 legislative measures in order to successfully establish the single market and, thanks to provisions allowing for wider use of QMV and the effective abandonment of the Luxembourg compromise, the target of adopting those measures before January 1, 1993 was met.

## Structural change

On the accession of new Member States the changes made to the treaties are generally limited to those inherent in enlargement, such as the composition of the Community institutions and to adjustments necessary to take account of particular features of the economies of the new Member States, including where necessary establishing transitional periods. More substantial changes to the structure of the Communities have been effected on three occasions, successively by the Single European Act (SEA) in 1986, the Treaty on European Union (TEU) in 1992 and by the Treaty of Amsterdam[67] in 1997.

Each of the three treaties is an exceedingly complex document reflecting hard won compromises and squaring of circles during the intergovernmental conferences leading to their adoption. Moreover, each treaty contains both new material dealing with areas not previously covered by the European Community treaties, and provisions amending the existing treaties. The latter material is often barely comprehensible without reference to the original texts which are being amended. Finally, each treaty has annexed to it numerous protocols and declarations whose importance or impact is often hard to guess at. Such complex documents are virtually impossible to read for any except a determined specialist with a good understanding of the background to their adoption. That lack of clarity certainly contributed to the hostile reception which they received in many Member States and the difficulties encountered in certain States in ratifying the treaties

66  Completing the internal market, White Paper from the Commission to the European Council.
67  The full title is "Treaty of Amsterdam amending the Treaty on European Union, the treaties establishing the European Communities and certain related acts".

once signed. It is therefore usually more profitable to consult consolidated texts of the treaties.[68]

*The Single European Act*

It is not clear whether the title "Single European Act" was intended ironically or as a genuine attempt at spin-doctoring so as to preserve an image of unity of purpose in a treaty (for it *is* a treaty despite the curious title) which emerged out of two separate but parallel intergovernmental conferences, brought about amendments to three different treaties and added a new inter-governmental area of activity to the work of the Communities, outside the scope of those treaties. Many of the effects of the Single European Act have now run their course or been superseded. Thus, for example, European Political Co-operation ("EPC") was superseded by the establishment of a Common Foreign and Security Policy ("CFSP") by the Maastricht Treaty[69] and likewise the rather coy reference to monetary union was replaced by provisions inserted in the EC Treaty by the Maastricht Treaty.[70] Nonetheless the Single European Act, despite certain shortcomings, has had a permanent impact on the organisation of the European Communities, and later upon that of the European Union which must be borne in mind when studying the current structure.

First the political drive to reform the Community treaties (some 30 years after they had been adopted) was driven partly by a European Parliament proposal for drafting a treaty on European Union, a proposal which was confirmed by a committee[71] which proposed the establishment of an intergovernmental conference taking the Parliament's draft as its starting point. Secondly, the Cockfield white paper mentioned above proposed certain legislative changes to facilitate the achievement of the single market, and again posited the establishment of an intergovernmental

---

68   Published for information purposes in the Official Journal of the European Communities even prior to the ratification of the amending treaty. Thus the TEU, together with the complete, amended text of the treaty establishing the European Community was published in OJ C 224, August 31, 1992, and the Treaty of Amsterdam together with a consolidated version of the Treaty on European Union and the treaty establishing the EC were published in OJ C 340, November 10, 1997. The earlier edition has the advantage of showing amendments in bold italic type so that they are instantly recognisable as such.
69   See above, p. 39.
70   Those articles have now been renumbered Articles 112 to 124.
71   Known as the "Dooge Committee" after the name of its Irish Chairman.

conference in order to bring about the necessary changes to the treaties.

In institutional terms the Single European Act first recognised the existence of the European Council[72] which had in practice already existed for nearly 20 years. It introduced into each of the three Community treaties an enabling provision for the Council to establish the Court of First Instance[73] and, by establishing European Political Co-operation ("EPC") it introduced the idea that certain intergovernmental activities could be carried on in close association with (although not under the auspices of) the European Communities, an approach later adopted in the Treaty on European Union.

So far as the creation of the single market was concerned, the important innovation was the extension of majority voting (QMV) in the Council to measures intended for the completion of the single market. This marked the effective end of the Luxembourg compromise[74] and a trend which continued into the Amsterdam Treaty. The Single European Act also introduced two new legislative procedures greatly enhancing the involvement of the European Parliament, in particular the co-operation procedure which requires, in brief, a unanimous vote of the Council to overcome an opinion of the European Parliament or to overrule a Commission opinion. A new so-called "assent procedure" was also introduced whereby the agreement of the European Parliament by an absolute majority[75] in case the Community intended either to enter into association agreements with non-Member States or where it intended to undertake enlargement on the application of candidate countries. Finally, the SEA introduced new powers for the Communities in a certain number of areas including measures concerning the environment, research and technical development and economic and social cohesion.

*European Union*

The *Treaty on European Union* ("TEU") signed at Maastricht on February 7, 1992 by establishing a European Union created a wholly new form of international organisation. Although the Union incorporates the three European Communities already in existence, it does not share their legal characteristics and although it shares the work of the institutions of the Communities (with the

72  See above, p. 63.
73  See Chapter 6, pp. 178 *et seq.*
74  See p. 60 above.
75  That is to say not a simple majority of those voting but that those voting had to constitute more than half of the current number of members of the European Parliament.

exception of the Court of Justice, whose jurisdiction is for all practical purposes excluded), the rules on majority voting in the Council do not apply and the Commission has no right of initiative. The European Parliament may ask questions of the Council or make recommendations to it. However, its role is merely consultative and its views need only be "taken into consideration". This means that the work of the European Union (outside the areas covered by the European Communities) is not subject to the democratic input and scrutiny of the European Parliament, supervision of the compliance of the Member States with their treaty obligations by the Commission nor, above all, to judicial review by the Court of Justice. Those areas therefore remain purely intergovernmental in character (see pp. 19 *et seq.* above).

It is therefore essential for all those dealing with European Union and European Community questions to be aware of and to maintain clearly the distinction between the Union and the Communities. This applies as much to journalists and politicians as it does to law students and legal practitioners. However convenient it may be to treat the abbreviations E.U. and EC as synonymous, they are not. Thus treating them as such results only in confusion or solecisms such as a recent headline in the *Financial Times* referring to the "E.U. Court".

As already mentioned, the European Union is composed of three elements which have come to be known as pillars from a popular, graphical way of showing the structure of the Union as the façade of a Greek temple based upon three pillars with the Union constituting the over-arching pediment. An alternative way of looking at it would be to regard the Union as a glass jar containing oil and water which stubbornly refuse to mix. The existing European Communities together constitute the first of the three pillars and indeed Article 1 (ex Article A) TEU[76] provides that "the Union shall be founded on the European Communities". The other two pillars are those of the Common Foreign and Security Policy ("CFSP")[77] which replaces the provisions on European political co-operation provided for by the Single European Act. The CFSP is outlined at pp. 39 *et seq.*, above. The third pillar

76  In order to maintain the distinction between the provisions of the TEU and those of the European Community treaties the Union provisions of the Maastricht Treaty were identified by the letters **A** to **S** (in bold type), the renumbering effected by the Amsterdam Treaty in the supposed interest of clarity has done away with this distinction. I propose to continue to use the rather cumbersome designation adopted by the consolidated text of the treaties published by the Official Publications Office. See Vade-mecum V.

77  Now contained in Articles 11 (ex Article J.1) to 28 (ex Article J.18) TEU.

consists of provisions on co-operation in the fields of justice and home affairs. This pillar has been substantially changed by the Amsterdam Treaty (see below) but as initially conceived included such matters as asylum policy, immigration policy and policy regarding nationals of third countries, measures to combat drug addiction and international fraud, judicial co-operation in civil and criminal matters, customs co-operation and police co-operation.

At the same time as establishing the Union, the Maastricht Treaty brought about substantial changes to the existing European Community treaties, in particular to the EEC Treaty. Even the name of the latter is changed to "Treaty establishing the European Community" (EC). The substantial additions to the EC Treaty included the provisions on Economic and Monetary Union outlined above, the establishment of citizenship of the European Union (curiously the notion of citizenship "of the Union" is nonetheless included in the text of the EC Treaty). An additional legislative procedure, known as the "Co-decision procedure" was created which, in the areas to which it is applicable effectively gives the European Parliament the final say on legislation so adopted thus enabling it, in practice, to veto positions adopted by the Council. Also at the institutional level the European Court of Justice was given the power to impose financial penalties on Member States which failed to comply with its own judgments.

It has always been the case that the demarcation lines between areas of Community competence and those remaining within the competence of individual Member States has been the area of greatest difficulty in relations between the Member States and the Community. In this context the notion of *subsidiarity* became increasingly important as constituting a reassurance that the powers of the Member States would not be gradually but systematically transferred to centralised European institutions. The principle holds that decisions should not be taken by a higher authority where they are capable of being effectively adopted at a lower level. This is put slightly differently in the preamble to the Treaty on European Union which refers to decisions being "taken as closely as possible to the citizen in accordance with the principle of subsidiarity". This was further translated into the text of the EC Treaty as follows:

"In areas which do not fall within its exclusive competence, the Community shall take action, in accordance with the principle of subsidiarity, only if and in so far as the objectives of the proposed action cannot be sufficiently achieved by the Member States and can therefore, by reason of the scale or effects of the proposed action, be better achieved by the Community" (Article 5 (ex Article 3(b)) EC).

As a political principle subsidiarity is unexceptionable, and, in different forms, appears in federal-style constitutions such as those of the United States or of Germany in which powers not expressly conferred upon the Union remain within the competence of the States or *Länder*.[78] As a political guideline the three institutions involved in the Community legislative process are committed to evaluating legislative proposals for their compliance with the principle of subsidiarity. However, it is doubtful whether the concept can be sufficiently well defined so as to form the basis for a legal challenge to an act of a Community institution on the ground that the principle had been infringed. The matter has not yet been brought before the Court of Justice which, if such a question ever is put, will have a more than usually slippery concept to grapple with.

Despite the emphasis on subsidiarity the Maastricht Treaty also provided for new areas of competence to be conferred on the European Community including several which one might have expected the principle of subsidiarity to exclude, such as, for example, social policy, education, vocational training and youth, culture, consumer protection and public health.

A summary of the impact of the Maastricht Treaty on the process of European integration would be incomplete if limited purely to its legal impact. The political fall-out which it provoked was considerable. First the complex structure of the treaty document itself (especially if unaccompanied by a consolidated version of the EC Treaty) meant that most people found it extremely difficult to comprehend what the treaty was about and what its effects might be. The inclusion of provisions relating to subsidiarity and a debate about what that concept might and might not mean was insufficient to allay fears of many citizens of the Member States that the powers of those States would not be diminished. Reservations about the feasibility and even the desirability of progress to monetary union (expressed in so-called "opt-outs" granted to Denmark and the United Kingdom) and even the very use of the word "Union" with its echoes of the recently demised and unlamented Soviet Union, or closer to British voters the Act of Union between England and Scotland, all gave rise to concern.

That concern was expressed most forcefully by the Danes who, in a referendum (required when the Folketing failed to ratify the treaty by the necessary majority of five-sixths of its members) also rejected the treaty. In addition to the matters already mentioned,

---

78   See for example Articles 30 or 72 of the German *Grundgesetz* (Basic Law) or the text of the Xth amendment (1791) to the U.S. Constitution.

many Danes were particularly concerned that the notion of citizenship of the Union would replace their own citizenship of Denmark of which (like the nationals of most countries) they are exceptionally proud. There was also concern that the provisions on CFSP would result in the establishment of a European army in which Danish soldiers might have to fight in places or for causes of no concern to the Danish people.

The Danish rejection, an unexpectedly narrow victory in a referendum in France, and a prolonged and bitter parliamentary debate in the United Kingdom (resulting in ratification of the treaty by a very narrow margin) shook the confidence of the Member States both in the aims which they were pursuing in the Maastricht Treaty and the means they were using. The Danish objections were later overcome by glosses added to certain parts of the treaty at the European Council held in Edinburgh. An important legal challenge before the Constitutional Court of Germany[79] failed when that court gave its judgment confirming the compatibility of the treaty with the German Constitution. The Treaty finally entered force on November 1, 1993 nearly 21 months after its adoption.

One positive outcome of these problems was an increased awareness by the Community institutions and the Member States of the need to explain their decisions and working methods more clearly to citizens upon whose compliance and support they depend for the effectiveness of their action.

Some of the weaknesses of the TEU may already have been recognised by the Member States at the time of its adoption since, although Article 51 (ex Article Q) TEU provides that the treaty is concluded for an unlimited period, Article N(2)[80] provided for an intergovernmental conference to be convened in 1996 "to examine those provisions of this treaty for which revision is provided". The delay in the ratification process meant that that IGC, opened by the European Council in Turin and now including representatives of the governments of the three new Member States of the Union, effectively opened barely three years after the entry into force of the Union Treaty. The result of that IGC was the Treaty of Amsterdam signed in that city on October 2, 1997. The ratification process had not been completed in any of the Member States at the time this book was written. However, it had passed what was thought to be its most risky test, a referendum in Denmark.

79  The second chamber of the Bundesverfassungsgericht (Federal Constitutional Court) gave its judgment in Cases 2 BvR 2134/92 and 2159/92, *Brunner and Others v. European Union Treaty* on October 12, 1993. An English translation of the judgment is published at [1994] 1 CMLR 57.
80  Which was deleted by the Treaty of Amsterdam.

*The Treaty of Amsterdam*

Despite the apparently modest objective of Article N(2) TEU, which appeared to envisage merely fine tuning of what was clearly a novel institutional and treaty structure, a huge amount of effort was invested in the preparation of the 1996 Intergovernmental Conference (IGC). Reports on their functioning and future prospects were elicited from each of the Community institutions and in June 1995 the European Council established a ministerial level reflection group in order to review the issues for discussion and to prepare the agenda for the IGC itself. The result of that work was that the IGC was invited to consider three principal areas, the first dealing with the relationship between individual citizens on the one hand and the Union and its Member States on the other. The second was to consider the efficiency of the Community institutional structure in particular in view of the likelihood of future enlargements and the third was to improve the Union's capacity for effective action in the field of common foreign and security policy. Two further issues were added to the list, namely the need for action to be taken at Union level to deal with unacceptably high levels of unemployment in the Member States and, particularly in the light of the British and Danish "opt outs" from aspects of the Treaty on European Union, as well as the existence of the Schengen Agreement outside the Union context, the possibility for certain Member States to proceed towards closer integration more rapidly than others. The Intergovernmental Conference itself was formally opened in Turin on March 29, 1996 and concluded at Amsterdam on June 17, 1997. Following the necessary technical drafting work and translations, the final texts were ready for signature on October 2, 1997.

Given the amount and duration of that preparatory work it is perhaps surprising that the results of the negotiation have been called variously "modest", "disappointing" and even, for those committed to a significant further integration, "retrograde". The biggest single lacuna in the new treaty is an almost total absence of institutional reform with a view to facilitating future enlargement. Although the Community's legislative processes have been somewhat simplified and the position of the European Parliament further reinforced, there are no provisions relating to the future development of the system for qualified majority voting in the Council or the composition of the European Commission. Recognising that these unresolved issues would not go away, a protocol was annexed to the new treaty entitled "Protocol on the Institutions with the prospect of enlargement of the European Union". The Protocol provides first, that at the date of the next enlargement of the Union, the Commission will be composed of one national of each of the Member States provided that certain changes have by then taken place in the weighting of votes in the Council. Perhaps more fundamentally it adds that at least one year before the membership of the European Union exceeds twenty, an IGC will be convened in order to carry out a comprehensive review of the provisions of the treaties on the composition and functioning of the institutions. Given that there are already six candidate countries engaged in firm accession negotiations such a review cannot long be postponed. Notwithstanding that protocol, Belgium, France and Italy added a joint declaration making clear their view that the Treaty of Amsterdam did not meet the need for substantial progress towards reinforcing the institutions and consider that such reinforcement is an indispensable condition for the conclusion of the first accession negotiations.

Nonetheless, the Treaty of Amsterdam, while leaving intact the three pillar structure of the European Union, has made a large number of changes, some substantial, others superficial, both to the European Union and to the European Communities. The full effects of these changes will not become apparent until the revised treaties have been operating for some time.

The most important single change is in the area of activities covered by the third pillar of the Treaty on European Union. This pillar has effectively been split into two, with one part being fully integrated into the Community structure (albeit subject to certain special rules and procedures) and the remaining part staying in the intergovernmental sphere while providing for increased involvement of the Community institutions. Article 2 (ex Article B) TEU now declares that one of the objectives of the Union is to develop "as an area of freedom, security and justice, in which the free movement of persons is assured in conjunction with appropriate measures with respect to external border controls, asylum, immigration and the prevention and combating of crime". To that end the former Title 6 of the TEU[81] is repealed and replaced with a new Title 6 entitled "Provisions on Police and judicial co-operation in criminal matters". Under that title the division between the respective roles of the Community and the Union is made clear by Article 29 (ex Article K.1) TEU. That article provides that the objective of providing citizens with a high level of safety within an area of freedom, security and justice is to be attained, without prejudice to the powers of the European Community, and that it will seek to prevent and combat crime, in particular organised crime and terrorism, offences against children, illicit trafficking in drugs, arms and persons, corruption and fraud.

---

81  Entitled "Provisions on co-operation in the fields of justice and home affairs" and including Articles K to K.9.

For its part, the EC Treaty receives a new Title IV headed "Visas, asylum, immigration and other policies related to free movement of persons". Under this heading, Articles 61 to 63 (ex Articles 73 i to 73 k)require the Council, within five years of the entry into force of the Treaty of Amsterdam, to adopt various measures in the fields of asylum, refugees and displaced persons, immigration policy and to safeguard the rights of nationals of third countries. Measures are also to be adopted in the field of judicial co-operation in civil matters including improving and simplifying the system for cross-border service of judicial documents and co-operating in the taking of evidence in cases involving more than one Member State. Since these matters now fall under the aegis of the Community, the Court of Justice clearly has jurisdiction on the interpretation and validity of measures adopted by the Council. However, only courts or tribunals in the Member States against whose decisions there is no judicial remedy under national law may request a preliminary ruling on such a point from the Court of Justice,[82] although those courts are obliged to make such a request. A new form of advisory jurisdiction of the Court of Justice is also created (similar to that contained in Article 300 (ex Article 228) EC in respect of the conclusion of international agreements) whereby the Council, the Commission or a Member State may request the Court of Justice to give a ruling on a question of interpretation of Title IV or of measures adopted under it.

In the same context, the Treaty of Amsterdam, in a particularly complex fashion, has brought the aim of the elimination of internal border controls on the free movement of persons as envisaged in the Schengen Agreement[83] within the scope of the European Union. Thus by a protocol annexed both to the Treaty on European Union and to the EC Treaty the Schengen *acquis*[83a] is incorporated into the legal and institutional structure of the European Union. That protocol will require particularly careful implementation since such implementation, as is recognised in the preamble to the protocol, must take into account the special position of Denmark, the fact that Ireland and the United King-

---

82   Compare in this regard the position of national supreme courts under the third paragraph of Article 234 (ex Article 177) EC.

83   See pp. 91 *et seq.*

83a   "*Acquis*" is a piece of Eurojargon meaning a body of rules, practices, policies and principles which have been accepted at a given date. Thus countries which are candidates for membership of the EU are expected to accept the "*acquis communantaire*" (*i.e.* the existing state of affairs) on the date of accession. More specifically the Schengen *acquis* is defined in the protocol to the Treaty of Amsterdam. See further, Vade-mecum IV B, p. 348.

dom are not parties to the Schengen agreements and that Iceland and Norway, non-Member States of the European Union but members of the European Economic Area, have both signed an agreement (falling short of accession) confirming their intention to become bound by the Schengen rules.

Other important changes to the Treaty on European Union include a new Article 7 (ex Article F.1) which enables the Council, acting unanimously (presumably with the exception of the incriminated Member State, to decide to suspend the rights of a Member State under the Treaty, in particular the voting rights of the representatives of the government in the Council where the Council finds that there has been "a serious and persistent breach by a Member State of the principles of liberty, democracy, respect for human rights and fundamental freedoms, or the rule of law".

A new Title VII TEU headed "Provisions on closer co-operation" enables the Member States which intend to establish closer co-operation between themselves to make use of the institutions, procedures and mechanisms laid down by the TEU and the EC Treaty. That possibility which clearly opens the way to what has variously been called "variable geometry" or a "two-speed Europe" is subject to various provisos, in particular that the action taken must concern at least a majority of Member States, it must be aimed at furthering the objectives of the Union and must respect the principles of the treaties and the single institutional framework of the Union while not affecting either the *acquis communautaire* or the competences, rights, obligations and interests of the non-participating Member States. States not participating in a particular area of integration may join it later.

Apart from the matters dealt with above the most important changes to the European Community treaties are those in the areas of social policy and employment. As already mentioned the problem of unemployment is of particular concern to the Member States, and the need to take steps to promote employment is referred to both in amendments to Article 2 (ex Article B) TEU which sets out the objectives of the Union, and Article 2 (ex Article 2) EC which states that one of the tasks of the Community is to promote "a high level of employment". To that end a new Title VIII headed "Employment" has been added to the EC Treaty. The six articles under that title (Articles 125 to 130 inclusive) require the Member States and the Community to work towards developing a co-ordinated strategy for employment to co-ordinate their action in this area within the Council and to take into account the objective of a high level of employment in formulating and implementing other Community policies and activities. The title does not require the Council to adopt any particular legislative measures to fulfil those aims but enables it to use the co-decision procedure to adopt incentive measures designed to encourage co-operation between Member States and to support their action in the field of employment. A new employment committee is to be set up with advisory status to promote co-ordination between the Member States and to monitor developments on the employment market and employment policy generally.

Elsewhere the change of government in the United Kingdom in May 1997 meant that the United Kingdom's tenacious opposition to the inclusion of social policy within the scope of Community activity was ended so that the substance of the social protocol to the TEU (which did not apply to the United Kingdom) could be integrated into the EC Treaty. As a result, the existing Articles 117 to 120 of the EC Treaty are completely replaced. It is worth noting that Article 136 (ex Article 117) now refers explicitly to the European Social Charter signed at Turin on October 18, 1961 and to the 1989 Community Charter of the fundamental social rights of workers. Those charters will therefore no doubt become a source of inspiration both for the Community legislature and for the Court of Justice called upon to interpret new legislation adopted under this title.

While the principle of equal pay for men and women was originally enshrined in Article 119 of the EEC Treaty and as it has always been treated as one of the fundamental elements of European Community law (as illustrated by the huge amount of case law which both that article and the related equal treatment and equal pay directives have given rise to), the more general goal of equality between men and women is now included in Article 2 (ex Article 2) EC as one of the goals of the Community. Article 149 (ex Article 119) itself is revised so as to make it explicit that men and women are to receive equal pay for "work of equal value" and, going beyond matters concerning pay alone, the Council may adopt measures "to ensure the application of the principle of equal opportunities and equal treatment of men and women in matters of employment and occupation". Such legislation may now be adopted through the co-decision procedure and by a qualified majority vote rather than on the basis of unanimity as was previously the case.

## THE EUROPEAN ECONOMIC AREA

As we have seen above, the European Free Trade Association ("EFTA") was established, at least in part, as a counterweight to the deepening integration pursued by the original six members of the European Communities. When, in 1986, Portugal (then an EFTA Member State) joined the European Communities at a time when the programme to complete the internal market was already well under way, the remaining EFTA States (see diagram on page

50) were anxious that their exclusion from that market might prove detrimental. For its part the European Community was keen to play down the suggestion that the creation of the internal market would lead to the creation of an economic "Fortress Europe" with a protectionist stance towards trade with outsiders.

The European Economic Area ("EEA") is a true hybrid of intergovernmental and integrationist organisations. It is dealt with in this chapter because of the closeness of the aims of the EEA to those of the single market aspects of the European Community and because of the similarities in its institutional arrangements, although as we shall see there are also important differences.

This hybridisation makes the EEA rather difficult to define and classify. However, its basic purpose is to extend the effect of most of the rules relating to the Community's internal market to the territory of the EFTA-EEA[83b] States. Thus it aims to ensure the free movement of goods, persons, services and capital throughout the EEA and, subject to a number of small exceptions, the entire *acquis communautaire* of the four freedoms is now applicable in the EFTA-EEA States.

The most important exception is trade in agricultural commodities which is not covered by the EEA agreement. In addition, the Community's rules on free competition are extended to the EFTA-EEA countries, thus the purpose of the EEA is summarised in Article 1 of the EEA Treaty as being to "promote a continuous and balanced strengthening of trade and economic relations between the Contracting Parties with equal conditions of competition, and the respect of the same rules with a view to creating a homogeneous European economic area".

Unstated in the Treaty is the political consideration that such arrangements would be likely to facilitate the acceptance by EFTA-EEA States of Community rules, and thus make the eventual transition to full membership of the European Union a smaller step to take. This is what actually happened when Austria, Finland and Sweden joined the European Union only one year after the entry into force of the EEA Treaty. Similarly hopes were expressed that future candidates for accession to the European Union, in particular the Central and Eastern European countries, might first apply to join EFTA, then adapt to the internal market rules through the operation of the EEA as a preparation to accession. Hence the reference to the EEA as "an ever closer waiting-room".[84]

83b  That is to say Iceland, Liechtenstein and Norway.
84  See Peers, "An Ever Closer Waiting-room? The Case for Eastern European Accession to the European Communities" (1996) 32 C.M.L. Rev 187.

It should be noted that the EEA (unlike the European Community) is not a customs union. Thus the European Community on the one hand and the individual EFTA-EEA States on the other maintain their own external customs tariffs and the free movement of goods between the various constituent parts applies only to goods originating in the EEA. As a result it is arguable that the effect of the EEA Treaty was for the European Community to join EFTA rather than for the EFTA countries to enter a closer association with the Community.

The (then) EFTA States and the EEC had already agreed in a declaration made in Luxembourg in 1984 to extend their cooperation beyond the existing bilateral trade agreements. That declaration included the first reference to the term *espace économique européen* (european economic area). Negotiations to formalise the relationship between EFTA and the EEC began in 1989 and resulted in a treaty signed in Oporto on May 2, 1992[85] by the then 12 EEC Member States, six of the seven EFTA States[86] and on behalf of the EEC and the ECSC.

Following a negative referendum result Switzerland failed to ratify the agreement, a situation which, in turn, caused problems for Liechtenstein as a result of its customs union with Switzerland. The agreement therefore came into force in respect of the five remaining EFTA countries, and what was by now the European Union, on January 1, 1994. Within a year however, Austria, Finland and Sweden had themselves joined the European Union, leaving only Iceland and Norway (joined in March 1995 by Liechtenstein) as the EFTA members of the EEA.

The interrelationship of the European Union, the European Communities, EFTA and the European Economic Area are apt to cause confusion and when dealing with the subject care should be taken to be sure that you know exactly which States and which organisation you are referring to. Thus EFTA now has four Member States of which one, Switzerland, is not a Member State of the EEA (although it does have a bilateral association agreement with

---

85   The delay in arriving at a signature was partly caused by the Commission's decision to request an opinion from the Court of Justice on the compatibility of the proposed EEA judicial supervision mechanism with the EC Treaty. The Court's carefully reasoned but negative opinion on that question (Opinion 1/91, [1991] ECR I 6079) meant that the institutional provisions of the Agreement had to be re-negotiated. For a summary of that opinion and for the later, positive opinion on the revised agreement (Opinion 1/92, [1992] ECR I 282) see Brown and Kennedy, *Brown and Jacobs' The Court of Justice of the European Communities* (4th ed., Sweet & Maxwell, London, 1995), pp. 232–240.

86   The arrangements for Liechtenstein to become a full member of EFTA had not yet been completed.

the EC). The European Union is not a member of the European Economic Area although all of its 15 Member States are. All of the activities of the EEA fall within the scope of the European Community pillar of the E.U. However, even that pillar contains matters which fall outwith the scope of the EEA agreement. The second and third pillars of the E.U. structure fall wholly outside the EEA although the incorporation of the Schengen *acquis* into the first pillar has involved special arrangements being made by Iceland and Norway.

Finally it should be noted that, since the EEA agreement takes the form of an association agreement concluded by the Community under Article 238 (now Article 310) EC it forms a part of the *acquis communautaire* which future candidate countries will be required to accept.

The institutional arrangements for the EEA are also complex consisting, on the one hand, of joint bodies with representatives both of the EFTA–EEA members and of the E.U.–EEA members. Two of the most important bodies however, the EFTA Surveillance Authority, and the EFTA Court remain exclusively EFTA bodies, although without participation of Swiss members. Of the joint bodies it should be noted that none has autonomous legislative power and that the EFTA–EEA States are therefore only bound by those decisions to the extent to which they agree to them. To that extent the EEA remains an intergovernmental type of organisation notwithstanding the enforcement machinery of the ESA and the EFTA Court. Of the joint EEA institutions the EEA Council composed of ministerial representatives of the governments of the Contracting States (*i.e.* all 18) and a member of the European Commission meets at least twice per year. It fulfils a similar role to that played by the European Council in respect of the European Union in reviewing progress towards the achievement of the treaty's objectives and in giving political impetus or resolving political difficulties through negotiation.

The EEA Joint Committee (similar to the Council of the European Union) is composed of senior officials of the signatory States who take decisions on a consensus basis and meets at least once a month. In addition there are two advisory bodies, an EEA Joint Parliamentary Committee consisting of members of the European Parliament and members of the Parliaments of the EFTA–EEA States. At its twice-yearly meetings it may make recommendations or adopt non-binding reports or resolutions on matters covered by the EEA agreement. The EEA Consultative Committee has a role analogous to that of the Economic and Social Committee of the European Community and indeed is partly composed of members of the latter.

Of the two purely EFTA bodies, the EFTA Court is dealt with in Chapter 6 below. The EFTA Surveillance Authority (ESA) has responsibilities with regard to the EFTA–EEA States broadly similar to those of the European Commission in respect of the European Community Member States. Thus the ESA will ensure that the EFTA–EEA States correctly implement, apply and interpret the EEA rules and has the power, if necessary, to bring the defaulting State before the EFTA Court for a declaration that that State has failed to fulfil its obligations under the EEA Treaty.[87]

The surveillance by the ESA of the activities of undertakings, and in particular of their compliance with the EEA competition rules (Articles 53 and 54 of the EEA Treaty which are for practical purposes identical to Articles 81 (ex Article 85) EC and Article 82 (ex Article 86) EC) are much more complicated. So far as the Community territory of the EEA is concerned, the competition rules are enforced by the European Commission which may take decisions in individual cases including the imposition of fines for infringement of the competition rules or granting exemptions in certain circumstances. Likewise the Commission must approve any proposals by the EC Member States to grant State aid to undertakings in difficulties.

The ESA has parallel competences in these areas in so far as the territory of the EFTA–EEA States is concerned. This is unlikely to cause difficulties in the matter of State aids. However, a complex scheme has had to be devised in order to determine which of the two bodies is to take the responsibility for supervising and, if necessary, regulating the activity of undertakings which may affect trade in both parts of the EEA territory. Thus the EEA Treaty and its protocols contain provisions requiring the ESA and the Commission to co-operate closely with each other and rules to determine which of the two authorities is responsible for the examination of, for example, a proposed agreement involving an undertaking established in the E.U. on the one hand and an undertaking established in the EFTA–EEA countries on the other. Thus, where the effect of an anti-competitive measure arises within the Community and in the EFTA area as a whole they will be dealt with by the Commission; if a measure or an agreement affects trade between the EFTA–EEA area and only one EC Member State it will be dealt with by the ESA, which will also deal with cases where more than one-third of the turnover of the operation concerned arises in the EFTA countries.

This Byzantine[88] arrangement is indicative of the difficulties in trying to arrange a marriage between two fundamentally different

---

87  See, for example, Case E–7/97 *EFTA Surveillance Authority v. Kingdom of Norway*, judgment of April 30, 1998, not yet reported.

88  The adjective, although appropriate, is not mine. See Cremona "The Dynamic and Homogeneous EEA: Byzantine Structures and Variable Geometry" [1994] 19 ELR 508.

organisations, the one based on a principle of integration and supranational institutions, the other being essentially intergovernmental with decision-making processes based on consensus and unanimity. For such a mismatch to work effectively it is essential that both parties should inform each other of their respective positions. Thus, on the Community's behalf, the Commission must take into account the positions of the EFTA–EEA countries in formulating proposals to the Council which in turn will have to give "due consideration" to those views when adopting final measures. This process is termed "decision shaping". Any of the EFTA–EEA countries retains the option of not being bound by a measure adopted at the Community level, again illustrating the difference between the two organisations inasmuchas, within the European Community a Member State finding itself in minority opposition to a proposed single market measure may nonetheless be bound by it if adopted by a qualified majority in the Council.

## THE SCHENGEN AGREEMENT

The Schengen Agreement is another example of the blurring of the distinction between intergovernmental and supranational organizations. When first adopted on June 14, 1985 the Schengen Agreement was based purely on intergovernmental co-operation between France, Germany and the three Benelux countries, without any involvement of the Community institutions, despite the fact that the subject-matter of the agreement was a logical product of the evolution of the Communities. By a Protocol to the Treaty of Amsterdam the original Schengen Agreement, as well as various subsequent agreements and protocols and certain decisions and declarations adopted pursuant to those instruments,[89] have now been incorporated into the legal and institutional structure of the European Union, including powers for the Court of Justice to exercise judicial review in certain matters. The Schengen Agreement can thus properly be regarded as part of European Community law.

Schengen itself is a modest little wine-producing village on the River Mosel in the bottom right-hand corner of the Grand Duchy of Luxembourg. It was this geographical position, rather than any other attribute, which led to the signature of the agreement there on June 14, 1985, while Luxembourg held the presidency of the European Communities. Thus the agreement was signed by the first five signatory States on board a boat moored in the middle of

89 The instruments concerned known collectively as "the Schengen *acquis*" are listed in an annex to the protocol and in Vade-mecum IV.

the River Mousel at the exact point where the borders of Luxembourg, France and Germany meet. This symbolic venue was deemed to be appropriate for an agreement whose purpose was the gradual abolition of controls at the common frontiers between the Member States. The provisions of the agreement thus include measures concerning the abolition of systematic checks, the easing of customs and other formalities, harmonization of visa regulations and closer co-operation and communication between the border police forces.

Five years later it was found that practical difficulties had resulted in little progress being made towards achieving those objectives and so an additional convention on the implementation of the agreement was signed, again in Schengen, on June 19, 1990. Subsequent accession protocols now mean that all of the Member States of the Union, with the exception of the United Kingdom and Ireland, have signed the agreement and that it has entered force in relation to the five original signatory States as well as Spain, Portugal, Italy and Austria.

The Schengen Protocol to the Treaty of Amsterdam substitutes the Council for the Executive Committee originally established by the Schengen Agreement, likewise the Schengen secretariat will be integrated into the general secretariat of the Council. The Council, acting unanimously (that is to say including the United Kingdom and Ireland) is to determine, *ex post facto*, the legal basis in the treaties for each of the provisions or decisions constituting the Schengen *acquis*. Other provisions in the Schengen context may be adopted by unanimity among the 13 signatory States meeting in the Council.

In order to enable Denmark, Finland and Sweden to take part in the Schengen arrangements, without at the same time disrupting the passport union which already existed between the Member States of the Nordic Council (see p. 32 above), the Accession Protocol signed by the three Nordic members of the European Union in Luxembourg on December 19, 1996 also provided for Iceland and Norway to be associated with the implementation of the Schengen *acquis*, and this provision too has been incorporated into the Protocol to the Treaty of Amsterdam. A separate agreement is envisaged in order to deal with the relations between Iceland and Norway on the one hand and the United Kingdom and Ireland on the other.

Because of fears that the unchecked movement of goods and people across the internal frontiers of the Community would benefit not only workers, traders and citizens going about their lawful business but also drugs traffickers, money launderers and other miscreants, the 1990 Convention set out various internal security measures in order to compensate for the loss of security arising from the abolition of border controls. Thus the Schengen

Information System (SIS) is a database allowing Member States, under carefully controlled conditions, to set up databases on persons and certain objects (such as firearms, banknotes and lost or stolen vehicles or identity documents). More rigorous checks may be carried out at the external borders of the Schengen group of States, and increased co-operation among the police forces responsible for border security is provided for through the build-up of better established communications, joint exercises, cross-border observation and the right of hot pursuit across borders. There is an obligation to supply the security forces of other Member States with information relating to crime prevention and increased co-operation in the fight against drugs and drug-related crime. These latter aims would be facilitated by the establishment of a European Police Office (Europol) located in The Hague and the European drugs monitoring agency in Lisbon.

# PART TWO: WHAT IS EUROPEAN LAW?

# 4. WHAT IS "EUROPEAN" LAW?

*"A definition is the enclosing of a wilderness of ideas within a wall of words", Samuel Butler,* Notebooks.

## PRELIMINARY MATTERS

Good question. It should already be apparent from the description of the various organisations covered in the previous two chapters that given the diversity of their aims, membership and working methods, it is a question which is unlikely to have a single neat answer. Indeed it is arguable that the expression is so general, including as it does, not only as many as four institutional legal orders but also aspects of the domestic laws of many European States, and both public and private international law, that it should rarely be used at all.

At the most general level the expression "European law" may be used to distinguish the law and legal systems originating in Europe from those say of Asia, Africa or the Americas. Even at that level the distinction may not be of much assistance given that the legal systems in many States in the latter regions owe their essential characteristics to the structures established by the former colonial powers in the image of their own domestic systems, including rules and institutions which have often survived many years of independence and even revolution and civil war.

Again regarding "European law" as the law applicable in Europe (apart from begging the question of the geographical extent of the Continent dealt with below) it will also include the municipal law of European States and the many bilateral relationships between those States as well as the law emanating from the various European or international organisations.

More usually however, the term "European law" is taken as defining the rules and arrangements made by, or pursuant to, certain international treaties entered into by European States.

Read in that way European law would include:

- the law of the European Communities;

- the law of the European Union;

- the laws of certain other groupings such as Benelux, the Schengen countries and the European Economic Area; and

- the law of the European Convention on Human Rights.

Clearly the first three categories are closely related and overlap to a considerable extent. Nonetheless, to apply the term "European law" to those areas collectively, would, on the one hand, ignore the importance of the Human Rights Convention and, on the other hand, obscure the important constitutional differences between the European Union as an intergovernmental organisation, the European Communities as being based on the principle of closer integration and the EEA as a hybrid.

It is in the collective sense that I have used "European law" in both the title of this book and of this chapter. Nonetheless, the use of the definition in that way does not bring us any closer to an understanding of the nature and characteristics of European law. Traditionally legal scholars describe and define different legal systems by reference to their sources. By this is meant the way in which legal rules are created. In the context of European law, this includes not only the rules establishing the various organisations and institutions but also the creation of specific rules giving rise to rights and obligations on the part of states, institutions or individuals. These sources will be examined below. In addition, one of the most striking characteristics of European law, in particular European Community law, is the way in which it has created rights and obligations which operate within the municipal law systems of the various Member States. This aspect is the subject of the next chapter. Before enumerating and describing the sources of European law it is, however, necessary to make a few remarks about geography and, particularly for the benefit of non lawyers, to explain what is meant by public and private international law.

**A Word about Geography**

It is tempting to assume that "European law" is the law applicable on the continent of Europe. Even if that were the case, there remains the difficulty of making or forming a precise geographical definition of "Europe". Scandinavia, Iceland and the archipelagoes of the Faroes and the British Isles clearly constitute the western extremity. Few would quibble either with the inclusion of the Atlantic Islands of the Azores, Madeira or the Canary Islands as forming part of Europe, although the Canaries lie closer to the coast of North-West Africa than to Spain to which they territorially belong.

The eastern border of Europe with Asia is far more difficult to define. Traditionally the Ural Mountains divide the Russian Federation into its European and Asian parts although that division has no political significance. Since the accession of the Russian Federation to the Council of Europe the division has even less meaning and now the European Convention on Human Rights and Fundamental Freedoms is applicable from Valencia to Vladivostok.

The territorial application of the EC Treaty is exceedingly complex. The basic rules are laid down in Article 299 (ex Article 227) EC, which provides, first, that the Treaty applies to the Member States which are listed and also specifies that the provisions of the Treaty apply to the French Overseas Departments,[90] the Azores, Madeira and the Canary Islands. However, the Treaty provides that "taking account of the structural, social and economic situation of the French Overseas Departments, the Azores, Madeira and the Canary Islands, which is compounded by their remoteness, insularity, small size, difficult topography and climate, economic dependence on a few products" ', the Council may adopt specific measures for the application of the Treaty rules to those regions. That article also provides that the treaties shall apply to territories for whose external relations a Member State is responsible but that it shall not apply to the Faroe Islands and shall apply to the Channel Islands and the Isle of Man only under certain conditions.[91]

Furthermore, Articles 182 (ex Article 131) to 188 (ex Article

---

90 Known as the *Départements d'outre-mer* or *Doms*. These *départements* are French Guyana on the South American mainland, Reunion Island in the Indian Ocean and Guadeloupe and Martinique in the Caribbean.

91 Those conditions were at issue before the Court of Justice in Case C–355/89 *Department of Health and Social Security v. Barr and Montrose Holdings* [1991] ECR I–3479, and in Case C–171/96 *Pereira Roque v. The Lieutenant Governor of Jersey* (not yet reported, July 16, 1998).

136(a)) provide for certain overseas countries and territories which have special relations with Denmark, France, the Netherlands and the United Kingdom to be associated with the Community. So far as Denmark is concerned this refers to Greenland since its secession from Denmark and the European Communities in 1985,[92] and for the rest various island territories including Aruba and the Netherlands Antilles, various French and British islands in the South Pacific, the South Atlantic and the British and French Antarctic territories. Under the association arrangements, whose aim is to "further the interests and prosperity of the inhabitants of these countries and territories", Member States must apply to trade with those countries and territories the same treatment as they accord each other under the Treaty and each of the overseas countries and territories must apply to its trade with Member States and the other territories the same treatment as that which it applies to the European State with which it has special relations. The European Union Treaties apply to the Årland Islands subject to certain derogations created by a protocol to the Austrian, Finnish and Swedish Accession Treaty. These derogations concern on the one hand restrictions on the rights to own real property on the islands and on the right of establishment and the right to provide services there, and on the other hand certain exemptions from the application of Value Added Tax, excise duties and other forms of indirect taxation.

Finally, some 70 developing countries in Africa, the Caribbean and the Pacific ("ACP countries") are linked to the European Union by the Lomé Convention originally entered into between the Member States of the then European Communities and 46 ACP countries in 1975. The Treaty whose aim is "to promote and expedite the economic, cultural and social development of the ACP States and to consolidate and diversify their relations with the European Union and its Member States" are revised from time to time. The Convention establishes a range of institutions to achieve those aims including an ACP–E.U. Council of Ministers, Committee of Ambassadors and a Joint Assembly.

Clearly the term "European law", even if one specifies that it includes European Community law and that of the European Convention on Human Rights, does not amount to a geographical designation of origin.

### Public International Law

Sometimes referred to as the "Law of Nations" or simply as "International law", public international law is the body of rules

---

92   See the Greenland Treaty, OJ L 29, February 1, 1985.

which govern the conduct of states[93] and their relationships with each other. Until the end of the nineteenth century, International law was concerned principally with the rules of diplomacy and the law of war. However, particularly since the Second World War, the massive growth in the number of international organisations means that the subject now includes the rules on the establishment, status and powers of such international organisations. As such the various forms of European law mentioned above may be regarded as sub-sets of International law.

The sources of International law are conveniently listed in Article 38(1) of the Statute of the International Court of Justice[94] which lays down the rules to be applied by that Court. Those sources are:

(a) International conventions (treaties), establishing rules expressly recognised by the Contracting States;

(b) International custom, as evidence of a general practice accepted as law;

(c) The general principles of law recognised by civilised nations;

(d) Subsidiary means for determining the rules of law including judicial decisions and the "teachings of the most highly qualified publicists of the various nations".

There is vast academic literature on the nature of those sources and on questions such as whether or not the list in Article 38(1) is exhaustive or whether the order in which the various sources are listed is significant as creating a hierarchical relationship between them. For present purposes it is only necessary to expand briefly on the nature of treaties.

*Treaties*

Treaties are agreements between states or occasionally between a state and an international organisation[95] laying down rules which are binding on the parties to the treaty. Such agreements may take many forms and have many differing designations. However, such differences of terminology have no influence on the effect of

93   The words "state" and "nation" are sometimes used interchangeably although they are not coterminous as, for example, any Scot, Welshman or Basque will soon explain. Even the United Nations is, in reality, an organisation of states.

94   See p. 197 below.

95   Such as the Headquarters Agreements in which a state allows an international organisation to be established on its territory and lays down the conditions under which the organisation may carry out its work.

the agreement as a matter of international law. Thus in the context of European law, in addition to the word "treaty" you may encounter "acts", "conventions", "agreements", "protocols", and "decisions" (for examples see the list in Vade-mecum IV).

Treaties, whether they have been entered into by two states (bilateral treaties) or several states (multilateral treaties) are binding only upon those states that enter into the agreement. They are not therefore analogous to legislation in the domestic legal systems within states which is imposed by the legislative authority on those subject to the law. Before becoming binding on states signatory to a treaty, it is usually necessary for the state to ratify a treaty whether by submitting it to approval by the people in a plebiscite or by seeking parliamentary approval according to the constitutional practice in the states concerned.

Once ratified, treaties owe their binding force to the principle that states will carry out the obligations which they have entered into in good faith in accordance with the rather tautologous Latin maxim *Pacta sunt servanda*, which means, simply that agreements shall be carried out. This general reliance on the goodwill of states, which on the whole works to ensure that treaties are observed, may be reinforced by the creation of a judicial authority — as in the case of the treaties establishing the European Communities, the European Convention on Human Rights and the European Economic Area, although the authority of those courts to ensure the observance of the treaties over which they have jurisdiction itself depends upon the terms of the treaties themselves. Likewise, the authority of the International Court of Justice depends upon the agreement of states who might submit a dispute on the interpretation of a treaty to that Court to do so. The methods used by courts for the interpretation of treaties are covered in Chapter 8 below.

*Legal Personality*

Although, as stated above, international law governs the relationships between states as such, the subjects of international law also include international organisations and individuals. So far as international organisations are concerned, their status as actors in the context of international law will depend upon the degree of legal personality which they have been given in their constitutive treaty. Thus the Marrakesh Agreement establishing the World Trade Organisation gives that organisation legal personality, although its predecessor, the General Secretariat of the GATT, did not have legal personality. The European Community has legal personality[96] and this is defined as meaning that "in each of the

96   Article 281 (ex Article 210) EC.

Member States, the Community shall enjoy the most extensive legal capacity accorded to legal persons under their laws; it may, in particular, acquire or dispose of movable and immovable property and may be a party to legal proceedings".[97] The Merger Treaty adds that the European Communities are to enjoy such privileges and immunities as are necessary for the performance of their tasks.

It may at first sight appear surprising that individuals (including both natural and legal persons) might be subject directly to international law. Although individuals may not have the capacity to exercise international personality, for example by negotiating with states, they may acquire or have conferred upon them both rights and duties at the international level. In the European context rights of individuals include the rights and freedoms protected by the European Convention on Human Rights (see Vade-mecum VI) or, for example, the right of men and women to receive equal pay for work of equal value (Article 141 (ex Article 199) EC). Obligations may also be imposed on companies, for example to respect certain international rules on navigation in the air or on the high seas, rules against discharging polluting substances in international waters or, in the context of European Community law, to refrain from anti-competitive activities (Articles 81 and 82 (ex Articles 85 and 86) EC).

*States*

Since states are the main building blocks of all of the organisations described in the last two chapters, it is useful to have some understanding of what constitutes a state. Moreover, since much of the debate on the merits of membership of European organisations, in particular the European Communities and the European Union, turns on arguments over the erosion of the sovereignty of states and the notion of sovereignty is a public international law concept, it is appropriate briefly to define it here.

According to the 1933 Montevideo Convention on the rights and duties of states,[98] a state for the purposes of international law must have a permanent population (there is no minimum number), a defined territory, a government and the capacity to enter into relations with other states. A typical sovereign state is therefore one with a central political authority, its government, which represents that state on the international plane and has paramount power within the territory of the state. In federal states, such as Germany, Switzerland, India or the United States of America, the individual constituent states of the federation retain

97   Article 282 (ex Article 211).
98   165 LNTS 20.

their powers to organise and regulate their internal affairs, subject to certain limitations laid down in the Constitution, whereas the Union has various institutions with powers of their own, some of which may operate internally within the constituent states. More importantly it is the federal government which exercises the exclusive authority to conduct foreign relations on behalf of the Union and to enter into treaties with other states. Although the European Communities have certain powers to enter into treaties in specified areas,[99] the individual Member States retain their treaty-making powers in other areas, although in some circumstances that power is exercised jointly by the Member States and by the Community.

*Sovereignty*

The impact of European law on the "sovereignty" of Member States is one of the most controversial aspects of its working which will be examined in more detail in the next chapter. Since, however, sovereignty is a central concept in international law it is appropriate briefly to define it here.

Sovereignty is generally taken to be the capacity of a state for independent action both within and outside its own territory. That definition may be broken down into three principal elements. First, and most importantly in the context of international law, comes external sovereignty or the capacity of a state freely to determine its relations with other states or international organisations. A state possessing such capacity is clearly independent of other states so, in this context, independence is a near synonym for external sovereignty.

The counterpart of (and necessary condition for) external sovereignty is internal sovereignty which is a state's exclusive right and jurisdiction to establish its own internal institutions, to make the necessary arrangements for their working, to legislate for all purposes and to secure observance of such legislation. Finally, territorial sovereignty is the exclusive authority which a state may exercise over anything or anybody within, above or beneath its territory. This includes the jealously guarded right to regulate

---

99   See for example Article 133 (ex Article 113) EC. The procedure for concluding such an agreement between the Community and one or more states or international organisations is laid down in Article 300 (ex Article 228) EC, which confers upon the Commission the power to conduct negotiations towards such a treaty pursuant to a mandate conferred on it by the Council, a requirement to consult the European Parliament and provision for obtaining the opinion of the Court of Justice as to whether an agreement envisaged is compatible with the existing provisions of the treaty.

access to the air space above the territory or, for example, to seize foreign submarines which encroach within the territorial waters of a maritime country.

Clearly, sovereignty as so defined cannot be absolute. All states must respect the sovereignty of others and accept limitations to their own sovereignty stemming either from their interaction with other states or, for example, from treaties which they have entered into. The rules of international law themselves, whether customary rules, the general principles of law recognised by civilised nations or treaties may all impose substantial restrictions on state sovereignty. Nowhere is this more evident than with the creation of the European Communities of which the Court of Justice has observed that "the Community constitutes a new legal order of international law for the benefit of which the States have limited their sovereign rights, albeit within limited fields, and the subject of which comprise not only Member States but also their nationals".[1] We will return to this matter in the next chapter.

**Private International Law**

Private international law is arguably not international at all since its rules form part of states' domestic law for the determination of cases involving a foreign element. Such a foreign element may arise when either or both of the parties to a dispute are outside the territorial jurisdiction of the court called upon to resolve the dispute, where issues of law from another legal system are invoked or where one or other of the parties claims that the courts of another jurisdiction are competent or may even have already decided the case. Clearly in a world where international contacts exist, particularly in trade and commerce but also given the increasing frequency of marriages between nationals of different states, such rules are increasingly important and therefore have a particular place in the consideration of European law.

The rules of private international law have three particular functions. First, to determine which courts have jurisdiction over a particular dispute; secondly to determine which municipal laws are applicable in order to resolve that dispute; and thirdly, where a judgment has already been delivered by a court in another jurisdiction, to determine the extent to which (a) that judgment may be recognised as conclusive and (b) the extent to which such a judgment may be enforced by the courts of a country other than by the one in which it was delivered. Since the court dealing with a particular case may have to reconcile the claims for jurisdiction of two legal systems, evaluate the competing arguments for the

---

1   Case 26/62 *Van Gend en Loos v. Nederlandse Administratie der Belastingen*, [1963] ECR 1.

application of the rules deriving from those legal systems or resolve a dispute as to whether or not the judgment of a foreign court ought to be recognised or enforced, the subject is often designated "conflict of laws".

Given that private international law is an element of domestic legal systems it is inevitable that the rules of private international law vary considerably from one country to another. Such a situation could, potentially, give rise to serious complications, for example if the courts of two different states each claimed jurisdiction to deal with the same dispute or each decided that different rules were applicable to it. Conversely, a denial of justice might result if all of the courts called upon declined jurisdiction based upon their own view of the powers of the others.

One approach to the reduction of such problems is the unification of the rules of private international law so as to ensure that a given case with a foreign element will be decided in the same way irrespective of the court before which it is tried. To that end the Hague Conference on private international law was established on a permanent basis in 1951 (whereas previously it had met on an *ad hoc* basis to discuss such issues) to examine and prepare proposals for the unification of private international law. A number of conventions have been drawn up by the Hague Conference to deal with private international problems in areas including succession, adoption, child abduction and many others. Such conventions, which only enter into force between countries which have ratified them, are arguably a source of European law in the wide sense used in this chapter.

Given that one of the principal objectives of the European Community is to secure the free movement of goods, persons, services and capital between Member States, it is inevitable that cross-border disputes and litigation, and consequently problems of private international law, will become more frequent. This is recognised in Article 293 (ex Article 220) EC which requires Member States to enter into negotiations with each other in order to secure *inter alia* "the simplification of formalities governing the reciprocal recognition and enforcement of judgments of courts or tribunals and of arbitration awards".

*Brussels Convention*

To that end the original six Member States adopted the Convention on Jurisdiction and the Enforcement of Judgments in Civil and Commercial Matters, usually known as the Brussels Convention, in 1968[2] and, three years later, a protocol concerning the interpretation of that convention by the European Court of Justice.

2    See Vade-mecum IV, Part D.

At each successive enlargement of the European Community and the European Union new Member States have signed accession conventions to the 1968 Brussels Convention and the 1971 interpretation protocol. Amendments are progressively made in order to take account of the specific features of the legal systems of the new Member States. In particular the San Sebastian Convention on the accession of Spain and Portugal made a number of significant changes in order to incorporate developments in the case law of the Court of Justice and the practice of other courts in the Member States. The Lugano Convention of September 16, 1988 mirrors the provisions of the Brussels Convention and extends its principles to the EFTA states. Since those states cannot accept the jurisdiction of the Court of Justice, the latter has no power to interpret the Lugano Convention. However, where it is called upon to interpret provisions of the Brussels Convention it must "pay due account" to rulings by courts in the EFTA States under the Lugano Convention. Conversely the courts in those states have a reciprocal obligation to "pay due account" to rulings of the Court of Justice and of the courts of the Contracting States to the Brussels Convention.

Although the Brussels Convention is a separate treaty and therefore strictly falls outside the scope of European Community law, it was, nonetheless, adopted for the furtherance of the purposes of the Community.[2a] It also constitutes in a sense the private international law of the Community as between its own Member States and the case law of the court in interpreting the Convention is published alongside the rest of the court's judgments. That law therefore firmly constitutes a part of European law.

Subsequently the Member States have included in the Treaty on European Union a provision (Article K. 3(2)(c)) enabling the Council to adopt conventions in areas covered by the "Third pillar" (Justice and Home affairs). These are now provided for in Article 65 (ex Article 73 m) of the EC Treaty.

## SOURCES OF EUROPEAN LAW

The notion of "sources" of law is, as has already been mentioned, a traditional tool for the classification and description of legal systems. It is a useful and effective tool and there is no obstacle to its use in the context of European law. However, before embarking on a description such as the one I have set out below, it is necessary to be aware of some of the limitations of the method.

First, the term "sources" is itself ambiguous, or rather it embraces several different shades of meaning. Thus in the first place it may refer both to the persons or institutions by whom the law is

2a   Pursuant to Article 220 (new Article 293) EC.

made (monarchs, parliaments, governments, judges, etc.) and to
the legal instruments by which they give effect to their intentions
(such as treaties, statutes, regulations or judgments). Since, generally, a given legal instrument presupposes a given institutional
structure from which it emanates, I have adopted the instrumental
approach below.

Secondly, the expression "sources" may also cover the questions of how law is made, whence it gains its authority or, quite
simply, where you can find it. The latter question is the subject of
Chapter 7 and, the question of its authority is connected with the
status of the persons responsible for creating it. Moreover, in the
field of European law, it is also closely concerned with the interaction between European law and the national legal systems of
the Member States dealt with in the next chapter.

Finally, it must be recognised that any attempt at classification
will inevitably be conditioned by the legal culture of the writer
attempting it, and this will affect not only the very categorisation
used but also the relative importance given to the various sources
which may be identified. Thus lawyers from countries whose law
and institutions are based upon a written constitution[3] will naturally look to find a source of European law which plays a similar
role to that of the constitution in their own legal system. The
announcement by the European Court of Justice that "the EEC
Treaty, albeit concluded in the form of an international agreement, nonetheless constitutes the constitutional charter of a
Community based on the rule of law"[4] would come as no surprise
to such lawyers. Alternatively, lawyers from the common law
traditions would have less difficulty in accepting the important
role ascribed to the case law of the European courts than would
some lawyers brought up in the civil law tradition. An Irish
lawyer combining both a common law approach with experience
of judicial review against constitutional standards might have yet
a different perspective. Then again, French lawyers and those
from other civil law systems accord the works of learned legal
writers (*"la doctrine"* in French) much greater weight than English
lawyers may do. With that background in mind what, then, are
the sources of European law? Broadly speaking,[5-6] five sources of
European law may be identified. These are:

3  Only the United Kingdom and New Zealand are without any form of
   written constitution. Israel has nine Basic Laws but as yet no consolidated constitution.
4  Opinion 1/91 on a proposed agreement to establish a European
   Economic Area [1991] ECR I–6079, at para. 2.
5–6 For more refined and detailed classification see Edward and Lane,
   *European Community Law: An Introduction* (2nd ed. 1995) at paras
   124–125 and Wyatt and Dashwood, *European Community Law* (3rd
   ed. 1993) at p. 52.

(i) Treaties which are the principal source of European law and provide its constitutional foundations. Because, as we have seen above, treaties are instruments adopted in accordance with international law, European law, in its various guises, is occasionally considered as a branch or a subset of international law;

(ii) Legislation. Legislation in the form of regulations, directives and legally binding decisions is an important source of law for the European Communities and the European Economic Area;

(iii) General principles of law. This is not as vague an expression as may at first sight appear;

(iv) The case law of the courts. This includes not only the judicial decisions of the European courts described in Chapter 6 but also judicial decisions taken by national courts;

(v) Learned writings.

**Treaties**

These are extremely numerous and the list contained in Vademecum IV is far from exhaustive. They fall into three categories. First, the principal or founding treaties which includes the three treaties establishing the European Communities: the European Economic Area Agreement, the Treaty on European Union and the European Convention on Human Rights and Fundamental Freedoms. The second category is that of treaties amending the principal treaties, including treaties providing for the accession of new Member States, the protocols to the Human Rights Convention, the Single European Act and the Treaty of Amsterdam. The Treaty on European Union falls into this category as well as the previous one since it effected substantial amendments to the earlier European Community treaties. Ancillary treaties form a third category and include, on the one hand, other Council of Europe conventions in so far as the various Member States have signed, ratified and implemented them, and on the other hand, agreements entered into either by the European Communities in the exercise of their autonomous legal personality under international law or entered into jointly by the Communities and their Member States. These include the agreement establishing the World Trade Organisation, the successive Lomé Conventions on trade relations between the European Community and the African Caribbean and Pacific (ACP) countries, association agreements between the European Communities and non-Member States including the Europe Agreements between the European Community and certain Central and Eastern European countries aspiring to membership of the European Union.

## Legislation

Legislation as a source of European law concerns only the European Communities and the European Economic Area.[6] The institutions of those two organisations may adopt various legal instruments, known as "acts". Such acts may be designated in different ways and may vary in scope or effect. Moreover, there is a variety of ways in which such legislative acts may be adopted although the particular procedure to be used for a given instrument will depend principally upon its subject-matter rather than its form. The different forms of legislation and the various procedures for their adoption are outlined below. First, however, it is useful to mention certain common characteristics of Community legislation.

### Characteristics of Community legislation

First, since all legislative measures of the European Community are "acts" of Community institutions (whether acting individually or in combination with each other), they are subject to judicial review of their legality by the European Court of Justice.[7] To that end the Court of Justice may annul legislation on one of three substantive grounds: that the institution or institutions responsible for the adoption of the act lacked the competence to do so; that although having powers to adopt the disputed act those powers had been misused; or, more generally, that in adopting the act the institution had infringed the treaty or "any rule of law relating to its application". Furthermore, the Court of Justice may annul acts if, during their adoption, the institutions concerned have infringed *essential* procedural requirements. Those procedural requirements are outlined below.

In addition, Article 7 (ex Article 4) EC requires each institution to act within the limits of the powers conferred upon it by the treaty and Article 253 (ex Article 190) requires regulations, directives and decisions to state the reasons upon which they are based. To satisfy those requirements, all Community instruments contain a preamble which is of vital importance both to the understanding of the act so as to enable it to be correctly applied, and for the Court to be able to carry out its task of judicial review outlined above. The presentation of Community legislation, what-

---

6   Acts adopted by the Benelux Union are not, strictly speaking, "legislation" since they require implementing measures at national level (see pp. 48–49 above). Many of the measures adopted at Benelux level have subsequently been superseded by European Union, European Community and Schengen Agreement measures.

7   Article 230 (ex Article 173) EC.

ever its precise form and content, will therefore always follow a standard pattern similar to that of the directive illustrated on p. 112. The title mentions the form of legislation (regulation, directive or decision), the date upon which it was adopted, the full descriptive title of the act concerned and its reference number for indexing or bibliographic purposes. In any sort of formal legal writing such as an article in a learned journal, an academic thesis, an official report or a court judgment, that full title should always be given when the instrument is first mentioned, accompanied by the reference to the relevant page of the Official Journal.

After the title the preamble takes the form of a long Cartesian sentence beginning with the indication of the adopting institution followed by a series of citations (the sentences beginning "Having regard to ... "),[8] the first of which normally indicates the treaty provision or provisions from which the institution draws its authority to adopt the act. The citations are followed by a series of recitals[9] which, particularly in the case of decisions implementing the Community competition rules, may be extremely lengthy. In legislative measures the recitals, each beginning with the word "Whereas ... ", set out the main policy considerations behind the adoption of the act including reference to the need for any exceptions to be made to the general rules which it lays down. The citations and recitals are in the form of subordinate clauses and the preamble ends with the adoption of the act, usually printed in capital letters. The operative part of the instrument consists of its various articles in which reference may be made to annexes containing lists of products for illustrations of standard forms and the like.

While the legislative process and the resulting enactments are quite complex, their redeeming feature is a substantial degree of transparency in their adoption. This takes two forms. First, the Commission in formulating its proposal will usually carry out extensive consultations with interest groups as well as with the national authorities responsible for the area of activity concerned. Both at this stage and during the adoption of the formal opinions by the European Parliament, the Economic and Social Committee and the Committee of the Regions, the relevant members of those institutions receive representations by lobbyists seeking to influence the eventual shape of the proposed legislation. Secondly, the Commission's proposal and the opinions or reports of the other institutions are all published in the Official Journal[10] and provide

8   Known in French as *visas*, each beginning with "*Vu ...* ".
9   In French known as the *considérants* because they each begin with the words "*Considérant que ...* ".
10  The references being given in the preamble to the final text of the legislation as adopted.

# The presentation of European Community legislation

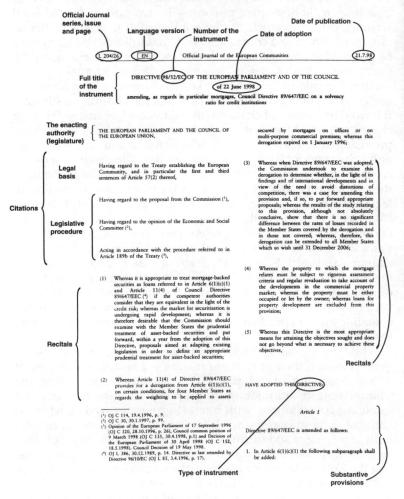

a useful "audit trail" of the progress of the legislation and of the arguments and ideas which may have influenced it. A range of other documents such as draft reports, white papers or other consultation documents may also be available in particular cases and, on the whole, institutions are very willing to provide them.

*Forms of legislation*

The scope and effect of the three main forms of Community legislation, regulations, directives and decisions are conveniently summarised in Article 249 (ex Article 189) EC, which provides:

"A regulation shall have general application. It shall be binding in its entirety and directly applicable in all Member States.

A directive shall be binding, as to the result to be achieved, upon each Member State to which it is addressed, but shall leave to the national authorities the choice of form and methods.

A decision shall be binding in its entirety upon those to whom it is addressed."

That text makes it clear that the differences between those three forms of legislation lie in their scope rather than in any ascending degree of authority in the way in which, in a Member State, a hierarchy of legislation may exist beginning with constitutional provisions and followed by parliamentary enactments and ministerial decrees (in descending order). Decisions carry the full authority of the Community institutions which adopt them. However, they are generally applicable only to those persons to whom they are addressed, although other persons who claim to be directly and individually affected by such a measure may also challenge it before the Court of Justice.[11] Decisions must be notified to those to whom they are addressed and do not come into effect until that notification has been effected.

Like decisions, regulations are adopted directly by the institutions exercising their autonomous powers and without the need for intervention, approval or ratification by the Member States. However, given that a regulation is of general application, binding in its entirety and directly applicable in all of the Member States, it represents the most extensive legislative power of the Community institutions. Nonetheless its use is permitted by the treaty only in relatively restricted and often highly technical areas, including such matters as the access of migrant workers to social security benefits in Member States of which they are not nationals,

11 See Article 230 (ex Article 173) EC, para. 4.

and regulations for the application of the treaty provisions on state aids or financial regulations covering the Community's own financial and budgetary organisation. Regulatory powers delegated to the Commission generally only allow the latter institution to adopt regulations in order to give effect to policies adopted by the Council. Chief among these are the Commission's responsibility for adopting regulations for the day-to-day management of the Common Agricultural Policy.

Directives are the most original, flexible and influential feature of the Community legislative system. Often the end product of lengthy and tortuous negotiations, replete with compromises and fudges, they represent, nonetheless, the collective will of the Member States to achieve certain objectives, usually laying down a time within which those objectives must be attained. It is however left to the individual Member States (some directives are not addressed to all of the Member States) to achieve that result in accordance with their own legal, constitutional or social circumstances. Thus, despite the somewhat authoritarian sounding tone of the word "directive", it will normally produce its effect through ordinary national legislation, regulation or other arrangements, the form of which will be familiar to the authorities responsible for applying it and to those to whom it must be applied.[12]

Nonetheless, because of its binding nature, a Member State may be open to legal action before the Court of Justice, which may ultimately result in the Court imposing a financial penalty, if the Member State fails to give effect to the directive within the time-limit laid down or, in giving such effect does so incompletely or wrongly. Furthermore, since only the Court of Justice has the authority to give definitive and binding interpretations of the wording of a directive, the effectiveness of the national measures giving effect to a directive will ultimately have to be tested against the interpretation arrived at by the Court of Justice. Finally, as we shall see in the next chapter, in the absence of implementation or faced with incorrect implementation of a directive, it may be given direct effect by the courts of the Member States as we shall see in the next chapter.

*Legislative procedures*

The Single European Act and the TEU each increased the number of different legislative procedures principally to accommodate the steadily extending powers and influence of the European Parliament. That the Member States have accepted this evolution is due

12   There is no convenient translation for the French word *"le justiciable"*.

in large measure to the realisation that the so-called "democratic deficit" in the Community decision-making process is unacceptable, and that such a deficit could only be remedied by giving the Parliament an increasing involvement in and responsibility for legislation. Nonetheless, the Member States (meeting as the Council) have sought to retain their final say in the content of legislation resulting in a further increase in the complexity of the procedures. However, as we shall see, in two of the procedures — assent and co-decision — the final word is now effectively shared between the Council and the European Parliament. The procedures were to some extent streamlined and rationalised by the Treaty of Amsterdam and it is the system as it now stands which is described below.[13] It should also be noted that much Community legislation, in particular all that which is concerned with the Single Market, must also be given effect in the European Economic Area. Therefore the adoption of legislation which has relevance for the EEA also requires the involvement and consultation of the EFTA–EEA States in a separate but parallel procedure.

Notwithstanding the apparent complexity of the procedures, involving as they do all three of the political institutions of the Community as well as, where so required, consultative bodies such as the Economic and Social Committee and the Committee of the Regions, each of the procedures nonetheless falls into three phases. First a proposal must be submitted by the Commission, secondly the proposal is examined by the Parliament, the Council and the consultative bodies, and thirdly the act is adopted or abandoned.

The Commission's monopoly of the power to make legislative proposals, known as its "right of initiative", is one of its most important prerogatives. Although the ultimate shape and wording of any piece of legislation will be determined by the contributions of the European Parliament and the Council during the course of the procedure, until the act is finally adopted the proposal remains that of the Commission which may withdraw it at any time during the procedure. This exclusive right of initiative does not mean that the Commission has a monopoly of new ideas for legislation, although many of its proposals do emerge from the Commission's own assessment of the Community's needs for regulation or change in a particular area of activity. It may, however, also receive suggestions for legislative measures from the Council, from individual Member States or even from specialised organisations or lobby groups. Since the Maastricht Treaty, the European Parliament may request the Commission to

---

13 Students or researchers who need to establish how earlier legislation was adopted should consult an older edition of one of the main textbooks on Community law.

submit any appropriate proposal on matters on which it considers that a Community act is required for the purposes of implementing the treaty.[14] Nonetheless even in this case it is still for the Commission to formulate and table its proposal, thus initiating the legislative process.

In making its proposal the Commission will indicate which of the five available procedures it regards as appropriate for the particular legislation envisaged, although it has little freedom of action in this regard since the choice of legal basis for the proposed legislation usually entails the application of one among the five possible procedures. The four available procedures, in ascending order of the degree of involvement of the Parliament, are:

(i)   the consultation procedure;
(ii)  the co-operation procedure;
(iii) the assent procedure; and
(iv)  the co-decision procedure.

Since the Treaty of Amsterdam, the co-decision procedure has been both simplified and extended in the range of subject matters which it may cover and is now the procedure which is most likely to be met with in practice. Although the other three procedures are still in existence, the scope and use of the co-operation procedure in particular has been significantly reduced. Those procedures represent, in ascending order: an increasing involvement of the European Parliament in the legislative process from the possibility of delivering an opinion on a proposal which might be simply disregarded by the Commission and the Council (consultation); a co-operation procedure which requires the Council to act unanimously if rejecting a Parliament amendment; the requirement for the Parliament to assent to a particular measure which gives it a *de facto* veto over certain decisions (assent is of particular importance for the approval of treaties to which the Community is a party, including accession treaties); and finally the co-decision procedure which raises the Parliament to a status of equality with the Council and gives the Parliament a power of veto. As a result, acts adopted under the latter procedure are, like the example on p. 112, known as acts of "the European Parliament and the Council".

Under the EEC Treaty, prior to the Single European Act, the consultation procedure was the only way in which the Parliament was involved in the legislative process.[14a] Such consultation was required by certain treaty articles. On other occasions the Council voluntarily consulted the Parliament. Although the Commission

14   Article 192 (ex Article 138(b)) EC.
14a  Except for its involvement in drawing up the Community's budget since 1975.

occasionally revised its draft in the light of recommendations by the European Parliament, both it and the Council could simply disregard a Parliament opinion. However, a failure to consult the Parliament at all, where so required by the Treaty, amounts to a failure to fulfil an essential procedural requirement and will entail the annulment of the resulting act.[15] The consultation procedure now applies principally to the adoption of measures under the Common Agricultural Policy and must be used where the Council acts under Article 308 (ex Article 235) in an area in which the Treaty has not provided express powers.

A conciliation procedure (which is not an independent legislative procedure, but a method for resolving difficulties under consultation) was introduced in 1975 in connection with the revised provisions for establishing the Community budget which represented the first step towards a genuine involvement of the European Parliament in the political decision-making processes. Under this procedure a conciliation committee consisting of representatives of the Member States in the Council and an equal number of members of the European Parliament, assisted by a representative of the Commission, would seek to resolve differences between the two institutions. This procedure, formerly limited to budgetary matters, was included in the co-decision procedure (see below).

The assent procedure was one of two new procedures introduced by the Single European Act, requires the European Parliament to give its assent to a measure acting by an absolute majority of its members.[16] The procedure now applies in two specific areas, namely the accession of a new Member State to the European Union (Article 49 (ex Article 0) TEU) and the conclusion of association agreements with non-Member States or international organisations.[17]

The co-operation procedure was also introduced by the Single European Act. The novelty of the procedure was in allowing the European Parliament a second reading of legislative proposals after the Council had adopted a common position following the European Parliament's opinion on first reading. If the European

---

15  See Case 138/79 *Roquette Frères v. Council* [1980] ECR 3333, known as the Isoglucose Case, in which the European Parliament intervened in support of the applicants' successful action for annulment of a regulation.

16  That is to say the measure must receive the affirmative votes of more than half of the total number of members of the European Parliament, not just more than half of those present and voting.

17  Article 310 (ex Article 238) EC, read in conjunction with the second sub-paragraph of Article 300(3) (ex Article 228(3)) EC.

Parliament either approved or adopted no position on the Council's common position the measure was adopted. If it rejected it by an absolute majority the Council could subsequently only approve it by unanimity. Finally, if amendments were proposed the Commission might revise its proposal in the light of those amendments and resubmit it to the Council which could then adopt by a qualified majority. This procedure has now been almost wholly superseded by the co-decision procedure except in matters relating to EMU.

The co-decision procedure originally introduced by the TEU in order to reinforce the role of the European Parliament has been both simplified and extended in scope by the Treaty of Amsterdam.[18] The two principal innovations of this procedure are first that an act may be adopted on first reading where there is agreement between the two branches of the legislature (*i.e.* where the Parliament proposes no amendments or any amendments which it does propose are accepted by the Council), and, since the Treaty of Amsterdam, the abolition of the Council's power to act unilaterally at third reading as under the co-operation procedure. It should, however, be noted that, although since the TEU the Parliament may veto legislation approved by the Member States in Council, it still cannot force the adoption of legislation contrary to the Council's wishes. As appears from the diagram on p. 119, an act may be adopted at one of four different stages in the procedure.

The co-decision procedure has brought 24 further subject areas within the scope of the co-decision procedure including eight of the newly created areas of legislation either introduced directly by the Treaty of Amsterdam or those moved from the third pillar.

The adoption of legislation with an EEA dimension (see Chapter 3 p. 86 above) entails close consultation and information being provided to the EEA authorities. However, given that the EFTA partners in the EEA operate on an intergovernmental basis they are not bound either by the decisions taken by the EC institutions or those taken by joint committees. Thus if for constitutional or other reasons one of the EFTA-EEA states is unable to implement an EEA act, then the operation of the EEA provision, including possibly the annex to the EEA agreement upon which it is based, is suspended with effect from the date upon which the EC equivalent legislation enters force.

### General Principles of Law

As mentioned above, the "general principles of law common to civilised nations" are one of the sources of international law to be applied by the International Court of Justice. This is not simply a

---

18  See Article 251 (ex Article 189(b)) EC.

## THE CO-DECISION PROCEDURE
## (Article 251 (ex Article 189 b) EC

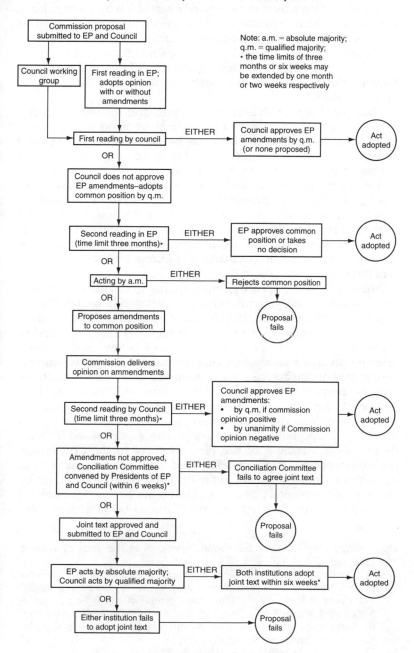

self-evident statement requiring the Court to apply the law but a reference to certain principles which underlie all legal relationships and which may not usually be overridden by other rules of law, even where expressly laid down in instruments such as treaties or regulations. The idea of general principles was perhaps in the mind of Edmund Burke when he said "there is but one law for all, namely, that law which governs all law, the law of our Creator, the law of humanity, justice, equity — the law of nature, and of nations".[18a]

There has been much academic debate over the definition and scope of general principles of law and there is no settled agreement on either issue. It can however be said that it is not a closed category and that international and European courts alike will, of necessity, have recourse to the general principles of law either in order to temper the unduly harsh effects of strict application of black letter law (see "proportionality" below) or in areas where other sources of law give no guidance as to how to resolve a particular problem. Those needs are equally present in the various systems of European law and, as a result, it is not surprising that the European courts, in particular the European Court of Justice, will have recourse to them.[19]

Although the European Human Rights Convention is itself a codification of the general principle that fundamental human rights must be protected, the Human Rights Court can and does look beyond the text of the Convention in seeking to interpret it. Thus the principle of proportionality (see below) is frequently referred to, particularly where states are allowed to impose restrictions on the exercise of convention rights. Such restrictions may be permitted to the extent that they are "necessary in a democratic society". However, to avoid giving States *carte blanche* to disregard those rights, the Court has held that any restrictions must be "proportionate to the legitimate aim pursued".[20] Similarly, where Article 1 of the First Protocol to the Convention prohibits a person from being deprived of his possessions "except in the public interest and subject to the conditions provided for by law and by the general principles of international law", it does not provide explicitly for such expropriation to be subject to com-

---

18a Speech, May 28, 1794. See Bond, Speeches at the Trial of Warren Hastings (1859), Vol. 4, p. 377.
19  For a more detailed treatment of general principles of law in European Community law see Brown and Kennedy, *Brown and Jacobs': The Court of Justice of the European Communities* (4th ed., Sweet & Maxwell, London, 1995) Chap. 15, and for the most extensive examination of the issue see Anthony Arnull, *The General Principles of EEC Law and the Individual* (London, 1989).
20  *Handyside v. United Kingdom* [1976] A. 24 at 49.

pensation. Nonetheless, the Court inferred such a right from the reference to "general principles" and from the fact that such compensation was generally provided for in "the legal systems of the Contracting States".[21]

In European Community law too, the Court of Justice has had frequent recourse to general principles of law in order both to fill lacunae in legislation and in the treaties themselves, and to curb unnecessarily draconian powers exercised by the institutions. Like the Statute of the International Court of Justice and the First Protocol to the Human Rights Convention, the EC Treaty incites the Court to have recourse to general principles of law. The only explicit reference is in the second paragraph of Article 288 (ex Article 215) EC which provides that "in the case of non-contractual liability, the Community shall, in accordance with the general principles common to the laws of the Member States, make good any damage caused by its institutions or by its servants in the performance of their duties". Taking as its starting-point national rules on non-contractual liability, the Court has established that for such liability to arise three conditions must be fulfilled:

(i)   an unlawful act by the institution concerned;
(ii)  loss or damage suffered by an individual; and
(iii) a direct causal link between the unlawful act and the loss or damage.

In like manner, the Court of Justice has developed the principles under which Community law infers a right to reparation by a Member State where an infringement of a rule of Community law has resulted in loss or damage to an individual. Thus the rule of law infringed must be intended to confer rights on individuals; the breach must be sufficiently serious; and there must be a direct causal link between the breach of the obligation on the state and the damage sustained by the injured parties.[22]

In addition to that explicit reference to general principles, two provisions of the Treaty couched in more general terms also incite the Court to look beyond the texts of Community law. Thus in Article 220 (ex Article 164) EC the task of the Court is defined as that of ensuring "that in the interpretation and application of this treaty the law is observed". This of course begs the question of what "the law" is, but it clearly cannot exclude the general principles of law. Similarly, Article 230 (ex Article 173) EC, which

21   See *James v. United Kingdom* [1986] 26 R.V.R. 139, European Ct. of Human Rights 98 and *Lithgow v. United Kingdom* [1986] A. 102.
22   Joined Cases C–46 and C–48/93 *Brasserie du Pêcheur S.A. v. Germany* and *The Queen v. Secretary of State for Transport, ex p. Factortame Ltd* [1996] ECR I–1029 at para. 51.

enables the Court of Justice to review the legality of acts of the Community institutions, enables the Court to annul acts of the institutions on grounds *inter alia* of infringement "of any rule of law" relating to the application of the treaty. Space precludes a detailed examination of the principles developed in the Court's case law. However, the five main principles (each of which has developed a number of subsidiary aspects) may usefully be enumerated here.

## Non discrimination

This principle is made explicit by Article 12 (ex Article 6) EC[23] which provides that "within the scope of application of this Treaty ... any discrimination on grounds of nationality shall be prohibited". The Court has held that other provisions of the Treaty which prohibit discrimination in particular areas, such as Article 34(2) (ex Article 40(2)) EC under which the common organisation of the markets for agricultural products must "exclude any discrimination between producers or consumers within the Community", or the requirement on Member States to ensure the application of the principle of equal pay without discrimination based on sex (Article 141 (ex Article 119) EC), are merely specific examples of "the general principle of equality" which is one of the fundamental principles of Community law.

The essence of the principle is that "similar situations shall not be treated differently unless the differentiation is objectively justified".[24] Conversely, treating clearly different cases in the same way may also amount to discrimination. From that starting point the Court of Justices has developed the principle of indirect discrimination whereby a rule which applies in apparently equal manner to two categories of persons, because of *de facto* differences in their situations, in fact has a discriminatory effect. Here the principle has been used to protect the rights of part-time workers, where such workers are, in practice, predominantly women and in other fields such as taxation or social security where a residence requirement for obtaining certain benefits *de facto* makes it easier for nationals of the country concerned to obtain those benefits.

## Legal certainty

This principle holds that those subject to the law, whether states, organisations or individuals, should be able to act and enter into

---

23    Prior to the entry into force of the Maastricht Treaty this provision was contained in Article 7 of the EEC Treaty.
24    Joined Cases 103 and 145/77 *Royal Scholten-Honig Ltd v. Intervention Board for Agricultural Produce* [1978] ECR 2037 at para. 27.

commitments in confidence. The principle has a number of specific aspects including the protection of legitimate expectations which, put colloquially, means that the goal posts should not be moved during the course of the game. Inasmuch as the principle of legitimate expectations includes the right of individuals and corporations to rely upon declarations made by Community institutions, it has a close affinity with the equitable doctrine of estoppel in English law. Another important aspect of legal certainty is the principle prohibiting the retroactive effect of rules imposing a penalty (a principle enshrined in Article 7 of the Human Rights Convention) and was applied by the Court of Justice in Case 63/83 *R. v. Kent Kirk*,[25] in which a Danish fisherman was fined for fishing in United Kingdom waters under a regulation adopted on January 25, 1983 and which purported to allow the United Kingdom to exclude fishing boats from other Member States from January 1, 1983. Kirk and his boat had however been arrested on January 6, 1983 and the Court found that the subsequent adoption of a regulation could not have the retroactive effect of making Kirk liable to a criminal sanction.

Other aspects of legal certainty include the requirement on states and institutions to act in good faith, to respect acquired rights and that it must be possible clearly to identify a person likely to be affected by a decision or other action.

*The rights of defence*

This principle, or rather group of principles, arises from the capacity of the Community institutions to take decisions having a direct impact on undertakings and individuals, and has therefore been developed principally through the case law relating to the application of the competition rules in the EC Treaty and of the staff regulations of officials of the Community institutions. The principles concerned correspond broadly speaking to the so-called "rules of natural justice" in English administrative law although they derive from concepts based in French administrative law, whence the expression *"droit de la défence"* (which might also be translated as a "right to a fair hearing") derives.

A right to a fair hearing presupposes "that a person whose interests are perceptibly affected by a decision taken by a public authority must be given the opportunity to make his point of view known".[26] In turn the application of that rule requires that a person whose interests are likely to be affected by such a decision be clearly informed, in good time, of the potential nature of the

25   [1984] ECR 2689.
26   Case 17/74 *Transocean Marine Paint Association v. Commission* [1974] ECR 1063.

decision and the considerations upon which it is based. The Court has further held that in the case of anti-dumping investigations the Community institutions must provide the undertakings concerned with all information which may be relevant to the defence of their interests, subject to the principle of confidentiality.

Especially in cases in which particularly large financial penalties or severe disciplinary measures might be likely to be imposed, the Court has held that there is a general legal principle that persons concerned have a right to legal assistance and that such legal assistance in turn implies that counsel should have access to the full case file and all relevant documents, and on the other hand that communications between lawyers and their clients should also be treated as privileged provided that the communications were made for the purposes of preparing the clients' defence and that they involve lawyers in independent practice not bound to the undertaking under investigation by an employment relationship.[27]

*Proportionality*

The principle of proportionality requires that, in exercising their powers, the means employed by institutions must be suitable for the purpose of achieving the relevant objective and must not go beyond what is necessary in order to achieve that aim. Put colloquially, institutions should not use a sledgehammer to crack a nut. By way of example, a Community regulation whose intention was to ensure that where refunds for exports of sugar were payable under the Common Agricultural Policy, those exports were effectively made. To that end exporters had to lodge a deposit, a measure which was not objectionable in itself. However, where an application for an export licence reached the Commission four hours past the deadline as a result of a clerical error, and a deposit of £1,670,000 was entirely forfeit. The Court found that such a forfeiture for a relatively trivial breach of the deadline was wholly disproportionate.[28]

The principle which derives from the German administrative law notion of *Verhältnismässigkeit*, was incorporated into the EC Treaty by the Maastricht Treaty as Article 5 (ex Article 3(b)) EC, the third paragraph of which provides that "any action by the Community shall not go beyond what is necessary to achieve the objectives of this Treaty".

---

27  Case 115/80 *Demont v. Commission* [1981] ECR 3147 and Case 115/79 *A. M. & S. v. Commission* [1982] ECR 1575.
28  Case 181/84 *The Queen v. Intervention Board for Agricultural Produce, ex p. Man (Sugar) Ltd* [1985] ECR 2889.

*Fundamental rights*

As early as 1969 the Court of Justice made reference to fundamental human rights as being "enshrined in general principles of
Community law and protected by the Court"[29] and the following
year that "respect for fundamental rights forms an integral part of
the general principles of law protected by the Court of Justice. The
protection of such rights, whilst inspired by the constitutional
traditions common to the Member States, must be ensured within
the framework of the structure and objectives of the Community".[30] In addition to that reference to "traditions common to the
Member States", the Court has frequently made reference to the
European Convention on Human Rights in which these principles
are codified.

Again, the Treaty on European Union, following the lead given
in the case law of the Court of Justice, incorporated the protection
of fundamental rights in Article 6 (ex Article F) (2) TEU which
provides that "the Union shall respect fundamental rights, as
guaranteed by the European Convention for the Protection of
Human Rights and Fundamental Freedoms ... and as they result
from the constitutional traditions common to the Member States as
general principles of Community law". As we have seen, respect
for human rights is among the conditions for a state to be admitted
to the European Union (Article 49 (ex Article O) TEU) and a serious
and persistent breach by a Member State of those principles may
lead the other Member States to suspend the offending State's
rights under the Treaty (Article 7 (ex Article F.1) TEU).

*Subsidiarity*

Subsidiarity, which has some affinity with proportionality, is
more a principle of legislative restraint than a source of law as
such. According to that principle decisions must be taken at the
lowest level within an organisation, consistent with effectiveness
of the proposed action. Although the principle has parallels in the
Constitutions of certain Federal States[31] and had been discussed

29   Case 29/69 *Stauder v. Stadt Ulm* [1969] ECR 419.
30   Case 11/70 *Internationale Handelsgesellschaft mbH v. Einfuhr- und
      Vorratsstelle für Getreide und Futtermittel* [1970] ECR 1125.
31   See, for example, the Tenth Amendment to the United States Con-
      stitution which says "the powers not delegated to the United States
      by the Constitution, nor prohibited by it to the States, are reserved to
      the States respectively, or to the people", or Article 30 of the German
      *Grundgesetz* (basic law) which says that "except as otherwise pro-
      vided or permitted by this basic law the exercise of governmental
      powers and the discharge of governmental functions shall be incum-
      bent on the *Länder*".

during the 1970s, it came to particular prominence in the Communities during the 1980s when it was regarded as a means of reassuring the governments of certain Member States, and their populations, that the continuing evolution of the Community and its development towards a European Union did not imply a continuing and inexorable erosion of the powers of States. As a result, the principle was added to the EC Treaty by the TEU and is now contained in Article 5 (ex Article 3(b)) which reads "In areas which do not fall within its exclusive competence, the Community shall take action, in accordance with the principle of subsidiarity, only if and in so far as the objectives of the proposed action cannot be sufficiently achieved by the Member States and can therefore, by reason of the scale or effects of the proposed action, be better achieved by the Community."

Although there is evidence that the inclusion of the principle in the Treaty has had certain practical effects, notably in the legislative process in which the three political institutions each assess the desirability of proposed legislation having regard to the principle of proportionality, the Court of Justice has not yet been called upon to annul a measure on the grounds that it infringes the principle of subsidiarity, and most writers incline to the view that the principle is too vague to be justiciable.

*The principle of good administration*

Like subsidiarity, this principle is a guide to good conduct rather than a source of law in the strict sense and, in general it may mean no more than ensuring that the administrative authorities respect the principles of non discrimination, legal certainty, the rights of the defence, proportionality and fundamental rights. Thus in a staff case the Court of Justice found that "it is in accordance with the requirements of good faith and mutual confidence ... [that the administration] should, as far as possible, put the official in a position to make his point of view on the projected decision known".[32] On numerous occasions the Court has also found that a failure by the administration to reply to a complaint or request within a given time-limit constituted poor administration even where, as is the case in the Community staff regulations, it is provided that such a failure is deemed to amount to an implicit rejection of the request. Where litigation has followed institutions have often been required to pay the applicants' costs even where the institutions' position was upheld, on the grounds that litigation might have been avoided by a timely response.

With a view to maintaining permanent vigilance over the Community administration the TEU enabled the European Parliament

---

32   Case 125/80 *Arning v. Commission* [check] [1981] ECR 2539.

to appoint an Ombudsman empowered to receive complaints concerning instances of maladministration in the activities of the Community institutions.

## Comparative law

Given the requirement for courts to tease out these general principles and the requirement in Article 38(1) of the Statute of the International Court of Justice and in Article 288 (ex Article 215) EC to derive inspiration from principles which are "common to the laws" of several states, it is inevitable that, in the development of both international law and European law, comparative law will play an important role. Comparative law, of course, is not a specialised subject area of the law in the manner of, for example, labour law or commercial law in a domestic legal system or even of international law or European law (with all the difficulties of definition which they entail) on the wider stage. It is more of a legal methodology, examining different approaches to the same or similar problems in order to find or adapt appropriate solutions to those problems under a particular legal system. As such the comparative legal method constitutes both a source of law in itself and an approach to problems of interpretation which, as we shall see in Chapter 8, may be very enlightening.

Furthermore, the involvement of comparative law in the development of international and European law is inevitable given that all of the courts described in Chapter 6 are composed of members drawn from different legal traditions,[33] each of whom will therefore inevitably draw upon their own individual legal experience and conceptual approaches.

The European Court of Justice, for its part, complements this inherent diversity with a research and documentation division which includes lawyers from each of the legal systems in the European Union and who are frequently called upon to provide comparative law research notes on particular issues. In addition, of course, the parties to court proceedings themselves live and operate in their own domestic legal context and will bring their experience before the European courts. Again, with particular reference to the European Court of Justice, the preliminary ruling procedure under Article 234 (ex Article 177) of the EC Treaty provides all of the Member States with the opportunity to take part in the proceedings and thereby to ensure that the Court has

---

33   The statute of the international Court of Justice requires that, in addition to their personal qualities of independence and legal expertise, appointments to the Court must be made in such a way as to ensure that the composition of the Court reflects the main forms of civilisation and the principal legal systems of the world.

an accurate and up-to-date picture of the legal position in their respective countries. For their part, an awareness by the national courts when making references to the Court of Justice that the latter Court takes into consideration the specific features of national legal systems, contributes to the legitimacy of the Community legal system and its acceptance by the courts and citizens of the Member States.

The Human Rights Court too will have careful regard to the legal conditions prevailing in the contracting States and, in accordance with its evolutive approach to the interpretation of the Convention, will take into account developments in social or moral standards, such as the disappearance of the stigma which formerly attached to children born out of wedlock[34] and the decline of prejudice and discrimination against homosexuals.[35] In taking such changes into consideration the Human Rights Court tends to err on the side of caution, preferring to confirm established practice by the contracting states rather than setting new standards of behaviour or protection of individual interests for the Member States to attain. Such caution is entirely consistent with the nature of the Convention which sets a series of minimum standards of protection of the rights which it enumerates. Lacking the resources of a specialised research division, similar to that of the Court of Justice, the Human Rights Court draws more heavily upon the individual experience of the judges as well as upon the comparative law expertise of non-governmental organisations such as Amnesty International, who may intervene in its proceedings.

Clearly the introduction of such principles as the protection of legitimate expectations or the principle of proportionality owe much to the comparative law method. Those two principles derive in particular from the concepts of *Vertrauensschutz* and *Verhältnismässigkeit* in German public law. While, at first sight, such concepts may seem unfamiliar to a lawyer trained in another legal system a closer scrutiny through the microscope of comparative law often reveals surprising similarities between concepts and institutions camouflaged by different linguistic expressions. Thus *Vertrauensschutz* has much in common with the principle of the *protection de la confiance légitime* and with the English doctrine of estoppel. *Verhältnismässigkeit*, usually translated into English as "proportionality", has much in common with the notion of "reasonableness" in English administrative law.[36] Clearly such

34  See *Marckx v. Belgium* [1979] A 31.
35  See *Dudgeon v. UK* [1981] A 45.
36  On this point see the Opinion of Advocate General Warner in Case 34/79 *R. v. Henn & Darby* [1979] ECR 3795.

cross-fertilisation of national and European legal systems is of benefit both to the development of European law and to that of the national legal systems of the Member States. European law is thus enabled to draw upon the deep well of experience of the national legal systems and thus compensate for its relative youth.

## Decisions of the Courts

Judicial decisions by the European courts, in particular the European Court of Justice and the European Court of Human Rights, undoubtedly constitute an important source of European law, just as decisions of the international Court of Justice are an important source of international law. Although this may seem self-evident to a lawyer or student familiar with the common law approach based on a system of binding precedents (*stare decisis*), this is not necessarily the case for international lawyers or those trained in the civil law legal systems of continental Europe.

Thus although Article 38(d) of the statute of the International Court of Justice mentioned above refers to judicial decisions, they are qualified only as "subsidiary means for the determination of rules of law". Moreover, their use for that purpose is "subject to the provisions of Article 59" which provides that a "decision of the Court has no binding force except between the parties and in respect of that particular case". This would appear to preclude ICJ decisions from being regarded as precedents and requires the Court to deal with every case afresh. Likewise, in France, Article 5 of the French *Code civil* provides that "judges may not decide cases submitted to them by means of generalised or law-making formulae".[37]

Nonetheless, it is an elementary principle of justice that like cases should be decided in like manner and legal certainty is an essential ingredient in both commercial and international relations. As the Court of Human Rights has put it, "it usually follows and applies its own precedents, such a course being in the interests of legal certainty and the orderly development of the Convention case law".[38] Similarly, one of the most frequently encountered phrases in the case law of the Court of Justice is "it is settled case law that ... " preceding a statement of legal principle which will in turn be followed by references to the previous case or cases in which that principle has been elaborated. In addition to the need to ensure consistency in decision-making, the European courts are faced with treaty and convention texts which, for the

---

37   "*Article 5. Il est défendu aux juges de prononcer par voie de dispositions générales et réglementaires sur les causes qui leur sont soumises*".
38   In *Cossey v. United Kingdom* [1990] A 184 at para. 35.

most part, are broadly programmatic in nature and do not set out to codify legal provisions which may be simply applied to a given set of circumstances. As Lord Denning put it in *Bulmer v. Bollinger*[39]:

> "the treaty is quite unlike any of the enactments to which we have become accustomed ... It lays down general principles. It expresses its aim and purposes. All in sentences of moderate length and commendable style. But it lacks precision. .... All the way through the treaty there are gaps and lacunae. These have to be filled in by the judges, or by regulations or directives."

The regulations or directives may themselves include gaps and lacunae and, not infrequently, ambiguities deliberately left by legislators unable to reach agreement on a clearer formulation. In filling such lacunae the courts will inevitably develop the law, often in ways which may have profound importance before the legal order concerned. The doctrines of direct effect and primacy of Community law outlined in the next chapter, are examples of jurisprudential developments which have shaped the very nature of the European Communities. In more specific areas the case law of the Court of Justice has preceded and influenced specific legislation in areas such as the recognition of academic diplomas (see Chapter 9, p. 287) and the freedom for lawyers qualified in one jurisdiction to work and establish themselves in another (see Chapter 10, p. 312 *et seq.*).

A detailed appraisal of the effect as precedence of the decisions of the European courts both in their own internal case law and in relation to the municipal courts in Member States is beyond the scope of this book.[40] Nonetheless, the following points should be borne in mind. First, in accordance with the civil law and international law approach, the European courts are not rigidly bound by their own previous decisions and may therefore depart from them if, in the words of the Human Rights Court in the Cossey case mentioned above, there are "cogent reasons for doing so", for example in order to "ensure that the interpretation of the Convention reflects societal changes and remains in line with present-day conditions". Similarly, the European Court of Justice has occasionally felt the need to bring up to date or adapt its case law in

---

39    [1974] 2 All E.R. 1226 at 1237.
40    For such a detailed examination see Neville March Hunnings, *The European Courts* (Cartermill, London, 1996) and Brown and Kennedy, *Brown and Jacobs' The Court of Justice of the European Communities* (4th ed., Sweet & Maxwell, London, 1995) Chap. 11.

particular areas,[41] or even to correct an earlier judgment.[42] In the context of the preliminary ruling procedure laid down in Article 234 (ex Article 177) EC, the ruling of the Court of Justice is binding on the Court which referred the question to it, and that court must dutifully apply the relevant rule of Community law as interpreted by the Court of Justice. The same does not apply to the "advisory opinions" given by the EFTA Court in response to questions submitted by domestic courts in the EFTA–EEA states. It seems unlikely that that formal distinction will make much difference in practice.

Given that the establishment of the European Economic Area involved the taking over of a very large part of the corpus of European Community law at the date of entry into force of the EEA Agreement, the EFTA Court is required to interpret EEA provisions in conformity with the relevant rulings of the Court of Justice delivered prior to the date of signature of the EEA Agreement, in so far as those provisions are identical in substance to corresponding rules of the EC Treaty. Further, the EFTA Court is required to pay "due account" to the principles laid down by the relevant rulings of the Court of Justice given after the date of signature of the EEA Agreement. Likewise, as we have seen above, the European Court of Justice and the municipal courts in the EFTA countries (including Switzerland) are required to pay due account to each other's case law on the Lugano Convention.

## Legal Writing

As with judicial decisions, so the weight given to legal writing[43] as a source of law varies significantly as between international and civil lawyers on the one hand and lawyers of the common law tradition on the other. Particularly in the early development of codified legal systems as well as in international law, prior to the proliferation of treaties which now dominate that field, learned commentaries provided an important source of ideas and inspiration in order to deal

41 For example, Case C–10/89 *CNL–SUCAL SA v. HAG GF AG* [1990] ECR I–3711 (known as *Café Hag II*); Joined Cases C–267 and 268/91 *Keck and Mithouard* [1993] ECR I–6097.

42 See, for example, Case C394/96 *Mary Brown v. Rentokil* June 30, 1998 (not yet reported) in which the judgment in Case C400/95 *Larsson v. Fotex Supermarket* [1997] ECR I–2757 delivered barely a year earlier was expressly overruled.

43 Article 38(d) of the Statute of the ICJ refers to "the teachings of the most highly qualified publicists", a cumbersome expression neatly covered by the French word *doctrine*, a usage which might conveniently be anglicised in the way that the French expression *jurisprudence* (meaning case law of the courts) is gradually penetrating English legal usage.

with cases not covered by explicit provisions of the codes. It would be an exaggeration to say that *doctrine* has had no influence on common law systems; as early as the thirteenth century by presenting the then English law in an orderly manner it greatly influenced its development. Glosses such as Cook's famous *Commentary upon Littleton* (1628) went through nineteen editions up until 1832, and Blackstone's *Commentaries on the Laws of England* (1765) were immensely influential both on the teaching and practice of the law. In more recent years it was permissible to cite legal commentaries to English courts if there was no case law directly in point and provided that the author of the text being cited was dead!

Although textbooks and commentaries by learned writers are almost never referred to in court judgments, whether municipal or at the European level, such writings may have great value to the judges as, in the words of Article 38(d) of the Statute of the ICJ "subsidiary means for the determination of rules of law" — in other words as a means of determining what the law is on a particular point in the absence of legislative or judicial texts. Moreover, all judges read copiously in treatises and legal journals and cannot fail to be influenced by what they read. The impact of such reading on their work (and consequently the weight of *doctrine* as a source of law) cannot really be measured. It will depend partly on the esteem in which the writer is held, the cogency of the argument put forward and its capacity to persuade judges and practitioners, and indeed the willingness of a particular judge, to be so persuaded.

Although legal writings are rarely, if ever, referred to by the courts, occasionally sustained and persuasive criticism of a particular judgment or line of case law may lead to a change. Thus the categorical refusal of the European Court of Justice in the *Kalanke* case[44] to allow national rules guaranteeing women absolute and unconditional priority for appointment over men to be regarded as a measure providing for equality of opportunity between men and women workers received sustained criticism in legal journals, which may well have influenced the Court of Justice in its later judgment in *Marschall*[45] in which the Court's earlier rigour was somewhat tempered.

In this context special mention must be made of the Advocates General at the European Court of Justice. Their precise rôle is described in Chapter 6 below (at p. 176). In terms of the sources of European law the Advocates Generals' Opinions may be situated somewhere between the "judicial decisions" and the "teachings

---

44 Case C–450/93 *Kalanke v. Freie Hansestadt Bremen* [1995] ECR I–3051.
45 Case C–409/95 *Marschall v. Land Nordrheim-Westfalen* [1997] ECR I–6363.

of the most highly qualified publicists" referred to in the Statute of the ICJ. They are not judicial decisions for they do not decide the cases with which they deal, nor is the European Court of Justice bound to follow them. However, they rank above academic writing in learned journals or treatises inasmuch as the Advocates General are members of the European Court of Justice, with the same qualifications and status as the judges of that Court.

Their Opinions are strongly influential on the Court of Justice and invariably form the starting-point of the reasoning of the Court in arriving at its decision. In a small number of cases the Court, or one of its Chambers, has simply endorsed the Advocate General's Opinion by stating that, "for the reasons given by Mr Advocate General . . . the answer to the question submitted to the Court must be . . . ". In many other cases, where the Court adopts the reasoning submitted by the Advocate General, it will cite the Opinion preceded by an expression such as "as the Advocate General pointed out" or "as stated by the Advocate General . . . ".

Even where the Court does not adopt either in whole or in part the Advocate General's views on a particular case the Opinion may have considerable value. First, the Advocate General may take a broader view of any particular case than the narrow requirements of solving a dispute between the two parties. He may thus situate the debate in its wider, economic, political, social or legal context and he is freer to discuss such issues than is the Court itself which must direct its reasoning to disposing of the case in hand. Secondly, in doing so, he may advance more radical ideas or criticisms of previous case law than are open to the judges called upon to decide a particular case. Such ideas may subsequently be developed by lawyers in later cases and thus may enter the corpus of the Court's case law.

Where the Court does not follow the Advocate General's reasoning the Opinion is, nonetheless, published alongside the Court's judgment and, given the status of the Advocates General it may be regarded, for all practical purposes, as a dissenting opinion which otherwise is not admitted in a court which gives its decisions on a collegiate basis.

Finally, in those extremely rare cases in which a case is withdrawn before a final decision is made by the Court of Justice the Advocate General's Opinion in such a case stands, like an unappealed judgment of the Court of First Instance, as an authoritative, if not definitive, statement of the law on that particular issue and the Opinion will be published nonetheless in the reports of cases before the Court.[46]

---

46 See, for example, the Opinion of Advocate General Jacobs in Case C–120/94 *Commission v. Greece* [1996] ECR I–1513.

## Soft Law

"Soft" law sounds like an oxymoron and its utility, indeed its very existence, is hotly contested by many scholars.[47] That dispute concerns two principal problems, first that the idea of "law" by very definition requires that there be enforceable commitments and that therefore the idea of "soft" law in which agreements are expressed in terms or instruments which are unenforceable, *ipso facto*, means that they do not amount to "law". At the other extreme, some politicians consider that the emergence of soft law amounts to a legalisation of international political intercourse which restricts their freedom of action. The extent to which soft law may be regarded as a source of European law is therefore, to say the least, debatable.

Nonetheless, the emergence of soft law as a phenomenon on the stage of international relations is undeniable. Roughly speaking (and it is really only possible to speak roughly) soft law emerges when none of the parties to a particular agreement accepts any enforceable obligations and when, in addition, none of the elements for the constitution of a binding obligation (including an enforcement system) are fulfilled. Put another way, a rule of soft law would have less legal effect than, for example, a provision of a treaty or a rule of established customary law but might nonetheless condition the behaviour of states which enter into it.

The existence of soft law thus raises the question of the boundaries of what must be called, for the purposes of making the distinction, "hard law", in other words raising the question of the legally binding nature of any instrument purporting to set out rights and obligations between certain parties. In the field of public international law soft law may emerge in a number of forms including resolutions adopted in the context of international organisations, codes of conduct and *communiqués* or declarations made following international summits or other negotiations.

So far as European law is concerned, soft law may include general declarations of goodwill (Americans might express this as being "in favor of motherhood and apple pie") such as emerge most often at the end of meetings of the European Council which, as we have seen, is a policy-making body but not a legislature. It may thereby determine the future orientation and even the content of "hard law" (legislation or treaty amendments) without creating commitments immediately.

---

47  For an interesting, if poorly edited, outline of the topic and the questions which it raises both in international law and in European Community law, see Wellens and Borchardt, "Soft Law in European Community Law" [1989] 14 E.L. Rev. 267.

So far as European Community law is concerned, as Wellens and Borchardt[48] put it:

"Community soft law concerns the rules of conduct which find themselves on the legally non-binding level (in the sense of enforceable and sanctionable) but which, according to their drafters, have to be awarded a legal scope, that has to be specified at every turn and therefore do not show a uniform value of intensity with regard to their legal scope, but do have in common that they are directed at (intention of the drafters) and have as effect (through the medium of the Community legal order) that they influence the conduct of Member States, institutions, undertakings and individuals, however without containing Community rights and obligations".

The first indication of the existence of soft law is contained in Article 249 (ex Article 189) EC which first empowers the European Parliament acting jointly with the Council, the Council itself and the Commission to "make recommendations or deliver opinions". The final paragraph of that article provides that "recommendations and opinions shall have no binding force". The Commission and the Member States in particular, have displayed a certain fertility of imagination in expanding the range of non-binding instruments while the Court of Justice has demonstrated a reciprocal rigour in determining whether, whatever the designation of a particular instrument, it was intended to have legal effects and therefore to be susceptible of judicial review. Thus there have been resolutions of the institutions, or the Member States, or both.[49] Other forms of soft law include programmes outlining steps to be taken to achieve Community objectives, the conclusions adopted at the end of the meeting of the European Council and certain decisions of the representatives of the Member States meeting in Council.

"Soft law" is clearly not a closed category and the effect of any given measure will have to be evaluated on a case by case basis. The emergence of soft law (which may of course with time develop into "hard law") must be accepted as a fact of life for all those interested in the subject.

---

48 See above, n. 47.
49 Including, for example, a joint declaration by the European Parliament, the Council and the Commission on the institution of a conciliation procedure of March 4, 1975, OJ C 89, April 22, 1975; the Joint Declaration by the European Parliament, the Council and the Commission on Fundamental Rights of April 5, 1977, OJ C 103, April 27, 1977 and Council Resolution of June 8, 1993 on the quality of drafting of Community legislation, OJ C 166 June 17, 1993, p.1.

## CONCLUSIONS

Are we any closer to answering the question which forms the title of this chapter? In formal terms, as indicated in the introductory paragraphs, "European law" comprises the rules included in or pursuant to a certain number of treaties made between various European states. It also includes, in varying degrees, legislation made by the institutions created by those treaties, the case law of the judicial institutions which they created, and the rules of public and private international law which underpin the organisations.

# 5. HOW DOES EUROPEAN LAW AFFECT NATIONAL LAW?

"*Droit interne, droit européén et droit international se mélangent, se superposent, se complètent, se renforcent, se concurrencent où se neutralisent*"[50], Grewe and Fabri, Droits constitutionnels européens.

This is a most complex, interesting and delicate question. It has given rise to a vast academic literature and a string of important cases decided both by the European courts and by domestic courts in the Member States both of the European Union and the Council of Europe. The complexity is caused, in part, because of the differing legal nature of the four orders of European law discussed in the previous chapter (that is to say European Union law, European Community law, the law of the European Economic Area and the law of the European Convention on Human Rights). The problem is then compounded by the fact that the precise effects of each of those fields of law in a particular State will depend upon that State's constitution and, in particular, the State's approach to fulfilling its obligations under public international law.

---

50    "Domestic law, European law and International law mingle with one
       another, overlay each other, complement each other, reinforce each
       other, compete with each other or cancel each other out".

In this chapter we will first distinguish between the "monist" and "dualist" constitutional traditions concerning the relationship between international law and municipal law and then examine, successively, the way in which the law of each of the four European legal orders interrelates with the domestic law of the States which are party to it. The closest attention will be focused on the relationship between European Community law and the legal systems of the Member States partly because of the wide scope of European Community law already mentioned in Chapter 1 but also because it is the depth of integration which membership of the European Communities entails which distinguishes them from the other organisations we have met with in this book. It is here that the difficulties of that relationship have been the most thoroughly explored and where the most original and far-reaching solutions have been found.

Thus in its case law the European Court of Justice has developed the twin doctrines of primacy and direct effect of European Community law which have shaped the entire evolution of the Communities. Moreover, through the preliminary ruling system provided for in Article 234 (ex Article 177) of the EC Treaty the Communities have a sophisticated judicial system in order to ensure the uniform and effective application of Community law.

Space will not permit giving more than a few references to specific examples of the ways in which the constitutions and courts of different states have approached the problem of the relationship between European law and their domestic law.[51] However, it is an instructive and interesting exercise to compare the approaches of different states in this area.[52] Thus if the reader is from a European Union or Council of Europe Member State, you might examine how in practice the different canons of European law have been integrated into your national legal system considering any specific problems which have arisen either for the

---

51 So far as European Community law is concerned there is a useful discussion of the effect of the primacy of European Community law on the United Kingdom, Germany, France and Italy in Weatherill and Beaumont, *EC Law* (2nd ed., Penguin, 1995) while the West Casebook, *Cases and Materials on European Community Law*, edited by Bermann, Goebel, Davey and Fox, contains an excellent and detailed account of the reception of Community law in France, the Benelux countries, Germany, Italy, Denmark, Ireland and the United Kingdom.

52 For the purposes of carrying out such an exercise, apart from the cases and constitutional provisions cited in the Casebook mentioned above, English language versions of most of those cases are available in the *Common Market Law Reports* and English translations of the constitutions of most of the countries of the world are contained in *Constitutions of the Countries of the World* Blanstein and Flanz, (Oceana, ).

legislature or the judiciary in the country concerned. For comparative purposes the same process could be carried out with two or three other Member States.

If you are from one of the states which is a candidate for EU membership you might consider whether any constitutional amendment will be necessary in the event of accession to the European Union (which automatically entails accession to the European Communities and the European Economic Area) and what constitutional obstacles may be encountered by your national courts. If you are from a country which is never likely to become a candidate for membership of one of the European organisations, consider how your country would cope with the constitutional challenges of joining such a regional system such as Mercosur in South America, the North American Free Trade Area (NAFTA) or the Economic Community of West African States (ECOWAS).

Finally, mention will briefly be made of the relationship between the fundamental rights defined and protected by the European Convention and its enforcement machinery, and the protection of fundamental rights as forming one of the general principles of law[53] which are protected by the Court of Justice in the European Community legal system.

## "MONIST" AND "DUALIST" STATES

Although, as we shall see, each of the four European legal orders operates in a different fashion, they were each created by multilateral treaties in accordance with the rules of public international law. Moreover, the treaties establishing the European Union, the European Communities and the European Economic Area all specify that they are to be ratified by the Contracting Parties "in accordance with their respective constitutional requirements".

Although those constitutional requirements, and especially the rules governing the effect of international treaty obligations within the various domestic legal systems will vary according to the precise terms of the constitution concerned, there are two basic approaches to the relationship known respectively as the "monist" and the "dualist" approach.

According to the monist approach, international law on the one hand and domestic law on the other are merely two aspects of a single legal order. Therefore once a treaty has been entered into and ratified by a monist state it becomes a source of law within that state's legal system and can be applied by domestic courts in the same way as other domestic rules. This has the great advantage, particularly in the context of application of the Human Rights Convention, that the national courts, at any level, may

---

53   See Chapter 4 above at p. 125.

provide a remedy themselves. Thus recourse to the Convention's own enforcement machinery in Strasbourg will only be necessary in the event of difficulties of interpreting the relevant Convention rule or if, for example, a procedural obstacle is raised against the complainant.

By contrast, according to the dualist tradition to which, for example, the United Kingdom, Denmark and the other Nordic countries adhere, international law and domestic law are considered to be two entirely separate and distinct legal orders. Under this view obligations, including treaty obligations, entered into by states are binding only on those states *qua* states. Even following ratification, according to parliamentary or other constitutional procedures, the existence of a treaty alone does not have any effect on legal relationships within the state except to the extent to which any particular rules have been directly incorporated into the national legal order.

The United Kingdom clearly illustrates the consequences of the dualist approach. Thus, on the one hand, although the United Kingdom was one of the prime movers of the Human Rights Convention and one of the first states to ratify it, it did not give effect to it in national law. It is however a firm commitment on the part of the Labour Government elected in May 1997 to enact the Convention into UK law and at the time of writing the Human Rights Act 1998 was awaiting the Royal Assent. The Act will enter force about one year later.

The consequences of not having enacted the Convention are illustrated in *Regina v. Home Secretary, ex p. Brind*.[54] The applicants, who were involved with broadcasting news and current affairs programmes, claimed that the Home Secretary's prohibition against the broadcasting of words spoken by persons representing terrorist organisations contravened Article 10 of the European Convention which enshrines the right to freedom of expression. The House of Lords dismissed the appeal stating that the Convention was not part of English law, although the presumption that Parliament had intended to legislate in conformity with the Convention might be used in order to resolve any ambiguity or uncertainty in British legislation.

Therefore a complainant who believes that his rights under the Convention may have been infringed in the United Kingdom cannot raise the Convention directly before UK courts but must, having exhausted domestic remedies, exercise his right of petition to the Court in Strasbourg.

By contrast, in order to give effect to its obligations under the European Community treaties the United Kingdom enacted the

---

54   *R. v. Secretary of State for the Home Department, ex parte Brind* [1991] 1 A.C. 696.

European Communities Act 1972, Article 2(1) of which provides that:

"All such rights, powers, liabilities, obligations and restrictions from time to time created or arising by or under the treaties and all such remedies and procedures from time to time provided for by or under the treaties, as in accordance with the treaties are without further enactment to be given legal effect or used in the United Kingdom, shall be recognised and available in law, and be enforced, allowed and followed accordingly."

The dualist approach is also illustrated by the European Communities (Amendment) Act 1993, adopted to take into account the ratification of the Maastricht Treaty. That act incorporates into United Kingdom law Titles II, III and IV of the Treaty on European Union amending the three founding European Community treaties. However, titles V and VI of the TEU providing, respectively, provisions on a common foreign and security policy and provisions on co-operation in the fields of justice and home affairs (before amendment by the Treaty of Amsterdam), are not mentioned in the act as they are the intergovernmental pillars of the European Union structure and, as such, have no effect in UK domestic law.

Like the distinction between integration and intergovernmentalism outlined in Chapter 2, the distinction between monism and dualism is by no means absolute. Thus the separation of international law and domestic law envisaged by the dualist approach is far from watertight. Nor do monist states unequivocally allow all self-executing international rules to operate directly in their legal systems. Nonetheless, the distinction has its use as a starting point for examining the effect of European law on the internal legal orders of various states. Of the Member States of the European Union the monists are generally considered to be France, the Benelux countries, Spain, Portugal and Greece, while Germany, Austria, Italy, the United Kingdom, Ireland and the three Nordic countries are generally considered to be dualists.

## THE HUMAN RIGHTS CONVENTION AND NATIONAL LAW[55]

It is consistent with the intergovernmental nature of the Council of Europe that, as originally envisaged, the purpose of the Convention was to bind the signatory States (called High Contracting Parties in

55 A useful study of the impact of the case law of the European Court of Human Rights in seventeen States which have formally incorporated the substantive provisions of the Convention into their internal law was made by Polakiewicz and Jacob-Foltzer, "The European Human Rights Convention in Domestic Law" (1991) 12 HRLJ 65 and 125.

the Convention) to setting and maintaining certain agreed minimum standards for the protection of human rights rather than to provide a direct remedy for individuals who believe that those rights may have been infringed. Thus there was at first no provision for individuals to bring their cases before the Court, nor even for them to take part in proceedings once they had been commenced.

The right of individual petition envisaged in Article 25 of the Convention (for those States which had made the required declaration allowing individuals to petition the Commission through the Secretary General of the Council of Europe) was a means for alerting the signatory states to a possible infringement of the Convention which would then be dealt with between the Contracting states through the machinery provided for. By the same token the involvement of a political authority, the Council of Ministers, in the enforcement machinery is another clear sign of the intergovernmental nature of the system.

As we shall see, that situation has now changed substantially. However, even at the outset, the High Contracting Parties were obliged under Article 1 of the Convention to "secure to everyone within their jurisdiction the rights and freedoms defined in . . . this Convention". Moreover, Article 13 of the Convention provides that there must be an effective remedy before a national authority in the event of a violation of the rights and freedoms in the Convention. It may be noted that that obligation to provide an effective remedy does not necessarily require that the remedy be a judicial one. Thus, according to circumstances, a system of administrative review or the existence of an Ombudsman might be regarded as sufficient provided that it was "effective".

Clearly, however, an enforceable remedy available through a national court system is likely to be more effective than having to have recourse to a rather cumbersome international supervision procedure. To ensure such effectiveness the majority of Contracting states have incorporated the Convention into their domestic law, although the precise scope and effect of the Convention once incorporated varies widely from country to country. Thus, for example, in the Netherlands the obligations under the Convention are regarded as being superior even to the constitutional law of that country while in Austria, which has a particularly strict hierarchy of legal norms, the Convention ranks at constitutional level. For its part Denmark gives the Convention the same status as a normal statute. While the precise status of the Convention in the United Kingdom following its incorporation remains to be seen, there is no provision for any form of legislation having a higher status than an act of parliament (which will be the vehicle incorporating the Convention) and therefore judges will be faced with the problem of how to reconcile it with any conflicting rules contained in other statutes.

Despite the limitations inherent in intergovernmental structures and the impossibility for courts in dualist states (especially the United Kingdom) to apply the Convention directly, the working of the Convention has had a substantial impact on the national laws of the Contracting Parties. Although it might appear that the obligation under Article 53 of the Convention for Contracting Parties "to abide by the decision of the Court in any case to which they are parties" might be limited to ending a violation in a specific case and providing appropriate redress, in practice, where a Contracting state's law has been found to be in contradiction with the Convention, states have generally changed their law in order to comply with their obligation under Article 1, albeit not always with great alacrity.

Apart from the resolution of individual cases and resulting changes in the law for states immediately concerned, a clear interpretation of one of the Convention guarantees should be taken into account by the other Contracting Parties who will know that a judgment of the Court may be relied upon by individuals in their respective countries in order to challenge laws similar to those concerned in a particular Court judgment. The speed and effectiveness of such cross-fertilisation is, however, far from perfect. When a new state applies to become a Member of the Council of Europe, its entire corpus of legislation is reviewed in order to ensure its conformity with the Convention, as interpreted in the case law of the Human Rights Court.

However, the Convention does not only work at the abstract or intergovernmental level but now also provides direct remedies for individuals through the Strasbourg machinery. Although, as noted above, this was not the original intention of the Convention and an individual applicant to the Human Rights Court must overcome some formidable obstacles before a case may be considered on its merits by the Court (see Chapter 6, p. 188 below), the sheer number of applications now made to the European Commission on Human Rights is evidence of the reliance which is now placed on the machinery. Nonetheless, given that Article 13 of the Convention requires an effective remedy before a national authority to be provided, and that Article 26 requires all domestic remedies to be exhausted before the Commission may deal with a case, it is clear that the national courts, subject to the reservations outlined above, have a vital role in ensuring the correct application of the Convention.

## EUROPEAN COMMUNITY LAW AND NATIONAL LAW

Like all intimate relationships, that between European Community law and the internal legal orders of the Member States is characterised by areas of synergy where partners work effectively together to achieve their objectives and by occasional conflicts which must be resolved. In the context of European Community law the synergy is expressed in the legal doctrines of direct applicability and direct effect, while potential conflicts are resolved by recourse to the doctrine of primacy. While direct applicability is mentioned in the EC Treaty, the doctrines of direct effect and primacy of Community law represent the most far-reaching jurisprudential creations.

### Direct Applicability

A directly applicable provision of European Community law is one which creates rights and obligations on the part of those to whom it applies without the need for any form of incorporation or implementation of the rule into the national legal order. According to Article 249 (ex Article 189) of the EC Treaty a regulation is of "general application" and "binding in its entirety and directly applicable in all Member States". As the Court of Justice has put it "owing to its very nature and its place in the system of sources of Community law, a Regulation has immediate effect and, consequently, operates to confer rights on private parties which the national courts have a duty to protect".[56]

In principle therefore, any national legislation purporting to give effect to a regulation is otiose and indeed runs the risk of restricting the scope or changing the effect of a regulation. However, some regulations may either require Member States to take certain steps or may not be sufficiently precise or unconditional (see under Direct Effect below) to be applied by national courts or administrative authorities. In those circumstances national implementing measures may be adopted provided that they are consistent with the regulation and do not purport to restrict its scope or limit its effects, matters which are in the last resort for the Court of Justice to determine as a matter of interpretation.

### Direct Effect

Direct effect is the capacity of a rule of Community law to confer rights on individuals which may be enforced by national courts. It should be noted that it is *the rule* which may be capable of having direct effect and not the instrument containing that rule. It is therefore possible, for example, for a directive to contain certain directly effective provisions while others are not directly effective. The question of whether or not a given rule in one of the treaties, a directive or other legal instrument is capable of having direct

---

56  Case 34/73 *Variola Spa v. Amministrazione Italiana delle finanze* [1973] ECR 981.

effect is a matter for interpretation of the specific provision concerned which is ultimately a question for the European Court of
Justice.

Treaty provisions, directives, regulations, decisions and international agreements entered into by the Community may all
contain rules having direct effect. The precise scope of the doctrine
varies somewhat according to the nature of the instrument concerned.

*Treaty provisions*

It was in connection with a treaty provision that the Court of
Justice first elaborated the doctrine of direct effect. When Van
Gend & Loos, a Dutch transport company, imported a consign-
ment of a chemical product into the Netherlands from Germany
the Dutch customs authorities imposed duty at 8% whereas, when
the EC Treaty entered force, the relevant rate had been 3%. Van
Gend & Loos sought to rely upon Article 12 of the EEC Treaty
which then provided "Member States shall refrain from introducing between themselves any new customs duties on imports or
exports or any charges having equivalent effect, and from increasing those which they already apply in their trade with each
other",[57] a "standstill" provision prior to the abolition of all duties
on trade between Member States. The question of whether or not
an individual might rely upon that article before a national court
or tribunal was referred to the Court of Justice by the Dutch
Customs Court.

In its judgment,[58] the Court of Justice said:

"The Community constitutes a new legal order of international
law for the benefit of which the States have limited their
sovereign rights, albeit within limited fields, and the subjects of
which comprise not only Member States but also their nationals. Independently of the legislation of Member States,
Community law therefore not only imposes obligations on
individuals but is also intended to confer upon them rights
which become part of their legal heritage".

The Court added that Article 12 "contains a clear and unconditional prohibition which is not a positive but a negative

---

57   That text was replaced by the Treaty of Amsterdam. Article 25 (ex
     Article 12) now provides "Customs duties on imports and exports
     and charges having equivalent effect shall be prohibited between
     Member States. This prohibition shall also apply to customs duties of
     a fiscal nature".

58   Case 26/62 *Van Gend en Loos v. Nederlandse Administratie der Belas-
     tingen* [1963] ECR I.

obligation. This obligation, moreover, is not qualified by any reservation on the part of States which would make its implementation conditional upon a positive legislative measure enacted under national law", the first expression of the "precise and unconditional" test mentioned above.

Subsequently, the Court has established the direct effect of a large number of treaty provisions, in particular those connected with "the four freedoms".[59] Moreover, the direct effect of treaty provisions may operate not only as between individuals and state authorities (known as "vertical direct effect") but also as against other private parties (known as "horizontal direct effect"). Thus, for example, Article 141 (ex Article 119) of the EC Treaty requires Member States to ensure the application of the principle of equal pay for men and women for equal work. In *Defrenne v. SABENA*[60] the Court first found that the principle of equal pay formed part of the foundations of the Community and added "since Article 119 is mandatory in nature, the prohibition on discrimination between men and women applies not only to the action of public authorities, but also extends to all agreements which are intended to regulate paid labour collectively, as well as to contracts between individuals".

*Directives*

Article 249 (ex Article 189) of the EC Treaty provides that "a directive shall be binding, as to the result to be achieved, upon each Member State to which it is addressed, but shall leave to the national authorities the choice of form and methods". In principle therefore, by contrast with regulations mentioned above, directives require national implementing legislation in order to produce effects within the national legal order. This means, in the normal course of events, that the rights upon which an individual may seek to rely or the obligations which he may seek to have enforced, stem immediately from the national implementing legislation and not from the directive. Indeed a party, an administrative authority or even a court before whom the matter is eventually brought, may be unaware that the legislation concerned derives from a directive.

The question whether or not directives could have direct effect, that is to say that they could be relied upon by individuals in the absence of national implementing measures or where such implementation was incorrect or incomplete, came before the Court of

---

59  See, for example, the *Reyners* and *Van Binsbergen* cases in connection with freedom of establishment outlined in Chapter 10 below at pp. 312 *et seq.*
60  Case 43/75 *Defrenne v. SABENA* [1976] ECR 455.

Justice in *Van Duyn v. The Home Office*.[61] Miss Van Duyn, a Dutch national, was refused entry into the United Kingdom because she intended to work for the Church of Scientology there. Although the Church of Scientology was not prohibited and there were no restrictions on British nationals working for it, the British Government had a policy of refusing admission to non-British nationals wishing to work for the Church. Miss Van Duyn brought an action claiming that her right of freedom of movement under Article 48 of the Treaty was being restricted. She also sought to rely on the Council directive providing for co-ordination between the Member States of restrictions on the movement and residence of foreign nationals based on considerations of public policy, public security or public health.[62] In particular Article 31 of the directive provides that "measures taken on grounds of public policy or public security shall be based exclusively on the personal conduct of the individual concerned".

The Court first rejected an argument based on the difference in the wording of the provisions of Article 189 (now Article 249) relating to the effects ascribed respectively to regulations, directives and decisions.

It then found that directives could have direct effect, saying:

"It would be incompatible with the binding effect attributed to a directive by Article 189 to exclude, in principle, the possibility that the obligation which it imposes may be invoked by those concerned."

Secondly, the Court pointed out, that "where the Community authorities have, by directive, imposed on Member States the obligation to pursue a particular course of conduct, the useful effect[63] of such an act would be weakened if individuals were prevented from relying on it before their national courts and if the latter were prevented from taking it into consideration as an element of Community law".

In the later case of *Ratti*[64] the Court added that "a Member State which has not adopted the implementing measures required by the directive in the prescribed periods may not rely, as against

61  Case 41/74 *Van Duyn v. Home Office* [1974] ECR 1337.
62  Council Directive 64/221/EEC of February 25, 1964 on the co-ordination of special measures concerning the movement and residence of foreign nationals which are justified on grounds of public policy, public security or public health, *OJ English Special Edition 1963–1964*, p. 117.
63  "Effectiveness" is now the usual translation for the French *effet utile*. See Chapter 8, at pp. 267 *et seq.*
64  Case 148/78 *Pubblico Ministero v. Ratti* [1979] ECR 1629.

individuals, on its own failure to perform the obligations which the directive entails."

In other words a state may not rely upon its own wrong as a defence to an action based upon a directive before its own courts. The Court of Justice has also held that, conversely, a Member State may not base criminal proceedings upon a directive which had not been implemented into national law.[65] It is also clear from the *Ratti* case that the direct effect of a directive may not be relied upon until after the expiry of the time allowed for its implementation, since it is only in the event of non-implementation after the expiry of that period that the Member State will be in default.

The approach in *Ratti* however leaves two questions open. First, what is "the State" for the purpose of relying on the direct effect of a directive, and secondly, is direct effect only available against the State as so defined (vertical effect) or can directives, like directly effective treaty provisions, also create rights and obligations as between private parties (horizontal effect)?

So far as the first question is concerned the Court has taken a broad view of the definition of a state for these purposes holding first, in *Marshall I*[66] that "where a person involved in legal proceedings is able to rely on a directive as against the State he may do so regardless of the capacity in which the latter is acting, whether employer or public authority." In a later case,[67] the Court held that the principle of direct effect against States included "all organs of the administration, including decentralised authorities such as municipalities". Finally, the Court laid down its broadest definition in *Foster*[68] where the Court said that:

"A body, whatever its legal form, which has been made responsible, pursuant to a measure adopted by the State, for providing a public service under the control of the State and has for that purpose special powers beyond those which result from the normal rules applicable in relations between individuals is included in any event among the bodies against which the provisions of a directive capable of having direct effect may be relied upon."

The question of the horizontal effect of directives was also addressed by the Court of Justice in *Marshall I* in which the Court pointed out that "the binding nature of a directive, which constitutes the basis for the possibility of relying upon the directive

65    Case 80/86 *Kolpinghuis Nijmegen* [1987] ECR 3969.
66    Case 152/84 *Marshall v. Southampton and South-West Hampshire Area Health Authority* [1986] ECR 723.
67    Case 103/88 *Fratelli Costanzo v. Comune di Milano* [1989] ECR 1839.
68    Case C–188/89 *Foster v. British Gas plc* [1990] ECR I–3313.

before a national court, exists only in relation to 'each Member State to which it is addressed'. It follows that a directive may not of itself impose obligations on an individual and that a provision of a directive may not be relied upon as such against such a person."

Despite such a clear rejection of the possibility of directives having horizontal effect, the issue has not gone away and the notion that directives may have such an effect is supported by much academic writing. This is not the place fully to canvass all of the arguments for and against horizontal direct effect, but they may be studied in three Opinions by three of the Court's Advocates General delivered in 1993 and 1994[69] in which they all urged the Court to reconsider the position it had taken in *Marshall I*. The issue came squarely before the Court in the *Faccini Dori* case[70] in which the Court first reiterated that the basis for giving directives direct effect is to prevent "the State from taking advantage of its own failure to comply with Community law" and added that:

"The effect of extending that case law to the sphere of relations between individuals would be to recognise a power in the Community to enact obligations for individuals with immediate effect, whereas it has competence to do so only where it is empowered to adopt regulations".

In other words, to attribute horizontal direct effect to directives would amount to assimilating the directive to a regulation.

Where a provision of a directive does not have direct effect, either because it is not unconditional or sufficiently precise or because it is sought to rely upon the provisions of a directive against an individual, it may nonetheless be possible to derive some benefit from the directive through the powers of national courts to interpret their own national legislation in such a way as to achieve the aims of the directive. This approach is known as "consistent interpretation" (from the French *interprétation conforme*) and has also been called "indirect effect". The Court of Justice has developed this approach on the basis of Article 10 (ex Article 5) of the EC Treaty which requires Member States to "take all appropriate measures, whether general or particular, to ensure fulfilment of the obligations arising out of this Treaty or resulting from action taken by the institutions of the Community". First in

---

69  Case C–271/91 *Marshall v. Southampton and South-West Area Health Authority II* [1993] ECR I–4367 (Advocate General Van Gerven); Case C–316/93 [1994] ECR I–763 (Advocate General Jacobs), and Case C–91/92 *Faccini Dori v. Recreb* [1994] ECR I–3325 (Advocate General Lenz).
70  Case C–91/92 *Faccini Dori v. Recreb* [1994] ECR I–3325.

*Von Colson and Kamann*[71] two women who had applied for posts as social workers in an all-male prison claimed that, by appointing less well qualified male applicants to the post their rights to equal treatment in access to employment under the Equal Treatment Directive[72] had been infringed. Although the German *Arbeitsgericht* (Labour Court) found that they had been discriminated against, it found that, under German law, it could compensate only the direct loss suffered by the applicants, in the particular circumstances of the case a paltry amount. The case, however, was referred to the Court of Justice which found that the directive was not sufficiently precise and unconditional as to have direct effect and thereby to create a right to a specific compensation that the applicants could rely upon in a national court. Nonetheless it held that any form of sanction provided for under the national implementing legislation had to be sufficient "such as to guarantee real and effective judicial protection". It then added that "it is for the national court to interpret and apply the legislation adopted for the implementation of the directive in conformity with the requirements of Community law, in so far as it is given discretion to do so under national law".

In a more recent case,[73] the Court of Justice first pointed out that the duty on Member States under Article 5 (now Article 10) of the EC Treaty to ensure the fulfilment of the obligation arising from a directive was binding on all of the authorities of Member States including, for matters within their jurisdiction, the courts. It continued that "in applying national law, whether the provisions in question were adopted before or after the directive, the national court called upon to interpret it is required to do so, as far as possible, in the light of the wording and the purpose of the directive in order to achieve the result pursued by the latter and thereby comply with the third paragraph of Article 189 of the Treaty".

*Other instruments*

In addition to the provisions of the main treaties and of directives, certain rules contained in other instruments are also capable of having direct effect, subject to fulfilling the usual requirements

71  Case 14/83 *Von Colson and Kamann v. Land Nordrhein-Westfalen* [1984] ECR 1891.
72  Council Directive 76/207/EEC of February 9, 1976 on the implementation of the principle of equal treatment for men and women as regards access to employment, vocational training and promotion, and working conditions, OJ L 39, February 14, 1976, p. 40.
73  Case 106/89 *Marleasing SA v. Comercial Internacional de Alimentación SA* [1990] ECR I–4135.

that they be sufficiently precise and unconditional. As we have already seen, regulations are endowed with direct applicability by Article 249 (ex Article 189) of the EC Treaty. Normally speaking, the directly applicable nature of a regulation will entail that it produces direct effect. However, as noted above, it is possible that a regulation might explicitly require Member States to take certain steps (thus making it conditional) or that a particular provision may be too vague to be capable of application by the Court.

The third binding form of act mentioned in Article 249 (ex Article 189) EC is the decision. That article provides that "a decision shall be binding in its entirety upon those to whom it is addressed". In *Grad*[74] the Court said that it would be incompatible with that binding effect to "exclude in principle the possibility that persons affected may invoke the obligation imposed by a decision, particularly in cases where ... the Community authorities by means of a decision have imposed an obligation on a Member State or all the Member States to act in a certain way, the effectiveness (*l'effet utile*) of such a measure would be weakened if the nationals of that State could not invoke it in the courts and the national courts could not take it into consideration as part of Community law".

Each particular case must be examined on its merits so as to ascertain "whether the nature, background and wording of the provision in question are capable of producing direct effects in the legal relationships between the addressee of the act and third parties".

The Court has also approached the question of the direct effect of certain international agreements entered into by the Community on a case-by-case basis. Thus, for example, the Court held that a prohibition on the free trade agreement between the Community and Portugal (before the latter became a Member State) which prohibited discriminatory taxation against goods imported from Portugal into the Community was unconditional and sufficiently precise to be relied upon by traders in the courts in the Member States.[75] Various provisions of association agreements concluded by the Community with Turkey, Cyprus and Morocco have similarly been found to be directly effective. By contrast it has decided that the provisions of the GATT do not have direct effect within the Community.

## Primacy

The three founding European Community treaties made no express provision to deal with the possibility of a conflict between

---

74   Case 9/70 *Grad v. Finanzamt Traunstein* [1970] ECR 825.
75   Case 104/81 *Hauptzollamt Mainz v. Kupferberg* [1982] ECR 3641.

a rule of European Community law and a rule of the municipal law of one of the Member States. Nonetheless, it was a principle of international law, codified in Article 27 of the Vienna Convention on the law of treaties that a party to a treaty "may not invoke the provisions of its internal law as justification for its failure to perform a treaty". Moreover, Article 10 (ex Article 5) of the EC Treaty imposes a general duty on the Member States "to ensure fulfilment of the obligations arising out of this treaty", to "facilitate the achievement of the Community's tasks" and to "abstain from any measure which could jeopardise the attainment of the objectives of this treaty".

The matter was decisively clarified by the Court of Justice in a case referred to it by an Italian court, *Costa v. ENEL*[76] in which Mr Costa, on the basis of a challenge to a modest electricity bill, sought to argue that the Italian legislation nationalising the electricity industry infringed both the Italian Constitution and various provisions of the EEC Treaty. In proceedings before the Italian Constitutional Court the latter ruled that in the Italian domestic legal order, the Treaty had the status of ordinary legislation since it had been ratified by a simple parliamentary act and that therefore any subsequent act which was in contrary terms automatically overrode it. The Court rejected that argument in forthright terms:

"By creating a Community of unlimited duration, having its own institutions, its own personality, its own legal capacity and capacity of representation on an international plane and, more particularly, real powers stemming from a limitation of sovereignty or a transfer of powers from the States of the Community, the Member States have limited their sovereign rights, albeit within limited fields, and have thus created a body of law which binds both their nationals and themselves.

The integration into the laws of each Member State of provisions which derive from the Community and, more generally, the terms and the spirit of the Treaty, make it impossible for the States, as a corollary, to accord precedence to a unilateral and subsequent measure over a legal system accepted by them on a basis of reciprocity."

Later the Court added:

"The precedence[77] of Community law is confirmed by Article

---

76    Case 6/64 *Costa v. Ente Nazionale per l'Energia Elettrica* [1964] ECR 585.
77    "Precedence" is the word used by the Court of Justice in *Costa v. ENEL* to express the primacy of Community law over national law; "supremacy" is also widely used as a synonym for this idea.

189 [now Article 249], whereby a regulation shall be binding and directly applicable in all Member States. This provision, which is subject to no reservation, would be quite meaningless if a State could unilaterally nullify its effects by means of a legislative measure which could prevail over Community law".

Far reaching though it is, the doctrine of primacy has not given rise to nearly as much academic discussion or case law as the doctrine of direct effect discussed above. By contrast the extent to which the doctrine has been accepted, particularly by the Supreme Court of the Member States, and the alacrity with which they have adjusted to it has varied considerably from one state to another.[78] The Court of Justice has, however, added two important refinements to the doctrine.

First, that it applies irrespective of the status of the national law which is in conflict with the Community rule, even where the national rule concerned had constitutional status or concerned the protection of fundamental rights. The Court said:

"The law stemming from the Treaty, an independent source of law, cannot because of its very nature be overridden by rules of national law, however framed, without being deprived of its character as Community law and without the legal basis of the Community itself being called in question. Therefore the validity of a Community measure or its effect within a Member State cannot be affected by allegations that it runs counter to either fundamental rights as formulated by the Constitution of that State or the principles of a national constitutional structure".[79]

To allay fears that by such a categorical statement the Community might override the cherished fundamental values consecrated in national constitutions, it added the proviso that "respect for fundamental rights forms an integral part of the general principles of law protected by the Court of Justice. The protection of such rights, whilst inspired by the constitutional traditions common to the Member States, must be ensured within the framework of the structure and objectives of the Community."

Secondly, the Court has dealt with the question of the approach of a national court confronted with a situation in which a rule of Community law appears to conflict with a rule of national law. First of all of course a national court is entitled to make a reference to the Court of Justice for a preliminary ruling on the correct

78   For an overview of the reception of the principle of primacy in the national legal systems see the sources mentioned at n. 51 above.
79   Case 11/70 *Internationale Handelsgesellschaft mbH v. Einfuhr und Vorratsstelle für Getreide und Futtermittel* [1970] ECR 1125.

interpretation of the relevant Community rule. It may emerge from such interpretation that there is in fact no conflict with the relevant national rule. In the second *Simmenthal* case[80] the Court pointed out that the effectiveness of the preliminary ruling procedure

> "would be impaired if the national court were prevented from forthwith applying Community law in accordance with the decision or the case law of the Court.
>   It follows from the foregoing that every national court must, in a case within its jurisdiction, apply Community law in its entirety and protect rights which the latter confers on individuals and must accordingly set aside any provision of national law which may conflict with it, whether prior or subsequent to the Community rule".

Since the *Simmenthal* case had been referred to the Court of Justice by a relatively low level court in Italy, where in principle, only the constitutional court had the power to declare domestic legislation void, the Court thereby made it clear that the duty to set aside conflicting national legislation was incumbent upon any court at any level in the national legal hierarchy. The *Simmenthal* rule was again relied upon in the first *Factortame* case[81] in which English courts were confronted with the problem that, as a matter of English law, they could not suspend an act of parliament, even where it appeared that it might be contrary to Community law. Again basing its argument on the requirement to ensure the "full effectiveness of Community law" the Court of Justice pointed out that that effectiveness would be impaired "if a rule of national law could prevent a court seised of a dispute governed by Community law from granting interim relief in order to ensure the full effectiveness of the judgment to be given on the existence of the rights claimed under Community law. It follows that a court which in those circumstances would grant interim relief, if it were not for a rule of national law, is obliged to set aside that rule".[82]

80   Case 106/77 *Amministrazione delle finanze dello Stato v. Simmenthal Spa (II)* [1978] ECR 629.
81   Case C–213/89 *The Queen v. Secretary of State for Transport, ex. p. Factortame Ltd (Factortame 1)* [1990] ECR I–2433.
82   The *sang froid* with which the House of Lords received that decision, in stark contrast to the comments of many politicians and newspapers (see in particular the speech of Lord Bridge of Harwich in the Report of the House of Lords judgment at [1991] 1 All E.R. 70; [1990] 3 C.M.L.R. 375), suggests that in putting the question to the Court of Justice the House of Lords may have been obeying the old advocates' maxim of never asking a question to which you do not already know the answer.

## State Liability

In a more recent development in its case law,[83] the Court of Justice has found that it is inherent in the scheme of the EC Treaty that where states cause loss or damage to individuals by infringements of Community rules they are liable to compensate the individuals for their loss. In the leading case *Francovich*,[84] a company, had fallen bankrupt with substantial arrears of salary owing to its employees. A Community directive[85] sought to provide protection for workers in such a situation by requiring Member States to establish guarantee institutions which would be able to ensure payment of employees' outstanding claims. The directive had not however been implemented in Italy as the Court of Justice had already found in proceedings successfully brought by the Commission for a declaration that Italy had failed to fulfil its treaty obligations.[86]

The Italian workers brought proceedings directly against the Italian State for compensation for their lost income and the national court referred the matter to the Court of Justice for a preliminary ruling. In its judgment the Court of Justice (referring to the *Van Gend en Loos, Costa v. ENEL Simmenthal* and *Factortame* cases mentioned above) first found that the directive could not have direct effect because, although it was sufficiently precise, it was also conditional on the establishment by the Member States of the required guarantee institutions. Nonetheless, on the basis of considerations of ensuring the full effectiveness of European Community law on the one hand and on the basis of the general duty on the part of Member States under Article 10 (ex Article 5) of the EC Treaty to ensure fulfilment of the obligations arising out of the Treaty, that it is a principle of Community law that Member States are obliged to make good the loss and damage caused to individuals by breaches of Community law for which they can be held responsible.

The Court found that there were three conditions to be satisfied for such liability to arise:

83 Although the possibility of State liability had been hinted at in earlier cases such as Case 6 60 *Humblet v. Belgium* [1960] ECR 559 and Case 60/75 *Russo v. AIMA* [1976] ECR 45.
84 Joined Cases C–6/90 and C–9/90 *Francovich and Bonifaci v. Italy* [1991] ECR I–5357.
85 Council Directive 80/987 of October 20, 1980 on the approximation of the laws of the Member States relating to the protection of employees in the event of the insolvency of their employer, OJ L 283 of October 28, 1980, p. 23.
86 Case 22/87 *Commission v. Italy* [1989] ECR 143.

(i)   that the result prescribed by the directive involved the granting of rights to individuals;
(ii)  that the content of those rights should be clearly identifiable from the wording of the directive;
(iii) that there was a direct causal link between the failure by the Member State to fulfil its obligations and the damage suffered by the individuals affected.

In a series of subsequent cases the Court has refined the concept of state liability drawing, in particular, on the principles under which the Community might be held liable for legislative acts under Article 288 (ex Article 215) EC and found that "Community law confers a right to reparation where three conditions are met: the rule of law infringed must be intended to confer rights on individuals; the breach must be sufficiently serious; and there must be a direct causal link between the breach of the obligation resting on the State and the damage sustained by the injured parties".[87] It also gave guidance to national courts confronted with such claims as to how to assess whether or not a particular breach was sufficiently serious.[88] In the *Faccini Dori* case,[89] in which, as we have seen above, the Court reiterated that directives were not capable of producing horizontal direct effect, the Court invited the Italian Court which had referred the case to it to seek to interpret its own national law in order to achieve the result prescribed by the directive (see the remarks on "consistent interpretation" above at p. 149), and suggested that if that approach failed to produce a remedy it might again be possible to award damages against the state for its failure to implement the directive correctly or at all.

### Role and Responsibility of National Courts

Although the doctrines of direct effect, primacy and state liability outlined above have been developed by the European Court of Justice through its case law it is evident that the principal responsibility for ensuring the effective application of Community law within the national legal systems lies upon the courts which make up those legal systems. The Court of Justice itself has said that:

---

87   Joined Cases C–46 and C–48/93 *Brasserie du Pêcheur SA v. Germany* and *The Queen v. Secretary of State for Transport, ex. p. Factortame Ltd* [1996] ECR I–1029.
88   See also on that point Case C–5/94 [1996] ECR I–2553 and Case C–392/93 *The Queen v. H.M. Treasury, ex. p. British Telecommunications Plc* [1996] ECR I–1631.
89   Case C–91/92 *Faccini Dori v. Recreb Srl* [1994] ECR I–3325.

"The development of the Community legal order has been to a large extent the fruit of the dialogue which has built up between the national courts and the Court of Justice through the preliminary ruling procedure. It is through such co-operation that the essential characteristics of the Community legal order have been identified, in particular its primacy over the laws of the Member States, the direct effect of a whole series of provisions and the right of individuals to obtain redress when their rights are infringed by a breach of Community law for which a Member State is responsible."[90]

Furthermore, the courts in the Member States, like the national administrative authorities who are responsible for the day-to-day application of the rules of Community law, are bound by the general obligation of co-operation laid down in Article 10 (ex Article 5) of the EC Treaty. So far as the courts are concerned in carrying out their tasks of settling disputes between private parties or in reviewing the administrative acts of other national authorities this general task includes ensuring that possible infringements of Community law are avoided, and ensuring the effective working of Community law. In *UNECTEF v. Heylens*[91] the Court asserted that where a decision of a national authority refused to allow the exercise of a right claimed under Community law, there had to be the possibility of a judicial remedy in the national legal system against that decision and, as a corollary, the decision had to be accompanied by a sufficient statement of the reasons upon which it was based to enable the national court to carry out its task.

Even in the absence of a claim based upon a right under European Community law national courts have a duty to raise such points of their own motion where appropriate.[92]

Beyond those general duties it may be helpful to summarise some of the specific duties of national courts when applying Community law, most of which have already been mentioned in the sections above.[93] First, in accordance with the doctrine of primacy, national courts must set aside conflicting rules of national law as well as national procedural rules which might make it impossible in practice or excessively difficult to vindicate

---

90 See "Report of the Court of Justice on certain aspects of the application of the Treaty on European Union", in *Annual Report of the Court of Justice 1995*, p. 19 at p. 25.
91 Case 222/86 *Union nationale des entraîneurs et cadres techniques professionnels du football v. Heylens* [1987] ECR 4097.
92 Case C–312/93 *Peterbroeck v. Van Campenhout & Co.* [1995] ECR I–4599.
93 For that reason full authorities are not given.

rights claimed under Community law. This may extend to the provision of interim relief in order to protect putative rights under Community law while their existence or scope is being tested through the preliminary ruling procedure.

Where appropriate, and subject to the test of sufficient precision and the absence of conditions, national courts must give direct effect to rules of Community law in whatever form they may be presented. In the absence of direct effect, or in the absence of national legislation implementing a directive, the courts must attempt to interpret any existing national law in such a way as to achieve the result envisaged by the directive. National judicial authorities, including those responsible for investigating and prosecuting offences must use the same diligence in pursuing offences under Community law as for offences committed under ordinary national law.[94] Where an infringement of a Community law right has occurred sanctions applied by the courts to the offending party must be sufficient to ensure the effective protection of Community rights, and therefore to have a real deterrent effect so as to guarantee real and effective judicial protection of the rights concerned.[95] Where financial compensation is the measure adopted in order to achieve that objective, it must be adequate, in that it must enable the loss and damage actually sustained as a result of the discriminatory dismissal to be made good in full in accordance with the applicable national rules.[96]

Such a sanction may include awarding damages against a state where the state has committed a sufficiently serious breach of its obligations under Community law and that infringement has caused loss to an individual.

In cases involving points of European Community law, the national courts should approach the relevant provisions in the same manner as the Court of Justice itself (see Chapter 8 on methods of interpretation), and must also apply the general principles of Community law (see Chapter 4 above), such as the principles of proportionality, legal certainty and protection of fundamental rights. Of course, in such areas courts at all levels may avail themselves of the preliminary ruling procedure in order to seek a ruling on the interpretation of any treaty provision or

94   Case C–68/88 *Commission v. Greece* [1989] ECR 2965.
95   Case 79/83 *Harz v. Deutsche Tradax* [1984] ECR 1921.
96   Case C–271/91 *Marshall v. Southampton and South-West Hampshire Area Health Authority II* [1993] ECR I–4367.

upon the interpretation and even the validity of any other Community measure.[97] However, should a national court have doubts about the validity of a Community measure it may not, itself, rule upon that question but must refer the matter to the Court of Justice for a preliminary ruling.[98]

## THE IMPACT OF EUROPEAN UNION LAW ON NATIONAL LAW

In so far as the Union is "founded on the European Communities", which constitute its first pillar, the relationship between European Union law and national law is covered by the outline in the previous section of this chapter. The second and third pillars comprising a common foreign and security policy and provisions on police and judicial co-operation in criminal matters respectively remain as traditional intergovernmental agreements effective at the international level and governed by the principles of international law.

As originally drafted Article L (now Article 46) of the TEU firmly excluded the Court of Justice from exercising jurisdiction over matters covered by the second and third pillars, subject to the minor exception that conventions drawn up by the Council in the areas of judicial co-operation in criminal matters, customs co-operation or police co-operation might stipulate that the Court of Justice should have jurisdiction to interpret them. Consequently, the remaining provisions included under the second and third pillars were justiciable, if at all, only before the International Court of Justice. The revised wording of Article 46 (ex Article L) TEU, following the entry into force of the Treaty of Amsterdam, does however give wider scope to the Court of Justice. In particular the powers of the Court of Justice apply to Article 6(2) (ex Article F(2)) TEU, according to which "the Union shall respect fundamental rights, as guaranteed by the European Convention for the Protection of Human Rights and Fundamental Freedoms signed in Rome on 4 November 1950 and as they result from the constitutional traditions common to the Member States, as general principles of Community law", although this jurisdiction concerns only the action of the institutions.

The provisions on common foreign and security policy (Title V, TEU) remain wholly outside the scope of the Court's jurisdiction.

---

97  The Court of Justice has published a note for guidance on references by national courts for preliminary rulings both in its weekly bulletin (Issue No.34/96) and in the *Annual Report 1996*, p. 21.
98  Case 314/85 *Firma Foto-Frost v. Hauptzollamt Lübeck-Ost* [1987] ECR 4199.

However, Article 35 (ex Article K7)[99] enables Member States to make a declaration accepting the jurisdiction of the Court of Justice to give preliminary rulings on the validity and interpretation of framework decisions and decisions, on the interpretation of conventions established under that title and on the validity and interpretation of the measures implementing them. A Member State which so accepts the jurisdiction of the Court is able to specify whether all of the courts in its legal system or only those against whose decisions there is no judicial remedy under national law may request the Court of Justice to give a preliminary ruling. How this system will work in practice and its effect on national legal systems remains to be seen.

## THE EUROPEAN ECONOMIC AREA AND NATIONAL LAW

As we have seen in Chapter 3, the European Economic Area consists of two groups of Member States. On the one hand there are the 15 Member States of the European Union and on the other hand, three of the four remaining EFTA states, namely Iceland, Liechtenstein and Norway. EEA law operates differently in each group. So far as the EC–EEA states are concerned those parts of the *acquis communautaire* which were taken over by the EEA Agreement upon its entry into force were and remain applicable to them in accordance with the principles of applicability of European Community law outlined above. Nonetheless, certain specific adjustments will have to be made so that EFTA-EEA nationals may benefit from the provisions of the agreement in EC Member States. To that end and in order to facilitate the implementation of the EEA Agreement in the national legal orders of the EC–EEA states, a Council regulation on arrangements for implementing the EEA Agreement has been adopted.

In accordance with the previous case law of the Court of Justice,[1] it is held that international treaties concluded by the Community are an integral part of Community law and that such treaties may have direct effect within the Community in so far as they are unconditional and sufficiently precise. Those parts of the *acquis communautaire* taken over by the EEA (some 1600 regulations and directives listed in the annexes to the agreement) already constituted fully binding Community law in accordance with the principles outlined above.

---

99  The text of this article following the Treaty of Amsterdam bears no relation whatsoever to the text as included in the original TEU.
1   Case 181/73 *Haegeman v. Belgium* [1974] ECR 449 and Case 87/75 *Bresciani v. Amministrazione Italiana delle finanze* [1976] ECR 129.

For the EFTA-EEA states the position is much more complex and remains to be fully worked out by the EFTA Court and the national courts in the EFTA–EEA states. First it must be noted that the EEA Agreement, unlike the EC Treaty, does not imply any transfer of sovereignty from the contracting states to any central authorities. Thus the EEA institutions have no legislative competence but under the decision-making procedure acts adopted at EEA level enter into force in the Member States in accordance with their respective constitutional requirements.[2]

Article 7 of the EEA Agreement, which faintly echoes the wording of Article 249 (ex Article 189) of the EC Treaty, first provides that the acts referred to or contained in the annexes to this agreement (*i.e.* those parts of the *acquis communautaire* taken over by the EEA Agreement) are binding upon the contracting parties, and then states how they shall become part of the internal legal order of those parties. Thus "an act corresponding to an EEC regulation shall as such be made part of the internal legal order of the contracting parties" and "an act corresponding to an EEC directive shall leave to the authorities of the contracting parties the choice of form and method of implementation". Those provisions were addressed essentially to the EFTA–EEA states since the regulations and directives upon which the EEA acts are based will produce their effects within the EC states in accordance with the rules of Community law outlined above. Given that the EEA Agreement essentially has the characteristics of a traditional international treaty, the effects of Article 7 in the legal orders of the EFTA–EEA states depends upon whether or not they belong to the monist or dualist tradition. Of the three EFTA–EEA countries, only Liechenstein belongs to the monist tradition and therefore the acts corresponding to EEC regulations can have direct applicability and direct effect there. By contrast, the two Nordic countries are from the dualist tradition and therefore such acts must be explicitly incorporated into their domestic law before they can produce any effects.

In both the EC and the EEA legal systems, states have a choice of form and method for implementation. Nonetheless, as we have seen under the EC system, a failure to implement a directive within the required time-limit may result in its provisions having direct effect. Moreover, the possibility of national courts awarding financial compensation for loss incurred by individuals as a result of non-implementation is a powerful force for the Member States to fulfil their obligations by implementing directives timeously.

2  See Article 103 EEA.

## THE HUMAN RIGHTS CONVENTION AND EUROPEAN COMMUNITY LAW

We have seen in Chapter 4 that the protection of fundamental rights is one of the general principles of law upon which the European Court of Justice may draw as a source of European Community law. Since the *Stauder* case[3] in 1969 the Court has stated on numerous occasions that fundamental rights form part of the general principles of law which are protected by the Court of Justice. In the *Rutili* case in 1975[4] the Court of Justice first made explicit reference to the European Convention on Human Rights and Fundamental Freedoms.

Two years after the *Rutili* case, the European Parliament, the Council and the Commission issued a joint declaration in which they stressed "the prime importance they attach to the protection of fundamental rights as derived in particular from the constitutions of the Member States and the European Convention for the Protection of Human Rights and Fundamental Freedoms. In the exercise of their powers and in pursuance of the aims of the European Communities they respect and will continue to respect these rights".[5] Subsequently the three amending treaties have each made more and more explicit reference to the principles of fundamental rights. Thus the preamble to the Single European Act refers to respect for the fundamental rights recognised, *inter alia*, in the Convention, and Article 6 (ex Article F(2)) TEU provides that "the Union shall respect fundamental rights, as guaranteed by the European Convention for the Protection of Human Rights and Fundamental Freedoms ... and as they result from the constitutional traditions common to the Member States, as general principles of Community law". Moreover, in the field of development co-operation, Article 177 (ex Article 130u(2)) provides that Community policy in the area of development co-operation is to "contribute to the general objective of developing and consolidating democracy and the rule of law, and to that of respecting human rights and fundamental freedoms". The political conditions for accession to the European Union laid down by the European Council at Copenhagen include respect for fundamental rights and the Treaty of Amsterdam reinforced this by providing that where a Member State was found to have committed a serious and persistent breach of, *inter alia*, the principle of respect for fundamental rights as guaranteed under the Conven-

---

3  Case 29/69 *Stauder v. Stadt Ulm* [1969] ECR 419.
4  Case 36/75 *Rutili v. Minister for the Interior* [1975] ECR 1219.
5  Joint Declaration by the European Parliament, the Council and the Commission of April 5, 1977, OJ No.C 103, April 27, 1977.

tion, the other Member States might decide to suspend certain of the rights deriving from the application of the Treaty.

It is therefore abundantly clear that the principle of respect for fundamental rights forms an integral part both of Community law and the law of the European Union, and that the list of fundamental rights set out in the Convention and its protocols[5a] have a special role as a source for the identification of those rights. The question remains however of whether or not the European Community should itself become a party to the European Convention. Such a move would have considerable symbolic importance, reinforcing by way of a legally binding and enforceable commitment the unambiguous declarations outlined above. It would, moreover, avoid the risk of divergent interpretation of the Convention by the Court of Justice in Luxembourg and by the Human Rights Court in Strasbourg, as has already happened on at least two occasions.[6]

As the late Rolv Ryssdal, President of the European Court of Human Rights, stated in a recent speech[7]:

"There are, however, more concrete benefits to be gained from [Community] accession. Accession would provide the constitutional basis for the protection of human rights within the Union which has been lacking hitherto and with it an increase in legal certainty. It would compel the Union's legislative and executive authorities to have regard to potential human rights issues before adopting a particular course of action. It would prevent the Court of Justice from developing case law on human rights which is inconsistent with the Strasbourg jurisprudence. Above all, it would open the way for the Union's citizens to seek redress in Strasbourg in respect of Community measures. Thus the Community's autonomous legal system would be subject to

---

5a  See Vade-mecum VI.
 6  Compare the judgment of the Court of Justice in Joined Cases 46/87 and 227/88 *Hoechst AG v. Commission* [1989] ECR 2859 in which the Court of Justice, noting that there was no case law of the European Court of Human Rights on Article 8(1) of the Convention, found that "the protective scope of that article is concerned with the development of man's personal freedom and may not therefore extend to business premises" with the subsequent judgment of the Human Rights Court in *Niemietz v. Germany* (1992) A 251–B. Compare also the judgment of the Court of Justice in Case C–159/90 *Society for the Protection of Unborn Children v. Grogan* [1991] ECR I–4685 and the judgment of the Human Rights Court in *Open Door and Dublin Well Woman v. Ireland* (1992) A 246.
 7  Address given on May 12, 1995 to a Round Table on the developing role of the European Court of Justice.

the same external scrutiny as the legal systems of its Member States."

In that latter point lies one of the difficulties for a mechanism would have to be found to accommodate the task of the Court of Justice under Article 234 (ex Article 164 of the EC Treaty) in ensuring the observance of the law in the interpretation and application of that Treaty as well as the exclusive competence of the Court under Article 292 (ex Article 219) EC with the need to defer to the Strasbourg Court on human rights issues. Notwithstanding those difficulties the Commission of the European Communities has repeatedly proposed to the Council that the Community should accede to the Convention and in its most recent report[8] it considered the questions of the legal basis of such a potential accession and the monopoly of jurisdiction of the Court of Justice.

Following pressure from the Commission and from the European Parliament the Council in April 1994 asked the Court of Justice for an opinion pursuant to Article 228(6) (now Article 300(6)) of the EC Treaty on the compatibility with the Treaty of accession of the European Community to the Convention. The Court first found that it had insufficient information for it concerning the arrangements by which the Community envisages submitting to the present and future judicial control machinery established by the Convention to enable it to give an Opinion on the compatibility of Community accession to the Convention. It did however give an Opinion on the competence of the Community to accede to the Convention.[8a]

In its opinion on the European Economic Area Agreement[9] the Court of Justice had already accepted the principle that "the Community's competence in the field of international relations and its capacity to conclude international agreements necessarily entails the power to submit to the decisions of a court which is created or designated by such an agreement as regards the interpretation and application of its provisions".

Nonetheless, in its opinion on accession to the Human Rights Convention, the Court found that there were no treaty provisions which conferred on the Community institutions any general power to enact rules on human rights or to conclude international

---

8  "Accession of the Community to the European Convention on Human Rights and the Community legal order" of October 26, 1993.

8a  Opinion No. 2/94 on the accession of the Community to the European Convention on Human Rights [1996] ECR I–1759.

9  Opinion No. 1/91 on an agreement to establish the European Economic Area [1991] ECR I–6079.

conventions in that field. Moreover, such accession, since it would have fundamental institutional implications for the Community and for the Member States, would be of constitutional significance and would therefore be such as to go beyond the scope of Article 235 (now Article 308) of the EC Treaty. That provision is designed to fill the gap where no specific provisions of the Treaty confer on the Community institutions express or implied powers to act, if such powers appear nonetheless to be necessary to enable the Community to carry out its functions with a view to attaining one of the objectives laid down by the Treaty. The Court therefore concluded that such competence could only be conferred upon the Community by way of treaty amendment and that, as Community law at present stands, the Community has no competence to accede to the Convention.

While reinforcing the commitment of Member States to the protection of fundamental rights by introducing the possibilities of sanctioning "serious and persistent breaches" as outlined above, the Treaty of Amsterdam has conspicuously not conferred such a power on the Community.

# 6. THE EUROPEAN COURTS

*"Courts and camps are the only places to learn the world in"*, Lord Chesterfield, *Letters to his Son* (1774).

In a recent round of a popular BBC radio quiz competition, the question master asked "In which city is the European Court of Justice based?". The four contestants, each of whom had already demonstrated wide-ranging general knowledge, answered successively "Brussels", "The Hague", "Strasbourg" and "Paris". While two of those cities are indeed host to one or more of the Courts dealt with in this chapter, the answers illustrate not only ignorance as to the geographical location of the various courts but also a lack of awareness as to their respective functions. Those misunderstandings are also illustrated by the correspondence received in particular by the Court of Justice and the Court of Human Rights. I have an envelope addressed to the Court of Human Rights, The Haigh (sic), Luxembourg, Belgium, and my favourite, originally addressed to the European Court of Human Rights, Brussels, Belgium, having been readdressed by the postal authorities successively to Luxembourg and then Strasbourg was, apparently in despair, referred to Amnesty International.

The purpose of this chapter then is to describe the jurisdiction of the various courts whose location is shown on the map on page 168 and whose full postal addresses are to be found in the Vademecum. As demonstrated by the quiz contestants and the correspondence referred to above, the International Court of

Justice at The Hague also contributes to, and no doubt suffers from, the general confusion surrounding these judicial institutions.[10] Therefore it seems appropriate to include a brief description of its functions in this chapter although, as we shall see, its jurisdiction extends far beyond Europe, however that nebulous concept is defined. Moreover, that Court has spawned certain offspring which it is appropriate to mention here for the sake of completeness.

The final section of this chapter will give a brief answer to the question frequently asked of the courts themselves, various information services and citizens advice bureaux: "How do I bring my case before the European Court?"

Anyone hoping to find a description of the role and functions of the European Court of Auditors in these pages will, I am sorry to say, be disappointed. Although it is one of the five principal institutions of the European Community with the vital task of ensuring that the Community's finances are lawfully and prudently managed,[11] it has no judicial function and therefore falls outwith the scope of this book. Suffice it to mention here that it is based in Luxembourg and that, in the Treaty of Amsterdam,[12] it was given the power to bring proceedings before the Court of Justice for the purpose of protecting its own prerogatives — for example, if one of the other Institutions were to refuse to provide it with any document or other information which it needed to carry out its task.

Before dealing with the specific characteristics of each of the courts it must be acknowledged that a good deal of the confusion surrounding them arises from careless use of terminology, misguided attempts to abbreviate what are admittedly sometimes cumbersome official titles and, perhaps most dangerous of all, the careless use of acronyms. Thus ICJ and ECJ are prone to confusion, while TPI (in French) may stand for *Tribunal de première instance* or *Tribunal pénal international*. To avoid contributing further to this morass and perhaps even to begin to redress the

10  Even so eminent a lawyer as Horace Rumpole has been known to fall into such error:

 " 'So we're off to The Hague, are we?'
 '*You* may be, Mr Rumpole, but the Court of Human Rights sits in Strasbourg.'
 'Of course! That's the one I meant. So you're going to brief me in Strasbourg, are you? It'll make a change from the Uxbridge Magistrates Court.' " John Mortimer, *Rumpole and the Rights of Man*.

11  Art. 246 (ex Art. 188a) EC is even more laconic than Art. 220 (ex Art. 164) EC (see below), consisting only of the nine words "The Court of Auditors shall carry out the audit".

12  See new Art. 230 (ex Art. 173) EC.

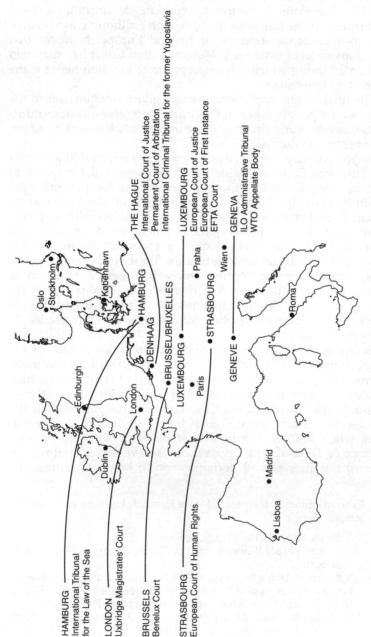

The European Courts

HAMBURG
International Tribunal
for the Law of the Sea

LONDON
Uxbridge Magistrates' Court

BRUSSELS
Benelux Court

STRASBOURG
European Court of Human Rights

THE HAGUE
International Court of Justice
Permanent Court of Arbitration
International Criminal Tribunal for the former Yugoslavia

LUXEMBOURG
European Court of Justice
European Court of First Instance
EFTA Court

GENEVA
ILO Administrative Tribunal
WTO Appellate Body

problem, it is suggested that readers of this book when writing undergraduate assignments, newspaper articles or letters to their Members of Parliament (especially of the European Parliament) should, when a particular court is first mentioned, give its full title, which is given as the heading of the sections below, indicating immediately afterwards which abbreviation or acronym (if you really must) you intend to use in the remainder of the text. Although in some languages the use of elegant variation (that is the avoidance of repetition by using different terms or euphemisms to describe the same thing) is encouraged, it is not a good idea and looks pretentious in English. So once an abbreviation has been selected it should be used consistently throughout the text. On a final point of style, there is no point in laboriously including in brackets after the first mention of a particular court "hereinafter referred to as ... " if you do not thereinafter refer to it.

## THE COURT OF JUSTICE OF THE EUROPEAN COMMUNITIES[13]

That full title may conveniently be abridged to "European Court of Justice" or just "the Court of Justice". The contractions "the European Court" or just "the Court" should only be used in circumstances where there is no ambiguity possible as to the Court which is meant. Some writers refer to the "E.U. Court", a term which invites confusion and is, in any event, inaccurate in terms of the jurisdiction of the Court of Justice. Many more writers, including specialists in the field, use the abbreviation ECJ. While this may be a convenient shorthand form for notetaking it is awkward to pronounce and is not a true acronym since it is itself based upon an abbreviated form of the title of the institution.

### Where is it?

Luxembourg. This was made clear in unequivocal terms by a decision of the representatives of the governments of the Member States on the provisional location of the Community institutions,[14] Article 3 of which provides that "the Court of Justice shall remain

---

13  For a detailed account of the organisation and jurisdiction of the Court of Justice see L. Neville Brown and Tom Kennedy, *Brown and Jacobs', The Court of Justice of the European Communities* (4th ed., 1994 with 1995 update).

14  Adopted on April 8, 1965 but, since it entered into force only on the same date as the Merger Treaty (July 1, 1967), not published in the Official Journal until 1967 (OJ 152 of July 13, 1967).

in Luxembourg". This was confirmed by a decision taken at the Edinburgh Summit in 1992.[15]

## When was it established?

The Treaty establishing the European Coal and Steel Community included, from the outset, a Court of Justice (Article 7). The appointments of the seven Judges and two Advocates General of that Court took effect on December 4, 1952 and that date is still regarded as the anniversary of the establishment of the Court of Justice.

On the same day as the signature of the EEC Treaty and the EURATOM Treaty (the Treaties of Rome) on March 25 1957, the Member States adopted a Convention on certain institutions common to the European Communities.[16] That Convention created a single Court of Justice with jurisdiction over the two new Communities and replacing the Court of Justice of the Coal and Steel Community. The triple jurisdiction of the single court is the reason for which the full title of the Court includes the word "Communities" in the plural. The members of the single court were sworn in on October 7, 1958 and that date still represents the beginning of the legal year for the Court of Justice, the date upon which the composition of the Chambers of the Court is settled each year and upon which, every three years, the mandates of one half of the members of the Court expire.

## Who sits on it?

The Court of Justice is currently composed of 15 Judges and nine Advocates General.[17] Although this is not formally required by the Treaty, the Court of Justice has always consisted of a number

---

15  Decision taken by common agreement between the representatives of the governments of the Member States on the location of the seats of the institutions and of certain bodies and departments of the European Communities of December 12, 1992 (OJ C 341 of December 23, 1992, p. 1).

16  Like the Treaties, this Convention has not been published in the Official Journal but is included in the volume of selected instruments taken from the Treaties published by the Office for Official Publications in all 11 languages.

17  For a detailed discussion of the composition of the Court of Justice see Tom Kennedy, "Thirteen Russians! – The Composition of the European Court of Justice" in *Legal Reasoning and Judicial Interpretation of European Law: Essays in honour of Lord Mackenzie Stuart* (Trenton Publishing, 1996) at p. 69.

of Judges sufficient for there to be one from each Member State.[18]

According to the Treaties,[19] "the Judges and Advocates General shall be chosen from persons whose independence is beyond doubt and who possess the qualifications required for appointment to the highest judicial offices in their respective countries or who are jurists of recognised competence", wording adapted from the equivalent provisions in the Statute of the International Court of Justice. This broad qualification has sometimes given rise to the criticism, particularly in the British press and from some in legal circles, that the Court is dominated by academics with no experience of senior judicial office. Such criticism is both erroneous[20] and misplaced since such a breadth of experience is a source of strength to the Court as a whole. This was recognised by the Select Committee of the House of Lords on the European Communities which noted that "a treaty amendment which would exclude professors or administrators would narrow the range of professional experience available to the Court and would be seen as trying to impose on other Member States a particularly British view of the best background for senior judicial office".[21]

Both Judges and Advocates General are appointed for a renewable mandate of six years. Most have their mandate renewed at least once and the average length of service on the Court is about nine years. It may be noted that a six-year mandate, which is shorter than the mandate of Judges on the International Court of

18   This was explicitly stated by the Member States in 1993 when they agreed that each Member State would propose one Judge for appointment. See conclusions of the European Council held at Brussels on December 10 and 11, 1993, *Bulletin of the EC* (1993), Vol. 26, No. 12, p. 17.

19   Article 223 (ex Article 167) of the EC Treaty. Article 139 of the EAEC Treaty is identically worded and the Convention on Common Institutions added a new Article 32(b) to the ECSC Treaty in the same terms.

20   Of the present 15 Judges, 12 have direct experience of senior judicial or quasi-judicial functions, including those of Attorney General, Advocate General of the Court of Justice itself or as a member of the Court of First Instance, while seven have held chairs of law (usually European Community law or Public International law) only two come from an almost exclusively academic background; six have held senior government appointments and two have held high political office. The total comes to more than 15 since it is common in many Member States for academics to be appointed to judicial posts and several have had distinguished careers in more than one field of activity.

21   Select Committee on the European Communities, Report on the 1996 Intergovernmental Conference (1996 H.L. 105) Session 94–95, 21st Report, at para. 260.

Justice (see below) is nonetheless longer than that of the European Parliament, European Commission or of any of the governments of the Member States.[22] Moreover, the dates of expiry of the mandates are staggered so that, every three years, those of half of the Judges expire. This, when combined with the possibility of renewal gives an important degree of stability and continuity to the composition of the Court.

**What does it do?**

According to the Treaties the task of the Court is to "ensure that in the interpretation and application of the Treaty the law is observed". While that wording may appear, at first sight, somewhat laconic, or even vague, it is that provision which underpins the Court's primary role as the constitutional court of the European Communities. In that capacity it may have to define the extent of the powers of the Community institutions as laid down in the Treaty, and establish the balance of powers between the political institutions among themselves or between the Community institutions on the one hand and the Member States on the other. It also acts as an administrative court reviewing the legality of acts of the Community institutions, as a court of appeal, from decisions of the Court of First Instance and even, in a sense, as a criminal court when it is called upon to establish whether the Member States have failed to fulfil their obligations under the Treaties. The various types of cases which may be brought before the Court of Justice are shown on the diagram on page 173.

Broadly speaking the jurisdiction of the Court of Justice may be considered to break down into three principal tasks. First, it ensures that the Member States fulfil the obligations which they have entered into under the Treaty. In this respect the European Commission acts in the manner of a public prosecutor, investigating alleged infringements, bringing cases before the Court of Justice pursuant to Article 226 (ex Article 169) of the EC Treaty and, if necessary, inviting the Court of Justice to impose a financial penalty on a Member State which fails to give effect to an earlier judgment of the Court.

Secondly, the Court ensures that the other institutions carry out their work lawfully, that is to say within the scope of the powers conferred upon them by the Treaties, in accordance with the procedures laid down for the exercise of those powers and in conformity with the Treaties themselves. In this context the Court of Justice is called upon to act both as an administrative court carrying out judicial review of the administrative acts of the institutions and as a constitutional court keeping the institutional

22   The President of the French Republic holds office for seven years.

## Jurisdiction of the Court of Justice of the European Communities

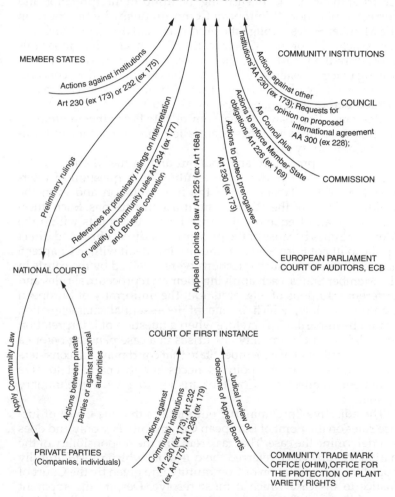

balance as between the various institutions as well as the balance
between the exercise of the powers of the institutions and those
remaining in the hands of the Member States.

Thirdly, perhaps the most important and influential task of the
Court of Justice is that of ensuring the uniform interpretation and
correct application of European Community law by the courts in
the Member States through the procedure laid down in Article 234
(ex Article 177) of the EC Treaty. It has been said that under this
procedure the Court has to hear cases which it does not decide,
arising in legal systems over which it has no jurisdiction, concerning the validity of legal rules of which it has no knowledge and
argued before it in a language which most of the judges do not
understand. The answer to that conundrum lies in the preliminary
ruling procedure which has been called the cornerstone of European Community law.

Under this procedure any court in any of the Member States
may request the Court to give a ruling on a question of interpretation of the Treaties or of the interpretation and even the
validity of acts of the other Community institutions. Such questions may, and frequently do, arise before the courts within the
Member States because of the principles of direct effect and direct
applicability of European Community law dealt with in Chapter 5
above. If, however, such questions were resolved by the courts in
the Member States, each applying their own procedural rules and
different traditions of interpretation, the uniformity of European
Community law, which is one of its essential characteristics,
would be imperilled. Therefore when a question of interpretation
(or validity) of Community law arises in a case pending before a
court or a tribunal of a Member State that court may, if it considers
that a decision on the point is necessary to enable it to give
judgment, request the Court of Justice to give a preliminary
ruling.

The adjective "preliminary" emphasises that the Court of Justice rules on the point of European Community law only and does
not determine the case. That task remains the responsibility of the
national court which referred the question, which must faithfully
apply the interpretation of Community law given by the Court of
Justice to the case which it must resolve. Despite the apparent
unwieldiness of this procedure it works extremely well and it is
for good reason that it has been called the keystone of the European Communities. Indeed it has been in cases submitted to it
under that procedure that the Court of Justice has developed all of
the main principles of European Community law and cases
referred under that procedure account for rather more than half of
the total work of the Court.

Although national courts from whose decisions there is no legal
redress are obliged to refer any question of European Community

law which arises before them to the European Court of Justice, it must be emphasised that the procedure is in no sense a form of appeal to the European Court. Rather it is a procedure in which the national courts and the European Court collaborate in establishing the correct interpretation of the law and then applying it for the solution of a particular case.

## How does it work?

Cases may be brought before the Court in two different ways. So-called "direct actions" arise when parties lodge their dispute directly before the Court of Justice itself or, to put it another way, one party asks the Court of Justice for a remedy against another. Examples of such direct action include proceedings brought by the Commission against a Member State for failing to fulfil its obligations, a Member State against an institution for allegedly acting outside the scope of its powers (*ultra vires*) or an appeal against a decision of the Court of First Instance. The other category of cases which may be regarded as "indirect actions" are those which originate before the courts of Member States resulting in a request to the Court of Justice for a preliminary ruling as outlined in the previous section.

It is not appropriate in this context to explain the details of the Court's procedure although some important points are mentioned in the section below on how to bring a case before the European Court and the handling of a typical case appears from the diagram on p. 177. However, three general points may be made.

First, the Registry plays a central role in the handling of all cases. In direct actions, documents are transmitted between the parties through the intermediary of the Court's Registry. Thus an applicant (whether a Member State, a Community institution or a corporation) serves its application on the Court Registry. The Registry then serves it on the defendant and in due course receives the defence which is then officially transmitted to the applicant. Similarly in preliminary rulings, the court of the Member State which needs the answer to a question of the interpretation of Community law sends its questions accompanied by a file setting out the circumstances of the case and the respective arguments of the parties before it to the Registry of the Court which notifies it to the governments of all of the Member States[23] and the other Community institutions. In turn all those who receive notification of a preliminary ruling are entitled to

---

23  And, since 1995, the three EFTA states which are members of the European Economic Area.

submit written observations to the Court as to how the national court's questions should be answered.

Secondly, the greatest part of the work carried out by the Court of Justice is conducted in writing. As a result, hearings before the Court of Justice are generally relatively short, rarely lasting more than two to three hours and they generally have limited importance in determining the outcome of a given case.

Thirdly, a particular feature of the procedure before the Court of Justice is the role of the Advocate General. Although there are analagous creatures in certain national legal systems, the role of the Advocate General in the Court of Justice is *sui generis*. So much so that he has been called "the duck-billed platypus of judicial zoology".[24] As we have already seen, the Court has nine Advocates General, one of whom is assigned to each case lodged before the Court. His task is to help the Court to arrive at its decision by delivering an Opinion in which he reviews the legal issues arising in the case and proposes a solution which the Court may adopt. He does so acting in complete independence and impartiality and, even where the Court disagrees with his Opinion, as it is quite entitled to do so, that Opinion is invariably the starting point for the Judges' deliberations. Moreover, given the standing of the Advocates General, who must hold the same qualifications as those of the Judges, they usually follow the Opinion wholly or to a very great extent. Even where the Court does not follow the Advocate General's Opinion its authority is such that it may be regarded in the same way as a dissenting opinion in courts where such dissent is permitted.

I am commonly asked in what proportion of cases the Advocate General is followed by the Court. However, unfortunately, there is no precise answer to that question. One may say that in particularly difficult cases there is more room for divergence of views. Therefore it may be more likely for the Advocate General's Opinion not to be followed in such cases. In other cases the Court might reach the same result as the Advocate General but for different reasons, or it might find that it can dispose of the case on one limited basis only whereas the Advocate General will have covered all of the aspects of the case.

**What language does it use?**

The Court of Justice may deal with cases in any of the 11 official languages of the European Communities or in Irish.[25] All languages are treated equally. However, the complexities which

24  By Advocate General (later Judge) Mancini.
25  See Article 29 of the Court's Rules of Procedure. It has not yet been called upon to deal with a case in Irish.

## Outline of Procedure Before the Court of Justice

---

### I. INITIATION OF CASE

**Cases Lodged:**
➡ in a direct action by application;

➡ In a request for a preliminary ruling by judgment or order of the national court;

**Notification by Court Registry;**
➡ to defendant;

➡ to parties in national proceedings, to EEA Member States, EC institutions and ESA;

➡ publication in Official Journal

---

### II. WRITTEN PROCEDURE

➡ In a direct action:
→ defence
→ reply by applicant
→ rejoinder by defendant

➡ In a preliminary ruling:
→ written observations submitted, by parties, member States and institutions who so wish.

---

### III. PREPARATION BY THE COURT

➡ Designation of Judge-rapporteur and advocate general;
➡ Judge-rapporteur draws up preliminary report;
➡ General meeting with all judges and advocates general for case management decisions (hearing by chamber or plenary session, date of hearing, etc.).

---

### IV. ORAL PROCEDURE

**Public Hearing**
➡ report for the hearing published
→ In a direct action
oral arguments on behalf of parties and interviewers.

→ In a preliminary ruling
oral observations submitted by parties, Member States and institutions who so wish.

**Advocate General's Opinion**
➡ Notified to judges in open court at a public sitting.

---

### V. JUDGMENT

➡ Deliberation by judges
➡ Adoption of text of judgment
➡ Delivery of judgment in open court

---

### VI. PUBLICATION

➡ Full text available in 11 languages immediately after delivery;
➡ Full text available at www.curia.eu.int in 11 languages later the same day;
➡ Court weekly bulletin contains summaries of all judgments;
➡ Authentic text, with Advocate General's opinion summary and indexing published in European Court Reports and CELEX datanase.

might arise from such a multilingual system, and the attendant costs, are attenuated by two practices. First, each case is dealt with in its own language known as "the language of the case" or "the language of procedure". In direct actions that language is chosen by the applicant save where the applicant is a Community institution in which the defendant selects the language of procedure. In cases referred for a preliminary ruling the language of the case is that used by the national court making the reference. Secondly, the members of the Court of Justice have adopted a common working language in which they conduct their deliberations and in which internal communications are drafted. For essentially historical reasons that language is French and that situation is unlikely to be changed. Nonetheless, since Community law must be uniformly interpreted and applied throughout the 15 Member States the judgments of the Court must be accessible to judges and lawyers in the Member States, therefore all of the Court's judgments and the Opinions of the Advocates General are translated into all 11 Community languages and published in the official series of reports (see Chapter 7 below).

## THE COURT OF FIRST INSTANCE OF THE EUROPEAN COMMUNITIES

Generally abbreviated to "Court of First Instance" in English, thus giving rise to the acronym "CFI". Like ECJ, this acronym is not easy to pronounce and is best avoided except for notetaking. Use of that acronym is discouraged by the Court of First Instance itself and it is never used in published documents emanating from either the Court of First Instance or the Court of Justice. In French the matter is simplified since the Court of First Instance is called *"Tribunal de première instance"* thus *le Tribunal* is distinct from *la Cour*.[26] Some writers import the French term *Tribunal* into English texts. However, to call the Court of First Instance "the Tribunal" is not accurate and, particularly to those familiar with the English legal system, may itself be a source of confusion and misapprehension as to the nature and status of that Court.

**Where is it?**

Luxembourg. This is implicit in Article 225 (ex Article 168(a)) of the EC Treaty which provides that "a Court of First Instance shall

---

26   In Spanish the two courts are called, respectively, *Tribunal de Justicia* and *Tribunal de Primera Instancia*.

be *attached* to the Court of Justice" (emphasis added). It was confirmed by the decision of the Governments of the Member States at Edinburgh. Article 1(d) provides that "the Court of Justice and the Court of First Instance shall have their seats in Luxembourg".[27]

The Court of First Instance thus occupies part of the same building complex as the Court of Justice and shares common administrative facilities (library, translation, personnel, finance, press and information and internal services) with the Court of Justice. The Court of First Instance, however, has its own independent Registry which carries out functions equivalent to those of the Court Registry in administering the procedure and ensuring the flow of documents.

**When was it established?**

Article 225 (ex Article 168(a)) was added to the EC Treaty by the Single European Act signed in Luxembourg and at The Hague in February 1986[28] and the details of the establishment of the new Court were laid down in a Council decision in October 1988.[29] The implementation of that decision and the appointment of the members of the new Court took a further year and so it was not until October 11, 1989 that the President of the Court of Justice was able to make the formal declaration that "the Court of First Instance has been constituted in accordance with law" which enabled it to start functioning.

**Who sits on it?**

Like its progenitor the Court of Justice, the Court of First Instance consists of 15 members, including one from each Member State. The qualifications laid down in Article 225(3) (ex Article 168(a)(3))

---

27  See n. 15 above.
28  OJ L 169 of June 29, 1987. For a full account of the establishment of the Court of First Instance see Kennedy, "The Essential Minimum: the establishment of the Court of First Instance" [1989] 14 E.L. Rev. 7 and "The Essential Minimum: a postscript" [1990] 15 E.L. Rev. 54.
29  Decision 88/591 (ECSC, EEC, EURATOM) establishing a Court of First Instance of the European Communities, 1988 (OJ L 319, November 25, 1988, published with corrigenda in 1989 OJ C 215 August 21, 1989).

again require the members of the Court of First Instance to be chosen from persons whose independence is beyond doubt but adds that they must "possess the ability required for appointment to judicial office". In order to ensure that this was not interpreted as including the lowest layers of the judiciary in the Member States the first recital in the preamble to the Council decision of October 24, 1988 emphasises that the Court of First Instance is to "exercise important judicial functions" and that its members should "possess the ability required for performing such functions". The Judges hold office for six years with the possibility of renewal and the mandates expire in staggered fashion every three years. The President of the Court of First Instance is elected for a three-year mandate by the other members of the Court.

Unlike the Court of Justice there are no permanent Advocates General. However, in certain cases one of the Judges of the Court of First Instance may be called upon to perform the task of an Advocate General if it is considered by the Court of First Instance, sitting in plenary session, that the legal difficulty or the factual complexity of the case so requires. This possibility has only rarely been called upon.

**What does it do?**

There were two reasons behind the establishment of the Court of First Instance. First, to relieve the Court of Justice of a part of its workload so as to enable it better to cope with its central tasks of ensuring the uniform interpretation of European Community law and second, to make the protection of individual rights (including rights of corporations) more like that provided in the Member States in which there is invariably the possibility of a two-tier judicial review. For the same reason, Article 225(1) (ex Article 168(a)) provides that decisions of the Court of First Instance shall be subject to an appeal to the Court of Justice, albeit limited to an appeal on a point of law only.

In its original drafting, Article 168(a) EC (now Article 225(1)) referred to "certain categories of cases brought by natural or legal persons", that is to say by private individuals or companies. That extra phrase had the effect of preventing cases brought by Member States or Community institutions from being lodged before the Court of First Instance. However, it was deleted by the Treaty on European Union (the Maastricht Treaty) so that it is possible that, at some time in the future, cases brought by the Commission against Member States for failure to fulfil their obligations, or cases brought by Member States against institutions for exceeding their authority may be brought before the Court of First Instance.

For the time being, the Council, by the establishing decision of

1988 and two subsequent amendments,[30] has transferred *all* cases brought by natural or legal persons against Community institutions to the jurisdiction of the Court of First Instance which now has the maximum scope of jurisdiction allowed to it under Article 168(a) of the EC Treaty in the wording prior to amendment by the TEU.

The cases it may now deal with therefore include:

- challenges to Commission decisions under the Community competition regulations, including challenges by undertakings to decisions concerning the award of aid by Member States (the Member States concerned may only challenge such decisions before the Court of Justice);
- cases brought under the ECSC Treaty;
- challenges to anti-dumping regulations adopted by the Commission or the Council;
- claims for compensation for damage caused by the Community institutions or their servants in the course of their duties;
- cases brought by Community officials against the institutions acting in their capacity as employers;
- challenges to the decisions of the appeal boards of the European Community Trademark Office or the Plant Variety Rights Office.

## How does it work?

Having been modelled closely on the procedure before the Court of Justice, the procedure before the Court of First Instance essentially follows that outlined in the diagram on p. 177 showing the procedure in the case of direct actions. Similarities with that procedure include the exchange of written pleadings which must contain all of the evidence and arguments relied upon and the language regime in which the applicant decides which language is to be used as the language of the case. The principal differences are that cases are immediately assigned to a Chamber of the Court of First Instance when they are lodged, only being referred to a larger Chamber or to the full Court where they are of sufficient importance to warrant such a course. A case referred to the full

---

30  By the first of those amendments made by decision of June 8, 1993 the Council decided to transfer to the Court of First Instance all cases brought by natural or legal persons with the exception of cases involving anti-dumping measures (1993 OJ L 144 of June 16, 1993, p. 21), and that remaining category was transferred to the jurisdiction of the Court of First Instance by a Council decision of March 7, 1994 (OJ L 66 of March 10, 1994, p. 29).

Court of First Instance will also be, by definition, sufficiently complex and important to warrant the assistance of an Advocate General as outlined above. Finally, because of the essentially factual nature of the disputes in many of the cases brought before the Court of First Instance, its rules of procedure provide explicitly for preliminary meetings or hearings at which factual issues may be settled prior to the hearing of the legal arguments. The language regime is the same as that of the Court of Justice.

## THE EFTA COURT[31]

For once it is appropriate to use the acronym in conjunction with this Court, partly because it is easy to pronounce but, more importantly because the acronym is included in the official title of the Court as it appears on its own publications and in the instrument by which it was established.[32]

### Where is it?

The seat of the EFTA Court has been in Luxembourg since September 1, 1996 having moved there from Geneva where it was originally established in January 1994. The EFTA Court has the necessary office facilities in one of the buildings of the European Parliament but holds its public hearings when necessary in a room rented from a local hotel.

### When was it established?

The EFTA Court was established under the agreement on the European Economic Area (EEA) of May 2, 1992.[33] During the negotiations for the establishment of the EEA it was originally planned to set up a separate EEA Court which would comprise both judges from the European Court of Justice and from the EFTA states. However, in an opinion requested pursuant to Article 228 (now Article 300) of the EC Treaty[34] the Court of Justice rejected

31    For a general account of the composition, jurisdiction and procedure before the EFTA Court following its reorganisation in 1995 following the accession to the EU of Austria, Finland and Sweden, see P. Christiansen, "The EFTA Court" (1997) 22 El Rev. 539.
32    Although EFTA is the acronym for the European Free Trade Association whose official language is English, it remains unchanged in the other official language versions of the Court's name which are "EFTA–Gerichtshof", "EFTA–dómstóllinn" and "EFTA–domstolen" in German, Icelandic and Norwegian respectively.
33    For the change in composition of the European Economic Area see Chapter II above and, in particular, the diagram on p. 50.
34    Opinion 1/91 of December 14, 1991 [1991] ECR I–6079.

that proposal and held that the system of judicial supervision which was envisaged was incompatible with the EEC Treaty. Following that negative Opinion, a separate EFTA court was set up with jurisdiction corresponding, in large measure, to that of the Court of Justice and the Court of First Instance of the European Communities. In a second opinion on the subject the Court of Justice found that that system was compatible with the EC Treaty.[35]

**Who sits on it?**

Since the accession of Austria, Finland and Sweden to the European Union and that of Liechtenstein to the EEA, the EFTA Court has, since July 1, 1996, consisted of three judges appointed by the governments of Iceland, Liechtenstein and Norway by common accord. In accordance with Articles 20 to 38 of the EFTA Surveillance Authority ("ESA") and Court Agreement the judges are chosen from persons whose independence is beyond doubt and who possess the qualifications required to appointments to the highest judicial offices in their respective countries or who are jurisconsults of recognised competence. Like their opposite numbers in the Court of Justice and Court of First Instance of the European Communities they are appointed by common accord of the governments of the EFTA states for a term of six years which is renewable, as is the three-year term of office of the President of the EFTA Court who is elected by the judges from among their number. Article 29 of the ESA/Court Agreement[36] provides that decisions of the EFTA Court are valid only when all of its members are sitting. Therefore in the event that one of the judges is disqualified from sitting or is otherwise unable to attend, an *ad hoc* judge is selected by the other two judges from a list drawn up by common accord between the governments of the Member States. A list comprising two qualified lawyers each from Iceland, Liechtenstein and Norway was drawn up by the governments of the three countries and they were sworn in by the EFTA Court in November 1997.

**What does it do?**

The duties of the EFTA Court correspond in essence to those carried out by the European Court of Justice and the Court of First Instance in respect of the European Community Member States.

Thus, like the Court of Justice, the EFTA Court may hear either direct actions or be asked for advisory opinions by courts of the

---

35  Opinion 1/92 of April 10, 1992 [1992] ECR I–2821.
36  OJ L 344 December 31, 1994, p. 1.

EFTA States (except those of Switzerland which is a member of EFTA but not of the EEA). Direct actions may be brought against a contracting EFTA State either by another state or by the ESA concerning either an infringement of the EEA Agreement or a dispute on the interpretation or application of that agreement. Although such actions correspond to the provisions of Articles 226 (ex Article 169) and 227 (ex Article 170) EC, unlike the latter provision, the EFTA states are not under an obligation to refer such a dispute to the ESA prior to bringing proceedings against an offending State. Secondly, actions may be brought for the annulment of decisions by the ESA under Article 36 of the ESA/Court Agreement which parallels Article 230 (ex Article 173) EC Curiously, none of the other organs of the EEA may be subject to such annulment proceedings so the EFTA Court cannot carry out judicial review of legislative acts adopted by the EEA Joint Committee. Thirdly, by analogy with Article 232 (ex Article 175) EC, actions may be brought against the ESA for its failure to act when legally required to do so. Finally, in the same way that national courts of the EC Member States may ask the Court of Justice for a preliminary ruling, those of the EFTA states parties to the EEA Agreement may request an advisory opinion from the EFTA Court on the interpretation of the EEA Agreement (see Article 34 of the ESA/Court Agreement). There are however two important distinctions between the EFTA procedure and the Community's reference procedure. First, although all courts in the EFTA-EEA states may ask the EFTA Court for an advisory opinion there is no equivalent to the third paragraph of Article 234 (ex Article 177) of the EC Treaty which *requires* courts from whose decision there is no legal redress to request a preliminary ruling. Secondly, whereas the preliminary rulings given by the Court of Justice are, according to the case law of the Court itself, binding upon the court making the request, the decisions of the EFTA Court are, as their name suggests, advisory and might, in theory at least, be disregarded by the national court which had asked for it.

**How does it work?**

The procedure of the EFTA Court laid down in the Statute[37] and its rules of procedure[38] is broadly similar to that of the Court of Justice and the Court of First Instance. The principle differences

37   Protocol 5 to the ESA/Court Agreement on the Statute of the EFTA Court.
38   Originally adopted by the EFTA Court on January 4, and February 1, 1994 and later amended on August 22, 1996 following the reorganisation of the Court after the accession of Austria, Sweden and Finland to the EU.

follow from certain specific features of the EFTA Court, thus, for example, there is no provision for an Advocate General's Opinion to be delivered. The language of the EFTA Court is always English and Article 25(1) of the Rules of Procedure specifies that this covers the whole procedure including deliberations, minutes and decisions of the Court. English must also be used in the written and oral parts of the procedure by parties, interveners, the EFTA states, the ESA, the European Community and the Commission of the European Communities in any direct action. However, where an advisory opinion is requested by a court in one of the EFTA EEA Member States it is submitted in the language of the referring court and the Court itself makes the arrangements for the request to be translated into English. The resulting advisory opinion given by the Court is made available and is authentic both in English and in the language of the referring court. In the report of the EFTA Court advisory opinions are published in both languages with the English on one side of the page and the equivalent text in German, Icelandic or Norwegian on the opposite page.

## THE EUROPEAN COURT OF HUMAN RIGHTS[39]

This is the other of the two main European courts which are so often confused with one another. Because of that confusion which I have already referred to several times, the epithet European Court should only be used in connection with it when absolutely no ambiguity is possible. Even then the contraction "Human Rights Court" is preferable and the acronym ECtHR should be used only for notetaking and footnote purposes. Note that ECHR refers to the European Convention on Human Rights and Fundamental Freedoms and ECnHR or ECommHR refers to the European Commission of Human Rights.

We have already seen in Chapter 2 that the European Convention on Human Rights and Fundamental Freedoms (hereafter "the Convention") and its related enforcement machinery (the Court and Commission of Human Rights) constitute the single greatest achievement (but by no means the only one) of the

---

39  For a general review of the Human Rights Convention, including the operation of the enforcement procedure, the practice and procedure of both the Commission and Court of Human Rights, see Harris, O'Boyle and Warbrick, *Law of the European Convention on Human Rights* (Butterworths, 1996). For a detailed account of the changes brought about to the control mechanism by Protocol No. 11, see Drzemczewski, "A Major Overhaul of the European Human Rights Convention Control Mechanism: Protocol No. 11", published in *Collected Courses of the Academy of European Law at the European University Institute, Florence* (1995), Vol. VI, Book 2.

Council of Europe. It does no harm to repeat that the Council of Europe is an intergovernmental organisation now consisting of forty European States with a further five having special guest status (see lists in Vade-mecum X). Just as the organisation, the Council of Europe, is frequently and understandably confused with the European Council, or the Council of the European Union, which are two institutions of the European Union, so also does the European Commission of Human Rights, part of the Convention enforcement machinery, suffer confusion with the European Commission, one of the principal institutions of the European Communities.

**Where is it?**

Strasbourg, which is the home of the Council of Europe and the meeting-place for its Parliamentary Assembly, Council of Ministers and Secretariat General. A separate building housing the European Court of Human Rights was opened in 1965. This building, now dwarfed by the building of the Parliamentary Assembly which is used equally for the plenary sessions of the European Parliament, proved chronically inadequate for many years. In 1995 the Human Rights Directorate, the Human Rights Court and Human Rights Commission moved into a magnificent new building designed by Sir Richard Rogers.[40]

**When was it established**

The European Convention on Human Rights[41] was adopted by the original 10 Member States of the Council of Europe on November 4, 1950. Article 19 of the Convention established the Court in order to "ensure the observance of the engagements undertaken by the High Contracting parties" and the Court was established on January 21, 1959 after eight Member States had made declarations recognising its compulsory jurisdiction.[42]

During the 1980s the workload of the Human Rights Court and the Commission increased exponentially and it was widely recognised that the average time of over five years taken by "the machinery" to deal with cases was unacceptable. Furthermore, the gradual re-establishment of democratic government and the rule of law in the Central and Eastern European countries, the Baltic States, and the former constituent States of the Soviet Union led to an increase in the number of Member States of the Council,

40   For Horace Rumpole's description of the building see Chapter 10, p. 311 below.
41   87 UNTS 103; ETS 5.
42   Articles 46 and 56 of the Convention.

signatories to the Convention and a massive foreseeable increase in the case load.

In order to deal with this situation it was decided to establish a single, full-time Court which would carry out the tasks both of the existing (part-time) Court and the Commission. Following lengthy and difficult negotiations between the Member States of the Council of Europe, Protocol No 11, restructuring the control machinery established by the Convention, was adopted on May 11, 1994.[43] According to Article 4 of Protocol No 11 it will enter into force on the first day of the month following the expiry of one year from the date on which all parties to the Convention have expressed their consent to be bound by the protocol. The last instrument of ratification, that of Italy, was deposited on October 1, 1997 and so Protocol No 11 took effect on November 1, 1998. The text which follows describes the situation following the entry into effect of Protocol No 11.

**Who sits on it?**

According to the new Articles 20 and 21 of the Convention, the Court will consist of a number of judges equal to that of the High Contracting parties (at present 40) who must be of "high moral character and must either possess the qualifications required for appointment to high judicial office or be jurisconsults of recognised competence", wording again similar to the statement of qualifications for judges of the European Community Courts, the EFTA Court and the International Court of Justice. The essential characteristic of the new court, by comparison with its predecessor, is that it will be permanent, thus judges are precluded from engaging in any activity which is incompatible with the demands of a full-time office. As in the past, the judges are elected by the Parliamentary Assembly of the Council of Europe on the basis of a list of three candidates nominated by each High Contracting party. The term of office of the judges is reduced to six years and a triennial renewal system similar to that of the Court of Justice of the European Communities is established.

For the purposes of considering cases brought before it the Court sits in committees of three judges, in Chambers of seven judges or in a Grand Chamber of 17 judges. The Grand Chamber

---

43  ETS 155. The text of Protocol No 11 is published as an annex to the current brochure of the Council of Europe which contains the text of the Convention and those of the first protocol and Protocols Nos 4, 6, 7, 9 and 10. For the background to the reforms and the eventual adoption of the 11th Protocol see the "Explanatory Report to the 11th Protocol, Council of Europe, 1994", published in (1994) 17 E.H.R.R. 514 and (1994) 15 H.R.L.J. 86.

will be the largest judicial formation called upon to deal with particularly serious or important cases referred to it and the complete Court or plenary will only sit for general purposes, such as the adoption or amendment of the rules of procedure, the election of the President of the Court and the Presidents of the Chambers.

When a case is dealt with by a Chamber or by the Grand Chamber the judge, who is a national of the State Party concerned, sits *ex officio* as a member of the Chamber; in the case of proceedings before the Grand Chamber this represents an exception to the rule that when a case is referred to the Grand Chamber, only the President of the Chamber which delivered the judgment under review will sit in the Grand Chamber.[44]

**What does it do?**

The role of the Human Rights Court remains that of ensuring the observance by the contracting states of the obligations imposed by the Convention. In carrying out that task it of course must interpret the Convention and in doing so contributes to the development of the law under the Convention as we have seen in Chapter 4. Ensuring the application of the substantive guarantees of the Convention (see Vade-mecum VI) is likely to prove a particular challenge as the number of cases arising in the Central and Eastern European countries which have recently joined the Convention begins to increase.

**How does it work?**

Under the new system, the procedure before the Human Rights Court has been considerably streamlined, ending the involvement of the Commission of Human Rights. It is difficult to be certain as to the functioning of the new system before the Rules of Procedure have been adopted. Nonetheless, it is likely that the system will comprise the same four essential stages, namely:

(i)   review of the admissibility of the application;

(ii)  establishment of the facts of the case and attempt at friendly settlement of the proceedings;

(iii) full review of the merits of the case by the Court, including possible referral to the Grand Chamber;

(iv)  execution of the judgment supervised by the Committee of Ministers.

---

44   Article 27(3) of the Convention as amended by Protocol No 11.

These stages are shown schematically in the diagram on p. 190, which shows the new procedure as envisaged by the explanatory report. Much of the detail of the procedure will remain uncertain until the newly constituted Court has adopted its own Rules of Procedure.

Applications to the Court may be made by states alleging that the provisions of the Convention have been infringed by one of the other contracting states or by individuals. The latter category includes non-governmental organisations or groups of individuals who claim they may be victims of such infringements. Each case will be referred to a Chamber which will register the case and designate a Judge Rapporteur for it. The Judge Rapporteur has a key role during the remainder of the proceedings. If he is in no doubt about the admissibility of the application and the importance of the issue which it raises he may refer the matter, of his own motion, directly to the Chamber for a full hearing. In the majority of cases however, the question of admissibility will first be considered by the three-judge committee formed within the Chamber of which that Judge Rapporteur is a member. In cases where such a decision can be taken "without further examination" and the three-judge committee unanimously concludes that the case is inadmissible, the applicant will be so informed and the case is concluded. There is no possibility of appeal from such a decision.

If the case is found to be admissible either by the Judge Rapporteur or by the committee or if the committee is unable to agree on admissibility, the case is referred to a Chamber of the Court composed of seven judges. Where necessary, the question of admissibility will be reconsidered by the Chamber, which again may conclude that the case is inadmissible, whereupon the matter ends. Up to this stage the proceedings of the Chamber are confidential and a decision on admissibility may be made by a bare majority. If the case has been declared admissible the Chamber, including the judge who is a national of the contracting state party concerned, will proceed to review the merits. First, under the guidance of the Judge Rapporteur, the parties will submit their written observations (known in Convention terminology as "memorials"). It may also order measures of investigation "for the effective conduct of which the States concerned shall furnish all necessary facilities".[45] It may also hold a hearing for the establishment of the facts and to hear argument on the merits of the case.

Following a declaration of admissibility and during this preparatory phase the Chamber is at the disposal of the parties with a view to securing a friendly settlement of proceedings where that

45  Article 38(1)(a) of the Convention.

## THE CONTROL MECHANISM OF THE HUMAN RIGHTS CONVENTION
### (following the entry into force of the Eleventh Protocol)

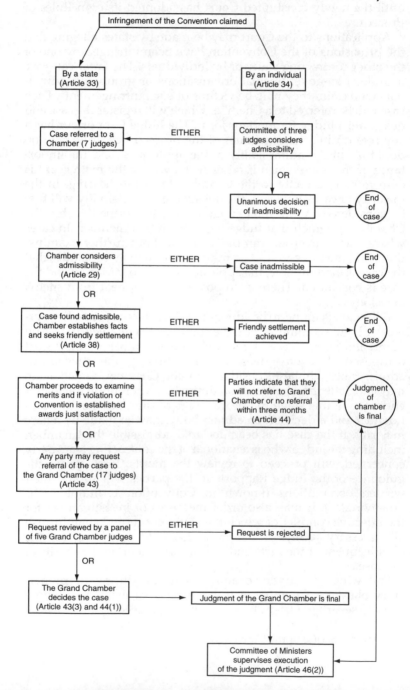

is possible, any negotiations aimed at securing such a settlement remain confidential. If a friendly settlement is arrived at the case is concluded at that stage. For reasons of principle, or to avoid political embarrassment, Member States are sometimes inclined to agree to friendly settlement on the basis of an *ex gratia* payment or other remedy to the alleged victim of an infringement without having to admit or have proved against it that it has in fact infringed the Convention.

In the absence of a friendly settlement the Court will continue to consider the merits of the case and reach a conclusion upon it. This conclusion may either result in a judgment which in turn will either reject the application or find that there has been an infringement of the Convention. In the alternative, where it feels unable to give judgment and, provided that neither of the parties objects the Chamber may decide to refer the case to the Grand Chamber. This may occur in cases where, for example, the result which it envisages to the case may diverge from the Court's previous case law or if a major or novel question of principle is involved.

If the Chamber has delivered a judgment in the case the parties may, within three months, themselves request that the case be referred to the Grand Chamber. In the absence of referral to the Grand Chamber the judgment of a Chamber becomes final:

- when the parties declare that they will not request such referral;

- or three months after the date of the judgment if no referral has been requested;

- or if the five-judge panel of the Grand Chamber rejects the request for a reference.

Where the Chamber dealing with the case relinquishes jurisdiction in favour of the Grand Chamber, the latter will proceed to deal with the merits of the case. Where, however, one or other of the parties ask for a judgment to be referred, a panel of five judges will determine whether the request for a rehearing is admissible, which it will do "if the case raises a serious question affecting the interpretation or application of the Convention or the protocols thereto, or a serious issue of general importance" (Article 43(2)). The decision of the five-judge panel of the Grand Chamber on whether or not to accept a referral, or the judgment of the Grand Chamber itself, is final.

**What language does it use?**

In accordance with the intergovernmental nature of the Council of Europe it has adopted a pragmatic language regime and therefore both the Council and in particular the Human Rights enforcement machinery operate in English and in French only. Both written and oral submissions to the Court (or its committees or chambers) should normally be made in one of those languages. However, where a party, or his lawyer, is unable adequately to express himself in one of those two languages leave to use a non-official language may be granted by the President of the Court. If a contracting state requests such leave it will be required to provide the necessary translation and interpreting facilities and to bear any costs thereby incurred. Where an individual applicant makes that request the Registrar of the Court will make the necessary arrangements for translation of written observations or interpretation of oral hearings into English and French. Verbatim records of the proceedings will be made in both official languages and submitted to the parties for rectification if necessary. Any participant before the Court, whether state or individual, should therefore include in their team at least one member with a good passive knowledge of one or other of the two official languages. It has been suggested that with the ratification of the Convention by countries from Eastern and Central Europe a case can perhaps be made out for increasing the number of official languages.[46] Given that the deliberations of the Court and the drafting of the judgment may be carried out in one of the two official languages, it is obviously desirable for any of those appointed as judges on the Court to be fully conversant with at least one and preferably both of those languages. Both the English and French versions of the resulting judgment are authentic.

## THE EUROPEAN COMMISSION OF HUMAN RIGHTS

Although the European Commission of Human Rights will cease to exist during the lifetime of this edition of this book, its vital role in securing the success of the European Convention and the massive amount of work it has carried out mean that it merits a proper description in this chapter. Moreover, the decisions which it has made on admissibility of cases and the Article 31 reports on the substance of applications remain an enduring legacy which will influence the Court of Human Rights and the national courts of the Member States of the Council of Europe for the future.

Part of the "control machinery" of the Human Rights Convention, the Human Rights Commission, is a court in all but name. That name clearly lends itself to confusion with the Commission of the European Communities and for that reason the abridgements European Commission or just the Commission should not be used unless there is not a scintilla of ambiguity. For note-taking

46   See Harris, O'Boyle and Warbrick at p. 658, n. 8.

or for footnote purposes the abbreviations HR Comm or ECnHR may be used.

Since its establishment it has developed as a unique legal institution capable of dealing with a massive case load and has made a substantial and distinctive contribution to the development of the law of the Convention.

**Where was it?**

Since its establishment the Human Rights Commission was based in Strasbourg in close proximity to the Human Rights Court, and like that Court, moved into the spectacular new Human Rights-building.

**When was it established?**

The Human Rights Commission was established by Article 19 of the Human Rights Convention which was signed on November 4, 1950 by the original 10 contracting states. It first sat in 1954. From the 1980s onwards the increasing number of Member States of the Council of Europe and a growing awareness of the extent of the protection afforded by the Convention led to an exponential increase in the number of complaints lodged from 3,007 in 1984 to 4,108 in 1988, 4,942 in 1990, 9,323 in 1993 and 10,201 in 1995. Although some two-thirds of such complaints are filtered out prior to formal registration (for the reasons for such exclusion see p. 209 below), the number of applications registered with the Commission had reached 2,037 by 1993 and 3,481 by the end of 1995. That trend, and the unacceptable length of time taken for a case to complete all the stages in the control machinery referred to above, had already made it clear that substantial reform of the control machinery was essential in order to ensure both its continued effectiveness and credibility.[47]

The solution adopted was the creation of the Single Court dealt with in the previous section and, therefore, the demise of the Human Rights Commission. Nonetheless, a transitional period is provided for by Article 5 of the 11th Protocol in order that work in progress may be completed and a smooth transfer to the new control machinery effected. Under those arrangements applications pending before the Commission which have not been declared admissible on the date of entry into force of the Protocol will be examined by the Court in accordance with the new control mechanism described above. Cases which have already been declared admissible will continue to be dealt with by the existing Commission for 12 months following the entry into force of the

47   See n. 34 above.

11th Protocol (that is to say from November 1, 1998 to October 31, 1999). Where the Commission adopts its Article 31 Report (see below) during that year the case may be referred to the Court or decided by the Committee of Ministers under the old scheme. Where a case is referred to the (new) Court, the panel of the Grand Chamber will decide whether the case will be dealt with by a Chamber or by the Grand Chamber. The European Commission of Human Rights will therefore cease to exist on October 31, 1999 or before that date if it has finished its work.

**Who sat on it?**

The qualifications for membership of the Human Rights Commission were, again, similar to those of the other European courts mentioned above, namely that "candidates shall be of high moral character and must possess the qualifications required for appointment either to high judicial office or be persons of recognised competence in national or international law".[48] There seems to be no significant difference between this definition and that of candidates for appointment to the Court who must equally be of high moral character and either possess the qualifications required for appointment to high judicial office or "be jurisconsults of recognised competence".[49] The number of members is the same as the number of contracting states and no two members may be nationals of the same state. The members of the Commission are elected by the Committee of Ministers from a list of candidates drawn up by the Bureau of the Parliamentary Assembly of the Council of Europe. Although the appointments are part-time and therefore all members of the Commission may continue to practise the professions upon which their qualifications for appointment were based (generally members of the national judiciary, academic lawyers or legal practitioners), they may not, during their term of office, hold any position which is incompatible with their independence and impartiality as members of the Commission, and various other provisions contribute to securing their independence.

**What did it do?**

In brief, the task of the Human Rights Commission was to examine the admissibility of all individual or state applications against a contracting state and, where applications were found to be admissible and no friendly settlement could be reached, the

48   Article 21(3) added to the text of the original Convention by Protocol No. 8 (ETS 118) which entered force on January 1, 1990.
49   Article 39(3).

Commission could express an opinion on the substance of the alleged violation. In the latter respect the Commission played a role similar to that of the Advocate General in the European Court of Justice, which, while not binding on the Court in its subsequent deliberation gave grist to its mill of reflection and a focal point for its consideration of the case. March Hunnings says of the Commission:[50]

"it is a filter, allowing only serious cases to reach the Court; it is a public prosecutor, preparing the case for presentation to the Court; it is a first instance court, dealing with all the issues of fact and law which need to be thoroughly examined before the case gets to Court; it is an arbitrator, dealing with the complaint in private and presenting its conclusions to the [Committee of Ministers] . . . ; it is an ombudsman, hearing complaints from the public and after examining them making recommendations to the Government; it is a mediator, using its good offices to reach a settlement between the complainant and the accused government."

While some of these comparisons may not be wholly apposite they give an idea of the range and importance of the Commission's work.

**How did it work?**

Even before the major reform introduced by the 11th Protocol, the 8th Protocol sought to address the problem of the overload of work faced by the Human Rights Commission. Therefore the 8th Protocol enabled the Commission to establish Chambers and also committees of three of its members, a structure taken over by the new arrangements under Protocol No 11.

The procedure before the Commission up to the stage of the adoption of its Article 31 Report was broadly similar to that which will now be followed by the permanent Court.

Thus individual applications were first subject to a preliminary filter by a committee of three members of the Commission who might refer the question on admissibility to a Chamber or to the plenary Commission. In the event that the three committee members were unanimous as to the inadmissibility of the application, the case was then closed. Taking both the preliminary filter by the Committee and the full review by a Chamber or the plenary Commission together, rather less than 10 per cent of all complaints were declared admissible.

50   *The European Courts* (Cartermill, 1996), p. 259.

In so far as the facts giving rise to the application have not already been determined or agreed upon by the parties the Commission's next task was to establish the facts. This could be done by way of affidavits and documentary depositions or the presentation of oral evidence by the applicant or other witnesses. Throughout the proceedings the Commission members used their good offices in order to establish whether a friendly settlement might be arrived at and, as indicated above, a certain proportion of cases were so concluded.

Under Article 31 of the Convention, an admissible case in which no friendly settlement has been found possible results in the Commission drawing up a report on the facts and stating its opinion as to whether or not the facts established disclose a breach by the state concerned of its obligations under the Convention. This report (the "Article 31 Report") was usually drawn up by one of the members of the Commission acting as Rapporteur and assented to by the others. Article 31(1) enables individual members of the Opinion to express their own opinions on the report, including dissenting opinions.

After adoption of the Article 31 Report and its transmission to the Committee of Ministers, the role of the Commission changes from that of a completely autonomous body operating as a combination of filter, investigating magistrate and conciliator to that of Judge Rapporteur and *amicus curia* putting the case before the Human Rights Court itself. Thus under Article 48 of the Convention the Commission must decide within three months whether or not the proceedings should be continued before the Court of Human Rights. In arriving at its decision it does not rely exclusively on the view expressed by the Commission as to whether or not there has in fact been an infringement of the Convention. For example, in the *Gibraltar Three* case[51] the Commission concluded by 11 votes to six that there had been no infringement of the Convention, nonetheless it was the Commission which brought the proceedings before the Human Rights Court.

It should be noted that, prior to entry into force of the 9th Protocol to the Convention,[52] individuals, groups of individuals or non-governmental organisations could not bring cases directly before the Court. This privilege was reserved to the contracting states and the Commission. Thus it was only through the agency of the Commission that the applicants' arguments could be put to the Court. Frequently however, the Commission included one or

---

51  *McCann and Others v. United Kingdom* Judgment of September 27, 1995.
52  Signed in Rome on November 6, 1990 (ETS No. 140) and entered into force on October 3, 1994.

more of the applicants' lawyers within its own legal team, thereby enabling the applicants' lawyer to address the Court directly.

Since the entry into force of the 9th Protocol, individual applicants have been able to seise the Court whether or not the Commission decided to do so after its Article 31 Report (provided, of course, that the Commission had found it admissible). Nonetheless, one further obstacle was then raised before such applicants in the form of a review of the case by a committee of three members of the Court whose task was to establish whether the case raised a serious question affecting the interpretation or application of the Convention or whether it did not, for any other reason, warrant consideration by the Court. If the panel unanimously reached that view the case would then be dealt with by the Committee of Ministers.

**What language did it use?**

Like the other Council of Europe bodies the official languages of the Commission are English and French and all proceedings are conducted in those languages. However, given that the Commission consists of one delegate from each of the contracting states and that the Secretariat also includes officials from the contracting parties, it exercises a degree of flexibility, using the languages of the contracting parties where appropriate in correspondence with them. Where a hearing is organised, interpretation will be provided into English and French by the Commission although the applicants' lawyer and any Commission member with knowledge of the language concerned may address the Court in another language.

**THE INTERNATIONAL COURT OF JUSTICE**

The International Court of Justice is one of the principal organs of the United Nations and is sometimes referred to as the World Court.

**Where is it?**

The International Court of Justice has been based at the Peace Palace in The Hague since it was established. The Peace Palace was constructed in 1913 with funds provided by the Scottish/American philanthropist, Andrew Carnegie, originally for the Permanent Court of Arbitration,[53] which still operates from the same premises.

---

53 See p. 202 below.

**When was it established?**

The United Nations Charter and the Statute of the International Court of Justice were signed in San Francisco on June 26, 1945. However, the antecedents of the World Court go back to the Treaty of Versailles of June 28, 1919 which embodies the peace settlement following the First World War. That Treaty established the Permanent Court of International Justice (PCIJ) whose Statute entered force on August 20, 1921. Although the PCIJ was established by the same instrument which created the League of Nations and had a close relationship with that organisation, it did not form part of its structure in the same way that the World Court forms part of the United Nations' structure. Despite the outbreak of war in 1939 which caused the demise of the League of Nations and ultimately the replacement of the PCIJ by the World Court, its creation was of considerable importance in that, for the first time, sovereign states became subject to the binding decisions of an international tribunal.

Unlike the League of Nations the PCIJ still existed at the end of the war and its position had been considered during the preparatory work for the San Francisco Conference. The Conference decided to incorporate a court (the International Court of Justice) in the structure of the new United Nations organisation and that its Statute should be an integral part of the charter. The Assembly of the League of Nations was convened for the final time in order to dissolve the PCIJ in 1946. However, the San Francisco Conference, wishing to ensure continuity between the PCIJ and the ICJ, ensured first that the drafting of the Statute of the ICJ was almost identical to that of its predecessor, a point which is also mentioned in Article 92 of the U.N. Charter. The new court was therefore able to operate in continuity with the old and to draw upon its established case law. Moreover, as noted above, the ICJ was established in the Peace Palace in The Hague and was therefore able to benefit from the infrastructure, including a ready-made staff, archives and library.

The members of the International Court were elected on February 6, 1946 at the first session of the U.N. General Assembly held in London. They met for the first time at the Peace Palace on April 3, 1946 when the first President, Vice-President and Registrar of the new court were elected. Its inaugural session was held on April 18, 1946, an event whose 50th anniversary was celebrated on April 18, 1996 by a special sitting.

**Who sits on it?**

The International Court is composed of 15 judges elected jointly by the U.N. General Assembly and the U.N. Security Council who, for the purpose, sit independently of each other. The first 15 judges were chosen separately by the two U.N. bodies from a list drawn up by the Permanent Court of Arbitration. Any candidate who was chosen by a majority vote of both bodies was elected to the Court, except that, if two persons of the same nationality had been chosen in that way only the elder of the two was appointed. Following the election of the first court lots were drawn to determine five judges who would hold office for three years, five for six years and the remaining five for the full nine-year term. Thereafter, every three years, the mandates of five of the judges expire and five new judges are elected by the same procedure, although any of the retiring judges may be re-elected.

The judges are appointed from a pool of candidates who must be qualified in their own country for the highest judicial office or be jurisconsults of recognised capacity in international law, wording which has subsequently been adapted for the qualifications for appointment to the various European courts discussed above. In addition to the individual qualities of the candidates for appointment the joint appointing bodies are required to ensure that the composition of the Court also reflects the main forms of civilisation and the principal legal systems of the world.

Given that there are 185 members of the United Nations but only 15 judges, it is highly likely that a state party to proceedings before the International Court of Justice will not have a judge of its own nationality as a permanent member of the Court. A state party to proceedings before the Court who does not have a permanent member of its own nationality may therefore nominate an *ad hoc* judge for the purposes of the case concerned. It has been observed that "this provision for *ad hoc* "national" judges can only be defended if it is necessary, as perhaps it is, for political reasons. It is a concession to the vicious theory that in some sense a judge ought to "represent" the parties and it places the "national" judge himself in a difficult position".[54]

**What does it do?**

The principal task of the International Court of Justice is to settle legal disputes submitted to it by sovereign states in accordance with the rules of public international law. The states parties to proceedings are usually (although they need not be) members of the United Nations. As a subsidiary task it may give advisory opinions on legal questions referred to it by authorised international organs and agencies. So far only organs and agencies of

54  J. L. Brierly, *The Law of Nations*, (6th ed.), revised by C. H. M. Waldock.

the United Nations have received the authorisation to ask for such an advisory opinion.

In resolving disputes the Court may be called upon to interpret and apply international treaties and conventions covering the particular dispute, customary international law, the general principles of law and, where necessary, judicial decisions (including its own previous case law and that of the PCIJ) and authoritative academic writing on international law.[55] This is referred to as "the teachings of the most highly qualified publicists" or, much more economically in French as *"la doctrine"*.

### How does it work?

In contentious proceedings only states may apply to and appear before the Court. This includes, by definition, the 185 Member States of the United Nations as well as Switzerland and Nauru which are not Member States but are nonetheless parties to the Statute of the Court. That requirement would exclude secessionist parts of states unless and until any secession was recognised by the state of which it formerly formed a part as well as by the wider international Community, including, where possible, admission to membership of the United Nations.

Unlike the Court of Justice of the European Communities, the International Court of Justice does not have automatic compulsory jurisdiction. It will therefore only be able to take cognisance of a case if both of the states concerned have accepted its jurisdiction by the conclusion of a special agreement to submit the particular dispute to the Court by the inclusion in a treaty or convention of a choice of jurisdiction clause. Under such a clause, in the event of a disagreement over interpretation or an alleged breach by one party, either party may bring the dispute before the Court. In the event of a dispute as to whether or not the Court has jurisdiction, the Court itself will decide the matter as in the recent case where the jurisdiction of the Court was a preliminary issue in the cases brought by the Libyan Arab Jamahiriya against the United States of America in connection with the bombing of the PanAm 747 over Lockerbie in Scotland.[56] The substantive question of law which the Court will now have to determine is whether or not the 1971 Montreal Convention entitles the country upon whose territory a terrorist act took place to try terrorist suspects from a third country.

The Court may also have jurisdiction in cases between two states which have made declarations according to which they

---

55  Article 38(1) of the Statute of the International Court of Justice. See Chapter 4, p. 101 above.

56  Provisional measures, Order of April 14, 1992.

accept the jurisdiction of the Court as compulsory in the event of a dispute with another state which has made a similar declaration. Only some 60 states have made such declarations and even those are frequently subject to reservations by which the state concerned refuses to accept compulsory jurisdiction of the International Court for certain categories of cases.

Under the Statute of the Court and its rules of procedure (which provided the model for those of the Court of Justice of the European Communities), the procedure before the International Court includes a written part during which the parties lodge successive pleadings (the application, the defence, a reply and a rejoinder) and an oral phase consisting of public hearings at which states appear through their government legal services or outside Counsel and submit oral argument to the Court. Following the oral proceedings the International Court deliberates upon the matter behind closed doors and then, usually several months later, delivers its judgment at a public sitting. The judgment is final and states parties are required to comply with it. If either of the parties fails to do so the other may lodge a complaint before the Security Council of the United Nations.

In addition to contentious cases concerning matters such as territorial borders on land or at sea, jurisdiction over fisheries matters or the interpretation of conventions covering diplomatic relations, the Court may also give advisory opinions. Such opinions may only be given at the request of international organisations authorised to do so. So far, the only such organisations are those within the organs and specialised agencies under the aegis of the U.N. Subject to an express provision in an agreement, convention or other legal instrument that such an advisory opinion will be binding, at least on the party or parties immediately concerned, the Court's advisory opinions are purely consultative although, given the authority of the International Court it is unlikely that such an opinion would be lightly disregarded.

## SOME OTHER INTERNATIONAL COURTS

The success of the courts briefly described above and in particular that of the European Court of Justice, the Human Rights Court and the International Court, have greatly strengthened the confidence of states both in Europe and the rest of the world in adjudication by independent tribunals as a means of resolving disputes between them. As a result, a number of new courts has sprung up mostly covering specialised areas of jurisdiction. Some, in particular the International Criminal Tribunals for the former Yugoslavia and for Rwanda, have special jurisdiction limited both geographically and in time, while others such as the Disputes

Settlement Body of the World Trade Organisation or the International Tribunal for the Law of the Sea have worldwide scope. Only the Benelux Court of Justice has a truly European vocation, nonetheless at least six such courts are based in European countries and therefore merit a brief mention here.

The models established, in particular by the two principal European courts have also been mirrored elsewhere. Thus both in Africa and South America organisations based on economic integration, including the Andean Pact,[57] Mercosur,[58] and in Africa ECOWAS (Economic Organisation of West African States) and UEMOA (*Union Economique et Monétaire Ouest Africaine*) have each included a court in their institutional structure. In the human rights field the inter-American Court of Human Rights and the African Charter on Human and Peoples' Rights have also put in an appearance.[59]

### The Permanent Court of Arbitration

The Permanent Court of Arbitration (PCA) is arguably neither permanent nor a court. It is however the world's oldest institution dedicated to resolving international disputes, having been established by The Hague Convention of 1899 (revised in 1907). Unlike the International Court of Justice it is not a United Nations organisation although it has the status of a permanent observer at the U.N. General Assembly and a strong history of collaboration with the U.N. Its task is to offer its services in order to resolve disputes between states as well as disputes between states and private parties. It may apply a wide range of dispute resolution procedures falling short of the full-scale legal proceedings available at the World Court. Thus it may act as an honest broker between the parties as a mediator or a conciliator, it may set up Commissions of Enquiry in order to establish disputed facts and it maintains a list of distinguished international jurists designated by the parties to the 1899 Convention. The parties may select from that list the members of a tribunal or a commission to undertake either a fact-finding enquiry or to try to resolve the dispute, if necessary by binding arbitration.

The permanent part of the Court is provided by its International Bureau which both ensures the day-to-day running of the PCA and acts as the registry for tribunals and commissions established

---

57  Chile, Bolivia, Colombia, Ecuador, Peru, Venezuela (Panama is an associate member).
58  Argentina, Brazil, Paraguay and Uruguay.
59  Also known as the Banjol Charter adopted in 1981. Its structure includes an African Commission on Human Rights but as yet no court. See (1982) 21 I.L.M. 59.

at the request of disputing parties. Thus, like the registries of the other courts dealt with in this chapter, it serves as the official channel of communication between the parties *inter se* and between the parties and the adjudicating body. It provides all of the necessary administrative infrastructure including, where necessary, translation and interpretation facilities, its own business being conducted in English and in French.

## The Benelux Court

As we have seen in Chapter 2, the Benelux Union despite its ambitions is essentially an intergovernmental organisation. That is to say all of its decisions are taken by representatives of the three Member States at governmental level acting unanimously. At the outset of the Benelux, therefore, it was not considered necessary to include a judicial body in the institutional structure. However, by the mid 1960s (after 20 years of operation of the Benelux Union and in the light of the experience of the European Communities), the three Member States concluded that the supervision of a court was desirable in the interest of ensuring uniformity in the application of those rules which were common to the three countries. They therefore decided to establish a Benelux Court, particularly in order to ensure that the national judiciaries did not interpret the Benelux treaties and Council decisions in a divergent manner. The Court was established by a treaty adopted on March 31, 1965.[60]

The Court is based in Brussels where it is supported by the infrastructure provided by the Secretariat General of the Benelux Economic Union. It is composed of nine judges, being a President, two Vice-Presidents and six associate judges as well as three Advocates General. The judges and associate judges are selected among the members of the supreme courts of each of the three countries, likewise the Advocates General are selected from the members of the Public Prosecutor's departments of the three member countries. They remain members of their respective judiciaries and receive no remuneration for the extra duties which they carry out as members of the Benelux Court.

The tasks of the Benelux Court are threefold: first, it must ensure uniformity of interpretation of rules laid down in the Convention between the Benelux countries or a decision of the Ministerial Committee established by the treaty establishing the Benelux Economic Union. For that purpose, if a court in one of the States is unable to rule on an aspect of Benelux law, that court has

---

60   "Traité relatif à l'institution et aux statuts d'une Cour de Justice Bénélux" 924 UNTS 30, which exists in French and Dutch, the two official languages of the Benelux.

the option (or in the case of a national court whose decisions are not open to any form of legal appeal in national law, the obligation) to refer the matter to the Benelux Court of Justice for a preliminary ruling which is binding on the national court making the reference. Even a Supreme Court in those circumstances may decide not to make a reference if it considers that the question concerned gives rise to no reasonable doubt or that the case is of special urgency.

Secondly, any of the three governments may request the Benelux Court to give a consultative opinion on the interpretation of one such rule. Thirdly the Court has jurisdiction in disputes involving officials of the Benelux Economic Union (slightly less than 100 at present).

## The Appellate Body of the WTO

The World Trade Organisation ("WTO") came into existence upon the signature of the Marrakesh Agreement on April 14, 1994. That agreement, as we have seen in Chapter 2, established the World Trade Organisation which included a new dispute settlement mechanism designed to reinforce the multilateral world trading system envisaged by the newly amended GATT. Thus in the final act of the Marrakesh Declaration, WTO members agreed not to take unilateral action against perceived violations of the trade rules but to seek redress through the new disputes settlement system. Like the GATT Secretariat, the WTO is based in Geneva (and took over many of the officials and internal bodies of the GATT) and the Disputes Settlement Body ("DSB") is also based there.

Where mediation or conciliation fail to resolve any dispute between parties to the WTO, a panel may be constituted from whose decisions an appeal on points of law may be lodged before a standing Appellate Body which is a court in all but name. By contrast the panels may be regarded as arbitration bodies since their composition is essentially dependent upon the will of the parties concerned.

Whereas panels are composed on an *ad hoc* basis, the Appellate Body is permanent. It is composed of seven people, three of whom sit on any one case. Members are appointed for a four-year term and any of them may be re-appointed once and once only. According to the Disputes Settlement Understanding (DSU), the Appellate Body membership must be broadly representative of the membership of the WTO. Thus within the limits imposed by such a small body, factors such as geographical balance, representation of different legal systems and the participation of countries or regions with different levels of economic development must be taken into account. The need for such a "court" and the willingness of states to submit to its judgments is demonstrated by the fact that since its establishment the Disputes Settlement Body has received some 140 requests for consultations. These have led to 27 panel decisions and 19 Appellate Body decisions.

## The ILO Complaints Tribunal

The International Labour Organisation (ILO) which was, like the League of Nations and the Permanent Court of International Justice established by the Treaty of Versailles, also deserves a mention. Although it was and remains a traditional intergovernmental organisation (based in Geneva) its membership constitutes not only governmental delegates but also representatives of the labour force (essentially through their respective trade unions) and of the employers' organisations in each Member State. Moreover, the Complaints Tribunal set up under the ILO is able to hear individual complaints (usually supported by a trade union or employers' organisation) against states, which makes the ILO the first forum to countenance such apparent *lèse-majesté*.

The ILO Complaints Tribunal continues to provide valuable service by providing a forum for international civil servants (other than those of the European Community institutions and the Benelux Union who have direct access to the Court of First Instance and the Benelux Court respectively) with an independent judicial tribunal in order to deal with disputes against international organisations acting in their capacity as employers.

## The International Tribunal for the Law of the Sea

After many years of negotiations the 1982 United Nations Convention on the Law of the Sea ("UNCLOS") entered force on November 16, 1994. That Convention established a new international court, the International Tribunal for the Law of the Sea ("ITLOS") based in Hamburg and appropriate procedural arrangements for the settlement of marine disputes, and an international seabed authority to settle disputes involving states, seabed mining contractors and any other relevant entities. The Convention has, at present, nearly 120 states party who, in accordance with procedures similar to those for the election of members of the World Court, have elected 21 members of the Law of the Sea Tribunal. Those members have in turn established three chambers in accordance with the Convention, a seabed disputes chamber, a chamber on fisheries matters and a chamber on the marine environment.

Like the EC Treaty (and going further in this respect than the U.N. Charter or the Protocol on the establishment of the World

Court) the Convention on the Law of the Sea makes it compulsory for convention parties to use the settlement procedure, including the Tribunal, in case of a dispute with another party.

## International War Crimes Tribunals

War Crimes, which, like elephants, are notoriously difficult to define (although "I know one when I see one"), have always proved a sensitive topic for international adjudication. There is a clear risk that the victor in any conflict may attempt to justify its treatment of the vanquished through the establishment of apparently independent legal channels. This problem has clearly exercised the international community ever since the Nuremburg War Crimes Trials. However, the questions raised and the lessons learned at Nuremburg were not seriously addressed until the late 1980s when the International Law Commission of the United Nations was requested to prepare a draft statute for a proposed international criminal court. The idea for such a permanent tribunal has received significant support from the various international Bar associations and the European Communities. At an international diplomatic conference in Rome which concluded on July 17, 1998, a Treaty on the creation of a Permanent International Criminal Court and the statute of that Court were adopted.[60a] When the Treaty has received the necessary number of ratifications the new Court will be set up at The Hague.

The heightening of interest is at least partly attributable to the ghastly civil wars which have erupted in the former Yugoslavia and in Rwanda in Africa. In answer to those two conflicts, the Security Council of the United Nations, which had decided that each of the two civil wars constituted threats to international peace and security, first established the International Criminal Tribunal for the former Yugoslavia ("ICTY")[61] and the International Criminal Tribunal for Rwanda ("ICTR").[62] The Yugoslav War Crimes Tribunal is based in The Hague which also seems likely to be the host city for any international war crimes tribunal that may be established by the U.N. in the future. The Rwanda War Crimes Tribunal is based in Arusha in Tanzania.

## "HOW DO I BRING A CASE BEFORE THE EUROPEAN COURT?"

The success of the Court of Justice of the European Communities and the European Court of Human Rights in protecting individ-

60a  See www.un.org/icc.
61    Security Council Resolution 827.
62    Security Council Resolution 955.

ual interests in their respective fields of jurisdiction, as well as a certain number of high-profile and highly publicised cases before each court, have given rise to a wide-spread perception that those courts provide a sovereign remedy for all manner of legal ills. As a result both courts, members of national and European parliaments, as well as other agencies and voluntary organisations are deluged with letters and telephone calls putting the above question. The letters range from delusional or paranoid ramblings accompanied by copious, usually irrelevant documentation, to genuine and distressing cases involving a real or perceived injustice in which the victim has been unable to find the correct form of redress. This section is designed to assist those to whom such persons may turn for advice or help to identify those cases in which judicial resolution of the problem, possibly including recourse to one of the European courts, might indeed be appropriate and the steps to be taken in order to seek a remedy.

**Preliminary Advice**

As already mentioned, persons with a legal problem very often turn directly to the court concerned. This is rarely, if ever, appropriate. Court officials (still less the judges) of the courts may not give advice relating to an individual's particular circumstances. Nor may they recommend lawyers or other advisers to whom it might be appropriate to turn. While the officials are invariably patient and courteous, the most they can do is to explain the jurisdiction of the respective courts in terms similar to those set out earlier in this chapter and suggest that the applicant seek advice elsewhere.

Normally speaking, such advice should be sought from a professional lawyer (in the United Kingdom a solicitor) who, if the matter falls outside his experience or expertise should be able to refer the client onwards to a colleague with the necessary knowledge. Where an individual or organisation does not have his or her own legal adviser a local Citizens' Advice Bureau, Law Society or Chamber of Commerce may be able to provide a list of practitioners in a particular geographical area possibly even with an indication of their areas of specialized practice. Failing that applicants may turn to trade unions or other professional associations to which they may belong and which may be able to provide the necessary legal or other professional advice or indeed help in resolving the matter themselves through negotiations with the appropriate authorities. There is also a wide range of voluntary associations in most Member States which may be able to give advice relating to such matters as consumer protection, women's rights, immigration or pensions and social security issues.

Many potential claimants, when advised to consult a lawyer,

raise the argument "Yes, I know, but I can't afford a lawyer". This is undoubtedly a deterrent to many people however most lawyers are prepared to give initial advice, at least to the point of assessing whether or not a potential legal claim exists, either free of charge or for a very modest fee. Voluntary organisations rarely charge for the services which they can provide and, in cases which fall within their area of interest may be prepared to assume the cost of full-scale legal representation in cases which they see as meritorious or in which litigation may determine or at least clarify an important point of law.

The availability of financial assistance or legal aid in order to obtain professional legal advice is a matter for the national legal system of the country in which the advice is sought. However, under Article 6.3 of the European Convention on Human Rights everyone charged with a criminal offence has the right, if he has not sufficient means to pay for legal assistance, to be given it free when the interests of justice so require. In the *Airey*[63] case the Court of Human Rights held that the right of effective access to a court, guaranteed by Article 6.1 of the Convention also extended to civil cases in situations in which a person was unable to plead his case effectively himself or where the law makes legal representation compulsory.

Once proceedings before the European courts are actually contemplated it may be possible to apply to them for legal aid for the purpose of those proceedings. It should be noted that neither court will provide legal aid for preliminary advice or for the purpose of investigation of a potential case. Any amounts granted are limited to the sums absolutely necessary for the preparation of proceedings to be lodged before the court or for representation directly before it. Thus the rules of procedure of the Court of Justice provide that "A party who is wholly or in part unable to meet the costs of the proceedings may at any time apply for legal aid".[64] Similar addenda to the Rules of Procedure of the Commission and the Court of Human Rights enable free legal aid to be granted respectively "where the Commission is satisfied: (a) that it is essential for the proper discharge of the Commission's duties; and (b) that the applicant has not sufficient means to meet all or part of the costs involved" or where the President of the Court is satisfied that "(a) the applicant lacks sufficient means to meet all or part of the costs involved; and (b) such a course is necessary for the proper conduct of the case before the Court".

63   *Airey v. Ireland* (A 32) (1979).
64   Article 76.1 of the Rules of Procedure, Article 94.1 of the Rules of Procedure of the Court of First Instance is worded identically as is Article 72.1 of the Rules of Procedure of the EFTA Court.

## Is it a "European" case?

This is a difficult question to answer since European law points, whether under the Human Rights Convention or European Community law, may crop up in the most unexpected ways. There is thus no infallible litmus test which will reveal whether or not either the Convention or Community law may be applicable in a particular case. Moreover, in the absence of a catalogue of fundamental rights in any of the European Community's founding treaties or in the Treaty on European Union, the Court of Justice can and does refer to the rights guaranteed under the Convention. While the Court of Justice (not always successfully) seeks to avoid interpreting the Convention this degree of overlap may be another source of confusion for the unwary and again specialist help should be sought to distinguish which of the two regimes may be relevant in a particular case.

So far as the Human Rights Convention is concerned, one of the helpful changes made by the Eleventh Protocol, mentioned above, is to have added headings before each article of the Convention and of the main protocols. That list of headings (which is reproduced at part VI of the Vade-mecum at the back of this book) constitutes a useful check-list of the rights which may be protected under the Convention. As is clear from the list these rights may all be categorised as concerning individual rights and freedoms.

Another guide is provided by the types of cases in which the secretariat of the Commission of Human Rights suggests, usually successfully, should *not* be proceeded with by the applicants. These categories account for about three-quarters of all complaints brought before the Strasbourg machinery and fall, broadly speaking, into six categories:

(i) Complaints about a right which is not protected under either the Convention or one of the protocols (see again the list in part VI of the Vade-mecum);

(ii) Complaints which are not directed against a state or the authorities of a state;

(iii) Complaints lodged before the remedies available in the state concerned have been exhausted;

(iv) Complaints lodged more than six months after the exhaustion of domestic remedies;

(v) Frivolous or vexatious complaints;

(vi) Complaints that national courts have wrongly evaluated the argument of the complainant.

So far as European Community Law is concerned the position is even more difficult. Perhaps the first question to be asked is whether or not there is a cross-border element involved, for example is the putative applicant or defendant a national of another Member State or does the case concern a transaction between people or undertakings in two or more Member States.[65] Alternatively, does it appear from the relevant national legislation that that legislation purports to implement the Community rules in the domestic legal system? Occasionally an enquiry will be prompted by reports of a decision of the Court of Justice or of an opinion delivered by one of the Advocates General. If the case can be sufficiently identified from what may be a rather garbled account, and if it presents parallels with the applicant's circumstances that too may be a guide. If the decision concerned can be sufficiently clearly identified a copy of the relevant document may be obtained from either of the courts. There have been cases where simply showing a copy of a recent judgment to the appropriate official has been enough to resolve a problem.

## Starting Proceedings

The only circumstances in which court proceedings are brought *directly* before one of the European courts is when action is envisaged against one of the European Community Institutions. This may involve a challenge to a decision or other act addressed to the applicant or, of direct and individual concern to him (this is a particularly hard test to satisfy). It may involve a claim by an official of one of the institutions against the institution for which he works in its capacity as an employer or a claim for compensation for damage or losses caused by an act of a Community Institution or by its officials acting in the course of their duties.

Any such case *must* be lodged before the Court of First Instance and the application *must* be drawn up and signed by a lawyer with rights of audience before a court in a Member State. This requirement is strictly adhered to, the only exception is an application for legal aid in order to enable the party to be represented (this in order to avoid a catch-22 situation — for legal aid see above). An application submitted by a party in person (even if he or she has legal qualifications) will be returned by the Registry of the Court of First Instance to be rectified before it can be registered. A defective application or an application for legal aid will not stop the time-limit for bringing proceedings from running.

With the exception of those cases which may be lodged before the Court of First Instance, all proceedings raising a point of

---

65  British lawyers are sometimes prone to forget that Ireland is a separate Member State.

European law must be commenced before the appropriate court within the Member State concerned. Where criminal proceedings are concerned (where potential infringement of rights under the Convention are the most likely to arise) of course it is the state authorities that initiate proceedings. Other cases may begin in the Court with appropriate jurisdiction such as local or regional courts which may have jurisdiction in civil proceedings involving relatively small sums in dispute, or courts of specialized jurisdiction such as labour courts or tribunals, tax courts, social security courts or family law courts.

It must be emphasized that neither the proceedings before the Court of Justice nor those before the Court of Human Rights constitute an appeal from the national courts where the case began. Any appeal from a decision of one of those courts will lie not to Luxembourg or Strasbourg but to the competent appellate court in the legal system concerned. Notwithstanding the requirement that domestic remedies must at first be exhausted, the Human Rights Court will declare inadmissible an application which simply alleges that the national courts have made erroneous findings of fact or of national law (this is known as the "doctrine of the fourth instance").

Any court, at any level of the judicial hierarchy of a Member State, is entitled to refer a case to the Court of Justice in Luxembourg for a preliminary ruling under Article 234 (ex Article 177) of the EC Treaty, however only a court sitting in an appellate capacity may make a reference under the Brussels Convention. Courts from whose decisions there is no legal redress within the national legal system must (subject to certain narrow exceptions[66]) make a reference where an issue of Community law is raised before them. The proceedings before the Court of Justice therefore constitute, in the phrase used by the court itself "a step in proceedings before the national court", which will ultimately have to decide the case as between the parties.

### Some Points of Procedure

Should the case go so far as a full set of proceedings before either of the European courts there will be many steps in procedure that will have to be dealt with.[67] Nonetheless it may be helpful to deal with some specific aspects of the procedure here.

---

66  As defined by the Court of Justice in Case 238/81 *CILFIT v. Ministry of Health I* [1982] ECR 3415.

67  So far as the Court of Justice is concerned see, in this respect, Brown and Kennedy, chapters 12 and 13; and, for the Human Rights Court, Harris, O'Boyle and Warbrick, *Law of the European Convention on Human Rights* chapters 22 and 24.

In the first place many inquirers from non-francophone countries appear to believe that the proceedings before either court must be conducted in French. Perhaps this misapprehension is due to the location of the two courts although to tell either a Luxembourger or a Strasbourger that he or she was a francophone might meet with a tart response. So far as the Court of Justice is concerned the language used in all stages of the proceedings will be the language of the court which referred the case to Luxembourg[68] thus any observations submitted (whether in writing or at the hearing) by governments of the Member States will be translated into the language of the case as will the Advocate General's opinion. The judgment of the Court will be authentic only in that language. So far as the Human Rights Court is concerned English and French are the official languages of that institution.[69] However the Registry of the Human Rights Court will make arrangements for written observations drafted in one of the languages of a contracting state to be translated into French and English and for oral observations to be interpreted from that language into the two official languages. The converse however, does not apply so it is necessary for the lawyer engaged by the applicant to be conversant with one or the other of the two official languages or else to provide the necessary interpretation facilities himself.

68　In the very rare cases of a direct action brought before the Court of First Instance the applicant will have the choice of any of the 11 official languages plus Irish in which to present his case.

69　Remember that, as pointed out in Chapter 2, the Council of Europe, of which the Human Rights Protection mechanism is a constituent part, is essentially an inter-governmental organisation and therefore does not have the direct contact with the legal systems of the Member States in the same manner as the Court of Justice.

# PART THREE: TOOLS

# 7. WHERE DO YOU FIND EUROPEAN LAW?

*"Non quaeras quis hoc dixerit: sed, quid diciatur attende".*[70]

*"When found, make a note of."*
Captain Cuttle in Dombey and Son, Charles Dickens.

A librarian from a major Swiss university once told me of an earnest young law student who had consulted her. He was about to embark on a course on international law and regarded the reading list provided by his tutor as inadequate. He therefore asked the librarian for a list of all the material on the subject held by the library. Having failed to dissuade him from this course of action she agreed to print such a list from the library's (fortunately) computerised catalogue. When the student returned the following day he was presented with a bibliography over 200 pages long, with each page detailing eight or 10 publications, some of which referred not to single volume monographs but to yearbooks or learned journals in series produced over many years or even decades.

---

70 "Seek not to know who said this or that, but take note of what was said." It perhaps offends the spirit of this epigram to reveal that its author was Thomas à Kempis in *The Imitation of Christ*, early 14th century.

Of course, not all libraries will have such extensive holdings as to make such a comprehensive approach so unrealistic. However, it will already be apparent from the earlier chapters of this book that European law is to be found in a number of different forms emanating from several different organisations, each with its own scheme of publications and varying language regimes. Thus the original documents include the texts of treaties and conventions, legislation in various forms and the case law of the various courts described in Chapter 6. These original sources are complemented by a large and growing number of compilations and digests, sometimes arranged thematically in order to facilitate use of the material, and finally there is the great bulk of legal commentary which may be descriptive, analytical or critical of the primary elements.

Legal materials are traditionally divided into primary sources, that is to say the texts of treaties, legislation and collections of case law and secondary sources including encyclopaedias, digests, textbooks, monographs and law reviews or other periodicals. Logically enough, primary sources are generally described first with the secondary sources described as a complement to the first. I propose however to reverse this order so as more accurately to reflect the real use that is made of these materials, both by experienced legal practitioners and researchers as well as by neophytes. That is to say almost all will seek first a general exposition of the area of law concerned, which will contain reference to the relevant legislation and case law as well as, importantly, any specialised terminology involved. Then, armed with those bibliographic "range-finders" he or she will either seek out more specialised literature or go to the original texts in order to check the accuracy and currency of the exposition. Moreover, because the adjectives primary and secondary are used in other contexts, in particular describing both national and Community legislation, for the sake of clarity I prefer to refer to original texts and legal publications respectively.

Obviously the approach to finding out European law will vary according to the needs of the enquirer. Thus a law student embarking on a course of structured study with the guidance of a tutor and a set reading list will take a different course from the research assistant to a parliamentarian looking for the answer to a constituency problem, or a general librarian faced with an enquiry from an environmental or other interest group. All of these may also face the daunting prospect of a wide range of publications presented in an unfamiliar layout and with their own distinctive, not to say idiosyncratic, indexing and cross-referencing systems. Thus faced with a task which may make searching for a needle in a haystack appear the easier option, the first stage in any enquiry will be to ask for advice.

## ASKING FOR GUIDANCE

This does not mean asking somebody else to do your work for you. All too often I receive letters from students informing me of the title of an assignment or dissertation they have been asked to prepare and asking me to provide them with all the relevant material. Such an approach is both lazy and as little likely to produce a constructive result as that of the international law student mentioned in the anecdote at the beginning of this chapter. It is also necessary to be sure that the person of whom an enquiry is made is himself in a position to give a reliable answer. Subject to that caveat, asking a fellow student who has already completed the course concerned or the information services of one of the institutions may well be the quickest way of identifying and locating either a specific piece of information or a library with the appropriate resources.

The representation offices of the European Commission both in the Member States and throughout the world can all provide basic information and brochures on the structure of the Communities and their main policies. They will also know where the main libraries (including European documentation centres and European reference centres mentioned below) are to be found. The larger offices, particularly those in the capitals of the Member States, themselves often have good libraries and reading room facilities which are open to the public.

Another resource of the Commission offices which may be of particular use to non-lawyers or to individual citizens with a legal problem is the Euro-jus network. Under this scheme an expert lawyer with experience in European Community law is available at each Commission office on one or two days a week to deal with legal questions put to them by telephone, in writing or in person. Very often it will be possible for an immediate answer to be given, either on the substance of the point or in giving an indication as to where the answer is to be found. Alternatively the lawyer may decide to examine the question further and carry out some research or may advise the enquirer to consult a practising lawyer who can take the necessary steps to resolve the particular problem. Even in the latter case the Euro-jus consultant will be able to define and categorise the problem and clarify whether or not a question of European law is in fact involved.

Despite their name the Euro-info centres do not have a general role as information providers but are focused more particularly on small and medium-sized enterprises and craftsmen. Nonetheless, since there are nearly 250 Euro-info centres in the Member States (there is a small number of such centres in the remaining EFTA Member States as well as in the countries of Central and Eastern Europe and some of the Mediterranean countries), such a centre may well be more accessible than the libraries mentioned below. For their target public the centres can provide information of particular interest to companies, including information on forthcoming legislative developments and the possibility of grants or technical assistance towards creating markets in other Member States, or taking part in public procurement procedures. The resources available to the Euro-info centre will depend upon its host organisation (very often Chambers of Commerce) but will include free documentation from the European Commission and other European institutions. They also enjoy preferential access to the European Community databases, including CELEX (see below).

## LEGAL PUBLICATIONS

The first port of call, even before crossing the threshold of a law library, is likely to be a general textbook. Many of these are available, particularly in the field of European Community law, although I have yet to find one in which all of the facets of European law as defined in Chapter 4 of this book are covered. Given the huge volume of publishing of materials in European law it would be impossible within the scope of a single chapter to give anything more than a brief indication of some of the materials available. The titles mentioned are intended as suggested starting-points for further reading and exploration and not as a Michelin-style recommendation. Still less should this list of materials be regarded as an alternative to the recommended reading lists provided by course directors or tutors. Most courses will recommend the use of a particular textbook and many courses will in fact be based upon such a work and draw heavily upon it. Nearly all such textbooks, at the very least, provide a sound and accurate account of the law and can be safely relied upon to provide a good grounding in the subject.

Some words of warning should however be borne in mind when reading any textbook. In the first place law is a fast-moving and dynamic field of study and nowhere is this more true than in the various fields of European law. Not only may a long-awaited regulation or directive transform a whole area of specific technical rules, but also the signature or ratification of an amending treaty or new accessions may change the very structure of the organisation and the way in which law applies within it and within the various Member States. The preface to most law books contains a sentence to the effect that the law is stated as at a given date, and occasionally adds that some later developments have been taken into account at the proof-reading stage. The signing of the preface on that date effectively encapsulates the author's view of the law, like a fly in amber, at that date and, given the time necessary for the practicalities of publication and distribution of a new work or a new edition, at the very least a number of months will elapse before the book is read. It is therefore *essential* to ensure that a statement of a particular proposition of law has not been superseded by treaty or legislative developments or an area of doubt elucidated by a court judgment. Obviously the greater the length of time between the date of the preface and the date upon which the textbook is read the greater the care which must be taken in checking original texts for changes in the law.

Secondly, given the pace of development of European law and the novelty of many areas of it, there is plenty of room for divergent views and approaches to particular topics. Most such textbooks are co-authored by two or more writers who may have had to paper over such disagreements in drafting their text. Other authors are happy to be more opinionated. Textbook pronouncements should not therefore be regarded as the "be all and end all" and, where time permits, it is helpful to read the same topic in another textbook which may approach it from a different angle. Thirdly, the author's style and even the presentation of the book may not be congenial to certain readers, in which case it is far better to seek an alternative than to be put off the subject completely.

As a final counsel of perfection those students who are able to may find it interesting to complement their reading in English textbooks by looking at the coverage of the same topics in another language. Not only may this shine new light on the subject concerned but it may be particularly important for those whose course includes a year studying in a university in another country.

## General Introductions

There are many general introductions to European Community law. Perhaps the most concise and at the same time comprehensive such work is Edward and Lane's *European Community Law, an Introduction* (2nd ed., Edinburgh, 1995). Originally intended as the introductory chapter to the title on "European Community Law and Institutions" for the Stair Memorial Encyclopaedia of the Laws of Scotland, it retains the structured presentation of such encyclopaedic works with each principal topic being dealt with in a separate numbered paragraph accompanied by the relevant references to legislation treaties and case law. Its succinct exposition and clear structure also makes it ideal as a basis for revision towards the end of a course. P.S.R.F. Mathijsen's *A Guide to European Community Law* (6th ed., London, 1990) is presented in a more traditional textbook style and is an accessible general introduction, while O'Neill and Coppell's *EC*

*Law for UK Lawyers* (Butterworths, London, 1994), as its title
suggests is intended specifically for the needs of British practitioners asked for advice in a specific situation. Therefore, after
general chapters explaining the Community legal order and the
various remedies available, the bulk of the book is devoted to the
specific impact of Community law in 15 specific areas including
business law, consumer protection law, environment and planning law and transport law.

### Textbooks

So far as textbooks are concerned, it is not the purpose of this book
to usurp the role of a course tutor in making recommendations,
nor to establish a critical bibliography of the many textbooks
available. A few general remarks are however appropriate. First,
by textbooks, as opposed to the general introductory works mentioned above, are meant those which provide an extensive and
fairly detailed treatment of all, or a large part of European Community law. Such works will usually begin with a general
historical introduction to the Communities tracing their development from the six members of the Coal and Steel Community to
the 15 members of the European Union, moving on to a description of the organisation of the principal institutions and their
respective powers as well as a more or less detailed account of the
Community legal order, in particular the principles of direct effect
of Community law and supremacy of Community law as well as
the various forms of action and remedies available for the enforcement of that law. The remainder of the book is likely to be devoted
to chapters covering certain specific topics of substantive law,
usually dealing with the four freedoms central to the internal
market, the basic elements of competition law and the application
of Articles 81 and 82 (ex Articles 85 and 86) of the E.C. Treaty,
possibly including a certain number of other topics of which one is
usually sex discrimination. It is relatively rare to find a chapter
devoted to the Common Agricultural Policy or to budgetary
questions. Depending upon the extent of their coverage and the
degree of detail in the treatment, some of these works are
extremely hefty tomes. However, this should not lead you to
select (or to reject) simply the slimmest.

As already indicated, a course will almost certainly have a
principal recommended textbook and such a recommendation
should not be disregarded lightly, first because the course may
well follow the structure of the book concerned and adopting
another approach may lead to confusion, and secondly because
the course may be being taught by one of the book's authors.
Nonetheless, for stylistic or other reasons you may find that the
recommended book does not suit or that a different approach

complements the main recommendation and facilitates study. In selecting a textbook it would be best, in an ideal world, to borrow two or three different textbooks either from fellow or former students or from your nearest law library and to read the general introduction to each book as well as the treatment of a particular topic. The final consideration, which may be conclusive in some cases, will be the date of the preface as mentioned above. This book was being written during the negotiations for and following the signature of the Amsterdam Treaty but before its ratification. Similarly, many general textbooks on European Community law, while aware of the developments of the Treaty on European Union (TEU) signed at Maastricht in February 1992 were forced by the delay in the entry into force of the treaty[71] to include various reservations in their prefaces.

If a specific area of law is being addressed either by a student or a practitioner confronted with a specific situation upon which to advise, monographs may be more helpful. These will deal with a specific area of European law, perhaps the free movement of goods, social security, the Common Agricultural Policy, taxation or competition. Into this category too must be included the various works on human rights in general and the European Convention and its case law in particular. General textbooks in this field are relatively rare. However, monographs (often based on academic theses on subjects such as the right to a fair trial and the right to freedom of expression and concomitantly the right to privacy) are legion, and any major law library will be able to produce a list of such works.

## Dictionaries, encyclopaedias and other reference works

Such works range from slim, single volume, paperback dictionaries giving succinct information about the different European organisations, treaties, institutions and personalities to multivolume reference works containing the original texts of all or most of Community legislation, occasionally with annotations or more extended commentaries. The latter works are generally extremely comprehensive, with each individual section written by an expert in the field concerned. The risk of instant obsolescence is minimised (although not altogether eliminated) by the fact that such works (whose acquisition is only within the reach of specialised law libraries or major law firms) are usually accompanied by regular (usually monthly) updating services which are often consolidated in an annual volume.

---

71  Itself caused by the negative referendum in Denmark, see Chapter 3.

In the field of European Community law it is, ironically, *Halsbury's Laws of England* which fulfils this role. As Lord Hailsham, the former Lord Chancellor, points out in a foreword to the relevant volumes, at the time of the planning and preparation of the fourth edition of *Halsbury's Laws*, the United Kingdom was not even a member of the European Community, still less was European Community law a part of "the laws of England'. By the time the fourth edition was nearing completion the penetration of European Community law into English law[72] was widely recognised. It was therefore decided to devote the two final volumes (Volumes 51 and 52) of *Halsbury's Laws* to European Community law. The volumes have also been published separately and now have their own up-dating service which, with its comprehensive indices and cross-referencing system, is probably the most reliable way to establish whether new legislation or judicial decisions may have changed the law in a given area.

**Law reviews**

Finally in this category one must mention the various law reviews which have a number of uses. The bulk of such reviews is taken up by learned articles on specific, and sometimes extremely narrow, areas of the law. While generally very erudite these articles may contain extremely contentious opinions whose validity should be carefully evaluated by any reader. Most also contain, in one form or another, reviews or surveys of recent developments in the field with which they are concerned including notes of cases recently decided by different courts and commentaries on new legislative interventions. These too are very often highly opinionated but are valuable as a source of stimulus to refer to the relevant texts. Book reviews in all fields of human endeavour (not just the law) are widely recognised as vehicles for settling old scores and setting out alternative views. Nonetheless, in law reviews as in other fields, they serve to alert readers to the most recent publications and of course they may provide guidance on whether or not to buy a particular textbook or monograph which may be of interest.

Although many general law reviews contain articles of interest to those in search of European law (indeed in the light of the arguments presented in Chapter 1 it would be hard for any law review to avoid including such material) certain among them stand out and may be regarded almost as required reading. In the

---

72   And of course Scottish law, as witness the inclusion of sections on
     European Community law in the Stair Society publication men-
     tioned above.

following paragraphs the full title of the law review is followed with its usual abbreviation which should be borne in mind when reading the section on citations below. The reviews referred to are mentioned in alphabetical order and the list is not intended to be either exhaustive or critical.

The *Common Market Law Review* (C.M.L. Rev.), despite its slightly anachronistic title is a wide-ranging journal dealing with all aspects of European Community law, the law of the European Economic Area and related issues concerning, for example, the second and third pillars of the European Union, the status of the Europe agreements and legal issues relating to the enlargement of the Union. In addition to analytical articles written by prominent academics, practitioners and senior national or European civil servants, the review contains substantial notes on important cases decided by the European Courts as well as decisions on points of European law made by the courts in the Member States. Although it is published from the University of Leiden in the Netherlands, all articles and reviews are published in English.

The *European Law Review* ([1996] 21 E.L. Rev.) sets as its aim to cover "the law of the European Union and the relevant legal developments in adjoining regions". It is aimed both at academics and legal practitioners and therefore, in addition to wide-ranging and useful general articles it includes a useful current survey of recent developments based upon a systematic classification of subjects covering developments in the European Communities, the second and third pillars of the Union, the 15 Member States and the Council of Europe.

In addition to those two journals devoted almost exclusively to European law issues, articles and notes on certain topics frequently appear in the International and Comparative Law Quarterly ((1997) I.C.L.Q.) as well as in more general law journals. The Yearbook of European Law ((1997) 17 Y.E.L.) is an annual publication, much like a law review in terms of its coverage and general presentation. However, the articles tend to be more substantial and reflective rather than aiming to provide current coverage.

In the human rights field the principal reviews in English are *The Human Rights Law Journal* ((1990) 11 H.R.L.J.), *The Human Rights Quarterly* (H.R.Q.) and *The Human Rights Review* (H.R.R.). Articles on human rights issues appear frequently in all international law journals as well as in general law reviews and certain specialist ones, particularly those specialising in criminal law and procedure. The "Yearbook of the European Convention on Human Rights" ((1997) Y.B.), in addition to commentaries on specific topics contains certain decisions of the European Commission of Human Rights on the admissibility of applications, and extracts from reports of the Commission and judgments of the

Court. That yearbook exists in both English and French versions (the French is called the *Annuaire des droits de l'homme*).

It should not be thought that English, despite its increasing role as a *lingua franca* in international academic exchanges, is the only or even the main language in which writing on European law is published. There is a wide range of publications in all of the major European languages and it will frequently be profitable to consult such works where your linguistic ability and available time and library resources so permit. Those whose courses include a year studying at a university in another Member State or who plan to travel abroad for postgraduate studies (see Chapter 9) should try to make a point of familiarising themselves with the legal materials which they will meet and with the language and drafting style of the country to which they are travelling.

## Casebooks

As Lord Mackenzie Stuart once pointed out in a foreword to a book of cases and materials[73] "in no field of legal study is descriptive writing a substitute for the basic texts". Means of accessing those basic texts are dealt with below. However, such casebooks have an important role to play, particularly for students. In the first place it is rarely possible to borrow such materials from the law library and photocopying may be prohibitively costly where large volumes of cases or treaty texts are required. Moreover, because of the cost and bulk of the materials required they may well be held only by the largest law libraries and those where such materials are in regular demand. *A fortiori* few students will be able to form their own personal collection of such materials. Therefore the reading list of most general or introductory courses to European law, especially European Community law, will include a volume of cases and materials chosen to accompany the textbook. Very often the recommended case book will have been compiled with a particular course structure in mind and, almost equally often, the process will have been reversed so that the course is built up from the recommended casebook.

Important and useful as these compilations are it should always be remembered that they are, by definition, selective, that the documents chosen may well be heavily edited and a clearer understanding of a judgment or legislative text will always be gained by reading the full document, including, for example, the preambles to legislation or the Advocates General's Opinions

---

73  Plender and Usher's *Cases and Materials on the Law of the European Communities* (3rd ed. by John A. Usher, 1993).

relating to particular judgments of the Court of Justice. Finally, even more than is the case with textbooks, volumes of cases and materials suffer from almost instant obsolescence and care should always be taken to establish whether or not there have been more recent developments in the area of law under investigation.

Given the close connexity between the structure of a given course and the case book concerned it will generally be rash to depart from the recommended work. However, where no such book is recommended, arguably the best available is, somewhat embarrassingly, an American publication entitled *European Community Law*.[74] The materials are comprehensive, clearly and systematically arranged and with excellent indexing. A separate volume of selected documents contains the full texts of various treaties, frequently encountered directives and Commission regulations. The extracts from cases are carefully chosen and each section is generally accompanied by an overview of the topic concerned while the cases themselves are accompanied by searching questions designed to encourage clear and independent thinking about the matter.

## ORIGINAL MATERIALS

No matter how comprehensive a case book may be or how detailed the commentaries in a text book or law journal, all students and other searchers after the law will sooner or later have to consult the actual wording used by the lawmaker, whether an intergovernmental conference of sovereign states, a legislative assembly or a court. However, as will already be apparent from earlier chapters, European law is a many-faceted field originating in public international law and including autonomous legal systems such as European Community law which itself operates in large measure through the domestic laws of individual Member States. Furthermore, the various organisations and institutions which generate European law have widely varying publications policies, resources and language regimes and consequently widely varying degrees of comprehensiveness or rapidity of documentation. So far as languages are concerned, English speakers are probably the best served since English is usually at least one of the official languages used in European relations, although this is not invariably so as demonstrated, for example, by the Benelux

---

74   Bermann, Goebel, Davey & Fox, eds. (West Publishing Company, Minnesota, 1993). The latest supplement was published in 1998 and takes into account The Treaty of Amsterdam.

(French and Dutch) or the Schengen Agreement (see below). It is therefore hardly surprising that there is no single comprehensive series or encyclopaedia within which all European law texts are neatly arranged and easily found.

Finally, it should be borne in mind that European Community law, which constitutes by far the most voluminous and pervasive constituent of European law as a whole, operates on two (at least) levels. Thus regulations and decisions are adopted by the institutions acting independently of the legal systems of the Member States and such instruments operate directly with no need for any further intervention by any national authorities. By contrast directives, while they are adopted at supranational level, must be implemented into domestic law in accordance with national constitutional arrangements. Thus the solution to a particular problem in an area covered by the directive may be found by studying the domestic law of the subject. Of course it may be necessary to compare the text of the directive and the national implementing legislation in order to ascertain whether the implementation (where it has been carried out) is correct and complete.

The remainder of this section will deal with finding the texts of treaties and conventions, then legislative texts such as directives, regulations and decisions and the case law of the various European courts. Such formal texts may not be the only institutional documents of interest to a student or researcher. Both the legislative and judicial processes generate numerous documents at various stages and which may be relevant to a research topic or, for example, in the case of legislative proposals serve as a stimulus to making representations (a polite word for lobbying) to the appropriate body.

### Treaties and Conventions

The texts of treaties and conventions are, with some exceptions, surprisingly difficult to find. The most comprehensive collection of treaties and international agreements is the United Nations Treaty Series (UNTS), started in 1946 pursuant to Article 102 of the Charter of the United Nations.[75] With the massive increase in exchanges between states the number of international treaties and agreements has increased exponentially and the UNTS now com-

---

75  The UNTS continued the work started under the League of Nations which registered and published treaties adopted between 1920 and 1946 in the League of Nations Treaty Series (LNTS).

prises over 1500 volumes. Thus the collection is likely to be held only by the best equipped research law libraries and for example in the libraries of Ministries of Foreign Affairs. Apart from the sheer scale of the series, its use is complicated by the fact that treaties are published in chronological order of the date upon which they are registered by the U.N. Secretariat, which cannot take place until the treaty or agreement concerned has entered force between two or more of the parties. This may therefore be many months or even years after the date upon which the treaty was made. In the context of treaties in the field of European law other sources should therefore be looked to first. Nonetheless the UNTS remains useful not least because each treaty is published both in the language or languages in which it is authentic as well as in translations both in English and in French. The series may therefore be useful in providing an authoritative (albeit not authentic) translation of a treaty which may otherwise be hard to find, such as the Schengen Agreement or the treaty establishing EFTA. Moreover, the UNTS may well be the only source for treaties and conventions establishing certain European or wider international organisations such as those dealt with in Chapter 2.

The European Treaty Series (ETS) does not have the same wide reach as the UNTS which aims to cover all treaties and agreements entered into by its Member States, but is limited to treaties and agreements negotiated within and entered into in the context of the Council of Europe. These documents are individually printed and numbered in sequence of their order of adoption and the series now includes some 60 conventions as well as various protocols and accession agreements. Thus, for example, the European Convention on Human Rights and Fundamental Freedoms is available as ETS No.5. Most states also collect and publish a series of the treaties to which they are parties, such as, for example, the United Kingdom Treaty Series (UKTS).

Many of the European organisations themselves publish editions of their constituent treaties in a convenient format for regular users. While these volumes or brochures do not constitute official or authentic sources for the texts of the instruments concerned (and are often accompanied by a disclaimer to that effect) they are invariably accurate and entirely reliable. Furthermore, in the interests of ensuring the widest accessibility of the instruments concerned these publications are heavily subsidised and therefore relatively inexpensive or may even be available free of charge altogether in the form of a brochure such as that distributed by the Council of Europe and containing the text of the European Convention on Human Rights with several of the main protocols. If you are likely to make regular use of the text of a particular treaty or convention it is therefore well worth obtaining such an edition.

Finally, certain periodicals also publish treaties, conventions and other legal instruments in formats which may be available more conveniently or more rapidly than the official sources or treaty series. Thus International Legal Materials (ILM)[76] provides a collection of current documents useful to any lawyers, academics or administrators concerned with the legal aspects of public and private international relations and which are not readily available in most libraries. In most cases I.L.M. reproduces the official documents by a simple photo offset process but will also publish an unofficial typescript where the official texts are unavailable or when a translation is given. The texts are sometimes accompanied by useful introductory notes by a legal practitioner or academic who has drawn the instrument to the attention of the editors. Since 1978, *Commercial Laws of Europe* (CLE) provides regular and systematic publication of new legal instruments of particular importance to lawyers advising businessmen or traders concerning matters such as company organisation, consumer protection, control of databases, intellectual property and taxation. In addition to European Community materials derived from the Official Journal, CLE publishes national legislation likely to have general interest outside the country concerned and where the legislation reproduced does not have an authentic English text both a translation and the original language text are reproduced. The original language version is published as a separate supplement (cited as CLE F) which is then bound together with the main issues in each annual volume. The news agency, Agence Europe, publishes a daily newsletter in French, English, German and Italian, which is required reading for all those who need to follow European Union affairs closely. As a most useful additional service the bulletin regularly includes a supplement entitled "Europe Documentation" which includes the text of newly adopted treaties or conventions or, for example, the conclusions of the Presidency following European Council meetings (summits).

## Legislation

Among the various European organisations only the European Community and the European Economic Area adopt and issue legislation which is of general application, such as directives,

---

76   (1991) 30 I.L.M. 68 is the reference for the text of the Schengen Agreement and the text of the Dublin Convention on Asylum may be found at (1991) 30 I.L.M. 425.

regulations and binding decisions.[77] Such legislation is sometimes referred to as "secondary legislation" by way of distinction from the primary sources of law which are the various treaties. The addition of that adjective is unnecessary and gives a false impression of the nature and effect of the legislation since the term "secondary legislation" is used in English law to designate delegated legislation such as statutory instruments and ministerial acts adopted without going through the full parliamentary procedures laid down for Acts of Parliament.

*The Official Journal*

Happily, in view of their close kinship, the European Union and the European Economic Area both publish their legislation in the *Official Journal of the European Communities* (usually cited in English simply as OJ, although in French and Italian, for example, this is extended to *JOCE* and *GUCE* respectively in order to distinguish the E.U. publication from the national official journals, the *JORF* and the *GURI* respectively).

The *Official Journal* is the official gazette of the European Communities and of the EEA in which are published the authentic texts of European Community legislation and a wide range of other documents and notices essential for the student or user of European law. Issues of the OJ are published daily in A4-sized format, each issue ranging from eight to several hundred pages in volume. The OJ is published in all 11 official languages, each version being distinguished by a stripe of colour on the spine,[78] the colour for the English version being pink. Each version uses the same numbering and pagination scheme. Therefore with very limited exceptions (in the case of individual documents which are only required to be published in one language) the same text will be found on the same page in each of the various language versions.

The two principal series of the Official Journal are known respectively as the L series (for legislation) and the C series (from the French *Communications*) containing notices and other documents.

---

77  See Chapter 4 above.
78  This simple and effective device for distinguishing the various language versions is becoming increasingly difficult as, for example, there are now three different blues, two greens and two yellows in use.

Most important is the L series in which all binding Community acts are published. These include all regulations, directives[79] and decisions as well as certain other binding acts such as the annual budget (invariably the biggest issue of the OJ each year, running to up to 1200 pages), amendments and corrigenda to pre-existing legislation, the rules of procedure of the institutions.

While the C series acts principally as a kind of official notice-board of the European Communities and the EEA, many of the documents published in it are of great importance and utility. In particular, the text of new Community treaties and acts of accession are published as individual issues[80] as are consolidated versions of acts amended by later treaties or legislation.[81] The C series also includes the texts of acts preparatory to the adoption of legislation, including the text of the Commission's proposals, the opinions of the Economic and Social Committee and the Committee of the Regions as well as common positions adopted by the Council. In addition, acts which are strictly speaking non-binding but in practice are adhered to, such as Council resolutions and declarations, exchange rates between the European Currency Unit and national currencies, are included.

A brief notice of every case brought before the Court of Justice, the Court of First Instance or the EFTA Court is also published in the C series and the importance of this for practitioners is that the three-month time-limit for intervening in cases before any of those three courts runs from the date of the publication of that particular notice. Until 1994 those notices were interspersed in the C series periodically, whenever space was available. However, since that time a specific issue devoted exclusively to court proceedings

---

79  Publication of directives has only been compulsory under Article 254 (ex Article 191) EC since the Maastricht Treaty. Although directives have always been systematically published in the L series their titles on the contents page were printed in light type indicating that publication was not obligatory, thus reflecting the intergovernmental nature of a directive as a form of legislation, *i.e.* it is an instrument adopted by the Council, composed of course of representative of the Member States, and addressed to the Member States. However, as Advocate General Lenz pointed out in his Opinion in Case C–91/92 *Faccini Dori v. Recreb*, such an approach was not consistent with the principles of the direct effect of directives as elaborated in the Court's case law. See p. 149 above.

80  Thus the Amsterdam Treaty is published in OJ C 340 of November 10, 1997.

81  Thus the Treaty on European Union, together with a complete and consolidated text of the EC Treaty as amended by the TEU, showing the amendments in bold italic type, was published in OJ C 224 of August 31, 1992.

appears approximately fortnightly, although it does not constitute a separate series and is numbered in sequence with other issues. These "Court of Justice" issues also include the text of the operative part of every judgment delivered by the three courts and of notices of withdrawals of actions. Finally, the Commission's annual report to the European Parliament on its monitoring of the application of Community law is published in the C series. This report includes, importantly, the status of the implementation of directives in the various Member States broken down by sectors, a list of judgments of the Court of Justice in infringement proceedings which have not yet been complied with, the state of infringement proceedings in progress and the application of Community law by national courts.

In addition to the two principal series there are a number of ancillary versions of the Official Journal. Of prime importance are the special editions issued on the accession of new Member States and containing official translations of the pre-accession legislation still in force. Thus in 1973 English and Danish special editions were published containing the legislation from 1952 to 1972. Similarly in 1981 a Greek special edition was published which was followed in turn by Spanish and Portuguese special editions in 1986 and Finnish and Swedish special editions in 1995. The S (for Supplement) series contains daily notices of public works and public supply contracts open to tender so as to enable contractors and suppliers to tender for such contracts in other Member States. The Annex to the Official Journal contains the full text of debates during the plenary session of the European Parliament in a so-called "rainbow" version, that is each speech is recorded and transcribed in the language in which it was delivered.

Finally, for those interested in potential employment in one of the institutions or other Community bodies or agencies, all notices of recruitment competitions are published in individual issues as a subset of the C series. Thus the main editions of the C series will contain, in every language, a brief mention of the vacancy and a reference to the issue in which further details and an application form can be found. The special issue is distinguished by a letter "A" after the number which corresponds to the number in the main C series. Where the post concerned is open only to applicants of a specific language, for example advertisements for the recruitment of translators or interpreters, the "A" issue of the C series will only be produced in that language. Individual issues of the "A" editions may be obtained free of charge from Commission offices or from the institution offering the job. A subscription to all such vacancy notices may be had for a very modest fee and should be available in all university careers departments.

Although the numbering system of individual issues of the OJ and the chronological arrangement of the published documents makes finding a document relatively straightforward, the sheer volume of material (in 1997 there were 357 issues published in the L series and 395 in the C series) makes a search for a particular document by browsing impracticable. Searches are therefore greatly facilitated by a sophisticated indexing system consisting of alphabetical tables and methodological tables published monthly with an annual consolidation. The alphabetical tables are particularly useful since they are not simply based on the initial letter of each instrument indexed but on an analysis of each published document which is then defined on the basis of certain key words and key expressions (descriptors) which constitute a rigorous thesaurus of Community terminology. Each document published in the OJ is indexed by up to six such key words or expressions and, in addition, the alphabetical listing contains so-called "non-descriptors", that is to say terms which are not used for indexing purposes but which guide the user to the relevant descriptor. Thus, for example, if you are searching for a regulation on tariff preferences the index under that "non-descriptor" will show "see: Preferential Tariff". Each time the document appears in the alphabetical index under any one of the possible six descriptors the reference will show the document number, the reference to the series, the number and the page in the OJ and the legal form and the institution which issued the document. Armed with this information it is then easy to find the full title of the document in the methodological tables or the complete text in the relevant part of the OJ itself.

If you are likely to have to make regular use of the Official Journal it is worth spending half an hour or so studying this indexing system and trying to track down a certain number of documents using the tables. Some examples of the presentation of the title of documents in the methodological tables and the indexing in the alphabetical tables as well as the list of abbreviations used are contained in the handbook.

**Case Law**

Reports of the decisions of the European courts described in Chapter 6 are of central importance to an understanding of the treaties and legislation with which each court is concerned. Moreover, such decisions themselves constitute an important source of European law,[82] particularly in circumstances where a treaty provision or legislative instrument is ambiguous or incomplete or where it is to be applied in novel circumstances not envisaged by the legislator.

---

82   See Chapter 4, p. 129, above.

Each of the courts makes its judgments in individual cases available immediately after delivery in a typescript form and in accordance with its respective language regime. Subsequently they are collected together and published periodically, often accompanied by summaries and by useful indexing and reference material. They may also become available subsequently on the Internet or through documentary data bases, of which more anon. Finally, many private publishers issue series of reports covering all or some of the activities of the courts. Generally speaking, wherever possible, reference should be made to the reports of decisions published by the courts themselves since those reports will contain the complete text of the judgment concerned, including associated texts such as a Report for the Hearing or Advocate General's Opinion. Moreover, any translations will have been carried out by the Court's own staff and verified by the members of the Court, and the text will not have been edited so as to fit available space or conform to the house style of a private publisher. That said, the private publishers perform a valuable service, sometimes ensuring that judgments are available more rapidly through their publications than the official reports, whereas others may specialise in a particular area of activity such as taxation or competition, grouping cases of particular interest to specialist practitioners in a convenient form.

*European Court of Justice*

The European Court of Justice is undoubtedly the most prolific of the European courts in terms both of the number of cases which it decides and, consequently, the volume of its reported cases. Initially a single series called "Reports of cases before the Court of Justice",[83] the advent of the Court of First Instance in 1989 and, subsequently, the need to reduce the volume of translations required by the Court have resulted in the reports being divided into two separate series, one of which is further divided into two parts.

Thus from 1954 to 1989 the European Court Reports contained only the reports of judgments of the Court of Justice, arranged in strict chronological order according to the date of the judgment and, where more than one judgment was delivered on a particular date, in numerical order of the cases concerned. Although the published judgments are issued in monthly paperback fascicles the pagination is continuous throughout the year and the number of each fascicle forms no part of the case reference. From 1990

---

83 Usually abbreviated (in English) to "European Court Reports" and referred to as ECR.

onwards the ECR is divided into Part I, containing the judgments of the Court of Justice itself and Part II, the judgments of the Court of First Instance. Initially, the two parts (each with its own pagination) were bound together in each monthly fascicle. However, once the Court of First Instance entered its stride the volume of the judgments which it produced made this system too cumbersome and so Parts I and II are now published separately.

Most recently, in 1994, in order to reduce the volume of translations required, it was decided no longer to translate reports of cases concerning community officials into all of the official languages (then nine, now eleven) but to publish them in a separate series known as the Reports of European Community Staff Cases, abbreviated to ECR–S.C. Given that the Court of First Instance retains the option of publishing full reports in all of the official languages of staff cases which raise a point of law of general interest (for example, a question of principle in administrative law or an interpretation of the rules of procedure), the reports published in the ECR–S.C. are likely to be of interest essentially only to highly specialised practitioners and it is not necessary to explain their rather complex structure and presentation here.

## The EFTA Court

If the jurisprudential output of the Court of Justice and the Court of First Instance have been prolific, not to say prodigious, that of the EFTA Court since its establishment at the beginning of 1994 can only be regarded as modest, at least so far. The reports of its decisions are therefore combined with an annual report which, as well as reports of the Court's decisions during the period covered, includes general information about the organisation of the Court, its jurisdiction and rules of procedure. The first report of the EFTA Court ([1994–1995] EFTA Rep.) cover the period from January 1, 1994 to June 30, 1995, the end of the transitional period following the accession of Austria, Finland and Sweden to the European Union on January 1, 1995. The judgments and other decisions reported in that volume are published only in the EFTA Court's official language, English. The second report covers the period from July 1, 1995 to December 31, 1996 and contains reports of the four advisory opinions delivered by the EFTA Court during that period both in English and in the language used by the courts which made the request for advisory opinions (all four cases were Norwegian) with the English language version being printed on the left-hand page and corresponding Norwegian text on the right-hand page with each version carrying corresponding page numbers. The third report follows the same pattern and, from that issue forth the reports will appear each calendar year.

European Court of Human Rights

The official reports of the European Court of Human Rights are published in English and French by a German publisher. There are two series of publications making up the reports, Series A which contains the judgments and decisions of the Court, including, since 1984 extracts from the Commission's report pursuant to Article 31 of the Convention. Series B containing the written submissions of the parties, the oral arguments and other documents, including the full text of the Commission's Article 31 Report, has always suffered from publication seriously in arrears and was finally discontinued in July 1995, the last volume containing documents relating to cases decided in 1987. The Commission's Article 31 Reports in cases that have been referred to the Court may now be obtained from the Registry of the Court in offset form, prior to the publication of the eventual Court decision. The original Series A was replaced, from January 1, 1996, by the "Reports of Judgments and Decisions".

The usual form of citation is *McCann v. United Kingdom* A (1989) 324. *McCann v. United Kingdom* (1989) (A 329) Com. Rep., followed by a paragraph number, will refer to the relevant number in the Commission's Article 31 Report. There appears to be no standard abbreviation for the new "Reports of Judgments and Decisions", which are however, published in strict chronological order of the date of their delivery or adoption. A reference to a case should therefore include the full names of the parties, the date of the judgment or decision concerned and the number of the volume of the reports in which it is to be found, if the latter information is available.

In the scheme of the control machinery of the Human Rights Convention prior to the entry into force of the Eleventh Protocol (see p. 187 above) the Commission of Human Rights played a highly important role, in recent years dealing with over 10,000 complaints a year. Partly because of the Commission's effectiveness in eliminating manifestly inadmissible complaints and applications and in identifying both admissible cases and those in which there were good grounds to suppose that there had been a breach of the Convention, the workload of the Court itself had been kept to manageable proportions. Since many of the cases dealt with by the Commission do not ultimately reach the Court of Human Rights, either because the Commission declares them inadmissible or because where they are admissible and apparently well founded, they may be dealt with by way of friendly settlement or resolution of the Committee of Ministers and hence not give rise to a decision of the Court itself published in the main reports series. Therefore, for a full picture of the law of the Convention access to the Commission decisions is necessary and will remain so even after the demise of the Commission itself in 1999.

These have been published since 1959, first in the collection of decisions of the European Commission of Human Rights (cd), superseded from 1975 onwards by the decisions and reports of the European Commission of Human Rights (dr). Both series are published in English and in French, contain selected Commission decisions as to admissibility, friendly settlement reports under Article 28 of the Convention and reports on the merits under Article 31 where the case is not referred to the Court. In such cases the Committee of Ministers' resolution closing the case is also printed. The volumes appear approximately monthly and are consecutively numbered. Since Volume 76 the volumes have been split into Parts A and B with the A volumes containing the original language version (*i.e.* English or French) of the document concerned, and the B series the translation, thus liberating at least the original language version from the delays inherent in a bilingual system.

*Privately published reports series*

Although not carrying the authority of the official series of reports published by the various courts, most such reports present at least one and sometimes several additional features enhancing their usefulness beyond that of merely duplicating the official reports. The main drawback of the unofficial reports is that they are invariably selective as to the materials published and therefore it is impossible to tell with confidence whether all the authorities on a particular point are available. Nonetheless, such reports may also include material unpublished elsewhere or may group material, such as judgments of the European courts together with other material such as judgments of national courts. They may also provide more comprehensive or user-friendly indexing and are frequently published more rapidly than the official series.

So far as European Community law is concerned, the main commercial series in English is the Common Market Law Reports (C.M.L.R.) which, from its establishment in 1962 to the accession of the UK and Ireland in 1973, provided the only reliable and reasonably comprehensive reports in English of the judgments of the Court of Justice. Since 1973, as well as including a selection of the more important judgments of the Court of Justice (and since 1990 those of the Court of First Instance) it has included decisions of national courts on points of Community law (whether they were referred to the Court of Justice for a preliminary ruling or not) both in the original language and, where that language was not English, in a useful English language translation. It also includes judgments of the EFTA Court and decisions of the

European Commission and the European Surveillance Agency applying the rules of competition in the EC Treaty and the EEA Agreement. It also publishes certain other documents such as the rules of procedure of the courts. The American publishing house CCH publishes European Community cases (CEC) which is highly selective, but particularly strong in its reporting of competition cases and related documents.

In 1995 Butterworths added a series entitled "European Cases" (All E.R. (EC)) to its popular all England Law Reports (All E.R.) series. The European Court Monitor (ECM) reviews, rather than reports, the decisions of the Court of Justice and the Court of First Instance as well as of selected Opinions of the Advocates General in particularly important cases. The cases are presented thematically and each "report" consists of a short and readable précis (more important cases are summarised at proportionately greater length) which occasionally includes helpful comment. The *Monitor*, like the Court of Justice' own weekly bulletin *Proceedings of the Court of Justice and the Court of First Instance*, is designed to enable practitioners to keep abreast of developments in the whole field of Community law and to identify rapidly those cases to which they will need to pay particular attention and of which they will need to read the full text of the judgment.

So far as Human Rights are concerned, since 1979 Sweet and Maxwell have published the European Human Rights Reports (E.H.R.R.) which contains full reports in English of all the Court's judgments as well as selected Commission reports and decisions. Since 1993 the latter have been published in a separate supplement (E.H.R.R. C.D.). The German publisher of the A and B series of the Human Rights Court reports (Carl Heymanns Verlag) produces an unofficial German version of the judgments of the Human Rights Court and the German journal *Grundrechte* also published German translations of the Court's judgments as well as Human Rights cases decided in other courts. Carl Heymanns Verlag also publishes a useful digest of Strasbourg case law relating to the European Convention on Human Rights a loose-leaf work jointly edited by the Council of Europe and the University of Utrecht containing extracts from the case law of both the Commission and the Court of Human Rights (including some Commission cases not reported elsewhere) arranged systematically following the scheme of the Convention.

## Other documents

In addition to the texts of law-making instruments, lawyers and other researchers often find it helpful to consult other documents containing reports on particular subjects, recommendations for legislative changes, the draft legislation to bring about such changes or other preparatory documents. As already mentioned, the C series of the Official Journal of the European Communities contains the so-called preparatory acts prior to the adoption of legislation. The contributions of the European Parliament to the legislative process are published at three separate levels. First the C series of the Official Journal contains the minutes of the plenary sessions of the Parliament, the resolutions adopted and written questions put by MEPs to members of the Council or the Commission and the answers supplied to those questions. Next the verbatim transcript of all of the debates of the European Parliament and the oral questions and answers during those sessions is published in a so-called "rainbow" version (that is to say that each intervention is published in the language in which it was made, with no translation) in an annex to the Official Journal.

Further upstream, and importantly if you are seeking to influence the content of proposed legislation or are advising those who do, are the session documents which are divided into three separate series which may be subscribed to in a microfiche format or may be individually requested from the Parliament. Series A contains the reports from committees of the Parliament. These are extremely influential reports, usually known by the name of the committee member responsible for drafting the report and carrying out the bulk of the research which goes into it. They are almost invariably adopted as an expression of the whole Parliament's position at a subsequent plenary session. Series B contains motions for resolutions while series C covers documents received from other institutions which are then renumbered for the Parliament's purposes. These are often referred to in committee reports and the documents may be more easily obtained through the Parliament's recording system than by traipsing around each individual institution or agency concerned.

The Commission's working documents, known as COM DOCs, are available in all 11 official languages and can be obtained either in hard copy or in microfiche format. The Commission's discussion documents and first policy formulations (known as green papers and white papers respectively following British parliamentary terminology, which is derived in its turn from the colour of the paper covers of these documents in Britain) in which a particular policy area or problem is described and the various options for dealing with it summarised. In the light of submissions made in response to a green paper the Commission will formulate its views more clearly with its policy guidelines and where necessary, draft legislation. Thus COM (93) 551 "Green Paper on European Social Policy – Options for the Union" was followed by the "White Paper on Social Policy -- A way forward for the Union" COM (94) 333 final, representing the Commission's considered view on the subject. As already mentioned, legislative proposals are published in the C series of the Official Journal. However, they will already have been contained in a COM DOC which, in addition to the draft legislation printed in the C series, includes an explanatory memorandum giving background information on the subject, the results of the consultative process undertaken and a summary of the policy considerations lying behind the draft legislation. Finally, COM DOCs may include retrospective reports on the implementation or effectiveness of a Community policy or legislative measure.

All Community institutions issue press releases on the day upon which new developments occur and, although of course these are principally for the use of journalists, they are available to any other person requiring up-to-date information on the activities of the institutions. They may be obtained on paper or by fax from the Press Office of the institution concerned However, all press releases of the Community institutions are published on the RAPID database which can be accessed free of charge through the Europa Internet site.

The *Bulletin of the European Union* is a monthly publication, in all 11 languages, giving details of the activities of the Commission and other institutions of the Union. In addition to a thematic section giving details of reports, decisions or new legislation in various areas of activity, the Bulletin contains extracts from important documents such as the conclusions of European Council meetings (summits) or policy statements by the Commission. References are also given to the activities of the other institutions, such as judgments of the Court of Justice and the Court of First Instance, reports from the Court of Auditors and resolutions of the European Parliament. Periodically a supplement is issued devoted to specific issues. Thus the Commission's "Agenda 2000" was published as a supplement at the same time as a series of ten reports, each covering one of the countries' candidates for the next round of accessions to the Union.

The written pleadings submitted to the Court of Justice, the Court of First Instance and the EFTA Court are confidential and remain so even after the case has been decided or withdrawn. It is possible for the parties to make their own pleadings and arguments public (but not those of the opposite party)[84] although it seems that they almost never do so. On the day of the oral hearing in each case, each of the courts publishes a Report for the Hearing in which the legislation at issue and the respective arguments of the parties, or of those submitting observations, is summarised.

---

84 See the judgment of the Court of First Instance of June 17, 1998 in Case T–174/95 *Svenska Journalist förbundet v. Council* (not yet reported) in which the applicant published the Council's defence on the Internet.

Until 1994 (except for 1987 and 1988) the Report for the Hearing was included in the final report of the case published in the ECR. Prior to 1987 it was re-presented in the form of the facts and issues section of the judgment. From 1989 to 1993 the Report for the Hearing was printed without amendment alongside the judgment. Such publication has now been discontinued. For its part, the Court of First Instance regarded the Report for the Hearing as a preparatory document whose contents, in so far as they were necessary for the pleadings, were incorporated into the judgment of the Court of First Instance, reflecting its important role as a Court required to establish the facts in the case. Both courts, however, will provide roneoed copies of the Report for the Hearing in a particular case, but only in the language of procedure of that case.

Since the EFTA Court does not yet suffer from the pressure of work of the two European Community courts it continues to publish the Report for the Hearing in the EFTA Court Report both in English and, where necessary, in the language of the referring court. As already mentioned, the arguments of the parties in cases before the European Court of Human Rights, accompanied by the Commission's Article 31 Report, were published in the B series of the European Human Rights Reports until 1995.

## A word about citations

The only purpose of including citations in legal writing, whether in course assignments, doctoral theses, academic journals or textbooks or parliamentary reports is to enable readers to identify and, if they wish, to find the sources of the authorities used so that they may be verified and the conclusions which are claimed to be based on those authorities confirmed. It is therefore indispensable that the abbreviations used for various publications, whether official documents or periodicals, be used consistently so that they may be recognised by anyone likely to read the document under consideration. If you are preparing notes exclusively for your own use or for the edification of a closed group of users, all of whom may be assumed to understand your shorthand or abbreviations, you may of course do as you like. However, even in those circumstances I would suggest that sticking to the orthodox abbreviations is a safer course since it will enable you to find the documents which you have used more easily in the future, if need be.

Unfortunately, there is, as yet, no uniform citation system for European legal materials and as a result a number of different ways of referring to the same document may be encountered. While the Community institutions and those of the Council of Europe endeavour to be reasonably consistent, structural changes and changes in publication policy over the years have inevitably led to variations, while in the Community context the different traditions of legal citation in eleven different languages must also be taken into consideration. Although this book is not the place to lay down such a uniform system, I would suggest that a basic rule of guidance is to use the style of citation contained in the document to which reference is being made. This is the approach followed throughout this book whenever a new document or publication is mentioned, as well as in the list of abbreviations contained in the Vade-mecum.[85] The importance of using citations consistently has increased rather than decreased with increasing use of legal databases and the Internet, since computers are more punctilious than the most "picky" of sub-editors. Thus, for example, the internal databases of the Court of Justice will reject an enquiry which omits the hyphen between the C or the T and the case number.

Many publishers of English language legal materials introduce variations into European law references in order to comply with their own house style or to make references look more like those to British or American materials and no doubt the same phenomenon occurs in other languages. Thus, for example, the All England Law Reports, when referring to a Court of Justice case, places the case number after the names of the parties rather than before and many publishers introduce fullstops after the letters ECR or OJ (O.J. was famously acquitted of murder). Therefore, although in strict grammatical usage a fullstop is used where a word is abbreviated to its initial letter, this is not necessary where the abbreviation consists exclusively of capital letters, as in OECD, ECR, EHRR or MEP. Inserting fullstops into acronyms which are formed solely from the initial letters of the organisation concerned actually looks ridiculous. Thus NATO, EFTA, CERN or GATT, are spelled in capital letters without stops. Fullstops are generally used when the abbreviation includes truncated words. Thus EL Rev., or Eur.Lr, or EFTA Rep.

Nicknames are sometimes given to organisations where the acronym of their initials is possible to pronounce, such as EURATOM (for the European Atomic Energy Community) or COREPER (for the Committee of Permanent Representatives of the Member States to the European Union – from the French *Comité des représentants permanents*) or Eur-op (for the Office for Official Publications of the European Communities). These nicknames take no punctuation, nor do they change according to language and are very often used in official texts.

85  Alphabet Soup, p 335.

Nicknames given to cases[86] may also cause problems. Apart from a very small number of particularly celebrated cases, such as *Cassis de Dijon*[87] or the *Gibraltar Three* case[88] (although even this case is occasionally called the *"Death on the Rock"* case) different writers are likely to give different names to the same case. Moreover, nicknames are hardly ever indexed and still less can computers cope with them. Nonetheless, nicknames or other labels can be useful, in particular in distinguishing between the many cases involving the same combinations of institutions or Member States. Thus, for example, Case 302/87 and Case C–70/88 were both actions brought by the European Parliament against the Council that are easily distinguished by calling them respectively the "Comitology" and "Chernobyl" cases respectively.[89] Cases brought by the Commission against Community Member States under Article 169 of the Treaty may often be conveniently distinguished by the product or area of activity concerned.[90] Also, cartel cases in which several applicants challenge a decision adopted by the Commission pursuant to Article 85 of the EC Treaty may again be most conveniently referred to by the name of the product concerned, such as Cement, PVC, Low Density Polyethylene (in French *PEBD*), Wood Pulp or Welded Steel Mesh. However, when resorting to such nicknames, it is essential always to give the full citation when the particular case is first mentioned and to use the nickname once adopted consistently throughout the text.

## LAW LIBRARIES

Despite the changes brought about through advances in information technology and the availability of relatively inexpensive textbooks, monographs and case books, the law library is, and is likely to remain, the main resource from which to find the answers to legal questions. However, for reasons of cost or available space, not all law libraries will hold complete or even extensive collec-

---

86  See Vade-mecum VII, p 370.
87  Case 120/78 *REWE-Zentral v. Bundesmonopolverwaltung für Branntwein* [1979] ECR 649.
88  *McCann & Others v. United Kingdom*, (A 324) (1989).
89  Case 302/87 *Parliament v. Council* [1988] ECR 5615 and Case C–70/88 *Parliament v. Council* [1990] ECR I–2041.
90  For example, Case 178/84 *Commission v. Germany* [1987] ECR 1227 is often referred to as "the German Beer case" (preferably not "the case of German beer") or "the Reinheitsgebot case" and of over 300 cases brought up by the Commission against the Italian Republic it may be helpful to distinguish, for example, those concerning the export of works of art or measures to control swine fever.

tions of European law materials, especially of the original materials. In larger cities or conurbations where two or more universities are within reasonable proximity to each other it is common for libraries to agree to a division of labour in order to avoid duplication of material in more specialised fields and thereby to save cost overall. Access to law libraries is often reserved to the members of the host institution. However, temporary access for a limited period for a specific purpose can usually be arranged on request. Similarly, it may be possible, by special request, to use the libraries of professional organisations such as Bar associations or research institutes.

So far as European Community law materials are concerned, the most complete collections will be held by European Depository Libraries (EDLs). These libraries, which automatically receive a copy of every official publication of the European Union in one of the official languages are generally attached to the National Depository Libraries. Although in principle there is only one European Depository Library per country, there are 24 in the Member States of the European Union, including three in the United Kingdom and two in Ireland. Of the 73 Depository Libraries spread throughout the rest of the world no less than 50 are in the United States.

After the Depository Libraries the most comprehensive collections of European Community documentation, including legal materials, are those held by European Documentation Centres. The network of EDCs is also the most extensive with some 300 centres in the EU Member States and a further 100 in the rest of the world. They are invariably attached to the libraries of universities which provide advanced courses and research facilities in European and wider international affairs.

The EDCs may receive all publications of the European Parliament, the European Commission and the other Community institutions. However, those attached to specialised research institutes often ask to receive only selected materials which correspond more specifically to their particular needs. Each centre has privileged access to the European Community databases and most will have at least one librarian who has received special training in the field of European documentation and in the interrogation of the European databases.

Finally, European reference centres are attached to public libraries or libraries which do not support a research function or to the libraries of universities with relatively limited needs for European materials. The role of the reference centres, of which there are 79 in the EU Member States and 126 throughout the rest of the world, is to make available both to the academic community (teachers, researchers and students) and the wider general public certain basic documents on the European Union and its policies and to provide references to other Community documents. They do not automatically have access to the Community electronic databases, although many of the libraries may do so.

It must be recognised that these three types of library, having been established by the European Community, have privileged access only to European Community information and publications. They do not automatically receive publications of the Council of Europe, such as the European Treaty series, or the reports of cases before the European Court of Human Rights. Nonetheless, the bigger libraries or those attached to major law faculties should also have such materials available.

Having found your library, what next? First, and particularly if you are likely to have to make regular use of it, it is as well to get to know the physical layout of the library and to locate the principal materials that you will need. Most large libraries publish a guide to their collections explaining the layout and classification systems used as well as the conditions under which books may be borrowed (if at all), databases consulted and photocopies made. Some larger libraries organise regular visits to introduce new readers to the holdings and catalogues. In others it may be possible to ask one of the librarians, or a more experienced reader, to show you where the various resources are held and how to use the bibliographies and catalogues. In any event, two or three hours spent on such a familiarisation exercise are likely to pay dividends later on.

It should be remembered that law libraries in general exist principally for reference purposes and it is therefore rarely, if ever, possible to borrow primary source materials such as legislative texts and volumes of the law reports. Although this means that if you wish to make a detailed study of a particular regulation or you wish to give a close reading to a lengthy case report you may have to take copies in order to pursue your research outside the library's reading room, it does have the advantage that if a given volume is not found at its proper place in the shelves it is likely that another user has it not too far away. A certain amount of flexibility and mutual tolerance is therefore called for by readers.

Most of the "how to study" books mentioned in Chapter 1 (see footnote 10 include a section or a chapter on how best to use a law library. More detailed accounts are in Jane Dean and Philip Thomas' *How to use a law library* (3rd ed., 1996) and Peter Clinch, *Using a law library: a student's guide to legal research skills* (1992).

The availability of a photocopying machine in, or in proximity to the law library is, without a doubt, a great boon when one wishes to continue to study a document outside the library's opening hours or where two or more readers wish to use the same document or volume simultaneously. Nonetheless, it can also act as a seductive and expensive trap if it is misused. To judge by the mesmerised expression on the faces of some students as they photocopy lengthy law review articles, they seem to hope that the blindingly satisfying flash of the machine will equally bring enlightenment and by some miraculous osmosis transmit the contents of the article into the mind of the reader. However, sadly, photocopying can never be a substitute for careful and thoughtful reading and the flash of the machine is no substitute for taking an accurate note of the document, be it a court judgment, legislative text or an article in a law review.

## ELECTRONIC SOURCES

The huge volume of documentary sources of European law clearly lend themselves to storage in computer databases and, since the 1960s, a large number of such databases and associated retrieval systems have been developed. The European Union's database directory alone lists 51 different databases. These databases present numerous advantages, particularly where extensive traditional library facilities are unavailable. First, they give access to unimaginably vast storehouses of information directly at the researcher's desk. Secondly, they are extremely up to date, being updated at least weekly and sometimes on a daily basis.

Nonetheless, such tools are not a panacea and do have certain drawbacks. First of all, the documents stored in these information retrieval systems are, for the most part, the same as the texts (whether treaties, legislation or case law) already available in printed form. Thus, having carried out a search in a database, the material which you will retrieve will be the same which you might have found in a well-equipped European law library. Therefore if you do not know how to use that material the documents churned out by the computer will be of no greater use to you. It is therefore essential to have a clear idea of what it is that you are looking for and what you are going to do with it once you have found it.

Secondly, most of the on-line databases, particularly the more sophisticated and well-stocked ones, are only available by subscription and the cost of such subscriptions when added to charges for use (that is to say the cost of the time actually spent consulting the database) is generally such that only institutions such as libraries, law faculties or medium to large law firms with a high level of use will find it economic to subscribe to them.

Many of the databases, despite the richness of the resources they contain, were developed during the 1970s and 80s and are therefore based on computer techniques which may be difficult to learn when they are not positively rebarbative. Although steps are being taken by nearly all database providers to make their materials more readily accessible, they still require some degree of specialised training to use profitably and the development of skills which only regular use will maintain adequately.

Finally, asking vague or general questions, such as the texts of all judgments of the European Court of Human Rights dealing with Article 6 of the Convention, or all of the case law of the Court of Justice on the free movement of goods, is likely to produce an avalanche of material exceeding even that obtained by the diligent law student mentioned at the beginning of this chapter. Moreover, where such large volumes of material are retrieved the time taken to download it and, if required, to print it can prove exceedingly expensive.

In the light of those drawbacks I would suggest first that the electronic sources should not be used as a port of call until you have some grasp of the basic principles of European law and at least a modicum of experience in using the printed versions of its source material. Secondly, I find that the databases are best used as a bibliographic or indexing tool enabling interesting or useful documents to be identified and, at least so far as mainstream materials are concerned, consulted and used in a normal library.

Broadly speaking there are two categories of electronic information sources, on the one hand, specially developed documentary databases, whether general or specialised, some of which may be available on CD-Rom as well as on-line. On the other hand there is the Internet. More even than is the case with printed publications, even a brief summary description of materials available electronically must be subject to the caveat that developments both in the range and content of what is available and the methods of accessing it are changing so rapidly that the only way to be certain of knowing what is available is to go and look. The distinction between on-line services and the Internet is becoming somewhat blurred since many on-line services are now available through the Internet (see, for example, CELEX below), thus doing away with the need for specially dedicated terminals which add to the cost of use of these materials. Nonetheless, it may still be necessary to pay for access to an on-line service via the Web (for example, by payment to be allocated a password) and, once having obtained access to a particular database, charges may be made for either the time used or the number of documents retrieved.

### On-line databases

As already mentioned, the European Union is particularly well served for on-line databases. Of the 50 or more databases providing for public access many are highly specialised, providing agriculture or energy statistics, information on tendering for public service contracts or on research and technical development activities of the Union. The databases mentioned below are those presenting a specific interest for lawyers. All of the databases are managed by the "Eurobases" department of the Official Publications Office in Luxembourg. However, access and subscription information is managed by an agent known as "a gateway" in each Member State as well as in certain non-Member States such as Japan, United States, Canada and Norway.

**CELEX** is by far the most important database for European lawyers covering, as it does, virtually the whole range of European Community law. Established in 1966 and open to the public since 1981, it includes all of the Community treaties and legislation from 1951 onwards, judgments and orders of the Court of Justice from 1951 onwards, opinions of the Court's Advocates General from 1965 onwards and a comprehensive (though not complete) range of preparatory documents, such as opinions of the various institutions, resolutions of the European Parliament and answers to questions. It is updated at least twice a week.

Given its antiquity (in data-processing terms) the retrieval methods and interrogation language required have earned a justified notoriety for their user unfriendliness. Nonetheless, the sheer richness of the material available (which covers all Community languages) means that the time taken to learn the interrogation system can be amply repaid for a regular user. Since 1997 it has been possible to access CELEX through the Internet, provided that the user has a personal identifier and password. In opening this possibility, the managers of the database have taken the opportunity to create a vastly improved and user-friendly graphical interface which contains useful hypertext links to other sources, including the possibility to order printed copies of the documents consulted. The cost for viewing a document is relatively modest at O.3 Ecus to see the bibliographic details (title and references, *etc.*) or 1.2 Ecus per document to see the full text. Licences to produce CD-Rom versions of the CELEX database (using the new simpler access technology) have been accorded to various private firms. The English version is published by Context Ltd and costs £1,250 per year including quarterly updates.

**EUDOR** is a recently introduced document delivery service on the Web which, on the basis of a very simple graphic interface, allows users to search for documents by titles, dates, document numbers or publication references, in particular to the L and the C series of the Official Journal. A cross link is provided from the CELEX database to EUDOR to enable documents which have been identified to be ordered. The searching and browsing functions of EUDOR are free of charge and documents can be ordered at a cost of 0.5 Ecu per page for delivery electronically, by fax or by snail mail.

**ABEL** is the existing on-line service for ordering documents published in the L and the C series of the Official Journal. At present its coverage is greater than that of EUDOR. However, because of the greater flexibility and better facilities offered by EUDOR, ABEL will be phased out as soon as EUDOR covers the whole of the two O.J. series.

**SCAD** and **ECLAS**, while not specifically legally oriented databases, may prove useful starting points for research on legal topics. SCAD contains bibliographical and other information about Community instruments and related preparatory documents, the publications of the E.U. institutions, references to articles from over 1,500 periodicals dealing with European affairs. ECLAS (European Community Library Automation Service) is the catalogue of the Commission library in Brussels which is the most comprehensive collection of European information and documentation available.

**EUROLEX/LEX**, which is accessible from the Europa Internet server* provides full access to the texts of all the European Union and Community Treaties, including those in the course of ratification. For legislation it gives full access to the Directory of Community legislation in force with the possibility of searching under various headings or for certain words. New legislation and other instruments published in the L and C Series of the Official Journal are available for the previous 20 working days.

Other private sector on-line services include Matthews E.C.J. Digest, providing summaries of all Court of Justice and Court of First Instance judgments, notes of new cases lodged and cases withdrawn since 1990. References are given to the relevant Community legislation and other background information. This service is also available from Context Ltd. More recently, E.U. Law Online includes summaries of decisions of the Court of Justice and the Court of First Instance in English, the full texts of court judgments in several languages, selected Advocates General's Opinions, a diary of forthcoming cases, feature articles on issues and developments in European Union law, a discussion forum and job information. The subscription charge is, at present, $1,250 per month with reductions for multiple users such as law firms or other companies.

**The Internet**

The Internet, with its almost unlimited capacity, is a wonderful resource and its use will become increasingly the norm both in professional circles and purely for entertainment. However, while it undeniably presents enormous potential and can already be of great practical utility, some words of caution are necessary. First, the possibilities of accessing information are so vast as to dwarf

---

\*   www.europa.eu.int/eur-lex/

the problem faced by the international law student mentioned at the beginning of this chapter. A certain degree of self discipline and a focused approach to searching the Web are necessary if it is to be used in a practical way. Secondly, response times are very variable and the time taken to download or to print documents located through the Internet may be considerable and also quite costly. As with on-line databases it is often more practical to use the Internet to identify useful or interesting documents and then to trace them in a traditional library.

Discussion groups and on-line journals may be useful sources of ideas but, since many such groups and journals are subject to little, if any, editorial control they may also contain extremely radical, uninformed or even completely barmy discussions.

Since completely free access to the documents produced by international institutions (including courts and legislative bodies) could disrupt commercial arrangements and publishing programmes established over decades, very few such institutions give more than limited access to such material free of charge on the Web. Nonetheless, information will usually be given on Web sites on how to obtain the documents or how to have access to them using a paid password. Often more useful is the general information provided about organisations and institutions which are not covered directly on a particular course and where a general description of the organisation and functions concerned is sufficient. A list of useful Web sites is contained in the handbook.

# 8. HOW DO YOU INTERPRET EUROPEAN LAW?

*"I don't know what you mean by "glory" ', Alice said.*

*"I meant 'there's a nice knock-down argument for you'".*

*"But "glory' doesn't mean a nice knock-down argument", Alice objected.*

*"When I use a word" Humpty-Dumpty said in a rather scornful tone ' "it means just what I choose it to mean, neither more nor less".*
*Through the Looking Glass*, Lewis Carroll.

As if a multiplicity of overlapping legal systems and courts were not enough, the methods and techniques for using European law differ significantly from those applicable to the national legal systems of individual states, whether members of the Union or not. While such approaches may appear strange to lawyers trained in a particular legal system, and even stranger to non lawyers, they nonetheless follow certain principles and maintain an internal consistency.

Do not be put off reading this chapter by the idea that an analysis of the methods of interpretation is merely an abstract and theoretical exercise for it may have many practical uses. In the first place, for a student or researcher with an assignment it will help you to analyse the materials which you have found to be relevant to the project in hand and to marshall your arguments and materials in such a way as to lead to a convincing result. For practitioners it will be important to be able to predict (as far as prediction is possible in any human undertaking) how one of the European courts is likely to respond to arguments based on treaty provisions or legislation. Perhaps more importantly, you may need to persuade a court in your own jurisdiction that what might appear an obvious approach to that court might not be quite so obvious to a European court called upon to adjudicate on the basis of the same materials.[91] Finally, for the more general reader an awareness of these different approaches may help to explain results in particular cases which may otherwise cause surprise.

Much ink has been spilt and the greatest minds exercised over creating a systematic framework for the theory of interpretation of European law. This chapter however is intended only to provide an outline of the main techniques of interpretation and their limitations. Unless otherwise stated it may be assumed that the remarks in the remainder of this chapter apply to the techniques used by both the European Court of Justice (including the Court of First Instance and the EFTA Court) and the Court of Human Rights (including the Commission of Human Rights).

## WHAT IS LEGAL INTERPRETATION?

Legal rules are not adopted in a vacuum. They are designed to be applied to practical situations. Given that the authors of a particular rule cannot foresee in advance all of the circumstances in which it may fall to be applied, rules are often couched in general terms. Although such a legislative approach allows a certain flexibility in the application of the law it throws an additional burden on the shoulders of those called upon to ensure that it is applied effectively. Thus it is fairly rare that a particular rule can be directly applied in a concrete situation. In order to be sure that it is applicable it is sometimes necessary to eliminate any ambiguities which it may contain in order to give the text its effective meaning. Thus the role of interpretation is to ensure that the rule concerned is given its correct scope and meaning, so that it can be correctly applied in a given set of circumstances.

It is clear that there is a large and indistinct grey area ranging from a mere explanation of the rule in question to the adoption of a virtually new rule by the judge in a particular case. If judges

---

91  See in this regard the warnings of the Court of Justice in Case 283/81 *CILFIT v. Ministry of Health* [1982] ECR 3415, or the famous gaffe of Lord Widgery, then the Lord Chief Justice, in the English proceedings in *R. v. Henn & Darby* [1980] 2 All E.R. 166 compared with the Preliminary Ruling by the Court of Justice in the same case reported as Case 34/79, [1979] ECR 3795.

stray consistently closely to the latter limit they may occasionally be accused of usurping the functions of the legislator and thereby damage their own credibility. The two principal European courts have frequently been the object of such criticism, and this matter is discussed further below. However, it is through the application of different techniques of interpretation that a court may shape or adapt the legal system and in many circumstances enable it to accomplish the tasks which it is required to do.

Much of the theoretical framework outlined below[92] concentrates on the so-called teleological or purposive method of interpretation. While it is true that the use of that method has resulted in some of the most important jurisprudential developments, its importance as a day-to-day tool is often overstated. Once again, it should be recalled that the task of an individual judge or of a collegiate court is to decide the case in front of it in a consistent fashion and so to be able to dispose of cases as expeditiously as possible. No judge will undertake a teleological or even a contextual approach if a ready answer to the problem at hand can be devised from a literal reading of the text itself.

Furthermore, although the three main approaches to interpretation are set out in a likely batting order below (literal, contextual (historical) and teleological) this does not mean that the three approaches are used necessarily in that order of preference but that they are tools to be used as required in order to complete the job in hand, namely deciding the instant case. When this is added to the infinite variety of circumstances and the vast volume of written law which may give rise to the need for interpretation it is clear that legal interpretation cannot be reduced to an exact diagnostic system in the way in which a faulty piece of electrical equipment might be tested in a series of ways, or a chemical analysis carried out on an unknown substance. There are no specific codes of interpretation and few explicit judicial pronouncements on methodology, although many of the cases in the various European courts contain clues as to the approaches adopted. Thus the courts may use all of the methods mentioned below, sometimes together and sometimes individually, sometimes as an alternative or using one to confirm the result arrived at by means of another.

Although a keen rock climber or mountaineer might select the most difficult or challenging route to get to the top of a particular

---

92  There is ample literature on the subject. See also Brown and Kennedy, *The Court of Justice of the European Communities*, Chap. 14; Harris, O'Boyle and Warbrick, *Law of the European Convention on Human Rights*; Timothy Millett, ' "Rules of Interpretation of EEC Legislation" [1989] *Statute Law Review* 163.

rock face simply for the sake of responding to the challenge, a judge faced with a problem of interpretation will be more like the hill walker who merely wants to enjoy the view from the top and, if an easier path exists around the back, will for preference take that. Of course if no such path exists, the judge will have to take the rock climber's approach using the available equipment.

Finally, as was explained in Chapter 4 above, the European Community treaties and the European Convention on Human Rights are all multilateral treaties adopted in accordance with the rules of public international law. Their interpretation is therefore subject to the same rules as that of other international treaties, the basic principles of which are laid down in Article 31 on the Vienna Convention on the Law of Treaties[93] which provides that a treaty "shall be interpreted in good faith in accordance with the ordinary meaning to be given to the terms of the treaty in their context and in the light of its object and purpose". That provision clearly enumerates the three main interpretative techniques which will be outlined below, namely the ordinary meaning or literal approach, placing the terms in their context (the contextual approach) and the object and purpose (purposive or teleological approach). It is interesting to note that, although the Court of Justice mentioned the three methods of interpretation contained in Article 31 of the Vienna Convention in its judgment in *Van Gend en Loos*,[94] it reversed the order of those methods when it said: "To ascertain whether the provisions of an international treaty extend so far in their effects it is necessary to consider the spirit, the general scheme and the wording of those provisions"; thus the three methods were entirely reversed in order, probably because this better suited the requirements of interpreting Article 12 of the EEC Treaty[95] in the circumstances of that particular case.

## LITERAL INTERPRETATION

It is little more than stating the obvious to say that any court faced with the problem of the interpretation of a legal instrument will first look to the wording it contains. This will be necessary in any event to ascertain whether or not the rule concerned may determine, or is at least relevant to, the issue under review. The literal approach requires the Court to look initially at the "ordinary meaning" of the words concerned. This may lead the Court to

---

93    1969, 1155 UNTS 331.
94    Case 26/62 *Van Gend en Loos v. Neerlands Administratie der Belastingen* [1963] ECR 1 at. 12.
95    Now Article 25 (ex Article 12) EC, the provision was substantially changed by The Treaty of Amsterdam.

adopt an almost dictionary-like approach. Thus in a case[96] concerning the Common Customs Tariff the Court of Justice was called upon to interpret the expression 'game' and declared that "the expression 'game' in its ordinary meaning designates those categories of animal living in the wild state which are hunted". Again in *Humblet v. Belgium*,[97] the Court said that "the words 'shall be exempt from any tax on salaries' indicate clearly and unambiguously exemption from any fiscal charge based directly or indirectly on the exempted remuneration".

Given that some words used in everyday language may differ slightly or significantly in their legal connotations in different countries or be required to bear a particular meaning in a given document (and subject of course to the variations of different languages dealt with below), the European courts may be led to adopt a specific, European law, definition. Thus in *Levin v. Staatssecretaris van Justitie*,[98] the Court of Justice said that "the terms 'worker' and 'activity as an employed person' may not be defined by reference to the national laws of the Member States but have a Community meaning". The Court concluded that those two terms were to be interpreted as including persons who worked on a part-time basis or who obtained remuneration lower than the minimum guaranteed in the sector concerned.

Likewise, in the Human Rights Convention many expressions have a plain meaning which has, on occasion, prevented the Human Rights Court from having recourse to other, more flexible, interpretation techniques. For example, in *Wemhoff v. Germany*[99] the Court held that Article 5(3) of the Convention (which provides for detained persons to be entitled to trial within a reasonable time or release pending trial) did not apply to appeal proceedings because of Article 5(1)(a) which allows a person to be deprived of his liberty after conviction by a competent court. As in the case of Community law certain Convention terms have an autonomous meaning which they must be given when they are being interpreted or applied in a context covered by the Convention. Such terms include the concepts of "civil rights and obligations", "tribunal" and "witness" in Article 6, or the term "vagrant" in Article 5(1)(e).

Apart from the ambiguities inherent in any language, and the use of certain words in a technical or autonomous fashion (that is jargon for "jargon"), there are two particular reasons why reliance on literal interpretation alone is insufficient in the context of European law. The first lies in the nature of the founding treaties

---

96   Case 149/73 *Witt v. Hauptzollamt Hamburg-Ericus* [1973] ECR 1587.
97   Case 6/60 *Humblet v. Belgium*, [1960] ECR 559.
98   Case 53/81 [1982] *Levin v. Staatssecretaris van Justitie ECR* 1035.
99   *Wemhoff v. Germany* (1968) A7.

and conventions as well as other instruments such as legislation or binding decisions and the way in which they are adopted. The second lies in the multilingual nature of the instruments themselves, the institutions called upon to apply and interpret them and of the context in which they operate.

As to the first point, neither the European Community treaties nor the Human Rights Convention constitute a complete programme of legislation with detailed rules for their application in a variety of circumstances. Far from it. The Community treaties set out an institutional framework and a number of aims and objectives. As Lord Denning put it in *Bulmer v. Bollinger*[1]:

"The Treaty is quite unlike any of the enactments to which we have become accustomed . . . It lays down general principles. It expresses its aim and purposes. All in sentences of moderate length and commendable style. But it lacks precision. . . . All the way through the Treaty there are gaps and lacunae. These have to be filled in by the judges, or by regulations or directives."

For its part the Human Rights Convention is in some ways little more than a "wish list" setting out certain minimum standards which the contracting states must seek to attain. Given that the scheme of human rights protection laid down in the Convention does not provide further detailed legislation spelling out each of these rights, a particularly heavy responsibility falls upon the Court of Human Rights in order to define them and to enable their wide generalisms to be applied to the myriad situations which human ingenuity, malice or carelessness can devise.

Moreover, the nature of the process by which treaties and certain other instruments such as decisions and directives which require unanimity are adopted (see Chapter 4 above) can have a profound impact on the resulting text. That process is essentially an intergovernmental one, based upon negotiation, in which governments for reasons of their internal politics may adopt firm and sometimes irreconcilable positions. Even in areas where particular governments may be thought to have no special interest (there seems no particular reason why Sweden would need to adopt any position in discussions over a directive on citrus fruit production, Luxembourg on Atlantic fisheries, or the Netherlands on agriculture in mountainous regions), nonetheless, all may be concerned where proposed legislation may have financial consequences. Alternatively, it may be expedient to support one or more of the other Member States in order to secure reciprocal

1   *Bulmer v. Bollinger* [1974] Ch. 401 at 425; [1974] 2 All E.R. 1226 at 1237.

support on different, possibly unrelated, issues of more immediate concern. The resulting necessity to square circles often requires recourse to "weasel words" or results in further lacunae of the kind regretted by Lord Denning and behind which may lie a genuine inability to find agreement or merely a wish by negotiators to leave "wiggle room". If it is true, as Sir Alec Issigonis[2] once remarked, that a "camel is a horse designed by a committee", one has to admit that much Community legislation and some of the more recent treaties are legislative camels. This phenomenon must naturally lead judges called upon to interpret such legislative camels to seek out or deduce the intention of the legislators (see below).

## THE LANGUAGE DIMENSION

The treaty texts and legislation of the European Communities are authentic in 11 official languages[3] and the European Economic Area Agreement was drawn up in 1992 in 13 equally authentic language[4] versions while the Human Rights Convention is authentic in English and in French. Despite the care taken in drafting legislative texts and the fact that each Community regulation or directive is scrutinised by teams of lawyer linguists in the Commission and the Council of Ministers, it is inevitable that linguistic divergences will arise. Although recourse may ultimately be had to other methods of interpretation, the courts confronted with linguistic divergency will first look at the literal meaning of the text. The approach of the courts in these circumstances is best shown by means of examples.

In its first judgment to mention that fundamental human rights were enshrined in the general principles of Community law the Court of Justice was required to interpret a regulation providing for the distribution of part of the Community's surplus butter stock at reduced prices to certain recipients of social benefits.[5] The regulation included a rule intended to ensure that only those properly entitled would be able to obtain butter at a reduced price. Of the four language versions of the regulation the Dutch and German versions stipulated that beneficiaries could only purchase butter on presentation of "a coupon indicating their names" while in the French and Italian versions it was only stated that "a

---

2  The engineer who designed the Austin Mini motor car.
3  With the exception of the ECSC Treaty, which is authentic only in French.
4  The then nine official languages of the European Community plus Icelandic, Norwegian, Finnish and Swedish.
5  Case 29/69 *Stauder v. Ulm* [1969] ECR 419.

coupon referring to the person concerned" had to be shown. The Court said:

"When a single decision is addressed to all the Member States the necessity for uniform application and accordingly for uniform interpretation makes it impossible to consider one version of the text in isolation but requires that it be interpreted on the basis of both the real intention of its author and the aim he seeks to achieve, in the light in particular of the versions in all four languages."

We will see below how the Court resolved the question.

In *Elefanten Schuh v. Jacqmain*[6] the Court was called upon to interpret Article 18 of the Brussels Convention.[7] The Court made it clear that it would not simply adopt an interpretation which was consistent with the majority of the languages used. In that case the Court followed the meaning of the French and Irish[8] versions of the Convention ignoring a more restrictive interpretation suggested by the wording in English, Danish, Dutch and German.

Another more recent example of the Court grappling with different language versions, by now increased to 11, is provided by Case C–72/95 *Kraaijeveld BV*[9] in which the Court reiterated that interpretation of a provision of Community law involves a comparison of the language versions. In the case of divergence between the language versions, the need for a uniform interpretation of the rule concerned requires that the provision in question be interpreted by reference to the purpose and general scheme of the rules of which it forms part. In that case the Court was called upon to interpret the term "canalisation and flood relief works" and examined the various language versions of that expression. It concluded that:

"the English and Finnish ('*kanavointi– ja tulvasuojeluhankkeet*') versions are similar, whereas the German, Greek, Spanish,

---

6   Case 150/80 *Elefanten Schuh v. Jacqmain* [1981] ECR 1671.
7   See Chapter 4 above.
8   Although it is not one of the official languages of the European Communities, the treaties and the principal conventions exist in authentic Irish versions. Irish may also be used as a language of procedure before the Court of Justice, or the Court of First Instance, although this has not yet happened.
9   Case C–72/95 *Aannemersbedrijf P.K. Kraaijeveld BV & Others v. Gedeputeerde Staten van Zuid-Holland* [1996] ECR I–5403.

French, Italian, Dutch and Portuguese versions refer to canalisation and regulation of water courses, the Greek version including in addition the French term *'canalisation'* in brackets after the Greek term *'Σιενθέτησης'*. The Danish and Swedish versions contain only a single expression reflecting the idea of regulating watercourses *('anlæg til regulering af vandløb'*, and *'anläggningar för reglering av vattenflöden'*)."

While the Human Rights Court does not have to cope with as many as 11 languages, it too is occasionally confronted with apparent linguistic divergences or even contradictions between the two versions of the Convention. Thus in *Brogan v. United Kingdom*[10] the Court, called upon to interpret Article 5(3) of the Convention, found that whereas the English version required an arrested person to be brought before a judge "promptly", the French version used the word *"aussitôt"* (which might be translated as "forthwith" or "immediately"). In such circumstances the Vienna Convention (Article 33(4)) requires courts to reconcile the two versions as far as possible. The Court's solution was to find that the use of *"aussitôt"* in the French version meant that "promptly" had to be interpreted strictly and even allowing for special features in a particular case (the *Brogan* case arose against the background of terrorism in Northern Ireland), a requirement of "promptness" was not satisfied where there had been a delay of over four days.

Given the nature of the Human Rights Convention as a set of minimum standards underpinning the protection of Human Rights which is, in principle, ensured by the domestic law of the Member States, recourse to detailed interpretation of the wording of the Convention is less frequent than is the case with the European Community treaties and legislation. Nonetheless, in applying the other methods of interpretation mentioned below, the Court of Human Rights will only exceptionally opt for an interpretation which cannot be accommodated by the wording of the Convention. One exception to that reluctance was in *Pretto v. Italy*.[11] The Court was called upon to decide whether the release by a court registry of the printed text of a judgment, rather than its oral delivery in open court, was compatible with the wording of Article 6(1) of the Convention which states that "judgment shall be pronounced publicly" (the French version reads *"rendu publiquement"*). There the Court said that in accordance with longstanding tradition in many Council of Europe Member States, courts of cassation (courts dealing with appeals on points of law)

10   (1988) A 145 B.
11   (1983) A 71.

did not generally read their judgments out in open court. Therefore "the form of publicity to be given to the judgment ... [had to]
be assessed in the light of the special features of the proceedings in
question". The Court therefore did not "feel bound to adopt a
literal interpretation" of Article 6(1).

The Court of Justice itself has summed up the difficulties
inherent in applying methods of literal interpretation exclusively
to one language version in its judgment in Case 283/81 *CILFIT v.
Ministry of Health*[12] in which it clarified the extent of the requirement of the third paragraph of Article 177 that courts from whose
decisions there was no judicial remedy under national law were
obliged to refer a question of Community law to the Court of
Justice. Here the Court spelled out the doctrine of so-called "*acte
clair*", that is to say a situation where the correct application of
Community law is so obvious as to leave no scope for any
reasonable doubt as to the manner in which the question raised is
to be resolved. However, the Court warned that:

"Before it comes to the conclusion that such is the case, the
national court or tribunal must be convinced that the matter is
equally obvious to the courts of other Member States and to the
Court of Justice. Only if those conditions are satisfied, may the
national court or tribunal refrain from submitting the question
to the Court of Justice and take upon itself the responsibility for
resolving it.

However, the existence of such a possibility must be assessed
on the basis of the characteristic features of Community law and
the particular difficulties to which its interpretation gives rise.

To begin with, it must be borne in mind that Community
legislation is drafted in several languages and that the different
language versions are all equally authentic. An interpretation of
a provision of Community law thus involves a comparison of
the different language versions.

It must also be borne in mind, even where the different
language versions are in accord with one another, that Community law uses terminology which is peculiar to it. Furthermore,
it must be emphasised that legal concepts do not necessarily
have the same meaning in Community law and in the law of the
various Member States.

Finally, every provision of Community law must be placed in
its context and interpreted in the light of the provisions of
Community law as a whole, regard being had to the objectives
thereof and to its state of evolution at the date on which the
provision in question is to be applied."

12  Case 283/81 *CILFIT & Another v. Ministry of Health* [1982] ECR
    3415.

## CONTEXTUAL INTERPRETATION

This approach seeks to clarify a rule, a concept or a legal term by placing it in its immediate context or in the broader scheme of the instrument of which it is a part. One might say that "a rule may be known by the company it chooses". This method, which may be complementary to or a precursor of a teleological interpretation[13] (it is hardly possible to examine the purpose of a provision without first looking at its context), may itself be helped by the ancillary techniques of historical interpretation and the examination of the provision in the light of comparative law. The process may include different degrees of abstraction. Thus a word may be looked at in the context of a sentence, an article or of the whole of a legislative act. The legislative act itself may be examined for its compatibility with the treaty provisions on which it purports to be based, or a treaty provision may itself be examined in the light of the position which it holds in the overall scheme of the treaty. The utility of this method will largely depend upon the degree of precision or generalisation of the higher texts with which comparison is drawn.

Different expressions have been used in the case law of the Court of Justice when referring to this method of interpretation, such as:

"The *framework* of Community law"[14];

"The *context of the Treaty*"[15] or

"The *general scheme* of the Treaty as a whole".[16]

The frequent reference by the Court of Justice to the "scheme" of the treaties leads some writers to call this the schematic method of interpretation.[17]

The contextual or schematic approach has certain corollaries. Thus, for example, an interpretation consistent with rather than contrary to a higher rule of law is always to be preferred. As

---

13  See below.
14  Cases 90 and 91/63 *Commission v. Luxembourg and Belgium* [1964] ECR 625.
15  Case 23/75 *Rey Soda v. Cassa Conguaglia Zucchero* [1975] ECR 1279.
16  Cases 2 and 3/62 *Commission v. Luxembourg and Belgium* [1962] ECR 425.
17  See for example Kutscher, *Methods of Interpretation*, as seen by a Judge at the Court of Justice, Luxembourg, 1976 (originally written and presented in German); T. Millett, "Rules of Interpretation of EEC Legislation" (1989) *Statute Law Review* 163.

Kutscher put it, "the interpretation of a provision in its relationship with others governing the same or related matters, that is to
say, its schematic interpretation, calls for it to be interpreted in
such a way as not to stand in contradiction to other rules of the
Community legal system which — just like national legal systems
— is to be regarded as a unity".

A further feature of this approach is that basic principles of the
Treaty are usually broadly interpreted, whereas exceptions to
those principles are interpreted a more strictly . Thus, for example,
Article 39(4) (ex Article 48(4)) of the EC Treaty provides that the
rules on freedom of movement of workers laid down in the first
three paragraphs of Article 39 (ex Article 48) shall "not apply to
employment in the public service". That provision first came
before the Court in Case 152/73 *Sotgiu v. Deutsche Bundespost*[18] in
which the Court first stated that, because of the "fundamental
nature" of the free movement of workers in the scheme of the
treaties and the principle of non-discrimination, the public service
exception to that freedom should be construed narrowly so as to
permit restrictions only on the initial employment of foreign
nationals and not as regards their conditions of employment once
they had been engaged. The Court later defined "employment in
the public service" very narrowly as referring only to "posts
which involve direct or indirect participation in the exercise of
powers conferred by public law and duties designed to safeguard
the general interests of the State or of other public authorities",[19]
and not merely the fact that the employer was a body governed by
public law. As a result, the Court held that nurses, electricians,
plumbers and gardeners employed by local government, or driv-
ers, signalmen, cleaners, painters, canteen staff, workshop hands
and nightwatchmen employed by the State railway were not
engaged in public service employment for the purposes of Article
48(4) (now Article 39(4)).

Although the Court made it clear in the *Levin* case referred to
above that a term in the Treaty could not be interpreted simply by
reference to its definition in national law, one of the features of
European law is that it operates in and through the national laws
of the Member States. In other words, the national legal environment is part of the context in which European law operates and is
therefore natural for the courts to have recourse to comparative
law analysis. Indeed, in the case of European Community law, the
Court of Justice is clearly pointed towards such an approach, both
by the general invocation to ensure that "the law" is observed
contained in Article 220 (ex Article 164) EC and, more directly, by
Article 288 (ex Article 215) EC which requires the Community to

18  [1974] ECR 153.
19  Case 149/79 *Commission v. Belgium* [1980] ECR 3881.

make good any damage caused by its institutions or by its servants in the performance of their duties "in accordance with the general principles common to the laws of the Member States".

A further subset of contextual interpretation is historical interpretation, that is an interpretation by reference to the actual or presumed intention of the authors of the text at the time at which it was drafted. This approach may occasionally provide a useful confirmation of results reached by other methods. However, it suffers from severe limitations and as a result is little used by either court. First, there is the difficulty of establishing the intention of the legislator. In the case of the founding European Community treaties, all of the preliminary drafts and other preparatory documents (*travaux préparatoires*) were destroyed once the text of the treaties had been adopted. Secondly, especially in the case of the Human Rights Convention, despite the fact that its *travaux préparatoires* are accessible,[20] they may themselves be silent, or even unhelpful, on a particular point. Moreover, they represent at best a snapshot of attitudes of the negotiating delegations at the time, attitudes which may be untenable in a contemporary context. It is thus inevitable that recourse to the *travaux préparatoires* will become increasingly rare with the effluxion of time.

That limitation is less significant in the context of European Community legislation since each adopted act contains a clear "audit trail" of its antecedents. Thus, the opening paragraphs of the preamble to a directive will state the provisions of the Treaty from which the Council, or the Council and the Parliament draw their legislative power in the particular act, followed by references to the proposal from the Commission, the opinion of the European Parliament and the opinion of the Economic and Social Committee with reference to those proposals and opinions as published in the C series of the Official Journal by way of footnotes. Lawyers or judges may refer to those documents and draw conclusions from any similarities or differences which the text of the instrument presents to them. For the reasons already given reference to those *travaux préparatoires* by the Court of Justice are relatively rare.

However, the Court does frequently quote the recitals in the preamble of the regulation or directive under review which every Community legislative instrument must contain in accordance with Article 235 (ex Article 190) EC These, however, are generally used in order to draw out the purpose of the rules under review rather than simply their historical context.

---

20  See collected edition of the *Travaux préparatoires* of the European Convention on Human Rights published in eight volumes by the Council of Europe.

## INTERPRETATION BY REFERENCE TO OBJECT AND PURPOSE

This method of interpretation is sometimes called the teleologi-cal[21] or purposive approach in which a court seeks to interpret a legal rule in accordance with its object or purpose rather than contrary to it. While this approach is unfamiliar in particular to lawyers in the common law legal systems it is really no more than is required by Article 31 of the Vienna Convention on the Law of Treaties[22] which, as already mentioned, provides that "a treaty shall be interpreted ... in the light of its object and purpose".

The difficulty arises however that, in determining the purpose or the scope of a treaty provision or a legislative instrument a court may substitute its own judgment as to what that purpose is or should be, or at least may appear to be doing so and thus encroaching upon, if not usurping, the legislative function. How-ever, courts do not deduce the purpose of an instrument or a rule in a vacuum. They will have regard to the stated aims of the treaty or the legislative act as contained in its preamble or any general objective set out at the beginning.

Thus in the context of the Human Rights Convention, the European Court of Human Rights will have regard to the fact that the preamble to the Convention states that "the aim of the Council of Europe is the achievement of greater unity between its mem-bers and that by one of the methods by which that aim is to be pursued is the maintenance and *further realisation* of human rights and fundamental freedoms" (emphasis added). The following recital in the preamble says that those fundamental freedoms "are best maintained on the one hand by an effective political democ-racy and on the other by a common understanding and observance of the human rights upon which they depend". Arti-cle 1 of the Convention requires the parties to "secure to everyone within their jurisdiction the rights and freedoms defined [in the] Convention".

It is hardly surprising therefore that the Human Rights Court has said that the object and purpose of the Convention is "the protection of individual human rights"[23] as well as the main-tenance and promotion of "the ideals and values of a democratic

---

21  From the Greek τέλος (telos) meaning end. Whether or not it is logical is a matter for individual judgment. Thus, teleology is the doctrine or study of ends or final causes, including the search for evidence of design or purpose.

22  Of May 23, 1969, 1155 UNTS 331, also published in the UK as Miscellaneous No. 19 (1971), Cmnd. 4818.

23  *Soering v. United Kingdom* (1989) A 161 at para. 87.

society".[24] The *Golder* case[25] is an example of the use made by the Human Rights Court of this approach. In that case a convicted prisoner had been refused permission to consult a lawyer with a view to bringing private civil proceedings against a member of the prison staff. Although on the face of it Article 6 of the Human Rights Convention only sets out a number of guarantees as to the fairness of legal proceedings, and does not therefore guarantee a right of access to a court, the Court found that a right to institute proceedings in the first place was implicit in the text of Article 6 which includes the words "everyone is entitled to a fair and public hearing" (or, in the French text, "*toute personne a droit à ce que sa cause soit entendue*"). The Court also found that access to a court was an essential element in the concept of "the rule of law" which was also referred to in the preamble to the Convention as forming part of the "common heritage" of the contracting states.

Although the Vienna Convention dates only from 1969 it is clearly intended as a codification of existing customary rules of interpretation of treaties. Thus from its earliest days as the Court of Justice of the ECSC, that Court has been accustomed to examining the purpose of the provisions which it is called upon to interpret. In the very first case to come before the ECSC Court, Case 1/54 *France v. High Authority*[26] the Court was called upon to interpret the powers of the High Authority under Article 60(2) of the Treaty. In his opinion to the Court Advocate General Lagrange, having failed to arrive at a conclusion on the basis of the wording of that provision or of an examination of the whole of that article, said that it was necessary to examine the provision "in relation to the Treaty in its entirety". He then asked:

"What then is the Treaty's immediate purpose (I am not speaking of its ultimate aim, which is to begin to unite Europe)? To create a common market in coal and steel, to define the rules for the functioning of that market, and finally to organise an institutional system suitable to ensure that functioning".

Those words are essentially a précis of Articles 2 and 3 of the ECSC Treaty and in its judgment the Court of Justice confirmed that those articles (as well as Article 4), which are explicitly mentioned at the beginning of Article 60, "constitute fundamental provisions establishing the common market and the common objectives of the Community". The Court concluded that the High Authority (and implicitly the Court itself) was obliged to take into

---

24  See *Kjeldsen, Buskmadsen and Pedersen v. Denmark*, (1976) A 23 at para. 53.

25  *Golder v. United Kingdom* (1975) A 18.

26  [1954–56] ECR 1.

account all the aims laid down in those three articles. There is therefore nothing new about the Court interpreting a provision by reference to its object or purpose.

The words of preambles to treaties, although couched in very general terms, amount to more than just a pious wish list. Article 31(2) of the Vienna Convention states that "the context for the purpose of the interpretation of a treaty shall comprise, in addition to the text, including its preamble ... ". Hans Kutscher,[27] formerly President of the Court of Justice, echoing the wording of the preamble to the EC Treaty, emphasised that:

"the Community Judge must never forget that the treaties establishing the European Communities have laid the foundations of an ever closer union among the peoples of Europe and that the [Member States] were anxious to strengthen the unity of their economies and to ensure their harmonious development. The principle of the progressive integration of the Member States in order to attain the objectives of the Treaty does not only comprise a political requirement; it amounts rather to a Community legal principle, which the Court of Justice has to bear in mind when interpreting Community law".

Therefore, where it has recourse to the aim and purpose of the treaties it cannot be complained that the Court is pursuing its own integrationist agenda when it draws inferences from the stated aims of the Member States themselves.

When using a teleological approach the Court does not necessarily have recourse to the level of abstraction of the preamble. Thus in the leading case on the application of the principle that men and women should receive equal pay for work of equal value, *Defrenne v. SABENA*,[28] the Belgian court dealing with the case referred a question as to whether or not Article 119 of the EEC Treaty[29] had direct effect. In its judgment the Court said:

"The question of the direct effect of Article 119 must be considered in the light of the nature of the principle of equal pay, the aim of this provision and its place in the scheme of the Treaty."

The Court found that Article 119 EEC had a double aim which was at once economic and social and concluded that the principle of equal pay formed part of the foundations of the Community. As

27  See n. 17 above at p. I–39.
28  Case 43/75 *Defrenne v. SABENA* [1976] ECR 455.
29  The relevant article is now Article 141 (ex Article 119) EC.

far as the economic aim was concerned, the purpose of the article was to avoid a situation in which undertakings in states which had implemented the principle of equal pay were at a competitive disadvantage by comparison with undertakings in states which had not done so. As to the second point, the Court emphasised that the Community was "not merely an economic union, but is at the same time intended, by common action, to ensure social progress and seek the constant improvement of the living and working conditions of their peoples", wording drawn directly from the preamble to the Treaty.

So far as Community legislation is concerned, the Court is assisted by the requirement in Article 253 (ex Article 190) EC that "regulations, directives and decisions . . . shall state the reasons on which they are based". Thus the preamble to a directive includes a summary of the problem which it is intended to address, the reasons why this must be done at a Community level and the policy considerations behind the proposed approach and any exceptions provided for in the text of the directive. A Commission decision in competition matters may typically have a very lengthy preamble setting out in detail the evidence which it has obtained and the conclusions which it draws from that evidence as to the conduct of the undertaking or undertakings concerned. Furthermore, so far as directives are concerned, the third paragraph of Article 189 of the EC Treaty makes it clear that they are "binding, *as to the result to be achieved*," upon the Member States to which they are addressed, making the task of establishing the result an inescapable one for the Court when it is subsequently called upon to interpret a provision of the directive.

The *Kraaijeveld* case[30] referred to above, provides an example of this approach. Having stated that, in the case of divergence between the different language versions of a directive, the provision in question must be interpreted by reference to the purpose and general scheme of the rules of which it forms part, the Court carried out the linguistic analysis mentioned above and continued:

"Given that divergence one must go to the purpose and general scheme of the directive. According to Article 1(2) of the directive, 'project' means 'the execution of construction works or of other installations or schemes' and 'other interventions in the natural surroundings and landscape, including those involving the extraction of mineral resources'."

---

30    Case C–72/95 *Aannemersbedrijf P.K. Kraaijeveld BV & Others v. Gedeputeerde Staten van Zuid-Holland* [1996] ECR I–5403.

According to Article 2(1), the directive is aimed at "projects likely to have significant effects on the environment by virtue, *inter alia*, of their nature, size or location". Article 3 provides that the environmental impact assessment is "to identify, describe and assess the direct and indirect effects of a project on human beings, fauna and flora, soil, water, air, climate and the landscape, material assets and the cultural heritage". The Court then concludes that "the wording of the directive indicates that it has a wide scope and a broad purpose. That observation alone should suffice to interpret point 10(e) of Annex II to the directive as encompassing all works for retaining water and preventing floods and therefore dyke works, even if not all the linguistic versions are so precise".

### Effet Utile

The doctrine of "*effet utile*" is an important aspect of the teleological method of interpretation. The French expression "*effet utile*" is difficult to translate. Usually rendered as "effectiveness", perhaps "efficacy" would be more accurate. Kutscher says that the rule has been borrowed from international law and that what the rule requires "is that the provisions of the Treaty are to be so interpreted that their purpose is, if possible, achieved, that they have a 'practical value' and that their 'effectiveness' can be developed. It can therefore be understood as meaning that preference should be given to the construction which gives the rule its fullest effect and maximum practical value". It may also be regarded as an application of the Latin maxim *ut res magis valeat quam pereat* or "it is preferable for a provision to be given effect than to be made void".

Here too, courts applying the principle run the risk of the accusation of forcing interpretation of treaties or legislation beyond the results intended by the authors. Kutcher however adds "but what are the criteria by which the effectiveness of a rule is to be judged? The only possible answer to this question is that these criteria must be gathered from the objectives of the Treaty. According to the principle of *effet utile* preference is to be given to the interpretation which is best able to further attainment of the objectives of the Treaty". The same observation applies, *mutatis mutandis*, to the interpretation of directives.

By way of example, in the *Van Binsbergen* case[31] the applicant in Dutch administrative proceedings engaged a lawyer who was qualified in the Netherlands but who subsequently became resident in Belgium. Under Dutch law legal representatives before

---

31  Case 33/74 *Van Binsbergen v. Bestuur van de Bedrijfsvereniging voor de Metaalinijverheid* [1974] ECR 1299.

Dutch courts were required to be resident in the Netherlands. In response to the issue of whether a state could require residence on its territory as a condition for the provision of services, the Court of Justice said:

"[A] requirement that the person providing the service must be habitually resident in the territory of the State where the service is to be provided may . . . , have the result of depriving Article 59 of all useful effect, in view of the fact that the precise object of that article is to abolish restrictions on freedom to provide services imposed on persons who are not established in the State where the service is to be provided".

The principle applies also in the case of the effectiveness or efficacy to be given to directives. Thus in Case 14/83 *Von Colson and Kamann v. Land Nordrhein-Westfalen*[32] the two applicants complained to a German Arbeitsgericht (Labour Court) that the defendant state had refused to engage them for social work in an all-male prison and that their right to equal treatment in access to employment under Council Directive 76/207 had thereby been infringed. The Arbeitsgericht found that there had indeed been discrimination but that under the relevant provisions of German law the available compensation for such discrimination was limited to the direct losses concerned and, on the facts of the case, Ms Von Colson was entitled only to reimbursement of her job application fee of DM7.20 (about £2) and Ms Kamann was entitled to no financial compensation. The Court stated that while the directive did not lay down any specific sanctions for breach of the principle of equal treatment, it did require Member States:

"to adopt measures which were sufficiently effective to achieve the objective of the directive and to ensure that those measures may in fact be relied upon before the national courts by the persons concerned. ... Although full implementation of the directive does not require any specific form of sanction for unlawful discrimination, it does entail that the sanction be such as to guarantee real and effective judicial protection. Moreover, it must also have a real deterrent effect on the employer. It follows that where a Member State chooses to penalise the breach of the prohibition of discrimination by the award of compensation, that compensation must in any event be adequate in relation to the damage sustained".

32  Case 14/83 *Von Colson and Kamann v. Land Nordrhein-Westfalen* [1984] ECR 1891.

Since the application of rules of European Community law is essentially the responsibility of the courts in the Member States, it follows that they too are bound to give application to rules contained in a directive in such a way as to ensure their *effet utile*. Thus in *Marleasing*[33] a Spanish court sought to establish whether or not it was required to interpret its national (Spanish) law in the light of the wording and purpose of the first Company Law directive.[34] After referring to the general obligation of Member States under Article 5 of the EC Treaty to take all appropriate measures to ensure fulfilment of the Treaty obligation and underlining that that obligation was incumbent also upon the courts of Member States in respect of matters falling within their jurisdiction, the Court said that "in applying national law, whether the provisions in question were adopted before or after the directive, the national court called upon to interpret it is required to do so, as far as possible, in the light of the wording and the purpose of the directive in order to achieve the result pursued by the latter and thereby to comply with the third paragraph of Article 189 of the EC Treaty".

It is equally necessary to ensure the effective protection of the rights guaranteed by the Human Rights Convention. Thus in *Artico v. Italy*[35] the Human Rights Court emphasised that "the Convention is intended to guarantee not rights that are theoretical or illusory but rights that are practical and effective". It then concluded that there had been a breach of Article 6(3)(c) of the Convention which requires that a person charged with a criminal offence, "if he has not sufficient means to pay for legal assistance, to be given it free when the interests of justice so require" to have been breached when a lawyer appointed by the State proved to be totally ineffective.

## ACTIVISM OR CREATIVITY?

The results arrived at through the use of these techniques of interpretation, particularly the teleological method allied to the doctrine of *effet utile*, periodically expose the Court of Justice in particular to accusations of judicial legislation or unacceptable

---

33  Case 106/89 *Marleasing SA v. La Comercial Internacional de Alimentación SA* [1990] ECR I–4135.
34  Council Directive 68/151, March 9, 1968 on co-ordination of safeguards which, for the protection of members and others, are required by Member States of companies within the meaning of the second paragraph of Article 58 of the Treaty, with view to making such safeguards equivalent throughout the community: OJ En.Sp.Ed. 1968 I, p. 41.
35  (1990) A 37.

judicial activism. While it is perhaps inevitable that such accusations will from time to time be made by politicians frustrated or
embarrassed by a particular judgment, similar observations are
made periodically by, often distinguished, academics. These in
turn tend to provoke rapid ripostes in the learned journals.[36]

Much (though not all) of the criticism is based upon the premise
that the Court of Justice "sometimes interprets provisions of the
treaties contrary to the natural meaning of the words used"
(Hartley) or, in the words of Sir Patrick Neill, that by its methods
of interpretation the Court has liberated itself "from the custom-
arily accepted discipline of endeavouring by textual analysis to
ascertain the meaning of the language of the relevant provision".
This appears to be a particularly English viewpoint which also
finds resonance with those British parliamentarians who are anti-
pathetic to European integration.

Not only does such devotion to the apparently infallible principle of literal interpretation completely overlook both the extensive
use which is made of it by the European courts and the limitations
of its application in the context of European law as indicated
above, it also disregards the degree of flexibility which even
English judges can and do show in their approach to the interpretation of statutes. While it is true that English judges generally
regard themselves as bound by the wording adopted by Parliament, where that wording is clear and unambiguous and is
equally clearly applicable to the case before them, they may also
examine a term in the context of the section in which it is found or
of the statute as a whole or even compare it with statutes or other
cases in which the term has been given a specific meaning in order
to see whether that meaning is applicable in the instant case. This
is no different in principle from the contextual or schematic
interpretation used by the European courts.

36   Thus the Danish Professor Hjalte Rasmussen's thesis "On Law and
     Policy in the European Court of Justice" attracted a response from
     Professor Mauro Cappelletti "Is the European Court of Justice run-
     ning wild?" [1987] 12 E.L. Rev. 3; Sir Patrick Neill, Q.C., Warden of
     All Souls College, Oxford, gave a paper at a conference entitled "the
     European Court of Justice: A Case Study in Judicial Activism", later
     published as part of the written evidence to the House of Lords Select
     Committee on the European Communities, 1996 Intergovernmental
     Conference (1994–5 H.L. Paper 88, p. 218), which received a reply by
     Judge David Edward "Judicial Activism — Myth or Reality?" in
     *Legal and Reasoning and Judicial Interpretation of European Law —
     Essays in honour of Lord Mackenzie Stuart* (1996); and Professor T. C.
     Hartley's "the European Court, Judicial Objectivity and the Con-
     stitution of the European Union" (1996) 112 L.Q.R. 95, was replied to
     by Professor Anthony Arnull in [1996] 112 L.Q.R. 411. It is always
     instructive to read both sides of the debate.

Similarly, the well-known "mischief rule", which dates back at least to the sixteenth century,[37] requires judges to consider the "mischief" which the legislation was intended to address and then to interpret the provision so as to deal with the mischief and ensure that the remedy is effective (compare *effet utile* above). Finally under the so-called "golden rule"[38] courts will avoid following a literal interpretation where that produces an absurd or patently unjust result.

Judicial activism is thus used as a pejorative epithet to cover jurisprudential developments with which the commentator disagrees. Those who approve of the results achieved will perhaps call the judicial approach creative. Conversely, where a court appears to eschew a radical approach in favour of a more limited one (by whichever technique of interpretation is used) the Court is said to be exercising judicial restraint or showing conservatism or even pusillanimity in an extreme case.

The utility of such terminology is, in my view, rather limited. As Pierre Pescatore, a former judge of the European Court of Justice, has pointed out:

" 'Judicial activism' is a slogan dear to those who have studied in the United States and it is essentially a subjective expression. It takes no account of the context of every judicial decision the purpose of which, *ex hypothesi*, is to settle a dispute between opposing points of view. 'Activism' means something fundamentally different depending on whether one puts oneself in the position of the strong or of the weak; of public authority or of the individual; of the general interest or of particular advantage; of the producer or of the consumer; of the polluter or of the environment; of a managed economy or of the free market, and so forth. What is described by one as activism is seen by another as a just and necessary safeguard".[39]

As Pescatore observes, the attempt to analyse a court's case law in terms of activism or conservatism is a particularly American predilection, particularly for journalists and political scientists examining the impact of the work of the U.S. Supreme Court. Thus the background of nominees to that court is examined to

---

37  See *Heydon's* case (1584) 3 Co.Rep. 7; 76 E.R. at 638.
38  George Bernard Shaw has said that "the golden rule is that there are no golden rules". *Man and Superman*, Act 4.
39  Pescatore *"Jusqu'où le juge peut-il aller trop loin?"* in *Festskrift til Ole Due* (Copenhagen, 1994) cited and translated by Judge David Edward in "Judicial Activism — Myth or Reality?", cited above n. 36.

establish whether or not the balance between liberal and con-
servative points of view is likely to be tipped. Even in the U.S.
Supreme Court, whose role and system for judicial appointments
perhaps lends itself to such an approach, analysis in those terms
can rarely be of more than historical interest and will be unlikely
to enable either observers or practitioners to predict the way in
which the Court will decide a particular case.[40]

Perhaps the key to understanding that neither of the European
Courts is engaged in pursuing some wider political agenda
whether of European integration or accruing greater powers to
itself at the expense of those exercised by the Member States of the
European Union or the contracting states of the Council of
Europe, is the realisation that, again as Pescatore has indicated,
the Court's principal task is to reach a legally convincing solution
to the particular case before it. Moreover, so far as the Court of
Justice is concerned, it has no control over the nature of the cases
that are submitted to it or the order in which they are presented.

Very often the answers given in a case will depend upon the
precise terms of the questions put by a national court and,
although the Court does quite often reformulate questions submitted by a national court, it does so in the interests of being able
to give an answer which will enable the national court to decide
the case before it or to make an otherwise inadmissible question
admissible. In the words of the Latin maxim *ne statuet iudex ultra
petita*, that is to say the judge may only rule within the context of
the case brought before him. Unlike the United States' Supreme
Court, the Court of Justice has no choice over the questions
brought before it. Similarly, the Human Rights Court, once the
European Commission of Human Rights has certified that the case
is admissible, must decide that case.

Patterns in the development of the case law are therefore only to
be discerned retrospectively. The courts, rather than following a
"paint by numbers approach", filling in gaps in the legal picture
according to a preordained scheme, is more like a colourblind
mosaic worker placing individual tesserae as seems most appropriate, leaving it to later commentators to discern any pattern
which might emerge.

Although the European Court of Human Rights has also been
the subject of the activist/restraint debate,[41] the criticism which is

---

40  Many Presidents of the United States have been surprised by the
    positions taken by judges they themselves have nominated to the
    Supreme Court. President Truman said "Whenever you put a man
    on the Supreme Court, he ceases to be your friend, I'm sure of
    that".

41  See Paul Mahoney, "Judicial Activism and Judicial Self Restraint in
    the European Court of Human Rights" (1990) H.R.L.J. 57.

levelled at it, while it may be extremely virulent, tends to be related more to the particular circumstances of the case concerned rather than the Court's methods of interpretation. Thus in the McCann case[42] the Court's ruling (by a narrow majority) that failures in the planning of a mission to prevent a terrorist attack amounted to an infringement of Article 2 of the Human Rights Convention (which safeguards the right to life) on the grounds that the use of lethal force by a state must be subject to strict safeguards, was greeted with howls of outrage as an irrational and indefensible judgment and led to calls from right-wing politicians and certain sections of the press for withdrawal of the United Kingdom from the Convention scheme.

---

42  *McCann and Others v. United Kingdom* (1995) A 324.

# PART FOUR: LEARNING AND EARNING

# 9. LEARNING EUROPEAN LAW

*"Tis well enough for a servant to be bred at an university. But the education is a little too pedantic for a gentleman." Congreve, "Love for Love".*

No doubt the most thorough education is that dispensed by the University of Life, however its courses are inordinately long and many of the diplomas are delivered only posthumously. Therefore "learning by study must be won"[43] and, so far as European law is concerned, there is a bewildering variety of courses, approaches and possibilities for such study reflecting the breadth and the diversity of the subject. Moreover, those embarking on the study of European law will have different requirements according to their status as undergraduate or postgraduate students, legal practitioners seeking to diversify their professional practice or a newly appointed judge or tribunal chairman likely to be confronted with practical problems of European law.

## PLANNING YOUR STUDIES

For undergraduates your choice of university is unlikely to have been determined, or even much influenced, by the availability and

---

43   John Gay, *Fables*.

structure of European law courses. Moreover, there can now be few, if any, universities whose law faculties which do not offer at least a basic course on the institutional and substantive law of the European Communities sufficient to satisfy the requirements for entry into the legal professions. Furthermore the need to acquire basic legal skills, a knowledge of the legal system and of some core legal topics for the understanding of your national legal system (again often driven by requirements for entry to the legal professions) means that the time available for more detailed treatment of subjects such as human rights and the law of international trade may have to be put off until the postgraduate level.

Nonetheless, when applying to universities it is worth enquiring how European law is treated and at what stage in the curriculum it is introduced. Although some universities successfully introduce European law at the very beginning of a degree course, on the basis that it is a discrete and *sui generis* subject, I would suggest that it is preferable to wait until students have acquired a basic knowledge of constitutional law, the national legal system and a modicum of substantive law. Until relatively recently there was a somewhat theological debate among law teachers as to whether or not European law, in particular European Community law, was best taught as a distinct subject or whether it should be dealt with in the context of courses on various relevant topics of domestic law. It is now generally recognised that the two approaches are not mutually exclusive and indeed that a judicious use of each method is both desirable and necessary. Thus the introduction of some substantive law in a field such as sex discrimination or the freedom of movement of workers can both illustrate and bring alive what might otherwise be a rather arid study of institutions, legislative procedures and judicial remedies while, conversely, it is hardly possible fully to understand those two areas of law without understanding the principles of direct effect of directives and of treaty provisions respectively.[44]

Judge David Edward[45] has outlined the necessary elements for a core course in Community law. These are:

"(1) The development and nature of Community law — a *brief* survey of:

44  See pp. 145–146 above.
45  In "The 'European' Content of British Law Degrees", [1995] 29 *The Law Teacher* 2 at 142. This article was written and published prior to the 1996 IGC and the adoption of the Treaty of Amsterdam. Obviously Judge Edward would expect courses to be kept up to date with both constitutional and other legal developments.

(i)    the origins and development of the Communities (from the Treaty of Paris through the Treaties of Rome and the Single European Act to Maastricht and the EEA);

(ii)   the 'political' institutions and the legislative process;

(iii)  the Court of Justice, its jurisdiction and forms of process, especially Article 177;

(iv)  sources (including general principles of law and fundamental rights) and interpretative methods;

(v)   methods of enforcement, Community and national, which can cover the ideas of primacy and direct effect;

(2) The structure and main provisions of the EC Treaty, which (in spite of Maastricht) is still a coherent text. This would involve a brief survey of, and explanation of the interrelationship between:

[(i)   'the Principles' . . . , emphasising that the Treaty sets out a programme of action;

(ii)   'the Foundations' — the Four Freedoms . . . , avoiding at all costs getting bogged down in the theology of Article 30;

(iii)  'the Common Rules' . . . , again avoiding the theology of competition;

(iv)  sex discrimination.''

He then proposes that specialised aspects of European Community law such as competition law, external relations and a more detailed treatment of each of the Four Freedoms could be offered as specialised optional courses at a later stage. The same would apply to the wider aspects of European law such as the law of the Human Rights Convention or of the European Economic Area.

Other factors which may influence the choice of the university for a budding European lawyer may be the availability of language learning facilities and whether or not the possibility of studying one or more languages is built in to the course with time being allowed for it and credit given towards a final degree. Many universities now offer courses in law with another European language which include a year studying at a university in the country where that language is spoken. Such courses, in addition to providing fluency and knowledge of legal terminology in the language concerned also give the opportunity of acquiring an understanding of a different legal system, an invaluable asset both for the continuing study of European or comparative law and for later practice. Note however that not all courses with law elements will contain a sufficient number of modules of legal subjects to provide exemption from the professional exams or admission to recruitment procedures for lawyers in the national or European civil service.

## Languages

The importance of a knowledge of one or more languages cannot be overstated. It is theoretically possible to become a practitioner or, for example, a civil servant in a government department (other than the Diplomatic Service) with a knowledge of only your mother tongue and a sufficient smattering of another language to order a drink in a bar while on holiday. The European Community treaties and legislation are equally authentic in all 11 official languages and the case law of the Court of Justice and the Court of First Instance is also available in each of those languages. Nonetheless a knowledge of other languages will make it easier to understand that there can be different approaches to and solutions for certain problems. It will often be easier to understand a legislative text or a piece of jurisprudential exegesis even in your own language if you are aware that its author may have been working within the linguistic and conceptual constraints of another language.[46]

It will be apparent from the description of the institutions and organisations in Chapter 2 that nearly all of them include English and French among their official or working languages and, in some cases, those are the only two official languages (*e.g.* the Council of Europe). Moreover, it is well known that the deliberations of the Court of Justice and the Court of First Instance are conducted in French and that the Court's judgments are initially drafted in that language even though they are only authentic in the language of the particular case. It is therefore tempting to assume that competence in English and French is sufficient linguistic expertise to be able to work effectively in this area. This is true up to a point and is comforting for those emerging from the British educational system in which languages are generally not accorded a very high priority and French is the language most likely to have been studied.

---

46 For an example of such an effect see Advocate General Elmer's Opinion in Case C–249/96 *Grant v. South-West Trains Ltd* [1998] ECR I–621. Mr Elmer's Opinion was drafted in his Danish mother tongue. However, English was the language of the case. In the English translation of his Opinion Mr Elmer systematically used the expression "gender discrimination" for "sex discrimination" despite the fact that the latter was the term used in the treaty article and directive which the Court of Justice was called upon to interpret (Article 141 (ex Article 119) of the EC Treaty and Council Directive 75/117 on the approximation of the laws of the Member States relating to the application of the principle of equal pay for men and women, OJ L 45, February 19, 1975, p. 19). The Advocate General perhaps took the view that the word "gender" (*køn* in Danish) more clearly referred to the sexual identity of individuals being either male or female.

Nonetheless, a good working knowledge of both English and French is really a minimum requirement for working in the field of European law (whether broadly or narrowly defined). Such a level of knowledge of those two languages is virtually taken for granted by German, Dutch and increasingly by Spanish and Italian professionals and, although those from the Nordic countries occasionally struggle with French they are invariably fluent in English and often in German as well. Lawyers from those countries are competing for business and jobs and candidates with a knowledge of several languages have a head start in competitions for recruitment to international organisations and institutions. Although in the European context German and Spanish are the most widely used languages after English and French it is often an advantage to have a knowledge of one of the less widely known and used languages. In that regard it should not be forgotten that both Portuguese and Dutch are used in various parts of the world as well as in the European territory of Portugal or of the Netherlands and Belgium respectively and that a good knowledge of one of the three Scandinavian languages provides a convenient gateway to and at least partial understanding of the other two. Occasionally, knowledge of such a language will provide direct financial rewards. Thus freelance translators or interpreters capable of working directly from, say, Finnish, Polish or Czech may command higher tariffs than those whose linguistic range is confined to the traditional Germanic or Romance languages. In the British Diplomatic Service special allowances are paid to officers with a knowledge of Slavic or Asiatic languages when they are posted to countries where those languages are used.

Where a degree course does include the possibility of a year abroad it is useful to check which are the partner universities and to seek to obtain some information about them. In that regard the European Law Students' Association (ELŞA)[47–48] publishes a guide to legal studies in Europe every two years which contains detailed

---

47–48   ELŞA (whose interests range far beyond European law, the name of the organisation meaning the "Association of law students in Europe" rather than the "Association of students of European law") provides a wide network of some 25,000 law students from around 200 universities in over 40 countries. It organises national and international seminars, study and traineeship exchange programmes and provides a number of useful publications. The existence of an ELŞA association is a useful asset to be considered when applying to universities.

information on law faculties and the universities in which they are situated.

## Mooting

Mooting is a traditional part of legal education in common law countries and provides valuable practice in the skills of preparing and presenting an articulate and intelligible argument while also helping to develop the self confidence which a lawyer will need when standing before a real court. The availability of a mooting society or facilities provided either by the faculty or, for example, by an ELŞA branch is worth taking into consideration. Moreover, it is worth enquiring about the success of teams from the university concerned in taking part in the various European and international law competitions. The most venerable of these competitions is the Jessup Moot Court Competition in public international law organised by the American Society of International Law Students (ASILS) whose finals take place in Washington each year.

The European Community Law Moot Court Competition, organised annually by a society established for the purpose, consists of regional finals in four different European cities each year, the winners of each regional final being invited to Luxembourg in order to plead the case before a bench composed of members of the Court of Justice and the Court of First Instance. The René Cassin Moot Court Competition, organised by Juris Ludi, sets problems based on the European Convention of Human Rights. Since 1995 the British Centre for English and European Legal Studies at the University of Warsaw has organised a Moot Court competition on a question of European Community law open to teams from universities in the Central and Eastern European countries and from the countries of the Commonwealth of Independent States.

## POSTGRADUATE POSSIBILITIES

Armed with a first law degree many graduates will naturally wish to complete their professional qualifications and embark on an earning career as quickly as possible. This is only natural. However, particularly for the European lawyer, some reinforcement of the basic legal education provided by a law degree is highly desirable. Thus a Masters Degree (LLM) or for example a French *Diplôme d'études approfondies* (DEA) will build on the foundations already acquired and possibly lead to specialisation, for example in the field of competition law or environmental law or any one of a wide range of others. Furthermore, particularly if your first degree has not included a period of study abroad, taking a

Masters Degree elsewhere can provide the benefits mentioned above of learning an additional language, gaining understanding of another legal system as well as a deeper or more specialised knowledge of an area of European law. Most universities provide a range of such courses and here again the ELSA guide to legal studies in Europe is the best source of information. There are in addition a number of educational institutions which have a European vocation and prestigious diplomas. Thus the *Collège d'Europe* in Bruges offers a one year and highly demanding course in European Community law requiring students to follow courses in both English and in French and to take the end of year exams in the language of the particular course. In addition there is a wide range of choice for the three optional seminars which must be followed and an emphasis on multidisciplinary studies including economics, history and politics. Although the demands of the courses do not leave a great deal of spare time or energy it should be remembered that Bruges is in the Flemish-speaking part of Belgium and so the opportunity exists to learn some Flemish, an asset for the reasons mentioned above.

The European University Institute in Florence is a postgraduate research institute established on the basis of a convention between the then nine Member States and opened in 1976. Through its teaching and research activities and links with universities throughout Europe (not only in the Member States of the European Union), it is intended to contribute to the development of Europe's cultural and academic heritage by the organisation and pursuit of interdisciplinary research programmes, in particular those relating to the development of European integration. The Institute is divided into four departments covering history and civilisation, economics, law and political and social sciences. Doctoral studies projects combining work in two or more of those departments are encouraged. In addition the law department has a one year LLM course in European Community law and an Academy of European law which holds summer sessions open to participants from outside the Institute. The EUI also organises a wide range of conferences on specific topics and has an extensive publications programme.

In selecting a university or European institute at which to follow an LLM or other postgraduate studies programme, you will be influenced first and foremost by the academic reputation of the university concerned and possibly by a wish to study under the guidance of a professor with a strong reputation in a specific field, or to follow a programme which will enable you to develop a specific subject interest. Where those considerations do not result in an automatic choice it is worth once again bearing in mind the language considerations already mentioned. Thus you should discover whether the teaching is dispensed in the local language — this will require you to have a good basic knowledge of the language before you start but following an academic course over an extended period provides an unrivalled way both of perfecting a general knowledge of the language and of obtaining a knowledge of a specialised legal vocabulary. Other regimes are those such as Bruges where two languages are used, or the Europa Institut in Basle in which teaching and written work may be done in French, English or German and participants are required to have an active knowledge of at least two out of those three. In Florence the majority of seminars are conducted in either English or French (sometimes both) but doctoral theses or LLM dissertations may be submitted in any of the 11 official languages of the European Union. Nearly all universities and other institutes require applicants either to demonstrate a knowledge of the relevant languages or to follow language courses in parallel with their legal studies. At the very least language learning facilities are made available to those who wish to avail of them.

Another approach is the increasing tendency for universities in different European countries to network with each other, a pooling of teaching resources and encouraging students to move between the universities in the network. Thus for example the PALLAS Consortium combines the law faculties of the Universities of Barcelona, Bologna, Essex, Konstanz, Lyon, Nijmegen and two universities in Rome, which also offers an LLM in European business law from its base in the University of Nijmegen. The one year programme covers eight main topics, which are all compulsory, covering different aspects of business law. In addition, participants must prepare a dissertation to be submitted at the end of the year. The working language of the course is English although facilities are available for studying Dutch. The PALLAS Consortium and the Europa Institute of the University of Basle both encourage Masters students to participate in the European Law Moot Court Competition already mentioned.

### Grants and Scholarships

Obviously spending time studying abroad entails some expenditure, including cost of travel to the place concerned, course registration fees, and board and lodging while there. These costs vary widely from country to country and between universities and some idea should be obtained beforehand of the costs concerned. The *ELSA Guide to Legal Studies in Europe* gives some idea of the likely cost of living and of the availability of university lodgings or other accommodation but accurate and up-to-date information should be obtained from the university to which you are applying. As for meeting those costs, the recognition both by the academic community and political authorities of the need to encourage the mobility of students and teachers means that there are more possibilities for obtaining financial support for such work than ever before. It may nonetheless require some persistence on a number of fronts in order to obtain sufficient financial help.

The objective of ensuring that as many students as possible in E.U. countries had the opportunity of study abroad was crystallised by the Member States in a new Article 149 (ex Article 126) of the EC Treaty which provides for Community action to develop the European dimension in education, particularly through the teaching and dissemination of the languages of the Member States and the encouragement of the mobility of students and teachers. Even prior to that change to the EC Treaty the ERASMUS programme for mobility in higher education has provided opportunities for study abroad, and since 1987 nearly half a million students have benefited from the programme.

ERASMUS is now one of the programmes included in the broader SOCRATES structure which is managed overall by the European Commission.[48-49] Procedures for the submission and selection of applications for support within SOCRATES (including ERASMUS) vary considerably, depending on whether the particular activity or project is managed directly by the Commission or, which is more likely, it is managed by the national authorities designated by the participating countries. The national agencies have specific responsibilities relating to the selection of projects and their supervision and financial management. Under the ERASMUS scheme support can be provided directly to universities to enhance the European dimension of the studies which they provide through organised exchanges of students for certain periods of study and through mobility and exchanges among teaching staff and by assisting curriculum development. ERASMUS can also provide direct financial aid to help cover the mobility costs (travel, language preparation and differences in the cost of living) for students carrying out an extended period of recognised study abroad. The addresses for further information on the SOCRATES and ERASMUS schemes may be obtained from your university grants office, the nearest European Commission information or representation office or on the Community's web site.[50]

Other sources of funding may include bursaries or grants awarded by the host institution or by the university in which you have completed your undergraduate study (where the undergraduate

48–49  Directorate General XXII Education Training and Youth, which has responsibility for managing a budget of 850 million ecus from 1995 to 1999.
50  Address: http://europe.eu.int/en/comm/dg22/socrates.html.

degree is itself a mixed one as outlined above the financial arrangements for the course as a whole will usually include the necessary support for the year spent abroad). A number of private philanthropic foundations may also provide support for overseas study projects. Thus for example the Shell foundation or *Volkswagen Stiftung* provide financial support for certain academic and research projects. The Rotary foundation graduate fellowship scheme supports hundreds of graduates from all disciplines who wish to undertake a period of study in another country. For information about the latter scheme you need only approach your local Rotary Club (whose support you will have to obtain in any event). Although acceptance of such an award brings with it certain obligations to attend Rotary meetings, to give talks about your home country or legal system, it is financially generous including, where necessary, paying for intensive language tuition prior to starting the course of study. Most importantly awardees are assigned a local mentor from among the members of the Rotary Club in the host city, thus facilitating the sort of social contacts which most foreign students would otherwise find difficult to make.

## "Stages" in EC Institutions

As a bridge between the academic part of education and the selection of a career path some form of traineeship (apart from those which are a mandatory part of qualifying to join one of the legal professions) can be invaluable. One of the best forms of such experience is to undertake a *stage*[51] which enables graduates (whether or not they have already passed or may be contemplating sitting an entry competition) to have first-hand experience of the working of one of the Community institutions. In both the Commission and the Court of Justice, *stages* last for five months and there are two cycles each year starting at the beginning of March and the beginning of October respectively. Details of the admission requirements and the necessary application forms can be obtained from the personnel divisions of each of the institutions. However, generally speaking, applications must be made at least six months before the start of the envisaged *stage* period, and must include evidence of having reached the required educational

---

51 Pronounced to rhyme with "Raj" not with "rage". This piece of Community jargon, based on French terminology, is equivalent to the English "traineeship" or, in American usage, "internship". Thus trainees or interns are known as *stagiaires* in Community jargon and, since the French versions *stage* and *stagiaire* are almost universally used in this connection they will be so used in the remainder of this section.

standard. In that regard candidates must have completed, by the closing date for applications, a course of university education and obtained a full degree or its equivalent according to the various national educational systems. For *stages* at the Court of Justice, that university qualification must be in law and preference is given to candidates with a proven record of achievement in, or a demonstrable special interest in, European Community law. Many bodies provide grants or scholarships to support *stagiaires*[52] and those who do not have such support may be paid a modest grant from the institution concerned subject to funds being available in the institution's budget. It may be an advantage if, when applying for a *stage*, you are able to demonstrate that you will not require such a grant.

Competition for *stages* is fierce because of the unrivalled opportunity which they give to observe the institutions at close quarters and to gain personal experience of their organisation and working methods. Such experience may serve to confirm your ambition to become a fully fledged official and may help to clarify ideas as to the particular department or area of activity in which you might eventually wish to specialise. The personal contacts made during a *stage* are also valuable. Equally the *stage* may lead a participant to decide that the international civil service is a totally inimical environment, nonetheless having taken such a *stage* gives a considerable advantage and is an asset when applying for jobs in other sectors.

## RECOGNITION OF DIPLOMAS

Of course, even a prolonged period of study abroad in a university or other academic institute will be of less value if on returning home to start legal practice or take up other employment the foreign diploma is not recognised at all or, conversely, if your diploma from your home state is not recognised in order to enable you to gain access to academic courses or professional training in another country. The authors of the EEC Treaty recognised the difficulties which might be caused by this problem and so, under the chapter dealing with the right of establishment, Article 47 (ex Article 57) of the EC Treaty, in order to make it easier for persons to take up and pursue activities as self-employed persons, requires the Council to issue directives for the mutual recognition of diplomas, certificates and other evidence of formal qualifications.

That legislative work had made little progress until, in 1974, the

---

52  For example each of the English Inns of Court has funds to support a *stagiaire* at the European Commission. The *stage* is recognised as equivalent to three months pupillage.

judgments of the Court of Justice in the *Reyners*[53] and *van Binsbergen*[54] cases made it clear that Articles 52 and 59 (now Articles 43 and 49) of the EC Treaty had direct effect at least in so far as rules preventing discrimination on grounds of nationality or of residence were concerned.

Difficulties were still encountered for lawyers qualified in one Member State but trying to join the legal profession in another, or trying to establish themselves under their home title in another country. Thus *Thieffry*,[55] a Belgian lawyer who had practised at the Brussels Bar for many years, moved to Paris. The University of Paris recognised his Belgian law degree as the equivalent of a French law degree thus entitling him to sit the French Bar examination, which he passed. Nonetheless, the Paris Bar Council refused his admission to the Paris Bar on the ground that he had not received a French law degree. Thieffry took legal action against that refusal and the case was referred to the Court of Justice in Luxembourg which found that the fact that national legislation provided for recognition of equivalence of his Belgian degree only for university purposes, could not of itself justify a refusal to recognise such equivalence as evidence of a professional qualification, especially since Thieffry's degree was supplemented by a professional qualifying certificate obtained in accordance with French law.

During the following decade a series of directives requiring mutual recognition of diplomas of nurses, dentists, veterinarians, pharmacists and midwives was adopted. However, this profession by profession response was found inadequate and in 1988 a directive providing for a general system of recognition of higher education diplomas[56] was adopted. The essence of the directive is that it requires Member States to recognise any diploma or certificate awarded by a higher education institution in any other Member State after a course of study of at least three years duration. Following successive enlargements of the European Communities and the creation of the European Economic Area this recognition now extends to diplomas from educational institutions in eighteen countries.

53  Case 2/74 *Reyners v. Belgium* [1974] ECR 631.
54  Case 33/74 *Van Binsbergen v. Bedrijfsvereniging voor de Metaalnijverheid* [1974] ECR 1299.
55  Case 71/76 *Thieffry v. Conseil de l'ordre des avocats à la Cour de Paris* [1977] ECR 765.
56  Council Directive 89/48 of December 21, 1988 on a general system for the recognition of higher-education diplomas awarded on completion of professional education and training of at least three years' duration (OJ L 19, January 24, 1989, p. 16). "Diploma" is extremely widely defined – see Article 1(a) of the Directive.

In a later case[57] the application of a Greek lawyer who had worked for many years for a German law firm to become a *Rechtsanwalt* was refused. Again on a reference to the Court of Justice that Court stated that a host country (in Germany such matters are dealt with at *Land* level) had to examine the educational qualifications and professional experience of a foreign lawyer applying to become a *Rechtsanwalt* and compare them with those of a German applicant, giving credit for those qualifications and experience where they were comparable to those required of a domestic candidate. Lest it be thought that only lawyers are affected by such matters it is worth mentioning that, in a case concerning the refusal by the French football authorities to recognise a Belgian coaching diploma,[58] the Court held that where the relevant authorities do refuse to recognise a diploma from another Member State they must state their reasons for that refusal and whether it relates to the whole or only part of the qualification concerned. Moreover there must be a possibility of seeking judicial review for the decision.

The diplomas directive regulates only the recognition of those diplomas which are awarded after at least three years of study. The LLM and many other postgraduate diplomas which may be awarded after one of the courses mentioned in the previous section are rarely so long. Nonetheless, the Court has recognised that a person holding a postgraduate law degree may have an advantage in entering a profession, obtaining employment or in professional advancement. In *Kraus*,[59] a German student had obtained an LLM degree following a one year course at the University of Edinburgh. He applied for the authorisation required under German law to use that degree (by including the letters "LLM" after his name on his headed paper and business card) and supplied a copy of his degree certificate. However he refused to pay the fee required by the German authorities on the grounds that that procedure restricted his freedom of movement under Article 48. The Court recognised that this situation was covered by Community law and was not simply an internal situation of a Member State regulating the behaviour of its own nationals. However, it found that an important public interest was served by the protection of the public from abusive references to foreign university degrees. Such an interest therefore justified a state creating an authorisation procedure governing the use of

---

57  Case C–340/89 *Vlassopoulou v. Ministerium für Justiz Baden-Württemberg* [1991] ECR I–2357.
58  Case 222/86 *Union nationale des entraîneurs et cadres techniques professionnels du football (UNECTEF) v. Heylens* [1987] ECR 4097.
59  Case C–19/92 *Kraus v. Land Baden-W(FC)rttemberg* [1993] ECR I–1663.

such degrees obtained in another state, provided that the procedure for so doing was relatively straightforward, the fees fixed at
a reasonable level, sanctions not excessive and as in the *Heylens*[60]
case that a right of appeal should exist.

Although these cases are instructive and provide a helpful
framework for securing recognition of a foreign diploma, litigation is a tedious and expensive business and should be avoided
where possible. If in doubt about the possibilities of your diploma
being recognised you should first seek the advice of the authority
whose recognition you seek (sometimes doing so before taking
the course concerned will avoid later headaches, by ensuring for
example an appropriate selection of optional subjects). Otherwise
most universities and certainly all Ministries of Education have
departments whose task it is to examine the recognition of diplomas. In 1984 the European Community set up a network of
national academic recognition information centres (NARIC)
which is responsible for providing institutions and citizens with
information on higher education systems and qualifications
throughout the European Economic Area. NARIC now operates
under the umbrella of the SOCRATES programme and initial
information on NARIC may be obtained from the same address as
for SOCRATES.

## CONTINUING EDUCATION

The advice above is all very well for undergraduates and those not
yet established in their professional careers. However, many,
possibly even the majority of practising lawyers and judges
throughout Europe, may have reached their present positions
without any formal training in European law at all. Although
many (including some of the most eminent) have "picked it up
along the way", one of the drawbacks of the University of Life, in
addition to those already mentioned, is that it is somewhat unfo-
cused. The European Communities recognised that the
completion of the Single Market required more than simply the
adoption of a vast amount of Community legislation up to the end
of 1992. The effective operation of that market would be compro-
mised if that legislation were not applied or were incorrectly
applied.

As we have already seen, one of the distinguishing characteristics of the Community legal order is the relationship between
national courts and the European Court of Justice. For that relationship to operate effectively the dialogue between the two must
not be a dialogue of the deaf and the need for legal practitioners
and judges in the Member States to develop the European law

60   Case 222/86 [1987] ECR 4097.

reflex or Euro-literacy is increasing rapidly in the light of a second generation of case law of the European Court of Justice. The latter having established and clarified the main principles of the treaties is increasingly addressing the consequences which domestic legal systems must draw from those principles in order to ensure that individual rights derived from Community law are protected within the national legal systems.

Thus the judges of courts in the Member States must be supported by legal professions able to identify situations in which their clients' rights under Community law may be infringed and correctly to present the European law issues to the judges before whom they appear. The scale of the problem becomes clear when it is recalled that in the European Union there are some 100,000 judges and about 450,000 legal practitioners of various sorts.

How, then, can an established practitioner acquire the necessary skills? In an ideal world it would be desirable to take a sabbatical year (even an academic year of say nine months) and read for an LLM, preferably in another country, thus, at a stroke, acquiring a sound knowledge of the foundations and main principles of European law, an acquaintance with another legal system and reinforcement of language skills. However this is not an ideal world and personal or professional constraints, not to mention the loss of income for a private practitioner, will in most cases make such a course impossible.

Open, or distance learning, which in terms of both teaching techniques and subject coverage has developed far beyond the undeservedly criticised correspondence courses of the past, is one alternative. Many universities offer such courses. Thus, for example, Leicester University offers a distance learning LLM spread over two years and covering the basic institutional and legal structure of the European Communities before encouraging a specialisation in either business related law or labour law and industrial relations from a business perspective. The course includes five residential weekends and a week long study tour of the European Institutions providing an opportunity for direct contact with course tutors and fellow students, including a wide mix of nationalities and professional backgrounds, including legal professionals, senior business managers and trade union officials.

The British Open University, through its business school, in collaboration with the College of Law[61] have recently developed a new programme of courses in legal studies. When the programme

61 One of the main professional legal training institutions in the UK. It is possible to register for courses with the Open University in any of the Member States of the EU or in Switzerland, but not, curiously, in the other three EFTA States which are members of the EEA.

is complete it will consist of four courses which, when taken together with other Open University courses or studies in other universities, will count as a Qualifying Law Degree for entry into the legal professions in England and Wales. The first course is called Understanding Law.[62] This introductory course is divided into 32 units (corresponding to 32 weeks of study), each of which requires 14 to 16 hours of study. Seven tutor-marked assignments count for half of the course credits, the remaining being dependent upon sitting an end-of-course examination. Nearly half of the course is devoted specifically to European law with two introductory units on an introduction to the European Union and EC law, and two on human rights and civil liberties. The final 11 units cover in more detail the workings of the European Communities and substantive law in the areas of social policy, free movement and trade, thus corresponding closely to the outline suggested by Judge Edward referred to above. While many of the other parts of the course, being devoted specifically to English law, might be superfluous for English practitioners and judges (thus lightening their burden of studying), they may well be of interest to lawyers qualified in other jurisdictions.

Even such a commitment to distance learning may be difficult to envisage for a hard-pressed professional with family responsibilities. Here, in addition to private study in snatched moments, one can recommend summer schools of three to six weeks duration and shorter seminars of a week or so organised in various law faculties all over Europe, some at introductory level, others covering specific areas in more depth or examining newly adopted legislation or contemporary problems. There is little systematic information about such courses although the ELSA legal studies handbook referred to above provides a useful starting point. Most such courses run for a period between about mid-June and early August, and cut-off dates for applications tend to be in early Spring. The best approach is probably to select a location and the dates between which you could set aside two, three or four weeks to follow such a course and then contact directly the university faculties concerned.

In this connection it is worth mentioning in particular the European University Institute which holds a summer academy of

---

62    Course code W200. Further information may be obtained from the regional offices of the Open University. There are 12 regional centres throughout the United Kingdom, and other Member States of the European Union are covered from the North Region based at Eldon House, Regent Centre, Gosforth, Newcastle upon Tyne, NE3 3PW. General information about studying with the Open University, including full course descriptions, can also be obtained from its web site at http://www.open.ac.uk.

European law each year where seminars are led by members of the Court of Justice, the Commission of the European Communities, the World Trade Organisation and other distinguished authorities in their fields. The Academy of European Law (ERA) in Trier organises both extended seminars for national legal practitioners and judges and one or two day seminars on specific topics. The European Institute for Public Administration (EIPA) based in Maastricht organises a wide range of four and five day seminars including one on using and finding European legal documentation aimed at law librarians in university libraries, EDCs, public administrations and law firms. At its Luxembourg branch the EIPA runs the European centre for the judiciary and legal professions which again organises frequent seminars providing an introduction to European law and institutions, methods of interpretation as well as specific aspects of substantive law.

Following a call by the Ministers of Justice of the Member States at a meeting in 1992 the EIPA, in co-operation with the Academy in Trier, the EUI in Florence and the College of Europe in Bruges organised a seminar on the training of judges in Community law which led ultimately to the definition of the Robert Schuman programme. That programme which is to run from 1997 to the end of 1999 and will in all likelihood be continued thereafter, is designed to stimulate and support activities designed to increase the awareness and knowledge of Community law on the part of judges and lawyers in the Member States. Under the programme financial support may be given for practical training in Community law whether at entry level or in terms of continuing training as well as support for the creation of information networks facilitating access to materials on Community law. Schemes may be put forward by courts, by the governing bodies of the judicial and legal professions, by other lawyers' organisations, by Ministries of Justice or by universities and other institutes which specialise in the training of lawyers and judges. A call for tenders for suitable projects is published annually and any of the bodies indicated above should be able to provide a list of successful projects and how to apply to join them. The main criteria for obtaining finance for such a project are its practical use for lawyers, and its accessibility in terms of both the academic level and geographical spread of participants. Seminars or other activities which bring together participants from more than one Member State are looked on particularly favourably.

Under the Grotius programme, which will last to the year 2000, the European Union can make funds available to support national professional bodies and other non-governmental organisations, especially those involved in legal and judicial training or research to organise exchanges for legal practitioners, again to increase awareness of laws, procedures, institutions and languages of

other Member States. This programme is not specifically concerned with the training of lawyers, and therefore does not
overlap with the Robert Schuman programme, but is concerned
with co-operation in the fields of justice and home affairs (the
third pillar of the Treaty on European Union) including judicial
co-operation in civil matters, the Brussels and Lugano Conventions, the enforcement and recognition of court decisions and the
transmission of legal documents.

## ASSOCIATIONS AND SOCIETIES

Learning European law need not be all hard slog. European
lawyers tend to be a clubbable group and have a better excuse
than most groups of professional specialists for holding convivial
conferences in various countries. Many of them also produce
useful newsletters or other publications and provide excellent
opportunities for making both professional and personal contacts.
Some of these are mentioned in the Vade-mecum but are worth
briefly mentioning here.

The *Fédération internationale pour le droit européen* (FIDE –
unhelpfully the same acronym as for the World Chess Federation)
consists of the national associations for European law in each EU
and EFTA Member State. Collectively they organise every two
years in the capital city of one of the Member States a major
conference on European law, including contributions from the
leading practitioners, academics and members of the European
institutions. Individual practitioners can attend the biennial conference by arrangement with their national association and
participants receive beforehand an impressively thick collection
of the conference papers and other documents.

The British Institute of International and Comparative Law has
a worldwide membership of legal professionals and academics
interested in the fields of public and private international law,
comparative law, and European Community law. It holds regular
conferences, manages an important library with major holdings in
the areas mentioned above and publishes the prestigious *International and Comparative Law Quarterly*. In addition members may
receive a fortnightly *Bulletin of Legal Developments*.

Finally, groups of lawyers interested in European law (usually
in the wider sense dealt with in this book) exist within each of the
main legal professions. Thus, for example, the English Bar European Group has about 650 members, is open to Bar students,
barristers in private practice or otherwise, and members of the
judiciary. Its annual conference is held outside the United Kingdom, usually in collaboration with the Bar of the country
concerned. It publishes a quarterly review containing articles by
leading Community lawyers and commentary on the most recent

developments in Community law and practice. It frequently holds evening seminars and lectures on specific topics presented in such a way as to be of interest also to non-specialists. The Scottish Lawyers' European Group is organised on a similar basis. And there are numerous specialist bodies such as the European Association of Insolvency Practitioners.

# 10. PRACTISING EUROPEAN LAW

*"One may seriously doubt whether the Treaty of Rome can have any bearing on the legal profession." Batonmier Brachers d'Hugo.*[62a]

As I have shown in Chapter 1, a sound knowledge of European law is essential for all legal practitioners and some understanding of its institutions and methods is, if not strictly indispensable, at least very useful for many other professions (see further under the heading "Miscellaneous" below). For those reasons the careers advice available to students in their schools and universities concerning access to and the educational requirements for the legal and other professions remains equally valid for those with a specific interest in European law matters. I do not therefore propose to rehearse such information in this chapter. Those who do not have ready access to such career advice may find help in a public library or, in the case of the legal professions, by contacting one of the addresses listed in part IX of the Vade-mecum. Here I propose rather to concentrate upon career opportunities in areas in which a knowledge of European law can be turned to particular advantage. These areas are principally in the legal professions or in the public service whether at national or international level. Two preliminary observations are however appropriate.

62a In the July/August 1958 issue of *Le Barreau de France*, quoted by Serge-Pierre Laguette, "Lawyers in the European Community", 1987 *European Perspectives*.

First, the advice given on career development, whether by careers advisers in schools and universities or professional organisations explaining opportunities to new entrants, tends to be based upon a strictly linear approach to career development and progress. Such advice is usually reflected in the assumptions made by those to whom it is given. Thus a European civil servant might expect to begin his or her career as an assistant administrator and then become successively an administrator, principal administrator, head of unit, head of division and ultimately director or director general. Similarly in the Diplomatic Service a new entrant will start as an attaché or junior attaché, work his or her way up through third, second and first secretary to counsellor, and ultimately to ambassador status. Likewise in the legal professions a trainee solicitor (formerly called an articled clerk) will expect, once admitted as a full member of the profession, to progress from being an assistant solicitor to an associate, a salaried partner, and finally a full partner enjoying a share of the partnership profits.

Real life is rarely so simple. At the purely professional level experience gained in a particular field (or even in an individual case) may confer special expertise or stimulate an interest for that field which might be better pursued or exploited elsewhere. Thus practising lawyers often become company secretaries or members of boards of companies, academics often gravitate towards the practical side of their field of study or research, poachers become gamekeepers and so forth. So far as the two legal professions in Ireland and the United Kingdom are concerned, there is regular traffic in both directions between the different branches. Moreover, the force of circumstance cannot be ignored. Unforeseen opportunities may arise, setbacks may occur for reasons wholly unconnected with your ability or personality, and an infinite variety of family circumstances may have a bearing on career decisions. A successful career will be marked by opportunities judiciously taken and even by setbacks in one direction being turned to advantage in another.

In similar vein, ambition, which is an important motivating force, should not make you blind to possibilities and opportunities which may not initially have occurred to you. Moreover, an unduly rigid fixation on reaching the pinnacle of a given profession which might, with dedicated effort and a fair wind result in such an achievement, might equally through ill luck or the untimely arrival of another even more brilliantly qualified candidate end in frustration or bitterness. Most organisational structures, whether in the private or the public sector, are pyramid-like in shape and, by definition, pyramids get narrower towards the top so the nearer you approach the pinnacle the fewer opportunities there are available to be shared among those who aspire to them. Nor should the holding of a cherished ambition over many years (particularly if it is not your own but a parental or family ambition) blind you to the possibility that the path you have embarked upon is not best suited to your particular talents or temperament and thus restrain you from pursuing other potentially more rewarding or gratifying paths.

The second is the question of languages already discussed in the previous chapter. Once again a knowledge of one or more languages in addition to your principal working language will contribute to your understanding of European law and will be an asset in recruitment procedures.

## SO YOU WANT TO BE A EUROCRAT?

Many careers advisers approached by a student for information on how to go about obtaining employment in one of the European institutions might advise the candidate to go and lie down quietly in a darkened room until the feeling wore off. Such advice would be inexcusable if it derived from ignorance or prejudice about the nature of the institutions but would have some justification if based on considerations of the complexity and slowness of the selection and recruitment procedures and the success rate among applicants. The entry path to employment in the institutions and the recruitment procedures are not widely understood and some of the constraints will be mentioned here.

Since the European Community institutions are by far the largest employers among the European and international institutions and the methods and conditions of recruitment are within my own experience, what follows in this section is related essentially to those institutions. Many of the general remarks made (including those relating to languages, above) are equally applicable to employment in, say, the Council of Europe, NATO or the OECD. The latter three organisations tend to recruit to individual posts and share their recruiting facilities. The number of posts arising in a given year is very small.

### Recruitment Procedures in the Community Institutions

The Court of Justice has drawn up a helpful guide to candidates taking part in recruitment competitions and that guide is published in the Official Journal each time an open recruitment competition is announced. It contains information on preparing an application, including explanation of what is required in the way of evidence of educational achievements and professional experience and an outline of the competition procedure.

The success rate in competitions is conditioned partly by the relatively small number of posts which will eventually be available for the appointment of candidates who are successful in the recruitment procedures (the number of posts in each institution is in turn determined by the budgetary authority of the Communities which, for most of the 1990s, has shown extreme reluctance to allow any growth in the overall size of the Community civil service). It is also partly conditioned by the large number of candidates tempted to apply for competitions by apparently generous terms of service and the reputation of the so-called "gravy train".

As a result, a recent competition organised by the Commission to recruit administrators (that is to say A grade officials with university level education) attracted some 55,700 applicants of whom about one-third were eliminated automatically as not satisfying the basic requirements for admission to the competition. A further substantial proportion was eliminated on the basis of a testing multiple choice general knowledge questionnaire, a crude device intended to reduce the number of candidates to manageable numbers to enable the selection board to carry out its work. Of the remaining 1,800 candidates who were admitted to take the full written tests, some simply failed to attend and about 1,200 were admitted to the oral tests (interviews). Finally 600 (*i.e.* just over 1 per cent of the initial number of candidates) were included on the list of successful candidates. Such a large number of candidates justifies the use of a rigorous procedure and enables the institutions to be confident that they recruit only officials of the very highest calibre. This confidence has been somewhat dented recently by the discovery of cheating by some of the 30,000 candidates in the latest commission competition.

In a competition jointly organised by the Court of Justice and the European Parliament for the recruitment of administrators with a British or Irish legal qualification (law degree or membership of one of the legal professions) of just under 300 candidates, 190 were admitted to the tests which were aimed at drawing up a reserve list of 14.

The numbers of candidates, the complexity of the procedures, and the necessity to ensure that those procedures are correctly carried out so that disappointed candidates will not subsequently be able to seek the annulment of the competition by the Court of First Instance, mean inevitably that competitions take a considerable time. In the example given above the competition took over two years to complete from the closing date for applications until the publication of the list of successful candidates. Such a delay inevitably causes problems for candidates and it frequently happens that even successful candidates have meanwhile found other employment and choose not to take up the offer of employment in the Communities. The Commission has therefore endeavoured to reduce the length of time taken to complete all competitions to one year and, for example, a recent competition organised jointly by the European Parliament and the Court of Justice with a closing date of April 1998 was intended to be completed by February 1999.

Furthermore, it must be emphasised that success in such a competition by no means guarantees immediate engagement as an official. As already mentioned, the availability of posts depends on the Community's budget and the availability of a vacancy. When vacancies arise they must automatically be published within the institutions and suitably qualified officials already in post in the institutions are given priority in filling them. Only when no such internal candidates emerge will the post be offered to candidates on the reserve list who will be contacted in accordance with the order of merit on that list. When the reserve list nears exhaustion a new competition cycle will be started with a view to ensuring that there is always a pool of candidates available for appointment to vacancies which may arise. Conversely, where a reserve list reaches the end of its validity (usually one year) and a substantial number of candidates still remains on that list its validity may be renewed for a certain period.

In parallel with that systematic approach to the appointment of candidates from the reserve list, the list is circulated to all directorates-general within the Commission who may thereby identify any candidates with particular qualifications or experience which might make them especially suitable for an appointment in a particular department. This process means that lobbying by candidates for posts is common and may be effective in securing an appointment to a desired post. Therefore, once your name has been placed on a reserve list and if you have strong ambitions to work in a specific field, you should identify the relevant directorate-general and seek out the head of unit concerned pointing out that you are a candidate on the reserve list, sending a copy of your curriculum vitae and explaining why it is you particularly want to work in that sector.

Such lobbying tactics are generally unfamiliar to British candidates, many of whom regard them as distasteful. Nonetheless it should be remembered that we are discussing candidates who have already successfully cleared the major hurdle of the competition procedure which is totally rigorous and transparent and is subject to judicial review if necessary. The kind of lobbying referred to here is not designed to subvert the recruitment process or reduce it to some kind of nepotism but to ensure that square pegs are duly inserted in the appropriately shaped hole.

The result of this process means that it may take anything between eighteen months and three years or possibly even longer for a suitably qualified candidate to be appointed to an active post in one of the institutions. This means that candidates and those who advise them must take a long view and that candidates should not invest all of their hopes and expectations in the possibility of such an appointment. Although appointments are sometimes made of newly fledged graduates, the fact that a candidate must present evidence of his or her qualifications by the closing date for applications combined with the inevitable length of time taken to run a competition, means that this is the exception rather than the rule.

Candidates are therefore faced with the problem of what to do between graduation and an eventual appointment. There is an infinite range of possibilities, from back-packing in the Andes to completing a professional qualification and gaining some experience in the desired field which may well carry weight when it is your turn for a vacancy to be filled. Here again, taking a *stage* in one of the institutions, as outlined in the previous chapter (p. 286), may provide both relevant experience and useful contacts.

**Translators and Interpreters**

Few, if any, students embarking on legal studies will have in mind a subsequent career as a legal translator or interpreter (see footnote 84 at p. 312 below for the difference). Nonetheless, just as it is evident from the rest of this book that the law is one of the main motive forces for European integration and one of the main mechanisms for ensuring effective intergovernmental co-operation, the numerous different languages used in the different European countries are capable of acting as grit in the machinery and bringing the whole mechanism to a halt. Competent linguists are the lubricant which ensure that this does not happen and with very few exceptions both translators and interpreters are engaged in the work of all the organisations covered in this book. Indeed, the European Community institutions their complex regime imposed by the requirements to treat 11 different languages equally are now the world's largest employers of professional linguists.

Many translators and interpreters, particularly at the European Parliament and the European Commission, are called upon to deal with a wide variety of work and therefore, although they may have degrees in various subjects including the social or natural sciences, history or purely linguistic qualifications, there is a special category in each institution of lawyer linguists. In the political institutions (European Parliament, Council and European Commission) the lawyer linguists' principal work is scrutinising the different language versions of proposed legislation in order to ensure not only that the language versions are consistent with each other, but also that legal terminology is used consistently and that the use of certain expressions will not give rise to specific legal problems in different jurisdictions. They therefore take a very active part in the legislative process. At the Court of Justice lawyer linguists are called upon to translate from two or more of the European official languages into their mother tongue the procedural documents necessary for the Court to be able to carry out its work, the preliminary rulings which are notified to the governments of each of the Member States in their respective languages, Advocate Generals' Opinions and, above all, the judgments of the Court of Justice and the Court of First Instance so they can be released simultaneously in the 11 official languages on the day of delivery of the judgment. Here again the essence of the work is to ensure that the judgment produces the same legal effect throughout the European Community irrespective of the language of the text concerned.

As with administrative grade officials, translators and interpreters are recruited through open competitions (although a number of experienced freelance interpreters and translators are used). In addition to their linguistic skills potential lawyer linguists must also either hold a law degree from a university in one of the Member States or be a member of one of the recognised legal professions. As a result of this dual qualification the starting grade for appointment is generally one step higher than that of ordinary administrative grade recruits. Particularly at the Court of Justice many lawyer linguists later move to the administrative branch and take up careers in research, information work, or management posts.

### Référendaires

Although the work of a *référendaire* is a short-term post rather than a career position it is worth mentioning in this context. Like *stagiaire*, the word *référendaire* is universally used rather than its equivalent which in English is the more cumbersome and slightly misleading "legal secretary". In the Court of Justice each judge and each advocate-general has three qualified lawyers to assist him and in the Court of First Instance there are at present two for each judge. Their role may be compared with that of the law clerks who assist the judges in American courts, in particular in the United States Supreme Court. Although each member of the two courts will organise his or her workload in the way that best suits and hence the work of the *référendaires* may vary slightly between the different chambers, their role is principally to assist the judge or advocate-general by doing research and by carrying out the preliminary drafting of opinions, judgments and other necessary documents.

Whereas in the United States courts law clerks are generally selected from among the best and brightest of Law School graduates before they enter professional practice, *référendaires* are, in the main, young lawyers who have already taken the first step on their chosen career path. Thus they include legal practitioners with two or three years experience, junior lecturers from universities, national civil servants on detachment or Community officials detached from other institutions or from within the Court of Justice itself. In a further departure from the American model, *référendaires* typically serve with their principal for three to four years before resuming their main career, although nominally they hold temporary contracts limited to the duration of the mandate of the member for whom they are working.

Given the closeness of the working relationship between the members of the courts and their *référendaires* it is essential that there be a close relationship of confidence between them and for that reason their selection and appointment is left in the discretion of the member concerned. He or she will generally consult widely among members of the legal professions and academics for recommendations as to able lawyers with a potential to act as a *référendaire*. More even than the *stagiaires*, the *référendaires* will work closely on the case files of the Court or of the Court of First Instance, and over a period of two to four years will follow several cases in different fields from their introduction to their conclusion. There can be a no better way of obtaining a deep and detailed knowledge of European Community law and of the workings of the Court of Justice and a spell as a *référendaire* is invariably an invaluable stepping-stone to a successful subsequent career. Indeed, four *référendaires*[63] have subsequently become judges on the Court of Justice and six have served on the Court of First Instance,[64] while dozens of others have obtained high academic distinction or made eminent careers in their national legal professions and judiciaries.

## THE LEGAL PROFESSIONS

It does no harm to reiterate that a sound knowledge of the main principles of European law, the remedies available and its methodology are nowadays essential elements in the toolkit of any legal practitioner. Although there are relatively few practitioners in any Member State that make a living either principally or exclusively by practising in European law, their number is steadily growing and those who do so practise are becoming increasingly specialised. Three particular areas may usefully be dealt with here. First, practising as a specialist in European law within your national legal system. This may include the second,

---

63 Jacobs, Gulmann, Saggio and Ruiz Jarabo.
64 Saggio, Biancarelli, Lenaerts, Kalogeropoulos, Jaeger and the Registrar Hans Jung.

namely appearing in proceedings before the European courts. Finally, practice in a country other than the one in which you are qualified.

## Staying at Home

In the popular perception, one lawyer is much like another and all fall under Ambrose Bierce's definition that a lawyer is "one skilled in circumvention of the law".[65] That impression of homogeneity may be reinforced by the wording of the Lawyers' Services Directive[66] and the more recent Lawyers' Establishment Directive,[67] both of which provide that "lawyer" means a person who is authorised to practise under the professional titles used in the different Member States. There then follows a list of various legal professions in the respective languages of the 15 EU Member States. Given that approach in the legislation, it might be thought that all the professions listed were interchangeable and that members of those professions carried out similar work to each other in their respective countries. In connection with the earlier directive this approach was called "a conceptual dog's breakfast since it is based on the false premise that equivalence of title implies equivalence of status, function and activity".[68] The list of the lawyers' professions mentioned in the directives is contained in the Vademecum along with the name and address of the relevant professional body to whom enquiries about joining that profession should be addressed.[69]

So, what specific advice can one give to a law student or young lawyer who desires to practise in the field of European law? You will already be aware that satisfactory completion of a course in

65  *The Devil's Dictionary* (1911).
66  Council Directive 77/249/EEC of March 22, 1977 to facilitate the effective exercise by lawyers of freedom to provide services.
67  Directive 98/5/EC of the European Parliament and of the Council of February 16, 1998 to facilitate practice of the profession of lawyer on a permanent basis in a Member State other than that in which the qualification was obtained, OJ L 77, of March 14, 1998, p. 36.
68  By D.A.O. Edward, *In Memoriam J.D.B. Mitchell* (1983), p. 231.
69  Further information on the organisation, work and entry requirements of those professions is available in J. Lonbay and L. Spedding, *International Professional Practice* (London, 1992) and Sheridan and Cameron, *EC Legal Systems: An Introductory Guide* (London, 1992). More up-to-date information is available on the Web Site of the Institute of European Law of Birmingham University at http://www.iel.bham.ac.uk. The *CCBE Cross Border Practice Compendium* by D.M. Donald-Little (Sweet & Maxwell) (a looseleaf updated every year) provides comprehensive coverage of the legal profession in Council of Europe Member States.

European Community law, during your university studies or preparation for professional exams is now an obligatory element for entry to either of the two principal legal professions in Britain[70] or Ireland. A similar requirement is imposed on German and Swedish entrants to their respective professions. However, that requirement is only sufficient to ensure that, in the fullness of time, all lawyers will have some familiarity with the main principles, methods and remedies of European law. Even this is vastly more than was available to many of today's leading practitioners who will freely admit that they first became interested in the subject through the chance circumstance of working on a particular case and that they "just picked it up as they went along". Clearly such a haphazard approach is no longer sufficient and those same leading practitioners would be unlikely to take on a young lawyer who felt that he or she could adopt the same approach.

What is required is what has been called Euro-literacy.[71] A working knowledge, or even a detailed knowledge of the rules of Community law and of the Human Rights Convention may be sufficient for a lawyer to be competent in European law. "The Euro-literate lawyer, as opposed to the merely Euro-competent lawyer, understands the structure of Community law, how it works and, even more important, how it thinks". How then is such Euro-literacy to be attained? In the first place a basic undergraduate course covering the European institutions, the four freedoms and perhaps an outline of the rules on competition can provide only a starting point. At least some postgraduate study should be undertaken and there is a wide choice of Masters Degrees which can provide a greater understanding of the European institutions, legislative processes, world trade and the competition rules.

Secondly, for the reasons already mentioned, a sound working knowledge of at least one, and preferably two, European languages should be obtained and consolidated. Third, where possible, some knowledge of the legal system of another country should be developed. Although this may sound like a tall order many opportunities exist and indeed by following a postgraduate course at a university in another Member State all three aims may be achieved in one fell swoop.

---

70  Solicitors and Barristers (Advocates in Scotland). There are in addition two notarial professions, for further information on which see the list of lawyers' professional organisations in the Vade-mecum IX.

71  By Peter Goldsmith Q.C., then Chairman of the English Bar, see the *European Advocate*, Quarterly Journal of the Bar European Group, Winter 1997/98, p. 7.

The next stage will be to make contacts among existing practitioners in the field, most of whom will be happy to provide advice and guidance or possibly short-term employment during university vacations which, like the *stages* in the European institutions, provide an invaluable opportunity for attaining first-hand experience of the practice of the law. Many of the main legal directories indicate the specialised areas of practice of particular firms or individual lawyers and the largest law firms will have a specialised European law department or division which may in turn be subdivided, for example, including teams working on intellectual property matters, competition law or employment law.

A further means of making contacts, learning more about the subject in all of its complexity and diversity as well as a relatively painless way of discovering whether or not you really want to work in the field is to attend the lectures, conferences and other events organised by the many associations of lawyers with European interests, whether within a single profession, at a national level or on a pan-European basis. Thus the British legal professions include the Bar European Group, the Solicitors' European Group and the Scottish Lawyers' European Group, all of which organise events both individually and in common. At the international level there are a number of associations of legal practitioners, some of which are listed in the Vade-mecum and there are several bilateral associations designed to foster contacts between lawyers of two different legal systems or between groups of countries with a shared language. The biggest conference of European law specialists is that organised every two years (even-numbered years) by the *Fédération internationale de droit européen* (FIDE) which is a confederate organisation based upon national associations in each EU Member State.

It is perhaps inevitable that the law firms and individual practitioners with substantial practices in European law are to be found in the capitals and principal cities such as London, Paris, Brussels and Frankfurt. So far as the English Bar is concerned, there are around 30 barristers (out of a profession of some 5,000 in total) who are occupied wholly or principally with European law. Over half of them are grouped in one set of chambers based in London but with a Brussels branch. Perhaps twice that number have some expertise in European law, often in a specialist subject area such as intellectual property, tax or social security.

The large City of London law firms often have immense resources and networks of contacts or corresponding firms in other Member States. In recent years this trend has been accelerated and intensified by a number of mergers of major law firms from the City of London and other countries, including Germany, France, Austria, Italy and Sweden.

Such large firms and specialist chambers inevitably create their own centre of gravity and, as their reputation and experience grow inevitably they attract the best work both in terms of quantity and quality. This unfortunately means that, with rare exceptions, practice in the provinces, even in substantial commercial or industrial cities, is unlikely to provide the opportunities for developing a specialised European practice.

## Appearing before the European Courts

The rules governing the rights of audience before the European courts are, on the whole, more flexible than those relating to rights of audience before the superior courts of the Member States of the European Union or the Council of Europe. Perhaps surprisingly, none of the European courts has attached to it a specialised Bar whose members have exclusive rights of audience before it and which a lawyer must therefore join before being allowed to plead. Thus in principle any lawyer who is entitled to practise before a court of a Member State may appear before the European courts.

In addition, states or international institutions who are parties to proceedings may be represented by an agent, often a member of the relevant government's legal service or one of the legal advisers to the Ministry of Foreign Affairs (France and Finland) or, in those countries where a special order of state advocates exists (for example, Spain and Italy), a member of that order.

In the European Court of Justice and in the EFTA Court, which may have to deal with cases referred from national courts, their Rules of Procedure[72] enable those courts to take account of the Rules of Procedure of the national court or tribunal which made the reference. Those provisions allow litigants in person to appear before the European court provided that their case has been referred by a court or tribunal in a legal system which so permits. This has occasionally happened.[73] Moreover, the statute of the European Court of Justice allows university teachers who are nationals of a Member State whose law gives them a right of audience, a right equally to appear before the Court of Justice.

---

72  Rules of Procedure of the Court of Justice, Article 104(2) and EFTA Court Rules, Article 97(2) respectively.

73  See, most recently, Case C–9/97 *Jokela*, judgment of October 22, 1998 (unreported), a case referred by the Finnish Maaseutuelinkeinojen valituslautakunta in which Mrs Jokela represented herself; Case C–61/97 *Egmont Film A/S and Others v. Laserdisken* judgment of September 22, 1998 (unreported), a case referred by the Danish Retten i Aalborg in which a proprietor of a video rental shop represented both himself and several fellow traders.

Examples abound of cases in which the lawyers concerned did not share the nationality of the parties they represented. This is of course necessary where a party is established in a non-Member State, as in the case of the applicants in the *Woodpulp* case.[74] In this case, the leading company was Finnish (prior to the accession of Finland to the EU.) which was represented by a German law firm which naturally enough took German as the language of the procedure. In Case 30/78 *Distillers Company Limited v. Commission*,[75] the company registered in Scotland was represented by a Belgian *avocat* while the Commission was assisted by two Scottish advocates and the Interveners (various Scottish companies) by an Italian *avvocato*. In preliminary rulings (or EFTA Court advisory opinions) one might expect that representation would be limited to those entitled to appear before the referring court. However, for example in *Cowan*[76] the English victim of an assault in the Paris Métro was represented by three lawyers, including two English solicitors, one of whom was a member of and practised at the Lille Bar and a Belgian *avocat* practising at the Liège Bar, none of whom would have had a right of audience before the *Tribunal de grande instance de Paris* which referred the case to the court in Luxembourg.

The rules on representation before the Strasbourg courts are, if anything, even more flexible. In proceedings before the Commission an applicant may be represented by a lawyer (with no restriction as to the title or professional affiliation of such a lawyer) or any other person provided that he or she is resident in a Convention country. Thus applicants may appear in person or be represented by a professional applicant or by any other adviser such as a trade union official or a representative of a non-governmental organisation such as Amnesty International or Inter-Rights.

In proceedings before the Human Rights Court itself the Rules of Procedure[77-78] require private parties appearing before the Court to be represented by an advocate (*sic*) authorised to practise in any of the Contracting States and resident in the territory of one of them. The President of the Court may however authorise any

74  Joined Cases 89, 104, 114, 116, 117, 125– 129/85 *Åhlström Osakeyhtiö and Others v. Commission* [1988] ECR 5193.
75  [1980] ECR 2229.
76  Case 186/87 *Cowan v. Trésor public* [1989] ECR 195.
77–78  Two sets of Rules of Procedure are applicable in the Court, the Rules of Court "A" and the Rules of Court "B", the latter are applicable to Protocol No.9 to the Convention. The rules on rights of representation are similar in each case. However, it is possible that those rules may be amended when the newly constituted Court takes up its duties after the entry into force of the Eleventh Protocol in November 1998.

other person to represent the applicant or give him leave to present his own case.

Finally, practising lawyers may be called upon to appear on behalf of clients before the Commission of the European Communities in the course of investigations of companies' compliance with the rules on competition. Although such hearings are vital in that they provide undertakings with the opportunity to explain the conduct which has given rise to the Commission's suspicions of an infringement, or to submit evidence in rebuttal of Commission's allegations, or again seek to mitigate any eventual penalty which the Commission might be minded to impose, there are no provisions in the Commission's Rules of Procedure either requiring parties to be represented or indicating the status to be held by any such representative. Nonetheless, in such circumstances which can result in very heavy fines and considerable adverse publicity for the undertaking concerned, they would be ill advised not to engage the services of a competent and experienced specialist.

## Being There

It is fairly unlikely that a total neophyte will be instructed to present a case before one of the European courts or the European Commission. Nonetheless, I recall a case in which a newly qualified solicitor was called upon to represent a truck driver required to appear before Magistrates on a charge of failing to comply with regulations on the use of tachographs. The young lawyer correctly identified a defence on the basis of Community law and secured an acquittal for the driver. The local police appealed, by way of case stated, to the Divisional Court which decided to refer a question on the interpretation of the regulation to the Court of Justice for a preliminary ruling. Although the solicitor, perhaps wisely, decided to instruct Counsel for the purposes of the proceedings in Luxembourg, the interpretation which the solicitor had put forward before the English Magistrates was accepted by the Court of Justice in its eventual judgment.

Lawyers should not therefore be unduly alarmed by the prospect of being called upon to appear before the Luxembourg or Strasbourg courts but should of course take care to prepare the case properly and in a manner appropriate to the specific features of each forum. This is not the place for a manual on the techniques of written pleading or oral argument before the courts.[78-79] Nonetheless, in this context, a few words to set the scene are appropriate. To obtain a clearer idea of how the courts work there

78-79 The Court of Justice and the Court of First Instance of the European
    Communities each publishes a set of "Notes for the guidance of

is no real substitute for visiting them and attending a hearing during the course of your legal education or professional training. In the absence of such a visit it is advisable to try to arrive in Luxembourg or Strasbourg as the case may be at least a day in advance to reconnoitre, find out in which court room you will be appearing, where the relevant robing rooms are and find out from the Registry which judges are sitting and whether there have been any last minute changes to the hearing schedule.

The layout and equipment of the courtrooms may also take a little getting used to, particularly for anyone more familiar with draughty, Gothic courtrooms fitted with hard wooden benches. The courtrooms used by the Court of Justice and the Court of First Instance are now all in the rather sprawling complex of annexes known as the Erasmus Building, the Thomas Moore Building and the C Building respectively.[80] The main courtroom housed in the C Building is used for plenary sittings of the Court of Justice and, if necessary, the Court of First Instance, or for Chambers hearings, particularly in large competition cases where no other courtroom is big enough. Its subdued décor with natural wood panelling and pale carpets and upholstery is extremely elegant and when combined with the perfect acoustics and up to 200 public seats, has perhaps more of the atmosphere of a concert hall than a courtroom. The Bench is arranged in a long flat curve, large enough to hold all 15 judges and nine advocates general for ceremonial occasions,[81] as well as the Court's Registrar. Finally, and most strikingly, the room is surrounded by 15 interpreters booths, enough to accommodate all of the existing official languages of the Court and three or four new ones after the next wave of

Counsel in the Oral Proceedings", which are automatically sent to lawyers appearing in cases before those courts. A series of useful, and still relevant essays was published in *Bar European News*, issue 17 May 1987 and issue 18 July 1987 with contributions from John Temple-Lang (from the point of view of a Commission representative), Advocate General Lenz (indicating what the Bench wishes to hear), and Tom Kennedy (on the role of the oral procedure). The introduction to *European Court Practice* (Butterworths, ) also contains two short essays on the subject by the former President of the Court, Ole Due and by Gerald Barling Q.C. who writes from the point of view of a regular practitioner before the Court of Justice.

80    The *Palais* or "Old Court Building" which was opened in 1973 on the accession of Denmark, Ireland and the United Kingdom to the European Communities, will shortly be closed for renovation and to have its asbestos lining removed. At present it houses the Chambers of the judges and advocates general of the Court of Justice, the Registry of that Court and the Library.

81    Also for hearings of requests for an Opinion on the legality of an international agreement under Article 228 (now Article 300) EC.

accessions. The output of the interpreters is relayed to listeners either on the Bench, at Counsels' tables, or in the public seats by lightweight headphones, each of which is equipped with a volume control and a button to choose the language which the listener wishes to hear. The other courtrooms are somewhat smaller, with fewer interpreting cabins and public seats, but follow essentially the same layout.

The EFTA Court, given the relatively small number of cases which it is required to hear, is now installed with its Registry in a small suite of offices in the conference centre behind the European Parliament's building complex in Luxembourg. When a hearing is organised it hires conference rooms in a neighbouring hotel which are suitably equipped and furnished so as to provide a public courtroom, a robing room for the judges and Registrar, and separate rooms for the parties and their lawyers. Since the EFTA Court resolutely works in English only there is no need for interpreting facilities.

The most strikingly futuristic of the European Court facilities is undoubtedly that in Strasbourg where the seat of the European Court of Human Rights was described by Horace Rumpole (who had apparently failed to take the precaution of spying out the land in advance) as follows[82]:

"The Court was a long, grey, concrete erection beside a river, with two circular towers like gasworks sawn off crookedly. Inside, we had wandered, uncertain of the way, in what looked like the vast boiler room of a ship, painted in nursery colours. We went up and down steel and wire staircases, and travelled in lifts whose glass sides let you see more of the journey than made you entirely comfortable. And then I was standing up at a desk in a huge courtroom. Across an expanse of blue carpet, so far away that I could hardly distinguish their features, sat the judges in black gowns[83] under a white ceiling, perforated like a giant kitchen colander. ... In some glass case halfway between us, lit up like tropical fish, the translators were noiselessly mouthing my words in various languages, which some of the judges put on headphones to catch, and others, either superb linguists or premature adjudicators, didn't bother to fit over their ears."

---

82 In John Mortimer, *Rumpole and the Rights of Man*, contained in the anthology *Rumpole and the Angel of Death* (Penguin Books, 1996), p. 178 at p. 206.

83 The judges' robes are in fact a deep blue colour but, given the extraordinary distance from the lawyers' tables to the judges' Bench this is a forgivable error by Rumpole.

Apart from the differences due to architects' whim or the requirements of working in a multilingual environment, the resemblance between hearings before the European courts and hearings before any other court or tribunal is a source of surprise for many first-time visitors. Thus the lawyers stand at lecterns to address the Court wearing the robes appropriate to the national legal system to which they belong.[83a] Their clients, assistants, and, if necessary, expert advisers, are ranged beside and behind them and there are the familiar piles of law reports, files of pleadings and documents, whispered conversations and the passing of scribbled notes. Given that in all of these courts hearings are preceded by a substantial written procedure, the Court is already fully apprised of the issues and principal arguments in the case. Hearings are therefore relatively short, rarely lasting more than a couple of hours. The pattern is essentially the same in each court, with the private parties, institutions and states each presenting their case in a speech of 20 minutes to half an hour. Lawyers who exceed such duration, without prior arrangement with the Court, are likely to do their case more harm than good. More importantly, it is quite inappropriate for a lawyer simply to come to the Court and either re-read his written pleadings (or memorials, as they are called at the Human Rights Court) or even to deliver a high flown rhetorical speech prepared specially for the occasion. In the first place, when reading a text it is natural to speak much more quickly than in ordinary spoken dialogue or when speaking off the cuff, and this makes life particularly difficult for the interpreters.[84] If the interpreters cannot keep up with your speech those judges listening to a given language will not follow your arguments, however persuasively framed and eloquently put and, for practical purposes, you might as well not be present. As Advocate General Lenz pithily put it[85]: "Do not read your written submissions. This is a hearing and not a lecture".

## Cross-border Practice

A lawyer who has had the opportunity of studying outside his home state, or who gains expertise in a branch of European law, is likely both to have a less insular view of legal practice than most of his colleagues and to attract clients from other countries. More personal considerations may also play a role. Thus Mr Gebhard, whose case before the European Court of Justice is mentioned

---

83a Robes are not worn before the Human Rights Court.
84 *Pace*, Mr Rumpole, translators deal with the written word; interpreters with speech.
85 In Advocacy before the European Court of Justice, *Bar European News*, May 15, 1987, p.11.

below, is a German *Rechtsanwalt*, married to an Italian national, who decided to settle in Milan where a large part of his clientele are Germans or Austrians. Practical considerations may also be important. Thus a lawyer specialised in European Community competition law or the rules on State aids and who may frequently have to appear before or negotiate with the European Commission, may find it convenient to set up an office in Brussels. There is also an increasing tendency for major law firms to merge with firms in other countries or to form less structured alliances[86] in order to be able to provide a wider range of services to clients.

These tendencies have been encouraged and facilitated, and indeed in many cases made possible by the application of the rules on freedom to provide services and freedom of establishment contained in the EC Treaty. Perhaps unsurprisingly, most of the leading cases before the Court of Justice on the interpretation of those provisions have involved lawyers and any lawyer or law student contemplating such a career or career move should carefully read the cases and directives briefly mentioned below. This narrow area of law also provides an excellent example of the way in which the European Community Single Market has evolved, from statements of principle in the Treaty, through legislative inertia progressively eased by decisions of the Court of Justice in cases brought by tenacious individuals keen to vindicate the rights conferred on them by the treaties, to the eventual adoption of a clearer legislative framework.

First it is necessary to distinguish between the rules on the freedom of establishment and those on freedom to provide services. As the Court made clear in *Gebhard*,[87] these two areas are mutually exclusive. Despite that categorical statement, the distinction between the two areas (which conceptually have much in common) is a somewhat fuzzy grey area rather than a sharp line of demarcation. For the purposes of the present summary it is perhaps sufficient to state that the freedom to provide services provided for by Article 49 (ex Article 59) EC is applicable where the provider and the recipient of the service concerned are based in two different Member States. It does not matter whether the provider, in our hypothesis a lawyer, travels to another Member State to provide services to a client there or whether the client travels to the Member State where the lawyer is established, or indeed whether no actual physical travel is involved and the services are provided by correspondence or other means of communication.

---

86   Such as European Economic Interest Groups (EEIGs).
87   Case C–55/94 *Gebhard v. Consiglio dell'Ordine degli Avvocati e Procuratori di Milano* [1995] ECR I–4165.

The concept of establishment on the other hand, although it may take different forms, implies that a lawyer who is a national of one Member State may participate on a stable and continuous basis in the economic life of another Member State usually on a permanent or long-term basis. Article 47 (ex Article 57) EC provides that, in order to make it easier for persons to take up and pursue professional activities in other Member States, the Council is to issue directives for the mutual recognition of qualifications and for the co-ordination of the regulatory framework (authorisation to practise, standards of training, professional standards and discipline). However, as a result of the great diversity of approaches even among the original six Member States concerning all professions (not only the legal profession) and the consequent inability of the Council to reach unanimity on these issues, little progress was made before 1974. It had been assumed, up to that time, that any progress in the field of freedom of establishment (and by analogy freedom to provide services) was dependent upon the adoption of such directives.

In *Reyners*[88] a Dutch national had obtained a Belgian law degree and had satisfied the other requirements in order to become a Belgian *avocat*. However, his application to join the Belgian Bar was rejected because a Belgian law allowed only Belgian citizens to become *avocats* in that country. In the case referred to the Court of Justice by the Belgian Supreme Administrative Court, the Court of Justice first held that Article 52 (now Article 43) was not dependent upon the adoption of implementing measures and that the prohibition against discrimination on grounds of nationality contained in that article had direct effect from the end of the transitional period. The Belgian authorities also sought to rely on Article 45 (now Article 55) EC, which provides that the rules on freedom to provide services shall not apply to activities which are concerned with the exercise of official authority in the state in which establishment is sought. The Court of Justice robustly rejected that argument holding that professional activities involving contacts with the courts, including even compulsory co-operation in their functioning, do not constitute, as such, connection with the exercise of official authority.

Shortly afterwards, the Court was given the opportunity to deal with the question of direct effect of Articles 59 and 60 (now Articles 49 and 50) EC on freedom to provide services. Thus Mr van Binsbergen[89] had instructed a Dutch lawyer to represent him in administrative proceedings in the Netherlands. During the course of the proceedings the lawyer moved to live in Belgium

---

88   Case 2/74 *Reyners v. Belgium* [1974] ECR 631.
89   Case 33/74 *Van Binsbergen v. Bedrijfsvereniging voor de Metaalnijverheid* [1974] ECR 1299.

whereupon the Dutch authorities refused to allow him to continue to act on the basis that Dutch law required legal representatives to be resident in the Netherlands. The Court unsurprisingly found that Article 59 became unconditional on the expiry of the transitional period and therefore could have direct effect, and that a residence requirement for the provision of certain services constituted a restriction incompatible with Articles 59 and 60 of the Treaty.

The lawyers in both *Reyners* and *van Binsbergen* unquestionably possessed the formal qualifications required to exercise their rights in Belgium and the Netherlands respectively. This still left the problem of nationals of Member States claiming the right to be established or to provide services in other Member States on the basis of their home state qualifications. Following *Reyners* and *van Binsbergen*, the Council adopted a number of directives harmonising the professional education and training standards for various professions throughout the Community so enabling a person duly qualified to practise a given profession in one Member State to establish himself or provide a service in any other Member State. Such "profession specific" directives covered, *inter alia*, doctors, veterinary surgeons, dentists, nurses, midwives, pharmacists and architects. Despite, or perhaps because of, the best efforts of the many legal professions in the Member States, it proved impossible to extend this approach to lawyers.

Shortly after the Court's judgment in *Thieffry*[90] the Council adopted the lawyer's services directive[91] which required Member States to recognise as a lawyer members of any of the professions specified in a list contained in the directive.[92] The directive concerns only the provision of services, not establishment and required lawyers providing services to comply with the conditions laid down for lawyers established in the host state. These conditions might include a requirement to be introduced, in accordance with local rules or customs, to the Presiding Judge or the President of the relevant Bar in the host state (but not to be registered with any professional organisation) or to work in conjunction with a lawyer practising before the judicial authorities concerned. The German implementing legislation for that

90  Case 71/76 *Thieffry v. Conseil de l'ordre des avocats la Cour de Paris* [1977] ECR 765, see Chapter 8, p. 000 above.
91  Council Directive 77/249/EEC of March 22, 1977 to facilitate the effective exercise by lawyers of the freedom to provide services (OJ L 78, of March 26, 1977, p.17).
92  The list, like the list in the subsequent lawyers' establishment directive (see below at p. 318, n. 99 and in Vade-mecum IX) refers essentially to the forensic legal professions and thus omits a number of other organised legal professions, in particular notaries.

directive was particularly strict and led the Commission to bring proceedings against Germany under Article 169.[93] The German rules required a foreign lawyer providing services in connection with litigation or in certain categories of administrative proceedings to collaborate with a German *Rechtsanwalt*, the latter being the authorised representative of the party concerned. Moreover, the assisting *Rechtsanwalt* had to be present at all times during the Court or administrative proceedings or when the foreign lawyer sought to visit a client in gaol. The Court found, however, that the obligation imposed on a "visiting" lawyer to act in conjunction with a local lawyer was intended to provide the former with the support necessary to enable him to act within a judicial system different from that to which he was accustomed. Therefore, since both were subject to the professional rules applicable in the host state, they had to be regarded as being capable, in compliance with those professional rules, and in the exercise of their professional independence, of agreeing on a form of co-operation appropriate to their client's instructions. The German rules were therefore disproportionate with the exception of those requiring the presence of the local lawyer for visits to persons held in custody for which such an arrangement might have public security implications.

The requirement in the directive for lawyers providing services to comply with the host state rules of professional conduct was reaffirmed by the Court in *Gullung*,[94] in which the applicant who held dual French and German nationality had been accused of misconduct and removed from the Register of Notaries in Alsace. He qualified as a *Rechtsanwalt* in Offenberg, a nearby city in Germany and then sought to establish himself as a *jurisconsulte* (legal adviser) in Mulhouse, France. After he had attempted to represent a client in a court in Colmar, in conjunction with a member of the Colmar Bar and therefore in accordance with the 1977 directive, the Colmar Bar Council prohibited any of its members from lending assistance to anyone who had been denied registration as an *avocat* on the grounds that he lacked the guarantees of good repute and integrity necessary, this being a reference to Gullung's removal from the roll of notaries. The Court found that the directive could not be relied upon by a lawyer established in one Member State with a view to pursuing his activities by way of the provision of services in the territory of another Member State where he had been barred from access to the legal profession in the latter Member State for reasons relating to dignity, good repute and integrity.

93    Case 427/85 *Commission v. Germany* [1988] ECR 1123.
94    Case 292/86 *Gullung v. Conseils de l'ordre des avocats du Barreau de Colmar et de Saverne* [1988] ECR 111.

Returning to the problems of establishment, a German *Rechtsanwalt*, Onno Klopp, practising in Dusseldorf, had attained a doctorate from the University of Paris in 1969. He passed the CAPA[94a] in 1980 and sought to set up a law office in Paris.[95] However, in France the Bar is organised on a regional basis with separate Bars being attached to each regional Court of Appeal. Under the rules of the Paris Bar, established in accordance with French legislation, a member of that Bar may not maintain an office outside the territorial jurisdiction of the Court of Appeal for the Paris region. Klopp, however, wished to maintain his *Rechtsanwalt* office in Dusseldorf, as he was entitled to do under German law, and to practise jointly out of both offices, dividing his residence between the two cities. In reply to a question submitted by the French *Cour de Cassation*, the Court of Justice[95a] acknowledged that, in the absence of specific Community rules in the matter, each Member State was free to regulate the exercise of the legal profession in its territory. While this enabled the authorities of the host country to require that lawyers enrolled there should conduct their practice in such a way as to maintain sufficient contact with clients and the judicial and professional authorities, those requirements could not prevent the nationals of other Member States from exercising properly the right of establishment guaranteed them by the Treaty. Article 52 therefore prevented the competent authorities from denying a national of another Member State the right to maintain chambers simultaneously in another Member State. While the cases outlined above and the directive on recognition of diplomas[96] no doubt represented some progress, there remained a considerable gap between the aim of freedom to provide services and freedom of establishment as set out in the treaties and the reality of the economic world.

94a  *Certificat d'aptitude à la profession d'advocat*, the qualifying certificate for the French profession of *avocat*.
95  Note that, since the removal of the possibility of restricted access to the legal professions on grounds of nationality by Articles 52 and 59, as interpreted in *Reyners* and *Van Binsbergen* above, it remains possible for a national of one Member State to follow the full qualification procedure and set up practice in another. What is at issue in the remainder of this chapter is the possibility to provide services or to set up an establishment in a host country on the basis of home country title.
95a  In Case 107/83 *Ordre des avocats au Barreau de Paris v. Klopp* [1984] ECR 2971.
96  Council Directive 89/48 of December 21, 1988 on a general system for the recognition of higher education diplomas (OJ L 19, January 24, 1989, p.16). See Chapter 9, p. 287 above.

Now only the effective implementation of the right of establishment of lawyers remained to be effected. After many years of discussion and negotiation between the legal professions of the (then) 12 EC Member States, in which a legitimate concern for the protection of public interest and the integrity of national judicial systems became a convenient camouflage for economic protectionism, the CCBE[97] submitted a proposed draft establishment directive to the European Commission. The Commission, in turn, drew up a proposal for a draft directive.[98] A more fruitful contribution by the CCBE was the adoption, in October 1988, of a common code of conduct setting out a minimum standard for rules of professional conduct and ethics. Finally, in February 1998, a lawyers' establishment directive was adopted by the European Parliament and the Council.[99] A measure of the difficulty in reaching agreement in this area can be obtained by carefully reading and comparing the CCBE and the Commission's draft with the directive as finally adopted.

Like the services directive, the establishment directive limits the definition of lawyer to members of certain named professions (see the list in the Vade-mecum at p. 383). First, it provides that a lawyer may carry on a practice in the host country under his home country professional title and under that title may give advice on the law of his home Member State, on Community law, on international law and on the law of the host Member State. Where activities involving the representation or defence of clients in legal proceedings are envisaged the host state may, as envisaged by the services directive, require lawyers practising under their home country titles to work in conjunction with a lawyer practising before the judicial authority in question and who would, where necessary, be answerable to that authority.

Secondly, the directive enables a lawyer registered in a host Member State under his home country professional title to practise as a salaried lawyer in the employ of another lawyer, an association or firm of lawyers, or a public or private undertaking under the same conditions as are applicable to host state lawyers. Finally, and most importantly, the directive enables fully qualified lawyers, after three years of professional practice in the host Member State to integrate into the host Member State's legal

---

97   Council of the Bars and Law Societies of the European Community.

98   Proposed on December 21, 1994 as a Commission document, COM(94) 572 final.

99   Directive 98/5/EC of the European Parliament and of the Council of February 16, 1998 to facilitate the practice of the profession of lawyer on a permanent basis in a Member State other than that in which the qualification was obtained (OJ L 77, March 14, 1998, p. 36).

profession after verification that he possesses the necessary professional experience. Meanwhile, in November 1995 the Court had delivered its judgment in the *Gebhard* case.[1] The Court, referring to many of the cases summarised above, reaffirmed the distinction between the establishment and the provision of services and clarified the conditions under which a national of a Member State might exercise his right of establishment which no doubt assisted those wrangling with the drafting of the establishment directive which was eventually adopted.

As already mentioned, Gebhard, a German *Rechtsanwalt*, had settled in Milan working as an associate member of a set of Italian lawyers' chambers. In 1989 he opened his own chambers in Milan in which Italian *avvocati* and *procuratori* worked with him. They were from time to time instructed to act on behalf of Italian clients in judicial proceedings in Italy. According to Mr Gebhard his activity was essentially non-contentious, covering assistance and representation of German speakers (65 per cent of his work), representing Italian speakers in Germany and Austria (30 per cent of his work) and about 5 per cent accounted for by assistance to Italian practitioners whose clients were faced with problems of German law.

A number of Italian practitioners, including the Italian practice in which Mr Gebhard had worked until 1989, lodged a complaint with the Milan Bar Council that he had used the title *avvocato* on the letterhead of notepaper which he used for professional purposes, of his having appeared using the title *avvocato* directly before the *Pretura* and the *Tribunale di Milano* and of his having practised professionally from *Studio legale Gebhard*. These complaints resulted in disciplinary proceedings being opened against him as a result of which he was suspended from pursuing his professional activity for six months.

Mr Gebhard appealed against that penalty and against an implied decision rejecting his application to be admitted to the Milan Bar. The *Consiglio Nazionale Forense* (National Bar Council) submitted two questions to the Court of Justice on the interpretation of the services directive, including the scope of the latter and whether or not a Member State might prohibit the establishment on its territory of chambers or a principal or branch office. The Court first pointed out that Mr Gebhard pursued professional activity on a stable and continuous basis in a Member State other than the one in which he was qualified and where he held himself out from an established professional base. Such a practitioner was covered by the provisions on the right of establishment, not on those relating to services. The Court rejected the argument that

---

1    Case C–55/94 *Gebhard v. Consiglio dell'ordine degli avvocati e procuratori di Milano* [1995] ECR I–4165.

establishment required membership of the relevant professional body of the host state. Nonetheless it accepted that the exercise of certain professional activities might be conditional on compliance with provisions laid down by law, regulation or administrative action which were justified by public policy considerations, such as rules relating to organisation, qualifications, professional ethics, supervision and liability. The rules might also lay down conditions for the use of certain professional titles, such as that of *avvocato*. However, where such requirements were imposed they had to be applied in a non-discriminatory manner, they had to be justified by imperative requirements in the general interest, they had to be suitable in order to secure the attainment of the objective pursued, and they must not go beyond what was necessary in order to attain it. As in *Vlassopoulou*[2] Member States had to take account of the equivalence of diplomas and, if necessary, compare the knowledge and qualifications required by their national rules and those of the person concerned.

## THE JUDICIARY

For readers from common law countries it may seem somewhat premature to give consideration to a judicial career given that, in those countries, a judicial appointment is usually attained only at the culmination of a successful career in one of the other legal professions. Nonetheless, as I pointed out in the first chapter, this book is not addressed only to university students but also to established practitioners whose education and training may not have included contact with European law and who may now be aspiring to judicial appointment and indeed to those members of the judiciary at every level who may find themselves in the same position. Moreover, in many countries the judiciary is a career distinct from that of the legal professions which is embarked upon as a career option following studies first at university level and then in a specialised judicial training institute. Finally, there is a growing number of quasi-judicial and regulatory authorities at national level which almost invariably include lawyers in their composition, some of which may have broad responsibilities such as, for example, national competition or mergers supervision or the monitoring and prevention of sexual or racial discrimination, while others may have more sectoral responsibilities such as the supervision of television broadcasting or air transport. Nor must it be forgotten that all national courts are, in addition, European courts. Thus it is for national courts in the first place to secure the protection of the individual rights provided for in the European

---

2   Case C–340/89 *Vlassopoulou v. Ministerium für Justiz Baden-Württenberg* [1991] ECR I–2357.

Convention and to ensure that the rules of European Community law are correctly applied in particular cases. The latter duty goes beyond simply assessing whether a particular set of circumstances falls within the scope of a known rule. It also, where necessary, requires the judges to raise relevant issues of Community law of their own motion, to interpret provisions of national law in accordance with Community law, to assess whether or not national implementing legislation correctly gives effect to Community law directives or, faced with incomplete or incorrect implementation, to disapply the national rules and give direct effect to the directive where it so allows. Most importantly of all it is for the national judges to assess when it is necessary to make a reference to the European Court on a point of interpretation or validity of a rule of European Community law and to frame the questions put to the Court in such a way as to make it possible for the Court of Justice to give a useful answer.

It follows that, if Euro-literacy is a necessary attribute of legal practitioners, the need is all the greater for members of the judiciary. Thus the "Euro reflex" consisting of the ability to recognise a point of European law, an understanding of the available remedies, and above all of the national court's role in the preliminary ruling process is not just a useful asset but a *sine qua non* both for members of courts of general jurisdiction and for those in specialised courts dealing with labour law, social security matters, commercial cases or a host of others. That in turn requires an understanding of the methodology of European law as outlined in Chapters 6 and 7 of this book.

It is appropriate also briefly to mention here appointments to the European courts themselves, even though the number of appointments available is infinitesimally small with barely half a dozen appointments available to any given country, taking all of the courts together. The formal qualifications required for each of the courts are mentioned in Chapter 4 and now, with the increasing maturity of both the Convention and European Community systems it may be assumed that, in practice, those responsible for making the appointments will require a demonstrable knowledge of the substance of European law as well. In most countries the candidates for appointment are selected at the highest political level, usually by the Minister of Foreign Affairs, sometimes acting in concert with the Minister of Justice and always subject to the approval of the Head of Government. The final appointments to the European Community courts and the EFTA Court are made by common accord of all of the Member States' governments whereas the appointments to the Human Rights Court are made by the Parliamentary Assembly of the Council of Europe to which each Member State submits a list of three candidates. In an interesting departure from the secrecy which has traditionally surrounded the procedures for selecting such candidates in the United Kingdom, the British Government placed advertisements for suitably qualified candidates to put themselves forward for appointment to the restructured Human Rights Court.

## THE NATIONAL CIVIL SERVICE

Litigation represents the pathological part of the working of the law, thus courts are only resorted to when disputes arise or legal arrangements break down. By far the greatest volume of work involved in the application of European law is therefore the task of the national administrative authorities, whether at state, regional or local level. The precise authority which is responsible for carrying out a particular task is a matter for the internal constitutional or administrative arrangements in each country. However all such authorities, within their respective areas of competence, will be responsible for ascertaining the relevant rules of European law and correctly applying them, subject to eventual judicial review. Some knowledge therefore of the relevant rules, if only in the specialised area concerned and of the relationship between the national rules and European rules in a given area are a requirement even for non-lawyers in the public administration. Nonetheless a general distinction can be drawn between the role played, in the European context, by the Ministries of Foreign Affairs of the Member States of various organisations and those of general administrative departments.

The Ministry of Foreign Affairs represents the interests of the state in the organisation concerned. Foreign Ministry officials must therefore provide the necessary legal and technical support for Ministers engaged in negotiating treaties, establishing new international organisations or taking day-to-day management decisions such as the adoption of budgets or making appointments to international bodies. In the European Communities context, while Ministers sitting in the Council meetings according to their respective responsibilities have the final political control and responsibility for adopting legislation, a considerable part of those responsibilities is exercised by delegation to the permanent representatives of each state sitting in the committee known as COREPER.[3] Each national delegation is headed by an ambassador empowered to negotiate on behalf of his or her Member State. The permanent representation has the dual task of preparing ministerial and COREPER meetings with proposed drafts and background papers on the issues to be decided and the positions of other

---

3   An acronym derived from the French *Comité des représentants perma-nents*, see Chapter 3, p.000, above.

national delegations. They must also report back to their respective governments on the progress or outcome of negotiations, new proposals made by the Commission and the different positions adopted by the Member States.

In the context of the Council of Europe the Committee of Ministers consisting of the Foreign Ministers of each of the 40 Member States is the key decision-making authority. Although the Committee meets only twice per year it may also hold extraordinary sessions for particular issues, but the regular work is carried out by the deputies of the Ministers with the support again of a permanent delegation. Thus the deputies establish the programme of work for the Council of Europe and adopt its budget and decide how to deal with proposals made by the Parliamentary Assembly, the Congress of Local and Regional Authorities or the results of special ministerial conferences on particular issues. Under the new Human Rights control machinery, the Committee of Ministers will still have the responsibility for supervising the execution of judgments of the Human Rights Court.

Before the European courts states are represented by an agent, usually a member of the legal department of the Ministry of Foreign Affairs and who has the authority to bind the state in the context of the proceedings concerned. In some countries (France and Finland) the agent also carries out advocacy on behalf of the government during the oral part of the proceedings, in others (for example, Spain and Italy) this task is conferred upon the State Advocates Department, whereas in others (such as the United Kingdom and Ireland) lawyers in private practice are instructed. In the United Kingdom the task of agent is carried out by the Treasury Solicitor's Department which co-ordinates litigation, including reviewing requests for preliminary rulings submitted to the European Court of Justice by courts in other Member States and consulting other government departments whose interests may be affected by the outcome of a particular case.

Virtually all other government departments will encounter European law in some shape or form. Thus the Justice and Home Affairs Ministries will have to be attentive to the rights of prisoners or others subject to judicial process in the light of the safeguards laid down in the Human Rights Convention. Treasuries or Finance Ministries must ensure that the Community's own resources are correctly collected and accounted for and that Community funds are protected against fraud,[4] and, for example, to ensure that legislation on VAT matters complies with the

---

4 Under Article 280 (ex Article 209(a)(2)) EC Member States must take the same measures to counter fraud affecting the financial interests of the Community as they take to counter fraud affecting their own financial interests.

numerous and complex directives on the subject. The customs authorities of each Member State administer the customs union and must apply the Community's common customs tariff to goods originating from outside the Communities. The Ministries of Agriculture have the principal responsibility for administering the Common Agricultural Policy and Fisheries Policies. Legal questions arising from the application of the Common Agricultural Policy give rise to the largest single category of cases brought before the Court of Justice. The Ministries of Trade and Industry will have responsibility for ensuring the correct application of the Community's competition rules, possibly with the help of independent supervisory bodies, and the rules on state aid, if necessary also reacting to applications for the approval of aid from other Member States or detecting and challenging the illegal grants of aid. All Ministries responsible for spending public funds (whether in connection with policy objectives in fields such as education or agriculture or simply in the matter of internal supplies of furniture, computers or stationery) must comply with the Community rules on public procurement, again implying some knowledge of those rules and the remedies available in case of dispute.

Recruitment to the civil service in most Member States is restricted to nationals of the state concerned and all governments have a public service ministry or department to whom particular enquiries may be directed. These departments may also be helpful in providing advice and preparation for taking part in recruitment procedures for the European Communities and other international organisations. In addition to formal appointments to international organisations, governments frequently second their own officials to international (including European Community) institutions to act as so-called national experts. This enables the institutions to have access to expertise in specific areas as well as providing the seconded staff with experience of the institutions which will be of value when returning to the national civil service. In the United Kingdom a so-called "European fast stream" has been created in which newly recruited civil servants with an interest in and some academic or other experience in European matters are given preferential treatment including experience in the European affairs divisions of various ministries, extra training in languages, secondment's to European Community institutions and preparation for taking part in recruitment competitions.

## OTHER PROFESSIONS

I have already emphasised that studying European law, in addition to specific technical expertise, is also of general cultural value, providing, as it does, an understanding of international relations,

European politics, the protection of individual rights and comparisons with the constitutional, political, economic and social organisation of other countries. It is not surprising therefore that such knowledge and "euro-literacy" may be of use in a number of other professions or career areas.

Thus in **accountancy** the giant multinational firms invariably have important legal departments, usually staffed by members of various legal professions from several countries. However, even in smaller firms, accountants without a formal legal qualification may be called upon to advise on VAT matters (an area exclusively based on European Community law) or aspects of company law and accounts in which European law plays a major part. In **banking** and **insurance** rules on competition, taxation, freedom to provide services across borders and freedom of establishment are likely to arise both for the banks and insurance companies themselves and on behalf of any clients they may have to advise.

In the **intellectual property** area much of the work is carried out by specialised legal practitioners. However, **patent** or **trade mark** agents must be aware of the European dimension of their work including the potential conflict between intellectual property rules and the rules on the free movement of goods within the European Community and on the competition rules. They must also know of the role and powers of the European Patent Office in Munich and the Office for the Harmonisation of the Internal Market (more usually known as the European Trade Mark Office) in Alicante, or even the Community Plant Variety Rights Office in Angers.

In **journalism** all too few journalists, even those responsible for reporting on court proceedings and other legal issues have legal qualifications which can help to avoid some of the journalistic howlers referred to elsewhere in this book. Even general political journalists will find a knowledge of international relations and institutions helpful and will better understand the respective powers of ministers, governments and international institutions and organisations for having studied European law. Closely connected with journalism are **press and information** officers, whether working in government departments, multinational corporations or even, as is increasingly the case, in law firms. Once again a basic knowledge of the structures and vocabulary of European law will enable you to give clear and accurate briefings on departmental or company policy or on the conduct of legal proceedings or political negotiations in which your employer may be involved.

**Lobbying** is a growth industry which has occasionally had its name somewhat tarnished in cases where the legitimate representation of a client's corporate or other interest to administrative or legislative bodies has crossed the line between persuasion and suborning. Lobbying involves collecting information on the legislative and other processes, developments, either in a specific industry such as aviation, brewing or car manufacturing or on industrial or social policy generally. Knowledge of the various institutions and their respective powers and procedures is obviously of great relevance here, as is an understanding of the different kinds of legislative instruments and the respective rights and obligations of individuals, companies and administrative authorities under that legislation. Obviously Euro-legal literacy, even falling short of formal legal qualification, can only be advantageous in such a context.

Particular **interest groups** supporting a specific cause or interest also engage in lobbying and usually have a legal officer or a legal department. They may also support litigation in test cases both in national courts and before the European courts where, as we have seen, they may have direct rights of audience. Thus Amnesty International and Inter-Rights closely monitor the observance of fundamental rights and civil rights under the European Convention as well as under national constitutions. The Equal Opportunities Commission monitors the correct application of the rules on equal treatment of men and women in the workplace, including support for individual cases or even challenges to official action by way of judicial review. Environmental and gay rights groups have also sought both to rely upon European law as it at present stands and to lobby and put pressure on legislative authorities in order to amend the law.

The dynamic and evolving nature of European law, in all of its manifestations and institutional structures means that **teaching** and **research** are fruitful and growing areas. The European Community also funds major research projects in fields such as nuclear energy and the marine environment, many of which have important legal aspects. The candidate countries for accession to the European Union and the more recent members of the Council of Europe are also hungry to acquire understanding and expertise in constitutional and legal processes given that progress on the establishment of democratic institutions and the protection of individual rights are conditions for their further integration into the European family. Again many such teaching projects are financed by the European Communities through its PHARE and TACIS programmes. In this context it is worth mentioning that, while many academically gifted law students (and those from other disciplines) progress naturally from successful undergraduate studies through postgraduate research to teaching, both research and teaching will benefit from some practical experience in the area of interest concerned.

# PART FIVE: VADE-MECUM

# PART FIVE: VADE-MECUM

## CONTENTS

# I  STYLE GUIDE

This brief style guide is not intended to be exhaustive. Still less is it intended to give any general prescriptions in the sense of correct English usage or points of grammar, syntax and typography. For such general guidance you should turn to such reliable style guides as *Gowers' Plain Words* or the immortal *Fowler*,[1] or those published by the *Financial Times* or *The Economist*. This guide therefore covers only certain specific terms concerning European law and recurrent solecisms that crop up in journalistic usage. A certain number of other style points are to be found in the main text.

**Abbreviation:** Given the cumbersome official titles of many European organizations, institutions or procedures, recourse to abbreviations, including curtailed words, initials, acronyms and neologisms is inevitable. Nonetheless such abbreviations should be avoided unless the meaning is absolutely clear and, in any event, in any text intended for publication upon the first mention of the abbreviated item, its official title should be set out in full with the abbreviation in brackets afterwards. It is not usually necessary to include the words "hereinafter referred to as . . . " except in the most rigorously formal texts.

**Acronym:** See **Abbreviation** above and **Alphabet Soup** at II.

**Appeal:** In legal parlance an appeal is the pursuit of a claim to a higher court after having failed to succeed in a lower court. The only circumstance in the context of European law where it is appropriate to use the

---

1    R.W. Birchfield (ed.), *Fowlers Modern English Usage* (3rd ed., Oxford University Press, 1996).

word is in cases in which an appeal is lodged before the European Court of Justice from a decision of the Court of First Instance. Note especially that none of the European Courts deals with cases by way of an "appeal" from courts in the national legal systems of the Member States. Thus questions referred to the European Court of Justice (*q.v.*) pursuant to Article 234 (ex Article 177) E.C. arise in cases in which an interpretation by the Court of Justice of European Community rules is needed by a court in a Member State to enable it to give judgment. The judgment of the Court of Justice in such cases is a preliminary ruling (*q.v.*). It is therefore incorrect to refer to such a case being "taken to the European Court". Old lawyers never die, they only lose their appeal.

**Brussels:** The capital of Belgium, and also the seat of the European Commission and the Council. This does not, however, justify its name being used as a euphemism for the European community or its legislature.

**Commission:** Confusion between the *European Commission of Human Rights* (see Chapter 6 p.000) and the *Commission of the European Communities* (see Chapter 3 p.000) is likely to diminish after the Human Rights body disappears in late 1999. When referring to the Commission of the EC. (which itself uses the short title "European Commission" for informal purposes) you should make it clear whether you are referring to the Commission itself, that is the "college" of 20 Commissioners, or to the institution as a whole including its services and their staff.

**Council:**This abbreviation should be used with care in order to avoid confusion between the Council of Europe (see page 30 above), the Council of the European Union (see page 57 above) and the European Council (see page 63 above).

**Court:** If you use this word on its own always be sure that it is clear *exactly* which court you are referring to. See European Court below and, generally, Chapter 6 above.

**England:** England is a part of the United Kingdom. It is not a Member State. There is therefore no "English" Government. In all contexts connected with the subject matter of this book reference should be made to the United Kingdom Government. Alternatively "British" may be acceptable as in "British nationality", "British passport", etc. English is the correct adjective for references to the English legal system (which however also covers Wales).

**EU Court:** There is no such animal. This abbreviation should not be used under *any* circumstances, whatever your house style manual may say. See further European Court below.

**European Court:** If you have read the book thus far, you will have realised that there are at least four different judicial bodies entitled to this designation. Their respective location, composition and jurisdiction are dealt with in Chapter 6 above and are summarized below. Always make sure that it is absolutely clear which of the European Courts you are referring to before using that abbreviation.

> *European Court of Justice* – permissible abbreviation for the Court of Justice of the European Communities which sits in Luxembourg and ensures the correct interpretation and application of European Community law (*q.v.*) (see page 169 above).

> *Court of First Instance* – short for Court of First Instance of the European Communities which was attached to the Court of Justice in 1989 and therefore also has its seat in Luxembourg. It hears cases brought by individuals or companies against decisions of the European Community institutions. These are not "appeals" (*q.v.*) (see page 178 above).

> *The EFTA Court* is now also based in Luxembourg and is competent to deal with challenges to decisions taken by the EFTA Surveillance Authority (ESA) and may deal with requests for advisory opinions (*q.v.*) submitted by courts in the EFTA–EEA Member States (see Chapter 2, page 28 and Chapter 6 page 182).

> *European Court of Human Rights* – part of the enforcement machinery for the European Convention on Human Rights and Fundamental Freedoms. Based in Strasbourg, it is an institution established by the Council of Europe and is not to be confused with the European Court of Justice. (See Chapter 6 page 185).

> *The European Commission of Human Rights*. A court in all but name this Commission carried out the role of a preliminary filter of cases submitted to the European Court of Human Rights (*q.v.*) until the entry into force of the Eleventh Protocol on the European Convention of Human Rights. It was also based in Strasbourg. (See Chapter 6 p. 192).

> *The International Court of Justice* is not a "European" court but it is based at The Hague. It is one of the principal bodies of the United Nations and applies international law to disputes between states. (See Chapter 6, p. 197).

**Footnotes:** Both a necessary evil and the bane of legal writing. Where they lighten the text by removing distractions in the form of cryptic references to documents which readers may (or may not) wish to pursue they are undoubtedly helpful and infinitely preferable to endnotes. When on the other hand an author uses them to qualify assertions because he is unable to accommodate or deal with counter arguments in his main text, or where the footnotes simply contain extracts of bibliographic references printed out from computer catalogues, they are worse than useless. A few articles in law journals take footnotes to excess with some pages containing only a few lines of substantive text at the top of the page, the remainder being taken up by closely printed footnotes.

**Interim measures:** Either the Court of Justice or the Court of First Instance may, if necessary, order that application of a contested act be suspended or prescribe any necessary interim measures. A request for such a measure can only be made where an action for the annulment of the act complained of has already been lodged, where the applicant is able to show that there is a prima facie case that that act is void and where there is a sufficient degree of urgency. The test for an applicant to demonstrate urgency is that a refusal to grant interim measures would lead to irreparable damage being caused to the applicant. These proceedings are therefore the equivalent of an application for a temporary injunction or an interdict in British domestic proceedings and are intended to maintain the status quo until the Court is able to make a final determination of the rights of the parties. Interim measures should not be confused with "preliminary rulings" (*q.v.*) or "Opinions of the Advocates General" (*q.v.*).

**Judgment:** A judgment is a final judicial decision which is binding on the parties involved in the proceedings which have given rise to it. Although preliminary rulings (*q.v.*) given by the Court of Justice in response to questions referred by national courts do not finally dispose of the case concerned, they are given in the form of a judgment of the European Court of Justice. Such a judgment is not subject to any form of appeal and represents a definitive statement of the law on the point concerned. It is therefore incorrect to refer to it as an "opinion" (*q.v.*) as is sometimes done in American usage.

**Opinion:** In ordinary usage the expression of a point of view or a belief which is sustainable on the basis of known information but which cannot be definitely established. In English this can be extended to include the professional opinion of a lawyer or another professional person. In American usage the word is used for the statement of a judge's reasons for a decision. In European law there are three main kinds of opinion:

(i) *Advocate General's Opinion.* Here "Opinion" is used for what the Treaty refers as the "reasoned submissions" which an Advocate General gives on each case before the European Court of Justice. Despite the use of the word "submission" the Advocate General must act "with complete impartiality and independence". His Opinion in this context gives guidance to the Court of Justice and is the starting point for the Court's deliberation in deciding the cases before it. It is not binding on the Court. Although it precedes the Court's eventual judgment it should *never* be referred to as a "preliminary ruling" (*q.v.*), or as an "interim" or "provisional judgment" or other euphemism. (See Chapter 4, p.132 and Chapter 6, p.176.)

(ii) The European Court of Justice may deliver an *Opinion on the compatibility with the Treaty of an agreement* which the Community envisages entering into with a non-Member state or an international organization (Article 300 (ex Article 228) of the EEC Treaty). This is more than a mere expression of a view since, if the Opinion of the Court of Justice is adverse, such an agreement may enter into force only in accordance with the procedure for revision of the Treaty itself.

(iii)    The EFTA Court may give *"advisory opinions"* on questions sub-
         mitted to it by courts in the EFTA–EEA Member States in
         proceedings similar to those for preliminary rulings (*q.v.*) in the
         European Community.

**Preliminary ruling:** A "preliminary ruling" is a judgment (*q.v.*) delivered
by the European Court of Justice in response to a question submitted to it
by a court in a Member State concerning the interpretation of a rule of
Community law, a decision upon which is necessary to enable that
national court to decide a case with which it is dealing. The procedure is
laid down in Article 234 (ex Article 177) E.C. See Chapter 6 above.

# II  ALPHABET SOUP — ABBREVIATIONS AND ACRONYMS

The initials and acronyms listed below are, for the most part, those used in the text of the main part of this book. Page numbers indicate a description of the organization concerned. For the sake of completeness or the avoidance of confusion I have added a few others. However the European Communities in particular have generated an astonishing number of committees and programmes and a full list (which would require constant updating) would be many hundreds of pages long. There are several dictionaries of such acronyms which I have found helpful, including Anne Ramsay, *Eurojargon: a dictionary of acronyms, abbreviations and sobriquets* (5th ed. 1997).

Acronyms are combinations of initials (NATO, EFTA, etc.) or truncated and composite words (Benelux, Intelsat, etc.) which form pronounceable words. Generally speaking they are written as words but with an initial capital letter like a proper name. However, those that are formed exclusively of initials or where the word might give rise to confusion with a word in ordinary usage are generally printed in capital letters and never with fullstops.

**ACP**      African, Caribbean and Pacific countries party to the Lomé Convention.

**AELE**     Association européenne de libre échange (See EFTA).

**Asean**    Association of South-East Asian Nations.

| | | |
|---|---|---|
| **Benelux** | Neither an abbreviation nor an acronym, this composite word is said to have been invented by a journalist working for the Economist in 1947 who was looking for a shorthand way of referring to the proposed customs union between Belgium, The Netherlands and Luxembourg. | 48–49 |
| **BERD** | See EBRD. | |
| **BIRD** | See IBRD. | |
| **BIS** | Bank for International Settlements. | |
| **CAP** | Common Agricultural Policy. | |
| **CCT** | Common Customs Tariff. | |
| **CEE** | See EEC. | |
| **CEPT** | *Conférence européenne de l'administration postale et des télécommunications* (European Conference of Postal and Telecommunications Administrations). | 20–46 |
| **CERN** | *Conseil européen pour la recherche Nucléaire* (European Organisation for Nuclear Research). | 20–44 |
| **CFSP** | Common Foreign and Security Policy. | |
| **Cites** | Convention on International Trade in Endangered Species of Wild Fauna and Flora. | |
| **CN** | Combined Nomenclature. | |
| **CSCE** | Conference on Security and Co-operation in Europe. | |
| **DSB** | Dispute Settlement Body (WTO). | |
| **DSU** | Dispute Settlement Understanding of the WTO (*q.v.*) agreement. | |
| **EAEC** | See Euratom. | |
| **EAGGF** | European Agricultural Guidance and Guarantee Fund. | |
| **EBRD** | European Bank for Reconstruction and Development (Banque européenne pour la reconstruction et le développement. | |
| **ECB** | European Central Bank. | |
| **ECE** | Economic Commission for Europe (U.N.). | |
| **ECR** | Reports of Cases before the Court of Justice of the European Communities and the Court of First Instance of the European Communities. | |
| **ECR– SC** | European Court Reports — Reports of European Community Staff Cases. | |

| | | |
|---|---|---|
| **Ecu** | European currency unit. | |
| **EDC** | European Defence Community. | |
| **EEA** | European Economic Area. | |
| **EEC** | European Economic Community (Communauté économique européenne). | |
| **EEIG** | European Economic Interest Grouping. | |
| **EFTA** | European Free Trade Association. | |
| **EIB** | European Investment Bank. | |
| **ELDO** | European Organization for the Development and Construction of Space Launch Vehicles. | |
| **EMI** | European Monetary Institute. | |
| **EMS** | European Monetary System. | |
| **EMU** | Economic and Monetary Union. | |
| **EPC** | European Political Co-operation. | |
| **ESA** | European Space Agency, or EFTA Surveillance Authority. | |
| **ESRO** | European Space Research Organization. | |
| **ETS** | European Treaty Services. | |
| **EURATOM** | European Atomic Energy Community (the acronym is the same in all languages). | |
| **Eurocontrol** | European Organization for the Safety of Air Navigation. | |
| **GATS** | General Agreement on Trade in Services. | |
| **GATT** | General Agreement on Tariffs & Trade. | |
| **IAEA** | International Atomic Energy Agency. | |
| **IBRD** | International Bank for Reconstruction and Development. | |
| **IEA** | International Energy Agency (OECD). | |
| **JET** | Joint European Tours. | |
| **Lingua** | Action programme to promote foreign language competence in the Community. | |
| **NATO** | North Atlantic Treaty Organisation. | 34, 37 |
| **NEA** | Nuclear Energy Agency. | |
| **OCDE** | See OECD. | |
| **OCTs** | Overseas countries and territories. | |
| **OECD** | Organisation for Economic Co-operation and Development (Organisation pour la co-opération et le développement économique). | 23–24 |

# III  KEY DATES FOR EUROPEAN LAW

| | |
|---|---|
| September 19, 1946 | In a speech in Zurich, Winston Churchill calls for a United States of Europe. |
| January 5, 1947 | General Marshall, in a speech at Harvard University, proposes that the USA should finance a European Recovery Program (Marshall Aid) to be administered by the European nations themselves. |
| May 7–11, 1948 | Hague Congress. A meeting of nearly 800 politicians from all over Europe gives the political impetus to the establishment of the Council of Europe. |
| May 5, 1949 | 10 European States, establish the Council of Europe, to be based in Strasbourg (Treaty of London). |
| May 9, 1950 | French Foreign Minister Robert Schuman proposes the creation of European Coal and Steel Community (ECSC). May 9, is therefore celebrated as Europe Day annually. |
| November 4, 1950 | The European Convention on Human Rights signed in Rome. |
| April 18, 1951 | The Treaty establishing European Coal and Steel Community (Treaty of Paris) is signed by Belgium, Germany, France, Italy, Luxembourg and The Netherlands. |

| December 4, 1952 | Court of Justice of the ECSC established in Luxembourg. |
|---|---|
| October 23, 1954 | Western European Union (WEU) created by the Paris agreements. |
| March 25, 1957 | The Six sign Treaties setting up European Economic Community (EEC) and Euratom (Treaties of Rome). |
| October 7, 1958 | Single Court of Justice of the European Communities inaugurated. |
| July 21, 1959 | Seven Member States of the Organization for European Economic Co-operation (OEEC), agree to set up EFTA (European Free Trade Association). |
| September 18, 1959 | European Court of Human Rights established. |
| May 3, 1960 | EFTA Treaty enters force. |
| July 20, 1963 | Yaoundé Convention signed between EEC and 17 African States. |
| April 8, 1965 | Treaty establishing a single Council and a single Commission of the European Communities (Merger Treaty) signed in Brussels. |
| July 1, 1967 | Merger Treaty enters force. |
| July 1, 1968 | Customs union completed and common external tariff established by the EC Member States |
| April 21, 1970 | Council of the EC decides that from 1975 EC will receive its own resources. |
| January 22, 1972 | Accession Treaties signed by Denmark, Ireland, Norway and the United Kingdom. |
| September 25, 1972 | In a referendum Norway rejects EC membership. |
| January 1, 1973 | EC formally enlarged to nine members. EC granted sole responsibility for common trade policy. |
| December 9 and 10, 1974 | In Paris Heads of State or Government agree to meet as European Council, (the "summit" which closes each six-month Presidency of the Council of the EC). |
| February 28, 1975 | EC and 46 ACP States sign first Lomé Convention granting financial and technical assistance and trade concessions. |

| June 5, 1975 | In a referendum United Kingdom votes to stay in EC. |
| May 28, 1979 | Act of Accession of Greece signed in Athens. |
| June 7–10, 1979 | First direct elections to European Parliament by direct universal suffrage held in the nine Member States. |
| January 1, 1981 | Greece joins the European Communities. |
| February 23, 1982 | In a referendum Greenland votes to leave EC. |
| June 12, 1985 | Acts of accession of Spain and Portugal signed. |
| June 14, 1985 | (1) Schengen Agreement signed. (2) Commission White Paper on completion of single market published. It marks the start of the campaign to abolish fiscal barriers and border controls by December 31, 1992. |
| December 2 and 3, 1985 | The European Council meeting in Luxembourg agrees institutional reform extending Community responsibilities and legal framework for co-operation on foreign policy. Treaty amendments are brought together in Single European Act. |
| January 1, 1986 | Spain and Portugal join Communities. |
| February 17 and 28, 1986 | Single European Act signed in Luxembourg and the Hague by Governments of the 12 EC Member States. |
| July 1, 1987 | Single European Act enters force. |
| October 24, 1988 | Council decision creating a Court of First Instance of the EC. |
| December 15, 1989 | Fourth Lomé Convention signed by EC and 68 ACP States. |
| June 19, 1989 | Schengen Implementation Convention signed in Luxembourg. |
| October 11, 1989 | President of the Court of Justice declares that the Court of First Instance has been constituted in accordance with law. |
| October 3, 1990 | Treaty between Federal Republic of Germany and German Democratic Republic enters force re-unifying Germany. The five new Länder become part of the EC. |

| | |
|---|---|
| June 25, 1991 | Spain and Portugal join Schengen Agreement. |
| February 7, 1992 | Treaty on European Union signed in Maastricht. |
| May 2, 1992 | EC and EFTA Foreign Ministers sign agreement establishing European Economic Area (EEA) in Porto. |
| December 6, 1992 | In a referendum the people and cantons of Switzerland votes against membership of the EEA. |
| January 1, 1993 | Single market largely completed. |
| March 17, 1993 | Additional protocol enables EC and EFTA to permit EEA Treaty to enter into force following withdrawal of Switzerland and provides special arrangements for Liechtenstein. |
| October 12, 1993 | German Constitutional Court rules in favour of Treaty on European Union. Ratification now completed in all Member States. |
| November 1, 1993 | Treaty on European Union enters force. |
| January 4, 1994 | EFTA Court inaugurated in Geneva. |
| March 16, 1994 | Accession negotiations concluded with Norway, after Austria, Finland and Sweden. |
| June 24, 1994 | Treaty of Accession of Norway, Austria, Finland and Sweden signed at Corfu. |
| November 27 and 28, 1994 | 52.2 per cent of Norwegians vote against joining EU. |
| January 1, 1995 | Austria, Finland and Sweden join EU. |
| March 26, 1995 | Schengen Agreement enters force. |
| September 1996 | EFTA Court re-locates to Luxembourg. |
| October 20, 1997 | Treaty amending the Treaty on European Union, the Treaties establishing the European Communities and certain related acts signed in Amsterdam. |

# IV PRINCIPAL EUROPEAN TREATIES AND CONVENTIONS

## A. THE EUROPEAN COMMUNITIES AND THE EUROPEAN UNION

| Place and date signed (entry into force) | Full Title | Short titles(s) | References |
|---|---|---|---|
| Paris, April 18, 1951 | Treaty establishing the European Coal and Steel Community | Treaty of Paris; ECSC Treaty | 261 UNTS 140 |
| Rome, March 25, 1957 (January 1, 1958) | Treaty establishing the European Atomic Energy Community | Euratom Treaty; the *other* Treaty of Rome | 298 UNTS 169 |
| Rome, March 25, 1957 (January 1, 1958) | Treaty establishing the European Economic Community | *The* Treaty of Rome, EEC Treaty; EC Treaty[1] | 298 UNTS 11 |
| Rome, March 25, 1957 (January 1, 1958) | Convention on Certain Institutions common to the European Communities | Convention on Common Institutions | 298 UNTS 269 |
| Brussels, April 8, 1965 (July 1, 1967) | Treaty establishing a Single Council and a Single Commission of the European Communities | Merger Treaty | OJ 152, June 13, 1967, p.2 |

---

1    The title of this treaty was amended to "Treaty establishing the European Community" by Article G.1 of the TEU.

| Place and date signed (entry into force) | Full Title | Short titles(s) | References |
|---|---|---|---|
| Luxembourg, April 22, 1970 (January 1, 1971) | Treaty amending Certain Budgetary Provisions of the Treaties establishing the European Communities and of the Treaty establishing a Single Council and a Single Commission of the European Communities | Treaty amending Certain Budgetary Provisions | OJ L 2, January 2, 1971, p.1 |
| Brussels, January 22, 1972 (January 1, 1973) | Act concerning the Conditions of Accession and the Adjustments to the Treaties – Accession to the European Communities of the Kingdom of Denmark, Ireland, the Kingdom of Norway and the United Kingdom of Great Britain and Northern Ireland | Act of Accession of Denmark, Ireland and the United Kingdom | OJ L 73, March 3, 1972 |
| Brussels, January 1, 1973 (January 1, 1973) | Decision of the Council of the European Communities of January 1, 1973 adjusting the instruments concerning the accession of new Member States to the European Communities | No short title. This decision takes account of Norway's failure to ratify the Act of Accession, above | OJ L 2, January 1, 1973, p.1 |

| Place and date signed (entry into force) | Full Title | Short titles(s) | References |
|---|---|---|---|
| Brussels, September 20, 1976 (July 1, 1978)[2] | Act concerning the election of representatives of the Assembly by direct universal suffrage | Direct elections Act | OJ L 278, October 8, 1976 |
| Brussels, July 22, 1975 (June 1, 1977) | Treaty amending Certain Financial Provisions of the Treaty establishing the European Communities and of the Treaty establishing a Single Council and a Single Commission of the European Communities | Treaty amending Certain Financial Provisions | OJ L 359, December 31, 1977 |
| Athens, May 28, 1979 (January 1, 1981) | Act concerning the Conditions of Accession and the Adjustments to the Treaties – Accession to the European Communities of the Hellenic Republic | Act of Accession of Greece | OJ L 291, July 19, 1979 |
| Brussels, March 13, 1984 (February 1, 1985) | Treaty amending, with regard to Greenland, the Treaties establishing the European Communities | Greenland Treaty | OJ L 29, February 1, 1985 |
| Madrid and Lisbon, June 12, 1985 (January 1, 1986) | Act concerning the Conditions of Accession and the Adjustments to the Treaties – Accession to the European Communities of the Kingdom of Spain and the Portuguese Republic | [Spanish and Portuguese Act of Accession; Act of Accession of Spain and Portugal] | OJ L 302, November 15, 1985 |

2   The first direct elections to the European Parliament on the basis of this Act took place on June 7 and 10, 1979.

| Place and date signed (entry into force) | Full Title | Short titles(s) | References |
|---|---|---|---|
| Luxembourg, February 17, 1986 and at the Hague, February 28, 1986 (July 1, 1987) | Single European Act | The same, or SEA | OJ L 169, June 29, 1987 |
| Luxembourg, October 24, 1988 (October 31, 1989)[3] | Council Decision of October 24, 1988 establishing a Court of First Instance of the European Communities (amended by Council Decision of June 8, 1993) | Decision establishing the Court of First Instance; CFI Decision | OJ L 319, November 25, 1988 p.1. corrigendum, OJ L 241 August 17, 1989, p. 4. (OJ L 144 June 16, 1993, p. 21.) |
| Maastricht, February 7, 1992 (November 1, 1993) | Treaty on European Union | TEU; The Treaty of Maastricht; the Maastricht Treaty | OJ C 191, July 29, 1992 |
| Corfu, June 24, 1994 (January 1, 1995) | Act concerning the Conditions of Accession and the Adjustments to the Treaties – Accession to the European Union of the Kingdom of Norway, the Republic of Austria, the Republic of Finland and the Kingdom of Sweden | Act of Accession of Austria, Finland and Sweden | OJ C 241, August 29, 1994 |

3   The Decision entered force on the day following its publication in the Official Journal (November 25, 1988) with the exception of Article 3 which entered force on the date of publication of the declaration by the President of the Court of Justice that the Court of First Instance has been constituted in accordance with law.

| Place and date signed (entry into force) | Full Title | Short titles(s) | References |
|---|---|---|---|
| Brussels, January 1, 1995 | Decision of the Council of the European Union of January 1, 1995 adjusting the instruments concerning the accession of new Member States to the European Union | No short title, this decision takes account of Norway's failure to ratify the Act of Accession above | OJ L 1, January 1, 1995 |
| Amsterdam, October 2, 1997 | Treaty of Amsterdam amending the Treaty on European Union, the Treaties establishing the European Communities and certain related acts | Treaty of Amsterdam | OJ C 340 of January 10, 1997 |

## B. THE SCHENGEN *ACQUIS*

The Schengen *acquis* is defined in the Annex to the Protocol Integrating the Schengen *acquis* into the framework of the European Union (the protocol itself is a part of the Treaty of Amsterdam) as including the Agreement, Convention and Accession Protocols listed below. In addition it includes "Decisions and declarations adopted by the Executive Committee established by the 1990 Implementation Convention, as well as acts adapted for the implementation of the Convention by the organs upon which the Executive Committee has conferred decision making powers". This last category runs to some 3000 pages, and at the time of hearings before the House of Lords Select Committee in March 1998[4] no definitive list or version of those acts existed. This in turn was causing problems from the distribution of those acts between the first pillar (immigration and asylum) and the third pillar (police co-operation).

| Place and date signed | Full Title | Short Title(s) | References |
|---|---|---|---|
| Schengen, June 14, 1985 (March 26, 1995) | Agreement between the Governments of the Benelux Economic Union, the Federal Republic of Germany and the French Republic on the gradual abolition of checks at their common borders | Schengen Agreement | |
| Schengen, June 19, 1990 (March 26, 1995) | Convention between the Kingdom of Belgium, the Federal Republic of Germany, the French Republic, the Grand Duchy of Luxembourg and the Kingdom of the Netherlands, implementing the Agreement on the gradual abolition of checks at their common borders, signed in Schengen on June 14, 1985 | Schengen Implementation Convention | |

4   See Defining the "Schengen *acquis*" (1997–98 H.L. 87).

| Place and date signed | Full Title | Short Title(s) | References |
|---|---|---|---|
| Paris, November 27, 1990 | Accession Protocol and Agreement to the 1985 Agreement and the 1990 Convention with Italy | Protocol on Italian Accession to Schengen | |
| Bonn, June 25, 1991 | Accession Protocol with Spain and Portugal | Protocol on Spanish and Portuguese Accession to Schengen | |
| Brussels, April 28, 1995 | Accession Protocol with Austria | Protocol on Austrian Accession to Schengen | |
| Luxembourg, December 19, 1996 | Accession Protocol with Denmark, Sweden and Finland | Protocol on Danish, Swedish and Finnish Accession to Schengen | |

## C. THE EUROPEAN ECONOMIC AREA

| Place and date signed | Full Title | Short Title(s) | References |
|---|---|---|---|
| Oporto, May 2, 1992 (January 1, 1994) | Agreement on the European Economic Area | EEA Agreement | OJ L1, January 3, 1994, p.3 |
| Oporto, May 2, 1992 (January 1, 1994) | Agreement between the EFTA States on the establishment of a Surveillance Authority and a Court of Justice | ESA/EFTA Court Agreement | OJ L344, December 31, 1994, p.1 |
| Brussels, March 17, 1993 (January 1, 1994) | Protocol Adjusting the Agreement on the European Economic Area | EEA Adjustment Protocol (to take account of Switzerland's failure to ratify the Agreement) | OJ L1, January 3, 1994, p.572 |
| Brussels, March 17, 1993 (January 1, 1994) | Protocol adjusting the Agreement between the EFTA States on the establishment of a Surveillance Authority and a Court of Justice | ESA/EFTA Court adjustment protocol | OJ L344, December 31, 1994, p.82 |

## D. COMMUNITY CONVENTIONS IN CIVIL AND COMMERCIAL LAW

The conventions listed below are treaties entered into by the EU Member States for purposes complementary to the EC Treaties. Although, as such, they fall outside the general institutional structure of the Community the interpretation protocols confer jurisdiction on the Court of Justice to give preliminary rulings. The Conventions and the resulting case-law of the Court may therefore properly be regarded as forming a part of Community law. Separate accession conventions are entered into by all of the Member States after each successive enlargement of the EC/EU. These accession conventions (not listed below) may make changes to the basic text in order to take account of specific features in the legal systems of new Member States or of problems which have emerged in the application of the Convention or again of matters of interpretation in judgment of the Court of Justice.

| Date and place signed | Full Title | Short title(s) | References |
|---|---|---|---|
| September 27, 1968, Brussels | Convention on jurisdiction and the enforcement of judgments in civil and commercial matters | The Brussels Convention, or the Judgments Convention | OJ C27, January 26, 1998, p.1[5] |
| June 3, 1971, Luxembourg | Protocol on the interpretation by the Court of Justice of the Convention of September 27, 1968 on jurisdiction and the enforcement of judgments in civil and commercial matters | The Interpretation protocol; the 1971 protocol or the Luxembourg protocol | OJ C27, January 26, 1998, p.24[5] |
| June 19, 1980, Rome | Convention on the law applicable to contractual obligations | Contracts convention; Rome convention | OJ C27, January 26, 1998, p.36[5] |

5    This reference is to a non-binding (but perfectly reliable) consolidated version of the convention following the accession of Austria, Finland and Sweden. At the page indicated there is a table giving the original references to the Convention, the interpretation protocol, and all four of the Accession Conventions in each of the 11 official languages as well as in Irish.

| Place and date signed | Full Title | Short Title(s) | References |
|---|---|---|---|
| December 19, 1988 | First protocol on the interpretation of the 1980 Convention by the Court of Justice | Interpretation protocol I to Rome convention; First interpretation protocol | OJ C27, January 26 1998, p.47[5] |
| December 19, 1988 | Second protocol conferring on the Court of Justice powers to interpret the 1980 Convention | Interpretation protocol II to Rome convention; Second interpretation protocol | OJ C27, January 26, 1998, p.52[5] |
| September 16, 1988, Lugano | Convention on jurisdiction and the enforcement of judgments in civil and commercial matters[6] | The Lugano Convention | OJ L319, November 25, 1988, p.9 |
| May 28, 1998, Brussels | Convention drawn up on the basis of Article K.3 of the Treaty on European Union on Jurisdiction and the Recognition and Enforcement of Judgments in Matrimonial matters | Brussels Convention II | OJ C221, July 16, 1998, p.2 |

6   This convention extends the principles of the Brussels Convention to the (at that time) six EFTA States. Importantly the Court of Justice does not exercise jurisdiction over the Lugano Convention but, in making rulings on essentially identical provisions of the Brussels Convention, must "pay due account" to rulings by Courts in the EFTA States under the Lugano Convention. The latter courts have a reciprocal obligation to "pay due account" to rulings of the Court of Justice and E.U. Member State courts on provisions of the Brussels Convention.

| Place and date signed | Full Title | Short Title(s) | References |
|---|---|---|---|
| May 28, 1998, Brussels | Protocol on the Interpretation by the Court of Justice of the European Communities of the Convention on Recognition and Enforcement of Judgments in Matrimonial matters | Interpretation protocol to Brussels II | OJ C221, July 16, 1998, p.19 |

# V TABLES OF EQUIVALENCES REFERRED TO IN ARTICLE 12 OF THE TREATY OF AMSTERDAM

Article 12 of the Treaty of Amsterdam provides for the renumbering of the Articles, titles and sections of the Treaty on European Union and the EC Treaty. Although this step is welcome in principle as a contribution to improving the clarity and, in Community jargon, the transparency, of the TEU and the EC Treaty the simplistic and unimaginative way in which it has been carried out will cause problems for all users of the Treaty for many years to come. As a result, in writing about or discussing cases or other subjects involving provisions of the Treaties, it will be necessary to exercise great care to ensure that the correct article has in fact been cited. Lawyers, students and anyone else needing to use the Treaties — other than those who wish to attempt prodigious feats of memory — will need to refer to the table of equivalences annexed to the Treaty and reproduced below.

The method chosen for the renumbering was first to add to the Treaties all of the new provisions and amendments made, both to the TEU and the EC Treaty by the Treaty of Amsterdam, then to delete all redundant articles and, finally, without reordering or restructuring the Treaty in any way, simply to renumber them from Articles 1 to 53 in the case of the TEU and 1 to 314 in the case of the EC Treaty. In the consolidated version of the Treaties published by the Office for Official Publications of the Communities, each article is referred to by its new number first with the old one in brackets and this is the usage I have followed in this book.

It may be useful to mention some of the specific problems which readers may encounter. First it must always be borne in mind that all legislation published and all judgments delivered prior to the date of entry into force of the Treaty of Amsterdam refer to the old numbering scheme. When dealing with new matters it will be necessary to cross-check the reference to the new provision and establish whether it has been amended and, in certain contexts, it may be necessary to adjust the form of citation suggested above and referred to, for example, "the Commission's decision under Article 85 EC (now Article 81)" or 'Article 32 TEU (formerly Article K4)".

The reference scheme will also cause problems for newly added articles which, in the consolidated version, are referred to in the same manner as all other articles, even though they did not exist in the post-Maastricht version of the Treaties. Thus, for example, faced with a reference to Article 61 (ex-Article 73(i)), you will look in vain for Article 73(i) in the earlier edition of the Treaties and instead you will have to look at Article 2 (15) in the Treaty of Amsterdam itself which adds the new title on Visas, Assylum, Immigration and Other Policies to the EC Treaty.

Teachers too will have to be particularly careful to indicate potential pitfalls to students. Thus, for example, a student reading the extensive case law on equal pay for equal work under Article 119 of the EC Treaty (old numbering) will be perplexed to discover that Article 119 now refers to procedures for Member States to deal with balance of payments difficulties. Undoubtedly however the master stroke of the begetter of this scheme was in renumbering former Article 36 of the EC Treaty (which provides for exceptions to the application of the principle of free movement of goods) to be renumbered Article 30, the provision under the old numbering laying down the principle itself. The perpetrator of such a potential source of confusion should be condemned to teach the free movement of goods to a class of truculent undergraduates in perpetuity.

Even greater care will be needed in referring to the provisions of the EC Treaty whose numbering had already been changed by the Maastricht Treaty. Thus Article 12 is referred to as "(ex Article 6)", however prior to the entry into force of the Maastricht the text of Article 6 was contained in Article 7. Good luck.

## A. TREATY ON EUROPEAN UNION

(*) indicates new Article introduced by the Treaty of Amsterdam
(**) indicates new Title introduced by the Treaty of Amsterdam
(***) indicates Title restructured by the Treaty of Amsterdam

| Previous numbering | New numbering |
|---|---|
| Title I | Title I |
| Article A | Article 1 |
| Article B | Article 2 |
| Article C | Article 3 |
| Article D | Article 4 |
| Article E | Article 5 |
| Article F | Article 6 |
| Article F.1 (*) | Article 7 |
| Title II | Title II |
| Article G | Article 8 |
| Title III | Title III |
| Article H | Article 9 |
| Title IV | Title IV |
| Article I | Article 10 |
| Title V (***) | Title V |
| Article J.1 | Article 11 |
| Article J.2 | Article 12 |
| Article J.3 | Article 13 |
| Article J.4 | Article 14 |
| Article J.5 | Article 15 |
| Article J.6 | Article 16 |
| Article J.7 | Article 17 |
| Article J.8 | Article 18 |
| Article J.9 | Article 19 |
| Article J.10 | Article 20 |
| Article J.11 | Article 21 |
| Article J.12 | Article 22 |
| Article J.13 | Article 23 |
| Article J.14 | Article 24 |
| Article J.15 | Article 25 |
| Article J.16 | Article 26 |
| Article J.17 | Article 27 |
| Article J.18 | Article 28 |
| Title VI (***) | Title VI |
| Article K.1 | Article 29 |
| Article K.2 | Article 30 |
| Article K.3 | Article 31 |
| Article K.4 | Article 32 |

| | |
|---|---|
| Article K.5 | Article 33 |
| Article K.6 | Article 34 |
| Article K.7 | Article 35 |
| Article K.8 | Article 36 |
| Article K.9 | Article 37 |
| Article K.10 | Article 38 |
| Article K.11 | Article 39 |
| Article K.12 | Article 40 |
| Article K.13 | Article 41 |
| Article K.14 | Article 42 |
| Title VIa (**) | Title VII |
| Article K.15 (*) | Article 43 |
| Article K.16 (*) | Article 44 |
| Article K.17 (*) | Article 45 |
| Title VII | Title VIII |
| Article L | Article 46 |
| Article M | Article 47 |
| Article N | Article 48 |
| Article O | Article 49 |
| Article P | Article 50 |
| Article Q | Article 51 |
| Article R | Article 52 |
| Article S | Article 53 |

## B. TREATY ESTABLISHING THE EUROPEAN COMMUNITY

(*) indicates new Article introduced by the Treaty of Amsterdam
(**) indicates new Title introduced by the Treaty of Amsterdam
(***) indicates Chapter 1 restructured by the Treaty of Amsterdam

| Previous numbering | New numbering |
|---|---|
| Part One | Part One |
| Article 1 | Article 1 |
| Article 2 | Article 2 |
| Article 3 | Article 3 |
| Article 3a | Article 4 |
| Article 3b | Article 5 |
| Article 3c (*) | Article 6 |
| Article 4 | Article 7 |
| Article 4a | Article 8 |
| Article 4b | Article 9 |
| Article 5 | Article 10 |
| Article 5a (*) | Article 11 |
| Article 6 | Article 12 |
| Article 6a (*) | Article 13 |
| Article 7 (repealed) | - |
| Article 7a | Article 14 |
| Article 7b (repealed) | - |
| Article 7c | Article 15 |
| Article 7d (*) | Article 16 |
| Part Two | Part Two |
| Article 8 | Article 17 |
| Article 8a | Article 18 |
| Article 8b | Article 19 |
| Article 8c | Article 20 |
| Article 8d | Article 21 |
| Article 8e | Article 22 |
| Part Three | Part Three |
| Title I | Title I |
| Article 9 | Article 23 |
| Article 10 | Article 24 |
| Article 11 (repealed) | - |
| Chapter 1 | Chapter 1 |
| Section 1 (deleted) | - |
| Article 12 | Article 25 |
| Article 13 (repealed) | - |
| Article 14 (repealed) | - |
| Article 15 (repealed) | - |
| Article 16 (repealed) | - |
| Article 17 (repealed) | - |

| | |
|---|---|
| Section 2 (deleted) | - |
| Article 18 (repealed) | - |
| Article 19 (repealed) | - |
| Article 20 (repealed) | - |
| Article 21 (repealed) | - |
| Article 22 (repealed) | - |
| Article 23 (repealed) | - |
| Article 24 (repealed) | - |
| Article 25 (repealed) | - |
| Article 26 (repealed) | - |
| Article 27 (repealed) | - |
| Article 28 | Article 26 |
| Article 29 | Article 27 |
| Chapter 2 | Chapter 2 |
| Article 30 | Article 28 |
| Article 31 (repealed) | - |
| Article 32 (repealed) | - |
| Article 33 (repealed) | - |
| Article 34 | Article 29 |
| Article 35 (repealed) | - |
| Article 36 | Article 30 |
| Article 37 | Article 31 |
| Title II | Title II |
| Article 38 | Article 32 |
| Article 39 | Article 33 |
| Article 40 | Article 34 |
| Article 41 | Article 35 |
| Article 42 | Article 36 |
| Article 43 | Article 37 |
| Article 44 (repealed) | - |
| Article 45 (repealed) | - |
| Article 46 | Article 38 |
| Article 47 (repealed) | - |
| Title III Chapter 1 | Title III Chapter 1 |
| Article 48 | Article 39 |
| Article 49 | Article 40 |
| Article 50 | Article 41 |
| Article 51 | Article 42 |
| Chapter 2 | Chapter 2 |
| Article 52 | Article 43 |
| Article 53 (repealed) | - |
| Article 54 | Article 44 |
| Article 55 | Article 45 |
| Article 56 | Article 46 |
| Article 57 | Article 47 |
| Article 58 | Article 48 |

| Chapter 3 | Chapter 3 |
|---|---|
| Article 59 | Article 49 |
| Article 60 | Article 50 |
| Article 61 | Article 51 |
| Article 62 (repealed) | - |
| Article 63 | Article 52 |
| Article 64 | Article 53 |
| Article 65 | Article 54 |
| Article 66 | Article 55 |

| Chapter 4 | Chapter 4 |
|---|---|
| Article 67 (repealed) | - |
| Article 68 (repealed) | - |
| Article 69 (repealed) | - |
| Article 70 (repealed) | - |
| Article 71 (repealed) | - |
| Article 72 (repealed) | - |
| Article 73 (repealed) | - |
| Article 73a (repealed) | - |
| Article 73b | Article 56 |
| Article 73c | Article 57 |
| Article 73d | Article 58 |
| Article 73e (repealed) | - |
| Article 73f | Article 59 |
| Article 73g | Article 60 |
| Article 73h (repealed) | - |

| Title IIIa (**) | Title IV |
|---|---|
| Article 73i (*) | Article 61 |
| Article 73j (*) | Article 62 |
| Article 73k (*) | Article 63 |
| Article 73l (*) | Article 64 |
| Article 73m (*) | Article 65 |
| Article 73n (*) | Article 66 |
| Article 73o (*) | Article 67 |
| Article 73p (*) | Article 68 |
| Article 73q (*) | Article 69 |

| Title IV | Title V |
|---|---|
| Article 74 | Article 70 |
| Article 75 | Article 71 |
| Article 76 | Article 72 |
| Article 77 | Article 73 |
| Article 78 | Article 74 |
| Article 79 | Article 75 |
| Article 80 | Article 76 |
| Article 81 | Article 77 |
| Article 82 | Article 78 |
| Article 83 | Article 79 |
| Article 84 | Article 80 |

| Title V | Title VI |
|---|---|
| Chapter 1 | Chapter 1 |
| Section 1 | Section 1 |
| Article 85 | Article 81 |
| Article 86 | Article 82 |
| Article 87 | Article 83 |
| Article 88 | Article 84 |
| Article 89 | Article 85 |
| Article 90 | Article 86 |
| Section 2 (deleted) | - |
| Article 91 (repealed) | - |
| Section 3 | Section 2 |
| Article 92 | Article 87 |
| Article 93 | Article 88 |
| Article 94 | Article 89 |
| Chapter 2 | Chapter 2 |
| Article 95 | Article 90 |
| Article 96 | Article 91 |
| Article 97 (repealed) | - |
| Article 98 | Article 92 |
| Article 99 | Article 93 |
| Chapter 3 | Chapter 3 |
| Article 100 | Article 94 |
| Article 100a | Article 95 |
| Article 100b (repealed) | - |
| Article 100c (repealed) | - |
| Article 100d (repealed) | - |
| Article 101 | Article 96 |
| Article 102 | Article 97 |
| Title VI | Title VII |
| Chapter 1 | Chapter 1 |
| Article 102a | Article 98 |
| Article 103 | Article 99 |
| Article 103a | Article 100 |
| Article 104 | Article 101 |
| Article 104a | Article 102 |
| Article 104b | Article 103 |
| Article 104c | Article 104 |
| Chapter 2 | Chapter 2 |
| Article 105 | Article 105 |
| Article 105a | Article 106 |
| Article 106 | Article 107 |
| Article 107 | Article 108 |
| Article 108 | Article 109 |
| Article 108a | Article 110 |
| Article 109 | Article 111 |

| Chapter 3 | Chapter 3 |
|---|---|
| Article 109a | Article 112 |
| Article 109b | Article 113 |
| Article 109c | Article 114 |
| Article 109d | Article 115 |

| Chapter 4 | Chapter 4 |
|---|---|
| Article 109e | Article 116 |
| Article 109f | Article 117 |
| Article 109g | Article 118 |
| Article 109h | Article 119 |
| Article 109i | Article 120 |
| Article 109j | Article 121 |
| Article 109k | Article 122 |
| Article 109l | Article 123 |
| Article 109m | Article 124 |

| Title VIa (**) | Title VIII |
|---|---|
| Article 109n (*) | Article 125 |
| Article 109o (*) | Article 126 |
| Article 109p (*) | Article 127 |
| Article 109q (*) | Article 128 |
| Article 109r (*) | Article 129 |
| Article 109s (*) | Article 130 |

| Title VII | Title IX |
|---|---|
| Article 110 | Article 131 |
| Article 111 (repealed) | - |
| Article 112 | Article 132 |
| Article 113 | Article 133 |
| Article 114 (repealed) | - |
| Article 115 | Article 134 |

| Title VIIa (**) | Title X |
|---|---|
| Article 116 (*) | Article 135 |

| Title VIII Chapter 1 (***) | Title XI Chapter 1 |
|---|---|
| Article 117 | Article 136 |
| Article 118 | Article 137 |
| Article 118a | Article 138 |
| Article 118b | Article 139 |
| Article 118c | Article 140 |
| Article 119 | Article 141 |
| Article 119a | Article 142 |
| Article 120 | Article 143 |
| Article 121 | Article 144 |
| Article 122 | Article 145 |

| Chapter 2 | Chapter 2 |
|---|---|
| Article 123 | Article 146 |
| Article 124 | Article 147 |
| Article 125 | Article 148 |
| **Chapter 3** | **Chapter 3** |
| Article 126 | Article 149 |
| Article 127 | Article 150 |
| **Title IX** | **Title XII** |
| Article 128 | Article 151 |
| **Title X** | **Title XIII** |
| Article 129 | Article 152 |
| **Title XI** | **Title XIV** |
| Article 129a | Article 153 |
| **Title XII** | **Title XV** |
| Article 129b | Article 154 |
| Article 129c | Article 155 |
| Article 129d | Article 156 |
| **Title XIII** | **Title XVI** |
| Article 130 | Article 157 |
| **Title XIV** | **Title XVII** |
| Article 130a | Article 158 |
| Article 130b | Article 159 |
| Article 130c | Article 160 |
| Article 130d | Article 161 |
| Article 130e | Article 162 |
| **Title XV** | **Title XVIII** |
| Article 130f | Article 163 |
| Article 130g | Article 164 |
| Article 130h | Article 165 |
| Article 130i | Article 166 |
| Article 130j | Article 167 |
| Article 130k | Article 168 |
| Article 130l | Article 169 |
| Article 130m | Article 170 |
| Article 130n | Article 171 |
| Article 130o | Article 172 |
| Article 130p | Article 173 |
| Article 130q (repealed) | - |
| **Title XVI** | **Title XIX** |
| Article 130r | Article 174 |
| Article 130s | Article 175 |
| Article 130t | Article 176 |

| Title XVII | Title XX |
|---|---|
| Article 130u | Article 177 |
| Article 130v | Article 178 |
| Article 130w | Article 179 |
| Article 130x | Article 180 |
| Article 130y | Article 181 |

| Part Four | Part Four |
|---|---|
| Article 131 | Article 182 |
| Article 132 | Article 183 |
| Article 133 | Article 184 |
| Article 134 | Article 185 |
| Article 135 | Article 186 |
| Article 136 | Article 187 |
| Article 136a | Article 188 |

| Part Five<br>Title I<br>Chapter 1<br>Section 1 | Part Five<br>Title I<br>Chapter 1<br>Section 1 |
|---|---|
| Article 137 | Article 189 |
| Article 138 | Article 190 |
| Article 138a | Article 191 |
| Article 138b | Article 192 |
| Article 138c | Article 193 |
| Article 138d | Article 194 |
| Article 138e | Article 195 |
| Article 139 | Article 196 |
| Article 140 | Article 197 |
| Article 141 | Article 198 |
| Article 142 | Article 199 |
| Article 143 | Article 200 |
| Article 144 | Article 201 |

| Section 2 | Section 2 |
|---|---|
| Article 145 | Article 202 |
| Article 146 | Article 203 |
| Article 147 | Article 204 |
| Article 148 | Article 205 |
| Article 149 (repealed) | - |
| Article 150 | Article 206 |
| Article 151 | Article 207 |
| Article 152 | Article 208 |
| Article 153 | Article 209 |
| Article 154 | Article 210 |

| Section 3 | Section 3 |
|---|---|
| Article 155 | Article 211 |
| Article 156 | Article 212 |
| Article 157 | Article 213 |
| Article 158 | Article 214 |

| | |
|---|---|
| Article 159 | Article 215 |
| Article 160 | Article 216 |
| Article 161 | Article 217 |
| Article 162 | Article 218 |
| Article 163 | Article 219 |
| **Section 4** | **Section 4** |
| Article 164 | Article 220 |
| Article 165 | Article 221 |
| Article 166 | Article 222 |
| Article 167 | Article 223 |
| Article 168 | Article 224 |
| Article 168 a | Article 225 |
| Article 169 | Article 226 |
| Article 170 | Article 227 |
| Article 171 | Article 228 |
| Article 172 | Article 229 |
| Article 173 | Article 230 |
| Article 174 | Article 231 |
| Article 175 | Article 232 |
| Article 176 | Article 233 |
| Article 177 | Article 234 |
| Article 178 | Article 235 |
| Article 179 | Article 236 |
| Article 180 | Article 237 |
| Article 181 | Article 238 |
| Article 182 | Article 239 |
| Article 183 | Article 240 |
| Article 184 | Article 241 |
| Article 185 | Article 242 |
| Article 186 | Article 243 |
| Article 187 | Article 244 |
| Article 188 | Article 245 |
| **Section 5** | **Section 5** |
| Article 188a | Article 246 |
| Article 188b | Article 247 |
| Article 188c | Article 248 |
| **Chapter 2** | **Chapter 2** |
| Article 189 | Article 249 |
| Article 189a | Article 250 |
| Article 189b | Article 251 |
| Article 189c | Article 252 |
| Article 190 | Article 253 |
| Article 191 | Article 254 |
| Article 191a (*) | Article 255 |
| Article 192 | Article 256 |
| **Chapter 3** | **Chapter 3** |
| Article 193 | Article 257 |
| Article 194 | Article 258 |

| | |
|---|---|
| Article 195 | Article 259 |
| Article 196 | Article 260 |
| Article 197 | Article 261 |
| Article 198 | Article 262 |
| Chapter 4 | Chapter 4 |
| Article 198a | Article 263 |
| Article 198b | Article 264 |
| Article 198c | Article 265 |
| Chapter 5 | Chapter 5 |
| Article 198d | Article 266 |
| Article 198e | Article 267 |
| Title II | Title II |
| Article 199 | Article 268 |
| Article 200 (repealed) | - |
| Article 201 | Article 269 |
| Article 201a | Article 270 |
| Article 202 | Article 271 |
| Article 203 | Article 272 |
| Article 204 | Article 273 |
| Article 205 | Article 274 |
| Article 205a | Article 275 |
| Article 206 | Article 276 |
| Article 206a (repealed) | - |
| Article 207 | Article 277 |
| Article 208 | Article 278 |
| Article 209 | Article 279 |
| Article 209a | Article 280 |
| Part Six | Part Six |
| Article 210 | Article 281 |
| Article 211 | Article 282 |
| Article 212 (*) | Article 283 |
| Article 213 | Article 284 |
| Article 213a (*) | Article 285 |
| Article 213b (*) | Article 286 |
| Article 214 | Article 287 |
| Article 215 | Article 288 |
| Article 216 | Article 289 |
| Article 217 | Article 290 |
| Article 218 (*) | Article 291 |
| Article 219 | Article 292 |
| Article 220 | Article 293 |
| Article 221 | Article 294 |
| Article 222 | Article 295 |
| Article 223 | Article 296 |
| Article 224 | Article 297 |
| Article 225 | Article 298 |
| Article 226 (repealed) | - |
| Article 227 | Article 299 |

| | |
|---|---|
| Article 228 | Article 300 |
| Article 228a | Article 301 |
| Article 229 | Article 302 |
| Article 230 | Article 303 |
| Article 231 | Article 304 |
| Article 232 | Article 305 |
| Article 233 | Article 306 |
| Article 234 | Article 307 |
| Article 235 | Article 308 |
| Article 236 (*) | Article 309 |
| Article 237 (repealed) | - |
| Article 238 | Article 310 |
| Article 239 | Article 311 |
| Article 240 | Article 312 |
| Article 241 (repealed) | - |
| Article 242 (repealed) | - |
| Article 243 (repealed) | - |
| Article 244 (repealed) | - |
| Article 245 (repealed) | - |
| Article 246 (repealed) | - |
| Final Provisions | Final Provisions |
| Article 247 | Article 313 |
| Article 248 | Article 314 |

# VI  RIGHTS AND FREEDOMS PROTECTED BY THE EUROPEAN CONVENTION ON HUMAN RIGHTS

Headings of articles to be inserted into the text of the Convention and its protocols by Protocol No. 11[1] which restructures the machinery established by the Convention. The wording of Section I (Articles 2 to 18) and of the protocols mentioned below is unchanged by Protocol No. 11, save for the addition of these headings. The existing text of Sections II to IV (Articles 19 to 56) is replaced by a new Section II (Articles 19 to 51) headed "European Court of Human Rights" which deals with the Organization, Powers and Procedures of the new unified Court. The remaining provisions are re-numbered Articles 52 to 59 and are grouped under a new Section III headed "Miscellaneous Provisions".

**The Convention**

**Section I**

| | |
|---|---|
| Article 1 | Obligation to respect human rights |
| Article 2 | Right to life |
| Article 3 | Prohibition of torture |
| Article 4 | Prohibition of slaver and forced labour |
| Article 5 | Right to liberty and security |

1    May 11, 1994, ETS No. 146, entry into force November 1, 1998.

| Article 6 | Right to a fair trial |
| Article 7 | No punishment without law |
| Article 8 | Right to respect for private and family life |
| Article 9 | Freedom of thought, conscience and religion |
| Article 10 | Freedom of expression |
| Article 11 | Freedom of assembly and association |
| Article 12 | Freedom of assembly and association |
| Article 13 | Right to an effective remedy |
| Article 14 | Prohibition of discrimination |
| Article 15 | Derogation in time of emergency |
| Article 16 | Restrictions on political activity of aliens |
| Article 17 | Prohibition of abuse of rights |
| Article 18 | Limitation on use of restrictions on rights |

**First Protocol[2]**

| Article 1 | Protection of property |
| Article 2 | Right to Education |
| Article 3 | Right to free elections |

**Fourth Protocol[3]**

| Article 1 | Prohibition of imprisonment for debt |
| Article 2 | Freedom of movement |
| Article 3 | Prohibition of expulsion of nationals |
| Article 4 | Prohibition of collective expulsion of aliens |

**Sixth Protocol[4]**

| Article 1 | Abolition of the death penalty |
| Article 2 | Death penalty in time of war |
| Article 3 | Prohibition of derogations |
| Article 4 | Prohibition of reservations |

**Seventh Protocol[5]**

| Article 1 | Procedural safeguards relating to expulsion of aliens |
| Article 2 | Right of appeal in criminal matters |
| Article 3 | Compensation for wrongful conviction |
| Article 4 | Right not to be tried or punished twice |
| Article 5 | Equality between spouses |

2  March 20, 1952, ETS No. 9.
3  September 16, 1963, ETS No. 46.
4  April 28, 1983, ETS No. 114.
5  November 22, 1984, ETS No. 117.

# VII NICKNAMES OF CASES

*"A nickname is the heaviest stone that the devil can throw at a man".* William Hazlitt, Sketches and Essays.

The main problem of referring to cases by a nickname or an abridged name is, as pointed out in the text of Chapter 7, that it makes it very difficult to trace the original text of the case later since nicknames are rarely, if ever, included in indices to textbooks (a worthy exception is Edward and Lane's *European Community Law – An Introduction* (Butterworths, 1995)) or in computer databases. Since there is no standardised usage for nicknames different authors occasionally give different names to the same case. Moreover the same nickname may apply to several cases (see, for example, *Bananas* below) or even to cases before two different courts (see, for example, *Gibraltar* below). Even where the same parties are before the same court they may be involved in two or more cases involving quite different principles of law (see, for example, *Defrenne* and *Factortame* below).

Nonetheless such nicknames can be a useful shorthand or may help to distinguish cases whose official names are confusingly similar, such as Community law cases involving the same combinations of institutions or Member States. In cases before the Human Rights Court or Commission, inter-state cases are often best referred to by the circumstances or the legal issue involved in the case. Again, particularly in human rights cases, applicants may wish to remain anonymous and be identified only by an initial. For some reason "X" is the preferred initial so that, for example, in the list of cases in a leading textbook there are over 250 cases with "X" as the applicant, as against, for example, 10 B's, 5 N's and 4 R's.

Wherever a nickname is used the same nickname should be used to refer to the same case throughout the text, and the first reference to it should include the reference to the full, official citation. By definition the list below cannot be exhaustive and is to some extent subjective. I have only included cases where the short name or nickname is not that of one of the parties. Nicknames of Court of Justice cases or Court of First Instance cases are given in italics, those of cases before the Court or Commission of Human Rights are shown in roman lettering.

| | |
|---|---|
| *Abortion services* | Case C–159/90 *SPUC v. Grogan* [1991] ECR I–4685 |
| *AETR* | see *ERTA* |
| *Art Treasures* | Cases 7/68 *Commission v. Italy* [1968] ECR 423 (the First Art Treasures Case) and Case 48/71 *Commission v. Italy* [1972] ECR 527 (the Second Art Treasures Case) |
| *Bananas* | Case 27/76 *United Brands v. Commission* [1978] ECR 207 also known as the *"Chiquita"* case. This judgment contains the immortal line that "bananas are a privileged fruit" and is a leading case on abuse of a dominant market position. However, bananas have also been the subject of a long running trade dispute between the EC and the USA which has given rise to dozens of cases before the Court of Justice and the Court of First Instance, as well as rulings by GATT panels and the DSU of the World Trade Organisation. It is better therefore to specify the particular case rather than using the generic "bananas" |
| *Bananas: Framework Agreement* | Opinion 3/94 |
| *Bangladesh* | Joined cases C–181/91 and C–248/91 *Parliament v. Council and Commission* [1993] ECR I–3685 |
| *Battery hens* | See *Laying hens* |
| *Bathing Water* | C–56/90 *Commission v. UK* [1993] ECR I–4109 |
| *Beer* | Case 176/84 *Commission v. Greece* [1987] ECR 1193<br>    Case 178/84 *Commission v. Germany* [1987] ECR 1227 |
| Belgian Linguistic Case | Always only referred to as such, A6 (1968) |
| *Bocksbeutel* | Case 16/83 *Prantl* [1984] ECR 1299. |

| | |
|---|---|
| *Brasserie du Pêcheur* | Joined Cases C–46/93 and C–48/93 *Brasserie du Pecheur SA v. Germany* and *The Queen v. Secretary of State for Transport, ex p. Factortame Ltd* [1996] ECR I–1029. See also *Factortame* below |
| *Bremer Vulkan* | Joined Cases C–329/93, C–62/95 and C– 63/95 *Germany and Others v. Commission* [1996] ECR I–5151 |
| *Buy Irish* | Case 249/87 *Commission v. Ireland* [1982] ECR 4005 |
| *Café Hag* | See *HAG* |
| *Cassis de Dijon* | Case 120/78 *REWE Zentral v. Bundesmonopolverwaltung für Branntwein* [1979] ECR 649 |
| *Cement* | see *VCH* |
| *Chernobyl* | Case C–70/88 *Parliament v. Council* [1990] ECR I–2041 |
| *Chiquita* | see *Bananas* |
| *Co-insurance* | Case 205/84 *Commission v. Germany* [1986] ECR 3755 |
| *Coloroll* | See Post-Barber cases |
| *Comitology* | Case 302/87 *Parliament v. Council* [1988) ECR 5615 |
| Corporal Punishment Case | *Tyrer v. UK* (A26) (1978). This is the leading case on corporal punishment, and relates to the use of such punishment by the state, but there have been several other cases concerning the use of corporal punishment in schools (e.g. *Costello-Roberts v. UK* (A247–C) (1993); *Warwick v. UK* (A247–C) (1993) (Commission Report); *Campbell and Cosans v. UK* (A48) (1982). These cases are sometimes collectively referred to as the "Corporal Punishment Cases" |
| (First) Cyprus Case | *Greece v. UK No. 176/56* (1956) 2 Y.B. 182, CM Res (59) 12 |
| (Second) Cyprus Case | *Greece v. UK No. 299/57* (1957) 2 Y.B. 186 |
| Northern Cyprus Cases | *Cyprus v. Turkey (I and II)* (1976) 4 EHRR 482 *Cyprus v. Turkey (III)* (1983) 15 EHRR 509 |

| | |
|---|---|
| *Defrenne* | Case 90/70 *Defrenne v. Belgian State* [1971] ECR 445–*Defrenne I*; Case 43/75 *Defrenne v. Sabena* [1976] ECR 455–*Defrenne II*; Case 149/77 *Defrenne v. Sabena* [1978] ECR 1365–*Defrenne III* |
| *Dim-Dip headlamps* | Case 60/86 *Commission v. UK* [1988] ECR 3921 |
| *Dutch Books* | Joined Cases 42/82 and 63/82 *VBVB and VBBB v. Commission* [1984] ECR 19 |
| *Dutch Courier Services* | Joined Cases C–48/90 and C–66/90 *Netherlands v. Commission* [1992] ECR I–565 |
| *Dyestuffs* | Case 48/69 *ICI v. Commission* [1972] ECR 619 |
| East African Cases | (1976) 3 EHRR 76 |
| ERTA (European Road Transport Agreement) | Case 22/70 *Commission v. Council* [1971] ECR 263 (the "*AETR*" Case) |
| European Economic Area (EEA) | Opinion 1/91 on the draft EEA Agreement [1991] ECR I–6079; and Opinion 1/92 on the revised draft EEA Agreement [1992] ECR I–2821 |
| *Factortame* | Case C–213/89 *The Queen v. Secretary of State, ex p. Factortame* [1990] ECR I–2433–*Factortame I*; Case C–221/89 *The Queen v. Secretary of State, ex p. Factortame* [1991] ECR I–3905–*Factortame II*; Joined Cases C–46/93 & C–48/93 *Brasserie du Pêcheur v. Germany* and *The Queen v. Secretary of State, ex p. Factortame* [1996] ECR I–1029–*Factortame III*, known to non-British lawyers as "*Brasserie du Pêcheur*"; see also *Regina v. Secretary of State, ex p. Factortame (House of Lords)* [1991] I All E.R. 70; [1990] C.M.L.R. 375 |
| *Fedechar* | Case 8/55 Fédération Charbonnière de Belgique v. High Authority [1955] ECR 245 |
| FEDETAB | Cases 209 to 215 and 218/78 van *Landewyck v. Commission* [1980] ECR 3135 |
| Five Techniques Case | See, Northern Ireland Case |
| *Flat glass* | Cases T–68/89, T–77/89 and T–78/89 *Società Italiana Vetro SpA and Others v. Commission* [1992] ECR II–1403 |

| | |
|---|---|
| *Flemish travel agents* | Case 311/85 *Vereniging van Vlaamse Reisbureaus v. Sociale Dienst van de Plaatselijke en Gewestelijke Overheidsdiensten* [1987] ECR 3801 |
| *Flemish Waste* | Case C–129/96 *Inter-environnement Wallonie v. Région Wallone* |
| *Foglia v. Novello* | Case 104/79 *Foglia v. Novello I* [1980] ECR 745<br>    Case 244/80 *Foglia v. Novello II* [1981] ECR 3045 |
| *GATS* | See *WTO* |
| GCHQ | *Council of Civil Service Unions v. UK* Appl. No. 11603/85 (1987) 50 D.R. 228 (Commission held that there was no violation and the case was therefore not referred to Court) |
| *Generalized tariff preferences* | Case 45/86 *Commission v. Council* [1987] ECR 1493 |
| *German Beer* | See *Beer* |
| *German property insurers* | Case 45/85 *Verband der Sachversicherer v. Commission* [1987] ECR 405 |
| Gibraltar/Gibraltar Shooting Case | *McCann, Farrell and Savage v. UK. The Times,* October 9, 1995 (or *McCann et al. v. UK*). See also Case C-298/89 *Government of Gibraltar v. Council* [1993] ECR I–3605, an action for the annulment of a directive on inter regional air services |
| *Gingerbread* | Cases 2/62 and 3/62 *Commission v. Luxembourg and Belgium* |
| (First) Greek Case | (1968) 11 Y.B.–II 690 |
| (Second) Greek Case | *Denmark, Norway and Sweden v. Greece* 12 Y.B. 1 |
| *HAG (or Café Hag)* | Case 192/73 *Van Zuylen v. HAG* [1974] ECR 731–*HAG* I;<br>Case C–10/89 *CNL-SUCAL v. HAG* [1990] ECR I–3711–*HAG II* |
| *Hormones* | Case 160/88 *Fedesa v. Council* [1988] ECR 6399 |
| *Human Rights Convention* | Opinion 2/94 |
| *Insurance* | See *Co-insurance* |

| | |
|---|---|
| *ILO Convention 170* | Opinion 2/91 [1993] ECR I– 1061 |
| *Irish souvenirs* | Case 113/80 *Commission v. Ireland* [1981] ECR 1625, see also *Buy Irish* |
| *Isoglucose* | Case 138/79 *Roquette Frères SA v. Council* [1980] ECR 3333; [1982] ECR 3159 |
| *Italian flat glass* | See Flat glass |
| *Japanese Ball Bearings* | Cases 118 … /77 *ISO and others v. Council* [1979] ECR 1277 |
| *Lappel Bank* | Case C–44/95 *R v. Secretary of State for the Environment, ex p. RSPB* [1996] ECR I–3805 |
| *Lawyers' Services* | Case 427/85 *Commission v. Germany* [1988] ECR 1123 |
| *Laying hens* | Case 131/86 *United Kingdom v. Council* [1988] ECR 905 |
| *Laying-up Fund for Inland Waterway Vessels* | Opinion 1/76 [1977] ECR 741 |
| *Leybucht Dykes* | Case 57/89 *Commission v. Germany* [1991] ECR I–883 |
| Little Red Schoolbook Case | *Handyside v. UK* A29 (1976) |
| *Local Cost Standard* | Opinion 1/75 [1975] ECR 1355 |
| *Mad Cows* | Case C–180/96 *UK v. Council* and C–157/96 *R v. Ministry of Agriculture, ex p. National Farmers' Union* |
| *Magill TV Guide* | Joined Cases C–241/91 P and C–242/91 P *RTE and ITP v. Commission* [1995] ECR I–743 |
| *Maize seed* | Case 258/78 *Nungesser v. Commission* [1982] ECR 2015 |
| *Metro* | Case 26/76 *Metro v. Commission* [1977] ECR 1875–*Metro I*; Case 75/84 *Metro v. Commission* [1986] ECR 3021–*Metro II* |

| | |
|---|---|
| *Milk Quotas* | Case 120/86 *Mulder v. Minister van Landbouw en Visserij* [1988] ECR 2321;<br>Case 170/86 *von Deetzen v. HZA Hamburg-Jonas* [1988] ECR 2355– *von Deetzen I;*<br>Case C–44/89 *von Deetzen v. HZA Oldenburg* [1991] ECR I–5119– *von Deetzen II;*<br>Case C–86/90 *O'Brien v. Ireland* [1992] ECR I–6251 |
| *Mulder* | see *Milk Quotas* |
| [British] Nationalisation Cases | *James v. UK* A98 (1986); *Lithgow v. UK* (A102) (1986) |
| *Non-existent acts* | see *PVC* |
| *North East Atlantic Fisheries Convention* | Joined Cases 3/76, 4/76 and 6/76 *Kramer* [1976] ECR 1279 |
| Northern Cyprus Cases | See under Cyprus |
| Northern Ireland Case | *Ireland v. UK* (A25) (1978), also known as the "Five Techniques Case" |
| *Nouvelles Frontières* | Joined Cases 209 to 213/84 *Ministère Public v. Asjes* [1986] ECR 1425 |
| *OECD* | Opinion 2/92 |
| *Pensions* | Case C–262/88 *Barber v. Guardian Royal Exchange* [1990] ECR I–1889, etc. |
| *Perfume* | Joined Cases 253/78 and 1/79 to 3/79 *Giry v. Guerlain* [1980] ECR 2327, etc.<br>Case 31/80 *L'Oréal v. De Nieuwe AMCK* [1980] ECR 3775 |
| *Philip Morris* | Joined Cases 142/84 and 156/84 *BAT and Reynolds v. Commission* [1987] ECR 4487 |
| *Pioneer* | Joined Cases 100 to 103/80 *Musique Diffusion Française v. Commission* [1983] ECR 1825 |
| *Polypropylene* | Cases T–1/89, etc. *Rhône Poulenc and Others v. Commission* [1991] ECR II–867;<br>C–137/92 P *Commission v. BASF* [1994] ECR I–2555 |

| | |
|---|---|
| *Post Barber cases* | Case C–109/91 *Ten Oever v. Stichting Bedrijfspensioenfonds voor het Glazenwassers en Schoonmaakbedrijf* [1993] ECR I–4879; Case C–110/91 *Moroni v. Collo GmbH* [1993] ECR I–6591; Case C–152/91 *Neath v. Hugh Steeper Ltd* [1993] ECR I–6935; Case C–200/91 *Coloroll Pension Trustees Ltd v. Russell and Others* [1994] ECR I–4541; Case C–57/93 *Vroege v. NCIV Instituut voor Volkshuisvesting BV and another* [1994] ECR I–4541; Case C–128/93 *Fisscher v. Voorhuis Hengelo BV and another* [1994] ECR I–4583 |
| *PVC* | Joined Cases T–79/89, etc. *BASF v. Commission* [1992] ECR II–315; C–137/92 *Commission v. BASF* [1994] ECR I–2555 |
| *Reinheitsgebot* | see *Beer* (*not* "Rheinheitsgebot") |
| *Returnable bottles* | Case C–302/96 *Commission v. Denmark* [1988] ECR 4607 |
| *Rubber Agreement* | Opinion 1/78 [1979] ECR 2871 |
| *Sheepmeat* | Case 232/78 *Commission v. France* [1979] ECR 2729 (first); Case 24/80 *Commission v. France* [1980] ECR 1319 (second) |
| *SLOM* | See Milk Quotas |
| Softenon | See Thalidomide |
| South Tyrol Case | *Austria v. Italy*, Appl. No. 788/60 (1961) 4 Y.B. 113 |
| *Spanish banks* | Case C–67/91 *Dirección General de Defensa de la Competencia v. AEB* [1992] ECR I–4785 |
| *(Spanish) strawberries* | Case C–265/95 *Commission v. France* [1997] ECR I–6959 |
| Spycatcher | *Observer and Guardian Newspapers v. UK* (A216) (1991). NB there is another case associated with *Spycatcher* affair, *Sunday Times v. UK (II)* (A217) (1992), and these cases are sometimes referred to together as the *Spycatcher Cases* |
| Storebael | Case C–243/89 *Commission v. Denmark* [1993] ECR I–3353 |

| | |
|---|---|
| Sugar | Joined Cases 40 to 48, 50, 54 to 56, 111, 113 and 114/73 *Suiker Unie v. Commission* [1975] ECR 1663 |
| *Sunday trading* | Case C–145/88 *Torfaen BC v. B & Q* [1989] ECR 3851, etc. |
| *Systembolaget* | Case C–189/95 *Åklagaren v. Franzén* [1997] ECR I–5909 |
| *Tachograph* | Case 128/78 *Commission v. UK* [1979] ECR 419, etc. |
| *Telespeed (British Telecom)* | Case 41/83 *Italy v. Commission* [1985] ECR 873 |
| Thalidomide | *Sunday Times v. UK* (A 30) (1979). Since Thalidomide was marketed under different names in different countries, the case is sometimes (even more confusingly) referred to by those names in other countries, *e.g.* as the *Softenon Case* in the Netherlands |
| *Titanium dioxide* | Case C–300/89 *Commission v. Council* [1991] ECR I–2867 |
| *Tourist Guides* | Case C–154/89 *Commission v. France* [1991] ECR I–659 (and C– 159/89 *Greece* and C–180/89 *Italy*) |
| *Transsexuals* | Case C–13/94 *P v. S and Cornwall County Council* [1996] ECR I–2143, see also Human rights cases *Rees v. UK* (A 106) (1986), *Cossey v. UK* (A 184) (1990) and *Sheffield and Horsham v. UK* (1998) |
| *TRIPS* | see *WTO.* |
| Turkish Case | *Denmark, France, the Netherlands, Norway and Sweden v. Turkey*, Appl, Nos. 9940–9944/82, (1983) 35 D.R. 143 and 44 D.R. 31 (friendly settlement). Note that here the applicants are listed in protocol order, however this case is often also listed (even more confusingly) as *France, Norway, Denmark, Sweden, the Netherlands v. Turkey* |
| Twenty-one detained persons v. FRG | Appl. No. 3134/67 *et al*, (1968) Y.B. 528 |
| Vagrancy Cases | *De Wilde, Ooms and Versyp v. Belgium* (A12) (1971) |

VCH

Case 8/72 *Vereeniging van Cementhandlaren v. Commission* [1972] ECR 977

*Waste/Waste disposal*

Case C–115/91 *Commission v. Council* [1993] ECR I–939

*Waste Removal*

Case C–187/93 *Parliament v. Council* [1994] ECR I–2857

*Welded Steel Trellis*

Cases T–141/89 to T–152/89 *Tréfileurope Sales v. Commission and others* [1995] ECR II–791 *et seq.* Case T–145/89 *Baustahlgewebe GmbH v. Commission* is the subject of an appeal before the Court of Justice as Case C–185/95 P (still pending at time of publication)

*Wild birds*

Case 236/85 *Commission v. Netherlands* [1987] ECR 3989; Case 339/87 *Commission v. Netherlands* [1990] ECR I–85; see also *Lappel Bank* and *Leybucht*

*Woodpulp*

Joined Cases 89/85 ... *A. Åhlström Osakeyhtiö v. Commission* [1988] ECR 5193; [1993] ECR I–1307

WTO (GATS and TRIPS)

Opinion 1/94 [1994] ECR I– 5267

# VIII ADDRESSES OF THE EUROPEAN COURTS

**COURT OF JUSTICE OF THE EUROPEAN COMMUNITIES**
Palais de la Cour de Justice
L–2925 Luxembourg

| Tel: (+352) | 43 03 1 | (Switchboard) |
|---|---|---|
| Fax: (+352) | 43 37 66 | (Registry) |
| | 43 03 2500 | (Press and Information) |
| | 43 03 2600 | (Other Departments) |

Internet:      **www.curia.eu.int**


**COURT OF FIRST INSTANCE OF THE EUROPEAN COMMUNITIES**
Rue du Fort Niedergrunewald
L–2925 Luxembourg

| Tel: (+352) | 43 03 1 | (Switchboard) |
|---|---|---|
| Fax: (+352) | 43 03 2100 | (Registry) |
| | 43 03 2500 | (Press and Information) |
| | 43 03 2600 | (Other Departments) |

Internet:      **www.curia.eu.int**

**THE EFTA COURT**
1 Rue du Fort Thüngen
L–1499 Luxembourg

Tel: (+352)   42 20 81      (Switchboard)
Fax: (+352)   43 43 89

Internet:     **www.efta.int./structure/court/efta-crt.cfm**


**THE EUROPEAN COURT OF HUMAN RIGHTS**
Council of Europe
F–67075 Strasbourg CEDEX

Tel: (+33)     3 88 41 20 00
Fax: (+33)     3 88 41 27 91
               3 88 41 27 62

Internet:     **www.dhcour.coe.fr**


**THE EUROPEAN COMMISSION OF HUMAN RIGHTS**
(See under European Court of Human Rights above)


**THE INTERNATIONAL COURT OF JUSTICE**
Peace Palace
Carnegieplein 2
NL–2317 KJ The Hague

Tel: (+31)     70 392 44 41
Fax: (+31)     70 364 99 28

Internet:     **http://www.icj-cij.org**


**THE BENELUX COURT**
Rue de la Regence 39
B–1000 Brussels

Tel: (+32)     2 519 38 11
Fax: (+32)     2 513 42 06


**THE APPELLATE BODY OF THE WORLD TRADE
ORGANISATION**
Centre William Rappard
154 Rue de Lausanne
CH–1211 Geneva 21

Tel: (+41)     739 5111

Fax: (+41)    739 5458

Internet:    **http://www.wto.org**


**THE ADMINISTRATIVE TRIBUNAL OF THE INTERNATIONAL
LABOUR ORGANIZATION**
Registry
Route des Morillons
Case Postale 500
CH–1211 Geneva 22

Tel: (+41)    22 799 87 28
Fax: (+41)    22 799 85 70

Internet:    **www.ilo.org**


**THE INTERNATIONAL TRIBUNAL FOR THE LAW OF THE SEA
(ITLOS)**
Wexstrasse 4
D–20354 Hamburg

Tel: (+49)    40 356 070
Fax: (+49)    40 356 072 45

Internet:    **http://www.un.org/Depts/los/los.io.htm#ITLOS**

# IX   LAWYERS' ORGANISATIONS

## A. PROFESSIONAL BODIES IN EEA MEMBER STATES

The professional bodies listed below are those with the main responsibility for regulating and administering the lawyers' professions as defined in Article 1 of the Lawyers Establishment Directive.[1]

| | | |
|---|---|---|
| **Belgium** | *Avocat/Advocaat* | **Ordre national des avocats de Belgique**<br>Avenue de la Toison d'Or,<br>B–1060 Brussels |
| **Denmark** | *Advokat* | **Det Danske Advokatsamfund**<br>Kronprinsessegade 28,<br>DK–1306 Copenhagen |
| **Germany** | *Rechtsanwalt* | **Bundesrechtsanwaltskammer**<br>Joachimstraße 1,<br>D–5330 Bonn 1 |
| **Greece** | *Αιηγόροζ* | **Dikigorikos Sylogos Athinon**<br>Akadimias Street 60,<br>GR–Athens |

---

1   Directive 98/5/EC of the European Parliament and of the Council of 16 1998 to facilitate practice of the profession of lawyer on a permanent basis in a Member State other than that in which the qualification was obtained: OJ L77 March 14, 1998, p.36.

| Spain | *Abogado/Advocat/ Avogado/Abokatu* | **Consejo General de la Abogacía Española** Calle des Serrano 9, E–28001 Madrid |
|---|---|---|
| France | *Avocat* | **Barreau de Paris Conférence des Bâtonniers Association des Avocats Conseils d'Entreprise Confédération Nationale des Avocats Fédération Nationale des Unions de Jeunes Avocats Syndicale des Avocats de France** c/o Délégation Française du CCBE, Maison du Barreau, 11, Place Dauphine, F–75053 Paris Louvre RP SP |
| Ireland | *Barrister* | **Bar Council of Ireland** Law Library – Four Courts, IR–Dublin 7 |
| | *Solicitor* | **The Law Society of Ireland** Blackhall Place, Dublin 7 |
| Italy | *Avvocato* | **Consiglio Nazionale Forense** Via Arenula 71, I–00186 Rome |
| Luxembourg | *Avocat* | **Ordre des Avocats à la Cour Supérieure de Justice de Luxembourg** Palais de Justice, Boîte Postale 361, L–2013 Luxembourg |
| The Netherlands | *Advocaat* | **Nederlandse Ordre van Advocaten** Postbus 30851, NL–2500 GW The Hague |
| Austria | *Rechtsanwalt* | **Österreichischer Rechtsanwalts-kammertag** Rotenturmstraße 13, A–1010 Vienna |
| Portugal | *Advogado* | **Ordem dos Advogados** 14, Largo de São Domingos-1°Dto, P–1194 Lisbon Codex |

| Finland | *Asianajaja/Advokat* | **Suomen Asiananjajaliitto**<br>Simonkatu 12 B 20,<br>FIN–00100 Helsinki |
|---|---|---|
| Sweden | *Advokat* | **Sverges Advokatsamfund**<br>Box 27321,<br>S–102 54 Stockholm |

**United Kingdom**

| England and Wales | *Barrister* | **The General Council of the Bar**<br>3 Bedford Row,<br>London WC1R 4DB |
|---|---|---|
| | *Solicitor* | **The Law Society**<br>113 Chancery Lane,<br>London WC2A 1PL |
| Scotland | *Advocate* | **Faculty of Advocates**<br>Parliament House,<br>Edinburgh EH1 1RF |
| | *Solicitor* | **The Law Society of Scotland**<br>26 Drumsheugh Gardens,<br>Edinburgh EH3 7YR |
| Northern Ireland | *Barrister* | **General Council of the Bar of Northern Ireland**<br>Bar Library, Royal Courts of Justice,<br>Belfast BT1 3JZ |
| | *Solicitor* | **Law Society of Northern Ireland**<br>Law Society House,<br>90–106 Victoria Street,<br>Belfast BT1 3JZ |

# B. PROFESSIONAL BODIES IN CANDIDATE COUNTRIES

| Cyprus | **Cyprus Bar Association**<br>Flat 47, 23 Leuki Akcritos Ave,<br>PO Box 1446, CY–Nicosia |
|---|---|
| Czech Republic | **Ceská advokátní komora**<br>Národní, tríd 16,<br>CZ–100 00 Prague 1 |

| | |
|---|---|
| Estonia | **Eesti Advokatuuri Juhatus**<br>Viru 19<br>Tallinn EE–0001<br>Eesti Vabariik |
| Hungary | **Országos Ugvédi Tanács**<br>Szemere Utca 8,<br>H–1054 Budapest V |
| Poland | **Naczelna Rada Adwokacka**<br>ul Swietojerska 16, 00–202 Warsaw |
| Slovenia | **Odvetniška Zbornica Slovenije**<br>Kotnikova 12,<br>Ljubljana<br>Slovenia |

## C. INTERNATIONAL ASSOCIATIONS FOR LAWYERS

**AEA or**    **Association Européenne des Avocats**
**OMNIJURIS**   Rue de Suisse 35,
B–1060 Brussels

Tel: (x32)2 534 16 80
Fax: (x32)2 537 27 41

**AIJA**        **Association Internationale des Jeunes Avocats**
Avenue Luis Lepoutre 59, Boite 20,
B–1060 Brussels

Tel: (x32)2 347 28 08/33 44
Fax: (x32)347 55 22

**AEPPC**     **European Association of Insolvency Practitioners**
Shelley House, 3 Noble Street,
GB–London EC2V 7DQ

Tel: (x44)171 606 7700
Fax: (x44)171 606 9887

**CCBE**      **Council of the Bars and Law Societies of the European Community**
Rue Washington 40
B–1050 Brussels

Tel: (x32)2 640 42 74
or (x32)2 640 09 31
Fax: (x32)2 647 79 41

Website:     **http://www.ccbe .org**

ECLA    **European Company Lawyers' Association**
Verbond van Nederlandes Ondernemingen, Boite 93093,
NL–2509 AB The Hague

Tel: (x31)70 349 73 97
Fax: (x31)70 381 95 08

ELSA    **European Law Students' Association International**
239 Boulevard Général Jacques,
B–1050 Brussels

Tel: (x32)2 646 26 26
Fax: (x32)2 646 29 23

e-mail:    **elsa@buc. inbe.vet**

ETLA    **European Trade Law Association**
Avenue de Tervueren 163,
B–1150 Brussels

Tel: (x32)2 735 89 45
Fax: (x32)2 735 22 51

FIDE    **Fédération Internationale pour le Droit Européen**
FIDE's principal activity is a conference every two years
on European law. Its members are the national
European law associations of each EC country.
Individuals can attend the biennial conference through
their national association.

UKAEL    **UK Association of European Law**
King's College London, Strand,
London WC2R 2LS

Tel: (x44)171 873 2890

IBA    **International Bar Association**
2 Harewood Place, Hanover Square,
London W1R 9HB

Tel: (x44)171 629 1206
Fax: (x44)171 409 0456

ICJ    **International Commission of Jurists**
P.O. Box 216
81A Avenue de Châtelaine
CH-1219 Châtelaine
Geneva

Tel: (x41) 22 979 38 00
Fax: (x41) 22 979 38 01

Internet:    **www.icj.org**
e-mail:    **info@icj. org**

ILA              **International Law Association**
                 Charles Clore House, 17 Russell Square,
                 London WC2B 5DR

                 Tel: (x44)171 323 2978
                 Fax: (x44)171 323 3581

UAE              **Union des Avocats Européens**
                 Corneliuss Strasse 9,
                 D–6000 Frankfurt

                 Tel: (x49)69 75 60 40
                 Fax: (x49)69 75 60 466

UIA              **Union Internationale des Avocats**
                 Avenue Charles de Gaulle 103,
                 F–92200 Neuilly-sur-Seine

                 Tel: (x33)1 47 38 13 11
                 Fax: (x33)1 47 38 61 38

UINL             **Union Internationale du Notariat Latin Permanent
                 European Secretariat**
                 37 Via Senato,
                 I–20121 Milan

                 Tel: (x39)2 86 41 51/52/53
                 Fax: (x39)2 28 10 12 81

                 **European Association of Labour Court Judges**
                 c/o Regional Office of the Industrial Tribunals
                 Crescent Centre
                 Temple Back
                 Bristol BS1 6EZ

                 Tel: (x44)117 929 82 61
                 Fax: (x44)117 925 34 52

# X  MEMBERSHIP OF EUROPEAN ORGANISATIONS

This table shows the European Member States of 10 of the orgainzations described in this book. It should, in addition be noted that Canada and the United States are members of the OSCE, NATO, EAPC and the OECD; the OECD also includes Australia, Japan, Korea, Mexico and New Zealand. The various states are listed for convenience in English alphabetical order.

"Obs" indicates observer status. In the WEU "A" designates "associate" while "Ap" refers to "associate partner".

| | OSCE | NATO | EAPC | WEU | EU | EFTA | EEA | OECD | Council of Europe | Nordic Council |
|---|---|---|---|---|---|---|---|---|---|---|
| Dates Established | 1975 | 1949 | 1997 | 1955 | 1992 | 1960 | 1994 | 1961 | 1949 | 1952 |
| Number of Members | 55 | 16 | 40 | 10 | 15 | 4 | 18 | 25 | 40 | 5 |
| Description at page: | p.38 | p.37 | p.38 | p.36 | p.49 | p.28 | p.86 | p.23 | p.30 | p.32 |
| Albania | ✓ | | ✓ | | | | | | ✓ | |
| Andorra | ✓ | | | | | | | | ✓ | |
| Armenia | ✓ | | ✓ | | | | | | | |
| Austria | ✓ | | Obs | Obs | ✓ | | ✓ | ✓ | ✓ | |
| Azerbaijan | ✓ | | ✓ | | | | | | | |
| Belarus | ✓ | | ✓ | | | | | | | |
| Belgium | ✓ | ✓ | ✓ | ✓ | ✓ | | ✓ | ✓ | ✓ | |
| Bosnia and Herzegovina | ✓ | | | | | | | | | |
| Bulgaria | ✓ | | ✓ | Ap | | | | | ✓ | |

| | OSCE | NATO | EAPC | WEU | EU | EFTA | EEA | OECD | Council of Europe | Nordic Council |
|---|---|---|---|---|---|---|---|---|---|---|
| Croatia | ✓ | | | | | | | | ✓ | |
| Cyprus | ✓ | | | | | | | | ✓ | |
| Czech Republic | ✓ | | ✓ | Ap | | | | ✓ | ✓ | |
| Denmark | ✓ | ✓ | ✓ | Obs | | | ✓ | ✓ | ✓ | ✓ |
| Estonia | ✓ | | ✓ | Ap | | | | | ✓ | |
| Finland | ✓ | | | Obs | ✓ | | ✓ | ✓ | ✓ | ✓ |
| France | ✓ | ✓ | ✓ | ✓ | ✓ | | ✓ | ✓ | ✓ | |
| Georgia | ✓ | | | | | | | | | |
| Germany | ✓ | ✓ | ✓ | ✓ | ✓ | | ✓ | ✓ | ✓ | |
| Greece | ✓ | ✓ | ✓ | ✓ | ✓ | | ✓ | ✓ | ✓ | |
| Holy See | ✓ | | | | | | | | | |
| Hungary | ✓ | | ✓ | Ap | | | | ✓ | ✓ | |
| Iceland | ✓ | ✓ | ✓ | A | | ✓ | ✓ | ✓ | ✓ | ✓ |
| Ireland | ✓ | | | Obs | ✓ | | ✓ | ✓ | ✓ | |
| Italy | ✓ | | ✓ | ✓ | ✓ | | ✓ | ✓ | ✓ | |
| Kazakstan | ✓ | | ✓ | | | | | | | |
| Kyrgyzstan | ✓ | | | | | | | | | |

| | OSCE | NATO | EAPC | WEU | EU | EFTA | EEA | OECD | Council of Europe | Nordic Council |
|---|---|---|---|---|---|---|---|---|---|---|
| Latvia | ✓ | | ✓ | Ap | | | | | ✓ | |
| Liechtenstein | ✓ | | | | | ✓ | ✓ | | ✓ | |
| Lithuania | ✓ | | ✓ | Ap | | | | | ✓ | |
| Luxembourg | ✓ | ✓ | ✓ | ✓ | ✓ | | ✓ | ✓ | ✓ | |
| Malta | ✓ | | | | | | | | ✓ | |
| Moldova | ✓ | | ✓ | | | | | | ✓ | |
| Monaco | ✓ | | | | | | | | | |
| Netherlands | ✓ | ✓ | ✓ | ✓ | | | | | ✓ | |
| Norway | ✓ | ✓ | ✓ | A | | | | | ✓ | ✓ |
| Poland | ✓ | | ✓ | Ap | | | | | ✓ | |
| Portugal | ✓ | ✓ | ✓ | ✓ | | | | | ✓ | |
| Romania | ✓ | | ✓ | Ap | | | | | ✓ | |
| Russian Federation | ✓ | | ✓ | | | | | | ✓ | |
| San Marino | ✓ | | | | | | | | ✓ | |
| Slovak Republic | ✓ | | | Ap | | | | | | |
| Slovenia | ✓ | | ✓ | Ap | | | | | ✓ | |
| Spain | ✓ | ✓ | ✓ | ✓ | ✓ | | ✓ | ✓ | ✓ | |

| | OSCE | NATO | EAPC | WEU | EU | EFTA | EEA | OECD | Council of Europe | Nordic Council |
|---|---|---|---|---|---|---|---|---|---|---|
| Sweden | ✓ | | Obs | Obs | ✓ | | ✓ | ✓ | ✓ | ✓ |
| Switzerland | ✓ | | Obs | | | ✓ | | ✓ | ✓ | |
| Tajikistan | ✓ | | ✓ | | | | | | | |
| The former Yugoslav Republic of Macedonia | ✓ | | ✓ | | | | | | ✓ | |
| Turkey | ✓ | ✓ | ✓ | A | | | | ✓ | ✓ | |
| Turkmenistan | ✓ | | ✓ | | | | | | | |
| Ukraine | ✓ | | ✓ | | | | | | ✓ | |
| United Kingdom | ✓ | ✓ | ✓ | ✓ | ✓ | | ✓ | ✓ | ✓ | |
| Uzbekistan | ✓ | | ✓ | | | | | | | |
| Yugoslavia (Serbia and Montenegro) | ✓* | | | | | | | | | |

* Suspended

# XI  USEFUL WEB SITES

The following, by no means exhaustive, selection is organised roughly in accordance with the order of the chapters in the main part of the book. *N.B.* Internet addresses are liable to change.

## A. INTERGOVERNMENTAL ORGANIZATIONS

| | |
|---|---|
| NATO (p.37) | **www.nato.int** |
| OSCE (p.38) | **www.osceprag.cz** |
| U.N. (United Nations Economic Commission for Europe) | **www.unece.org** |
| WTO (p.25) | **www.wto.org** |
| Council of Europe (p.30) | **www.coe.fr** |
| OECD (p.23) | **www.oecd.org** |

## B. THE EUROPEAN UNION

| | |
|---|---|
| General – the Europa website provides a vast store of access to information about the EU and the EC and access to the sites of various other institutions | **www.europa.eu.int** |
| IDEA – Directory of officials of all E.U. & E.C. institutions | **www.europa.eu.int/ ideae.html** |

| | |
|---|---|
| Eurostat | **europa.eu.int/<br>eurostat.html** |
| European Environment Agency | **www.eea.eu.int** |
| European Monetary Institute (EMI)<br>(will become European Central Bank<br>(ECB) | **www.ecb.int** |
| Court of Auditors | |
| EMUNET (Information and<br>documents on Economic and<br>Monetary Union) | **www.euro-emu.co.uk** |

## C. THE EUROPEAN COURTS

| | |
|---|---|
| Court of Justice (p.169) and Court of<br>First Instance (p.178) of the European<br>Communities | **www.curia.eu.int** |
| EFTA Court (p.182) | **www.efta.int/structure/<br>court/efta-crt.cfm** |
| European Court of Human Rights<br>(p.185) | **www.dhcou r.coe.fr** |
| Yugoslav War Crimes Tribunal (ICTY) | **www.un.org/icty** |
| International Court of Justice (p.197) | **www.icj-cij.org** |

## D. FINDING EUROPEAN LAW

| | |
|---|---|
| CELEX (see p.247) (access to databases<br>requires user id and password) | **http://europa.eu.int/celex** |
| EUR-Lex – Directory of EC legislation<br>in force; all Official Journals for past20<br>days – free access (see p.248) | **http://eur opa.eu.int/eur-<br>lex/en/index.html** |
| SCAD Plus – contains summaries of<br>developments in EC legislation | **http://europa.eu.int/<br>scadplus** |
| OEIL – legislative observatory shows<br>status of legislative proposals in<br>progress | **http://www.europarl.eu.<br>int/dors/oeil/en** |
| SCAD – Bibliography of official EC<br>publications | **http://europa.eu.int/scad** |

EUDOR – Document delivery service free to search for references but downloading must be paid for (see p.297)  http://www.eudor.com

ECLAS – Commission Library catalogue  http://europa.eu.int/eclas

Court judgments – see part C above.

Treaties – see EUROPA or CELEX above

## E. STUDYING EUROPEAN LAW

European University Institute,Florence  http://www.iue.it

Collège d'Europe, Bruges  http://www.coleurop.be

European Institute for Public Administration  http://www.eipa.nl

Eurotext (selection of full text EC documents of special relevance to students)  http://eurotext.ulst.ac.uk

ELSA – European Law Students Association  http://www.Ins.nl/elsa

European Law Moot Court Society  http://www.elmc.org

Concours René Cassin  http://www.sdv.fr/jurisludi

## F. LEGAL PROFESSIONS

See also Vade-mecum IX above

CCBE  http://ccbe.org

The Law Society of England and Wales  www.lawsociety.org.uk

The Bar Council  www.barcouncil.org.uk

# XII  G-SPOT

With the striking lack of imagination which diplomats can show when they really put their minds to it, encouraged by journalists and sub-editors for whom a nickname or acronym may facilitate headline writing, a number of loose organisations has developed known as "G" with a number attached. "G" in this context is merely shorthand for "group of", and the number is equal (sometimes approximately) to the number of participating states. The frequent use of the letter "G" implies no central organisation of these groups which have little in common with each other.

The subject matter discussed by the "G" groups is, principally, the highest level of international macro-economic policy – occasionally including broader issues of international affairs such as regional crises in the Balkans or the Far East. They are listed here in numerical order since European States are often active participants, and decisions taken may have important financial or political consequences in Europe.

G-3     Finance ministers and central bankers from Germany, Japan and the United States, the states with the world's three strongest currencies. The director of the European Central Bank and the President of ECOFIN may participate in future, after the introduction of a single currency, in the European Union.

G-6     Established in 1984 to work for nuclear disarmament. Consisting of Argentina, Greece, India, Mexico, Sweden and Tanzania – it may also be the leading candidate for the group with the most disparate membership. Presumably India's membership has lapsed since its nuclear tests in 1998.

**G-7**      Meets regularly at the level of Heads of government, foreign
             ministers or finance ministers of the United States, Japan,
             Germany, France, Canada, Italy and the United Kingdom.

**G-8**      G-7 plus Russia.

**G-10**     G-7 plus the Benelux countries (counting as one), Switzerland
             and Sweden – central bankers (who provide the principal
             funding for the International Monetary Fund (IMF)) meeting
             regularly.

**G-15**     A group of developing countries comprising representatives
             of Algeria, Argentina, Brazil, Egypt, India, Indonesia, Jamaica,
             Kenya, Malaysia, Mexico, Nigeria, Peru, Senegal, Tanzania,
             Venezuela. The group aims to encourage dialogue between
             the developing countries themselves in a spirit of mutual
             encouragement and support in order to reduce their
             dependence on Northern hemisphere countries.

**G-22**     Allegedly a "one-off" meeting (refreshingly also known as
             "the Willard Group" after the hotel where the meeting was
             held) including G-8 and 14 other nations, namely: Argentina,
             Australia, Brazil, China, Hong Kong, India, Indonesia, South
             Korea, Malaysia, Mexico, Poland, Singapore, South Africa and
             Thailand.

**G-24**     G-8 plus representatives of the other 16 board members of the
             IMF.

**G-77**     Established in 1967 and now comprising 128 developing
             countries plus the Palestine Liberation Organization. Its
             purpose is to co-ordinate the policies of developing countries
             at sessions of the United Nations.

# INDEX